Differentials

Differentials

Poetry, Poetics, Pedagogy

MARJORIE PERLOFF

THE UNIVERSITY OF ALABAMA PRESS
Tuscaloosa

Copyright © 2004
The University of Alabama Press
Tuscaloosa, Alabama 35487-0380
All rights reserved
Manufactured in the United States of America
Typeface: Minion
∞
The paper on which this book is printed meets the minimum requirements of American
National Standard for Information Science-Permanence of Paper for Printed Library
Materials, ANSI Z39.48-1984.

Library of Congress Cataloging-in-Publication Data

Perloff, Marjorie.
    Differentials : poetry, poetics, pedagogy / Marjorie Perloff.
        p. cm. — (Modern and contemporary poetics)
    Chiefly essays previously published in various sources.
    Includes bibliographical references and index.
    ISBN 0-8173-1421-0 (alk. paper) — ISBN 0-8173-5128-0 (pbk. : alk. paper)
    1. Literature, Modern—History and criticism. 2. Poetics. I. Title. II. Series.
    PN511.P47 2004
    809'.04—dc22

                                                        2004001811

Contents

Acknowledgments

The following essays appeared, most in different form, in the following publications and are reprinted here by permission:

"Crisis in the Humanities? Reconfiguring Literary Study for the Twenty-first Century," as "In Defense of Poetry: Put the Literary Back in Literature," *Boston Review* 24: 6 (Dec.–Jan. 1999–2000): 22–26.

"The Search for 'Prime Words': Ezra Pound as Nominalist," *Paideuma: Studies in American and British Modernist Poetry* 32, Numbers 1–3 (fall 2003), 205–28.

"'But isn't *the same* at least the same?' Wittgenstein on Translation," in *The Literary Wittgenstein*, ed. John Gibson and Wolfgang Huemer (London: Routledge, 2004), 34–54. In an earlier version, this essay appeared in *Jacket*, http://www.jacketmagazine.com/14/perl-witt.html, and in *Salt* 14: *The Jacket Issue*, ed. John Tranter (2003): 17–43.

"'Logocinéma of the Frontiersman': Eugene Jolas's Multilingual Poetics and Its Legacies," *Kunapipi* 20 (1999): 145–63.

"'The Silence that is not Silence': Acoustic Art in Samuel Beckett's Radio Plays," in *Samuel Beckett and the Arts: Music, Visual Arts, and Non-Print Media*, ed. Lois Oppenheim (New York: Garland, 1999), 247–68. "The Beckett/Feldman Radio Collaboration: *Words and Music* as Hörspiel," *Beckett Circle* 26, no. 2 (fall 2003), 7–10. Used by permission of Routledge/Taylor & Francis Books Inc.

"Language Poetry and the Lyric Subject: Ron Silliman's Albany, Susan Howe's Buffalo," *Critical Inquiry* 25 (spring 1999), 405–34.

"After Language Poetry: Innovation and Its Theoretical Discontents," in *The World in Time and Space: Towards a History of Innovative American Poetry, 1970–2000*, ed. Joseph Donahue and Edward Foster (Talisman House Press, 2000), 333–55.

"The Invention of 'Concrete Prose': Haroldo de Campos's *Galaxias* and After," *Contemporary Literature,* special issue: *American Poetry of the 1990s,* ed. Thomas Gardner, 42, 2 (summer 2001): 270–93.

"The Oulipo Factor: The Procedural Poetics of Christian Bök and Caroline Bergvall," *Textual Poetics,* 17.3 (winter 2003).

"Filling the Space with Trace: Tom Raworth's *Letters from Yaddo,*" *The Gig,* ed. Nate Dorward, 13–14 (May 2003): 130–44.

"Teaching the 'New' Poetries: The Case of Rae Armantrout," *Kiosk: A Journal of Poetry, Poetics, and Experimental Prose,* 1 (2002): 235–60.

"Writing Poetry/Writing about Poetry: Some Problems of Affiliation," *Symploke* 7: 2 (2000): 21–29; rpt. in *Affiliations: Identity in Academic Culture,* ed. Jeffrey R. Di Leo (Lincoln: University of Nebraska Press, 2003), 133–43.

The author gratefully acknowledges permission to reprint excerpts from the following sources:

Rae Armantrout, *The Pretext* (Los Angeles: Green Integer, 2001). Used by permission of Sun & Moon Press.

Christian Bök, *Eunoia* (Toronto: Coach House Books, 2001). Used by permission of Coach House Books.

Jorie Graham, "Evolution," in *Never* (New York: Ecco/HarperCollins, 2002), copyright © 2002 Jorie Graham. Used by permission of HarperCollins Publishers Inc.

Susan Howe, "Secret History of the Dividing Line," in *Frame Structures: Early Poems, 1974–1979* (New York: New Directions, 1996), copyright © 1974, 1975, 1978, 1979, 1996 Susan Howe. Used by permission of New Directions Publishing Corporation.

Harryette Mullen, *Muse & Drudge* (Philadelphia: Singing Horse Press, 1995).

Frank O'Hara, "Lana Turner Has Collapsed!" in *The Collected Poems of Frank O'Hara,* ed. Donald Allen (Berkeley and Los Angeles: Univ. of California Press, 1995), copyright © Frank O'Hara. Used by permission of City Lights Books.

Ezra Pound, "Canto LXVIII," in *The Cantos* (New York: New Directions, 1993), copyright © 1934, 1937, 1948, 1956, 1959, 1962, 1963, 1966, and 1968 Ezra Pound. Used by permission of New Directions Publishing Corporation.

Tom Raworth, *Collected Poems* (Manchester, Eng.: Carcanet Press, 2003). Used by permission of Carcanet Press, Ltd.

Joan Retallack, *How to Do Things with Words* (Los Angeles: Sun & Moon, 1998). Used by permission of Sun & Moon Press.

Jacques Roubaud, *Quelque chose noir* (Paris: Gallimard, 1986). Used by permission of Gallimard; and Rosmarie Waldrop, trans., *some thing black* [from "Unlikeness," a section of her translation of *Quelque chose noir*] (Elmwood Park, IL: Dalkey Archive, 1990). Used by permission of Dalkey Archive.

Ron Silliman, "Albany," in *ABC* (Berkeley, CA: Tuumba Press, 1983); and "Under *Albany*" (Detroit: Gale Research Center, 1997, in *Contemporary Authors Autobiography Series,* vol. 29, ed. Joyce Nakamura, Gale Research, Detroit, MI, 1998). Used by permission of Ron Silliman.

William Carlos Williams, "The Young Housewife," in *The Collected Poems of William Carlos Williams,* vol. 1, 1909–1939, ed. A. Walton Litz and Christopher MacGowan (New York: New Directions, 1986), copyright © 1938 New Directions Publishing Corporation. Used by permission of New Directions Publishing Corporation.

Introduction

Differential Reading

Reading Closely

Not long ago I was teaching a graduate course called "Theory of the Avant-Garde," which covered such major movements as Futurism and Dada as well as two individual American "avant-gardists"—Gertrude Stein and William Carlos Williams. The course material was largely unfamiliar to the class: F. T. Marinetti's *parole in libertà,* Velimir Khlebnikov's *Tables of Destiny,* Marcel Duchamp's *Large Glass* and the "notes" for its execution in the *White Box,* Kurt Schwitters's collages and sound poems, and Raoul Haussman's political satire. The students were remarkably astute on the larger aesthetic and ideological issues involved and especially perceptive about visual works. I was therefore astonished when at semester's end we came to what I took to be the more familiar American modernist exemplars and found that the same students who could discuss with great aplomb the relation of the Milky Way to Bachelors in the *Large Glass* were largely at a loss when it came to Williams's short lyric poems like "Danse Russe" or "The Young Housewife"—both, incidentally, well-known anthology pieces. Here is "The Young Housewife":

> At ten A.M. the young housewife
> moves about in negligee behind
> the wooden walls of her husband's house.
> I pass solitary in my car.
>
> Then again she comes to the curb
> to call the ice-man, fish-man, and stands
> shy, uncorseted, tucking in
> stray ends of hair, and I compare her
> to a fallen leaf.

> The noiseless wheels of my car
> rush with a crackling sound over
> dried leaves as I bow and pass smiling.[1]

In the self-consciously feminist eighties, readers often objected to what they perceived as the rape fantasy in this poem: if the young housewife is comparable "to a fallen leaf," and the "noiseless wheels" of the poet's car "rush with a crackling sound over / dried leaves," he is evidently longing to "ride over" the young woman, to possess her. This analysis, I shall suggest later, is not incorrect, but the reference to rape ignores the wry humor of the poem's tone, the delicacy of its irony.

In 2002 the response was much more bizarre. A number of students, for example, took the young housewife to be a prostitute because she comes to the curb and calls men. She is, moreover, in a state of undress—"in negligee" and "uncorseted." And the poet compares her to a "fallen leaf"—that is, a fallen woman. But, I asked these students, what about those men the young housewife actually calls from the curb: "the ice-man" and "fish-man"— which is to say, delivery men who bring daily domestic goods to the house? And why is she doing these things, shyly "tucking in / stray ends of hair" at 10 A.M.? Again, why does the poet "bow" to this prostitute or call girl and "pass smiling"? Why such respectful—and distant—behavior?

This last question prompted mere dismissal on the part of the class, for, it was argued, there must be something funny going on here, because you can't bow in a car! In response I started driving in my chair and doffing my imaginary hat, as was the habit in early-twentieth-century America, so as to show them that all "bows" are not Japanese deep bows of the kind they have seen in the movies. Indeed, I've been practicing the Williams bow and smile in my car ever since.

Another reading proffered by the class was that the poet-speaker has been having an ongoing affair with the young housewife. Otherwise, how would he know that she wears negligees in the morning? No doubt he is jealous of the husband who owns her, the husband behind whose "wooden walls" she is forced to perform her daily tasks. And he is bitter about being "solitary" in his car and hence fantasizes about "crushing" her.

This reading is really not much more convincing than the first. One doesn't refer to one's mistress as "*the* young housewife," and a "shy" one at that. If the speaker, who evidently doesn't know her by name, is passing "solitary in [his] car," he can only surmise—or imagine—what she might be wearing. When he does see her as he passes, she is outside the front door, shyly calling the ice-man and fish-man; so, if the two are indeed lovers, she is behaving peculiarly indeed. More important—if the poet were her lover, why does he merely "bow and pass smiling"? Why no interaction between the two?

But surely, it will be argued, there isn't one "correct" reading, is there? If post-structuralism taught us anything, it's that the reader can construct the text in a variety of ways. True enough, but that is not to say that anything goes. For example, if someone argued that "The Young Wife" deals with trench warfare, at its height in 1916 when this poem was written, everyone would agree that this is nonsense.

How, then, does one proceed? Perhaps there is finally no alternative to what was called in the Bad Old Days, *close reading.* Today's students may have no idea what close reading entails, but surely their teachers vaguely remember close reading or *explication de texte,* as it was known in French, as some sort of New Critical or Formalist exercise whereby readers performed dry, boring, and nitpicking analyses on given "autonomous" texts, disregarding the culture, politics, and ideology of those texts in the interest of metaphor, paradox, irony, and what a leading "close reader" of the 1950s, Harvard's Reuben Brower, called the "key design" of a literary work.[2] But would a *far reading,* then, be better than a close one? Well, not exactly, but perhaps *reading* is itself passé, what with the possibility that a given poem or novel could serve as an exemplar of this or that theory, in which case one might only have to focus on a particular passage. In the case of T. S. Eliot's "Gerontion," for example, one need only discuss the specifically anti-Semitic passages so as to demonstrate Eliot's racism.

But close reading was hardly confined to the New Critics or to Formalists of various stripes. There have been stunning Marxist close readings—for example, those by T. J. Clark of specific modernist paintings from Manet's *Bar at the Follies Bergère* to DeKooning's *Suburb in Havana.* And the best close readings we have of Williams are probably those of Hugh Kenner, who understood that poetry was not the equivalent of metaphor or a "key design" waiting to be unpacked. Indeed, in his readings of Joyce and Beckett, Pound and Williams, Kenner relied just as heavily on biographical and cultural information as he did on rhetorical analysis. You could not, for example, understand the minimalist lyric "As the cat," he noted, unless you knew what a "jamcloset" was.[3]

Formalist reading, we are regularly told, goes hand in hand with the premise that the poem is an autonomous artifact. But the privileging of the poetic function has never meant that knowledge—of the poet's life, milieu, culture, and especially his or her other poems—is not relevant. Roman Jakobson's great essay on Mayakovsky's poetic called "The Generation That Swallowed

Its Poets" is a case in point. In the case of "The Young Housewife," it surely helps to know that each morning, Dr. Williams, a busy pediatrician, left his house at 9 Ridge Road in suburban Rutherford, New Jersey, and headed for his office, proceeding, later in the day, to make house calls and hospital calls that naturally involved a good deal of driving. Poems were something he wrote on the run, between patients, generally leaving a page in the office typewriter and composing a verse or two when he had a free moment.

There is currently much speculation about Williams's love life. By his own admission, in poems like "Asphodel that Greeny Flower" and the *Autobiography,* he had his share of affairs, but for obvious reasons they had to be highly circumspect: Williams was a married man, the father of two sons, in a small suburban town. There are indeed poems that allude to specific incidents—for example, poem IX in *Spring and All,* with its address to a hospital nurse: "O 'Kiki' / O Miss Margaret Jarvis / The backhandspring" (*Collected Poems* 1 200). But "The Young Housewife" is written in the third person, its tone one of bemused, clinical detachment. The title itself suggests that the woman in question is one the poet barely knew, someone he merely saw fleetingly on his daily drive to the office.

Williams's poem has none of the difficult references and allusions we find in Pound or Eliot; there seems to be nothing to "look up." Indeed, the New Critics found Williams's poetry so "flat," so prosaic, that they dismissed it as inferior to the poetry of Robert Frost or Hart Crane. But the references that were obvious to Williams's contemporaries may now be as obscure as Pound's Chinese ideograms or references to Eleusis in *The Cantos.* In the twenty-first century, the ice-man and fish-man are no longer familiar figures. Was there really a time when people did not have refrigerators and hence needed to have a block of ice delivered to their homes? When the milk-man delivered the requisite quarts every morning? And when the fish-man delivered fresh fish on demand? Williams's reader needs to know that in the early twentieth century, home delivery—now pretty much reserved for the newspaper—was the order of the day. The calling of the ice-man and fish-man is thus simply part of the housewife's morning routine. Or take the phrase "as I bow and pass smiling" which my students found unrealistic. In 1916 men routinely wore hats outside their homes, and when they greeted someone, especially a lady, they inclined their heads slightly and doffed their hats. It is a scene played out in any Humphrey Bogart or Fred MacMurray film you care to see.

Inevitably, then, we cannot separate a close reading of the poem from at least some reading of the poet's culture. In another well-known Williams poem, "Danse Russe" (1916), the poet tells us that it's his inclination, "when my wife is sleeping / and the baby and Kathleen / are sleeping," to retire to his "north room" and "dance naked, grotesquely / before my mirror . . . sing-ing softly to myself, 'I am lonely, lonely, / I was born to be lonely, / I am best so!'" (*Collected Poems* 1 86–87). To assume, as some students did, that Kathleen, clearly the baby's nurse, and the poet are lovers, is to ignore the speaker's consuming desire to be alone, to assert his independence from the daily household routine. On the other hand, this transient desire has its comic side, as we know from the poem's conclusion that even as the poet does his eccentric little naked dance, he declares, "Who shall say I am not / the happy genius of my household?" The poet is smiling at his own antics.

Indeed, a droll, tongue-in-cheek humor is central to these early Williams lyrics, as their language and genre suggest. Because poetry now tends to be taught, when taught at all, without recourse to convention and genre, readers fail to recognize that "The Young Housewife" is to be read as an updated ver-sion of the *chanson courtois:* the "solitary" physician at the wheel of his car is a modern version of the knight on his charger, approaching the fortified castle where his lady is kept in captivity by the tyrannical lord of the manor. The "young housewife," pictured "behind / the wooden walls of her hus-band's house"—a deliciously long-winded circumlocution—is inaccessible to the poet. But his "Complaint" is more parodic than real; he does not pene-trate the "wooden" castle before him; indeed he merely passes by. And he will not languish or wither away from unrequited love; on the contrary, the poem ends with a smile. After all, as neighboring poems make clear, he has, for better or worse, his own wife—another young housewife, incidentally, who must negotiate with ice-men and fish-men.

Given these generic markers, the poem itself is a triumph of tone. The three-stanza free-verse poem begins matter-of-factly:

> /   / /\   //   /   /   /\
> At ten A. M.   the young housewife

It sounds like a lab report, but Williams slyly makes the second word group echo the first by repeating its stress pattern in elongated form, as if to equate the anonymous woman with a mere time signal.[4] After this casual opening, the second line deviates from the colloquial norm:

> moves about in negligee behind

Normal syntax would demand an article or possessive pronoun before "neg-ligee"; its absence suggests that "in negligee" is this young woman's inherent state—a supposition borne out by the curious break after "behind" that gives us a double entendre, focusing on the woman's "in negligee behind." The same phenomenon occurs in lines 7–8, where the poet, passing "solitary in [his] car," first surmises (or imagines) that the young housewife is "uncorseted" and then observes her "tucking in" what the line break anticipates will be her flesh, deliciously not yet tucked into her corset, but that turns out to refer to "stray ends of hair."

With the image of those sexually charged "stray ends of hair," the poet's erotic fantasy reaches its peak. Williams's lyric form, James Breslin observed in what is probably still the best general book on the poet, "renders prosaic subjects with a tough colloquial flatness."[5] But what is interesting is that this "colloquial flatness" so easily moves—and this is a Williams trademark—into a quasi-surrealism, a fantasy state. The young housewife's appearance, uncorseted and "in negligee," may be largely a projection of the poet's own desire. And the comparison that now follows—"and I compare her / to a fallen leaf"—is patently absurd, since no one could seem fresher, younger, more shyly inexperienced than this young, probably newly married woman, performing her housewifely tasks. The poet may well wish that she would come to the curb and call out, not to the ice-man or fish-man, but to him! It is only in foolishly comparing her to a fallen leaf that he can distance himself from her presence.

And so, in the final stanza the "noiseless wheels of [his] car / rush with a crackling sound over / dried leaves"—a puzzle, for how do noiseless wheels crackle? Perhaps the poet-doctor is just imagining the sound? He knows, in any case, that normalcy must prevail, that it is 10 A.M. on an ordinary weekday morning and probably time to make hospital rounds. The desire to "rush with a crackling sound over / dried leaves" is thus fleeting and subliminal, a momentary wish to "have" what belongs to another man. But within the suburban context of the poem, nothing is going to happen. The driver merely "bow[s] and pass[es] smiling." Time to move on.

It is only by looking closely at line breaks, syntactic units, and word order that the delicately comic/erotic tone of "The Young Housewife" can be understood. If the poet's is a rape fantasy, it remains firmly in the poet's mind, the irony being that the young woman seems largely unaware of his presence. Indeed, the poet's self-assertion is itself comic, as in the silly internal rhyme:

Stray ends of *hair,* and I com*pare* her

And this line also contains an echo of "Shall I compare thee to a summer's day?" In the same vein, the alliteration of *h*'s in lines 2 and 3—"be*h*ind," "*h*er," "*h*usband's *h*ouse"—gives the lines a breathlessness connoting anticipation rather than any kind of serious plot.

Then, too, consider the relation of line to stanza in "The Young House-wife." The poem's twelve lines, ranging from five to nine syllables, are divided into three stanzas of four, five, and three lines, respectively. Given the purposely prosaic rhythm of such lines as

    / || /\ / || /   /\
    Shy, uncorseted, tucking in

whose eight syllables carry only three primary stresses, broken by caesurae, one wonders why Williams felt he had to group these irregular lines into stanzas at all. I think there are two reasons. First, these are, in Hugh Kenner's words, "stanzas you can't quite *hear*. . . . They are stanzas to see, and the sight of them, as so often in Williams inflects the speaking voice, the listening ear, with obligations difficult to specify."[6] Then, too, there is a time gap between each of the stanzas. In the space between stanzas 1 and 2, the young housewife makes her appearance. Between stanzas 2 and 3, the doctor driving by finally makes eye contact with her. "Smiling" is the key word in this context—the moment when she seems to finally acknowledge the man's presence—although that too may be his imagination.

"Close reading" moves readily between such detail and larger cultural and historical determinants. What was the role of wives in pre–World War I America? What sort of decorum was observed between men and women, and when was it violated? If we read "The Young Housewife" against Williams's own short stories, poems, and autobiographical writing, a more complex picture of the Rutherford scene emerges. Eccentricity, for example, was wholly frowned upon, as we see in "Danse Russe." Again, if we read "The Young Housewife" against, say, the work of Williams's friends Wallace Stevens and Marianne Moore, we note a willingness to trace the curve of actual emotions and sexual fantasies that Stevens would have shied away from and that Moore would have rendered in much more symbolic/allegorical terms. Here class and gender considerations come into play, as do issues of nationality when we read Williams against his expatriate friend Ezra Pound. The young housewife is not compared to a Greek goddess or a figure in a Renaissance painting, and she is, significantly, never given a name, whether realistic like Eliot's Miss Helen Slingsby or fanciful like Stevens's Nanzia Nuncio. Rather, it is location that counts for Williams—the suburb, a word that rhymes with the *curb* from which his housewife calls. And that suburb, epitomized by the wooden walls of her husband's house, acts to *curb* her very activity.

Did British poets of 1916 write this way? And if not, why not? What historical constraints and cultural markers were operative? It would be fascinating to explore such questions, but current discourse about poetry is reluctant to ask them. *Using everything,* as Gertrude Stein enunciated the principle, is out of favor. And speaking of Stein, students who took the young housewife to be a prostitute and the Kathleen of *Danse Russe* to be Williams's girlfriend were even more misled by Stein's "Miss Furr and Miss Skeene." In the course of this brilliant and witty tale of a lesbian affair and its breakup, we read:

> She [Helen] went to see them where she had always been living and where she did not find it gay. She had a pleasant home there, Mrs. Furr was a pleasant enough woman, Mr. Furr was a pleasant enough man, *Helen told them* and they were not worrying, that she did not find it gay living where she had always been living. [my emphasis][7]

I received one student paper called "How Mrs. Furr became Miss Furr," arguing that Helen Furr and Mrs. Furr are one and the same and that the latter divorces Mr. Furr because she needs to escape from her stifling bourgeois milieu. Such wholesale misconstruction of "Miss Furr and Miss Skeene" (whose names play so nicely on "fur" and "skin") suggests that before we jump off into speculations about Stein's epistemology, her treatment of gender, or her situation as a secular Jewish expatriate, we had better *read* the text in question. Fortunately, "Miss Furr and Miss Skeene" is only five pages long.

Reading Contemporaneously

For the New Critics, who are often considered to be the exemplary practitioners of close reading, the guiding assumption, as I noted above, was that the given poem would yield up a "key design"—what Reuben Brower called "the aura around a bright, clear centre." Cleanth Brooks, for example, based his reading of Keats's "Ode on a Grecian Urn" on the "central paradox" conveyed by the phrase "Cold Pastoral!" in the final stanza:

> The word "pastoral" suggests warmth, spontaneity, the natural and the informal as well as the idyllic; the simple, and the informally charming. What the urn tells is a "flowery tale," a "leaf-fring'd legend," but the "sylvan historian" works in terms of marble. The urn itself is cold, and the life beyond life which it expresses is life which has been formed, arranged. . . . It is as enigmatic as eternity is, for like eternity, its history is beyond time, outside time, and for this very reason bewilders our time-ridden minds: it teases us.[8]

It is from this recognition that Brooks now moves to the enigmatic ending of the Ode: "Beauty is truth, truth beauty,—that is all, / Ye know on earth and all ye need to know." "The urn," writes Brooks, "is beautiful, and yet its beauty is based—what else is the poem concerned with?—on an imaginative perception of essentials. Such a vision is beautiful but it is also true" (*Well Wrought Urn* 164).

This is an admirable reading of Keats's *Ode*, but it begins with three premises few of us would accept today: (1) that the language of poetry is, as Brooks himself puts it, "the language of paradox"; (2) that this central truth remains the same across the ages—and, by implication, that it is unrelated to culture, gender, and a given poem's historical moment; and (3) that poetics is equivalent to hermeneutics, the critic's role being to determine what it is a given poem says. True, Brooks himself was aware of what he called, in a chapter of *The Well Wrought Urn*, the "heresy of paraphrase" and insisted that a poem is "a pattern of resolutions and balances and harmonizations, developed through a temporal scheme" (203). But the resolutions and balances he speaks of are all thematic—very little is said of rhythm and syntax or, for that matter, of *language* itself—and in any case they must be "resolutions and balances and harmonizations"—which is to say the poem (or novel or drama) must be *centered*.

But what happens when, as in so much of the innovative writing of the present, there is no "aura around a bright, clear centre," no "balance" between given "tensions," no "resolution" of "opposites"? Critical discourse has had a very difficult time with such poetry: either it dismisses the new work out of hand as simply too opaque, obscure, and disorganized to reward any kind of sustained attention, or it is satisfied to talk around questions of meaning and value, relating the poetic work in question to a particular theory or an alternate discourse—say, from anthropology or ecology.

The work of English poet Tom Raworth is a case in point. Now in his sixties, Raworth has long been regarded as an important outsider poet, an experimentalist, with a following primarily in the United States, where he has published dozens of small-press books, given readings, and held major residencies and visiting lectureships. In the United Kingdom there have been a few respectful and serious essays on his work by such leading academics as John Barrell and Colin MacCabe, both of whom have discussed the dissolution of lyric subjectivity in Raworth's poetry from the perspective of poststructuralist and cultural theory.[9] But even though the Carcanet Press has now published Raworth's *Collected Poems* (2003)—a volume of almost six hundred pages—there remains, as I discovered when I was asked to review the book for the *Times Literary Supplement,* almost no sustained discussion of the poetry itself. The one exception is a recent special issue of Nate Dorward's excellent but little known Canadian journal *The Gig* (summer 2003), and even Dorward has remarked, in an essay for the *Chicago Review,* that in the case of a poetry like Raworth's, "any act of 'close reading'—of 'reading for content'—would either be willfully synthetic or merely document the trace of private associations (mine) that are both unstable and of doubtful value to another reader." To submit a poem or short passage to "a quick and contained 'close reading' before extrapolating to a larger poetic entity," Dorward argues, suggests that any other text by the poet in question would do just as well—that they are all the same. Moreover, "close reading is . . . problematic in dealing with highly open-ended poetry, since close reading often carries within it ideals of a 'complete' reading that are at odds with poetries that emphasize open-endedness and arbitrariness." Indeed, as in the case of John Ashbery, it is a mistake to expect that "every detail in the poem can or should be *justified.*"[10]

This is an appealing argument: why shouldn't open-ended poetry be subject to open-ended, more free-wheeling readings? Why submit an Ashbery or Raworth poem to a "close reading" that may distort the larger parameters of the poet's oeuvre? Dorward inadvertently answers his own question when he admits, "In proportion to the length of Raworth's career [the *Collected Poems* covers the period 1966 to the present] and the evident importance of his work to several generations of poets from the UK, North America, and Europe, there has been remarkably little substantial criticism about his poetry," a poetry, Dorward admits, that remains largely "elusive" ("On Raworth's Sonnets" 18). If, after more than three decades of publication, a poet's oeuvre continues to be little known and largely "elusive," surely something must be wrong. For either Raworth's work really *is* tediously obscure, as his detractors think, or there must be a way of accounting for the strong appeal of his poetry, especially to a younger generation.

Suppose, then, that we take a stab at reading an early (1968), little-known Raworth poem called "These Are Not Catastrophes I Went out of my Way to Look for":[11]

corners of my mouth sore
i keep licking them, drying them with the back of my hand
bitten nails but three i am growing
skin frayed round the others white flecks on them all

no post today, newspapers and the childrens'
comic, i sit

in the lavatory reading heros the spartan
and the iron man

flick ash in the bath trying to hit the plughole
listen to the broom outside examine
new pencil marks on the wall, a figure four

the shadows, medicines, a wicker
laundry basket lid pink with toothpaste

between my legs i read

   levi stra
    origina
   quality clo

   leaning too far forward
into the patch of sunlight (*Collected Poems* 37)

Like Williams's "Danse Russe," this is a domestic poem, expressing a certain malaise about domesticity. But it resembles neither the work of Raworth's closest poet-friend, the American Ed Dorn, nor the "domestic" lyric of his British contemporaries. Philip Larkin has a poem called "Home Is So Sad," that mourns the family house, bereft of its dead owners, with the words, "You can see how it was: / Look at the pictures and the cutlery. / The music in the piano stool. That vase."[12] What pictures, what sheet music, what vase? Raworth's own little domestic poem refuses Larkin's patronizing contract with the reader ("We know how dreary Mum and Dad's décor was, don't we?"), giving us a devastatingly graphic Portrait of the Artist caught up in the domestic round, a kind of latter-day Leopold Bloom reading *Photo-Bits* as he sits on the toilet.

"These Are Not Catastrophes I Went out of my Way to Look for" is a typical Raworth title: this poet's titles tend to be short, single words like "Ace" or "Writing" or "Act," or deliciously bombastic long ones like "My Face is My Own, I Thought," "You've Ruined My Evening / You've Ruined My Life," or "Come Back, Come Back, O Glittering and White!" The word *catastrophe* comes to us from Greek: *kata* (down) plus *strophe* (turn)—a *strophe* that also designated the first section of a Greek choral ode and, later, simply a structural unit in a given poem. If *catastrophe* originally referred to the dénouement of tragedy and hence a "sudden disaster," it has more recently come to mean "an absolute failure, often in humiliating or embarrassing circum-stances."[13] And in this sense, Raworth does have his daily domestic catastro-phes. His one real decision, the poem suggests, is to have let three of his nails grow—one does need nails for various physical acts—even as there is "skin frayed round the others white flecks on them all." "Lick" and "fleck" prepare the ground for the "flick" of "flick ash in the bath trying to hit the plughole." Accedia is a state of licking the corners of one's mouth and listening to the broom outside the lavatory door (evidently his wife is trying to tidy up), while examining "new pencil marks on the wall, a figure four." Our man on the toilet does not consider erasing these child graffiti; he just looks at them. And in this context, the "wicker / laundry basket lid pink with toothpaste" alludes slyly to Robert Creeley's "A Wicker Basket," that now-classic ballad of drunken regression and solipsism. But whereas Creeley's speaker hides from the world inside his "wicker basket," Raworth's, scanning comic books with titles like *Heros the Spartan* and *The Iron Man,* may be said to keep in touch with the catastrophe of Greek tragedy.

The poet's reading "between my legs" is especially apposite in this regard:

> levi stra
> origina
> quality clo

Literally, one surmises, the poet is contemplating not his navel but the label affixed to his jeans: "Levi-stra[uss] / origina[l] / quality clo[thes]." But "clo" can also refer to closet (as in water-closet) or to the "closure" Levi Strauss was always looking for in his structuralist systems—and that Raworth him-self rejects. "Origina[l]" is thus ambiguous, pointing to the poet's own *writ-ing* as well as his reading, for example his justifying the right margin here so as to produce the column *a-a-o,* which gives us Raworth's own alpha and omega. But let's not get carried away: what happens when you lean too far forward on the toilet? Well, it may mean one misses—and that would be lit-erally going out of one's way to produce a "catastrophe" one certainly hadn't been looking for.

Is it foolish or pedantic to try to justify the detail in such a seemingly casual little poem? Perhaps not, for every word and morpheme, I would sug-gest, is carefully chosen, beginning with those "corners of my mouth" that relate to the corners of the lavatory and of the newspaper page as well. And further, the first syllable of "corners"—rhyming with "sore" plays on the word "core," as if to say it is my very core that is sore. Meaning is not what

Raworth does away with—on the contrary—but he does avoid those causal networks to which readers of magazine verse and popular anthologies are still accustomed. Why is the speaker letting three of his fingernails grow rather than two or four? There can be no rational answer to such a question. And why doesn't he have anything better to do than to flick ash into the tub's plughole? Again, we cannot point to a "cause"; the condition simply *is*, and the poem's aim is to define it as accurately as possible.

"Accuracy"—what Pound called "constatation of fact"—is reflected in the very rhythms of "These Are Not Catastrophes." The poem's nineteen seemingly diaristic lines are grouped into stanzas as follows: 4, 4, 3, 2, 1 (3 half lines)—2. The poem's forward push seems to be toward this fragment (ll. 15–17), whose epiphany is no more than the truncated recitation of the designer label "Levi Strauss / original / quality clothes." But it is after this "discovery" that the poet can lean forward "into the patch of sunlight"—a phrase highly figured in its alliteration of *t*'s—and discharge his duty. The anticipated "catastrophe" would seem to be behind him.

Raworth's later poems develop this mode with increasing complexity and resonance; many take their cue from the long columnar poem (between one and four words per column) of more than two thousand lines called *Ace*,[14] whose four sections are suggestively titled "in think," "in mind," "in motion," and "in place," and whose coda, "Bolivia: another end of ace," has shorter sections called "in transit," "in part", "in consideration," and "in love." The challenge is to see how these parts relate: is "in think" the same as "in mind"? And how does "in love" relate to being "in transit"? Within the poem itself, these syntactic conundrums are worked out.

When Raworth performs *Ace* orally, he recites it at top speed, no change of inflection, and no pause for breath—a bravura performance that has been imitated by a score of younger poets. The even tone has often been interpreted as the absence of affect: everything seems to be as important as everything else. But when one reads *Ace* a few times, it reveals itself as curiously emotional in that its forward thrust, its drive toward change, is everywhere short-circuited by refrain (e.g., "SHOCK SHOCK"), repetition, rhyme, echolalia, and double entendre so that the asserted continuity is increasingly difficult to maintain. Accordingly, the poem's meditation on identity, time, and memory, varied in myriad ways, becomes a complex process in which the Ace never trumps for long. Raworth's pronouns shift from "I" to "you" to "he," the referents never being specified; and the language oscillates between straightforward abstract phrase to found text, citation, allusion to film plots and pop recordings, and every manner of cliché. *Ace* opens with a rhyme for the title—"new face"—and continues "from my home / what do you think / I'll voice out / of the news." A record is played "with a light pickup" and we read:

> bless you brother
> yours
> till the energy
> gaps again
> let light
> blink
> history think
> leaves some thing
> like a bomb
> relief again
> to sail
> against depression
> i glow
> and flicker
> change
> but first
> a present
> that
> fits me
> to a t
> no mist
> but sky
> and we
> beneath it (*Collected Poems* 201–02)

The predominant vowel of this passage is the short *i* following or preceding the consonant *t* as in *till* or *fits*. This minimal pattern is heard again and again, its structural control in tension with the poem's dominant rhetorical device, which is the non sequitur. Nothing here "follows," and yet almost every phrase echoes a more familiar one, as when "Let there be light" becomes "let light / blink" or when the "I" is seen to "glow / and flicker" like the proverbial burnt-out candle. A "present" is given "that / fits me / to a t / no mist," the letters almost spelling out the word *gift*, synonymous with "present." And this is followed by the mock-astute observation about "sky / and we / beneath it."

In the *I-T-T* context of the column, the two words that stand out by contrast are "bomb" and "depression." What's a bomb doing in this "history think" (perhaps an echo of Eliot's "Gerontion," where history forces the poet to "Think now") context? And why and how does one "sail / against depression"? The refrain "SHOCK / SHOCK" now comes as a reminder of the world lived in with its constant talk of bombs, but the blinking light turns into a "thinking light" and then a "painted light," while the word "energy" recurs a number of times to suggest that even after the bomb we just have to keep going. The short, fragmented units equivocate continually between all that is fixed and frozen and the motion that breaks through the ice. Despite the presence of "the home / service/ the light / programme / the third programme" and other deadly daily routines, "words / clutter / me / me / face enters / not me / use / no / mad / for feeling / me / and / it / is a song / cloud/ white / night / moon" (*Collected Poems* 206–07). *Ace* tracks a Beckettian process of "I can't go on, I'll go on," using everyday lingo and a steady *stream* of allusions. It regularly breaks into song and concludes (in the second, or Bolivia conclusion) with the words "by delight / in softness / heart / and heart / so far / a / part," where the pauses at line break provide a kind of Wittgenstein cum pop song conclusion.

If such writing looks random, think again! For one thing, no two sequential lines of *Ace* have exactly the same syntax. Unlike Gertrude Stein, Raworth is not partial to prepositions at the expense of adjectives or adverbs; it's just that each line unit is separate from the one before and after, because it has a different syntactic shape. As Raworth puts it after the first four hundred lines or so, "why / not / a little / difference / each / time / certain / gambles"—where in eight lines there is no repetition of grammatical form. *Difference,* for this brilliant poet, is the source of poetic inspiration—"think / leaves some thing"—even as his structural markers (mostly sonic but also metonymic) are always in place. Indeed, when "in mind" and "in motion" come together, "in place" can follow. But being so regularly "in transit," we don't always recognize when we have arrived.

Reading Differentially

My "close reading" of a few pages of *Ace* has touched only on the "profound / weight less ness" of this complex work, whose structure of dislocations might be profitably compared to that of such related poetic sequences as Ashbery's *Flow Chart* on the one hand, Creeley's *Pieces* on the other. If *Ace* seems more uncompromising than either of these, it may well be that Raworth's relationship to institutions is much slighter than theirs: this poet has never been a card-carrying academic and has been peculiarly reluctant to grant interviews, "explain" the sources of his poetry, or participate in discourse on poetics. Living in near poverty, he has largely gone his own way, although his Web site, featuring his recent political collages and obituaries for poet-friends, is surprisingly genial and reader-friendly, his radical politics presented as high comedy. Indeed, reading Raworth suggests that given the endless discourse of *isms* and *izations* (as in *globalization*) that confronts us today, perhaps the most fruitful task is to discriminate *difference*, both within a given work and within the larger categories of artworks. I am well aware, of course, that the choice of works to be so read in the first place is inevitably based on larger theoretical assumptions; otherwise, there is no way to get beyond empiricism. Still, now that the long twentieth century is behind us and many of our sacred texts are ripe for revaluation even as other newer ones crowd the field, it may be a good moment to focus on what Marcel Duchamp called the *infrathin*.

What is *infrathin*? In the later thirties, when Duchamp was restoring his *Large Glass* after it was shattered and was beginning work on his *Boîte en valise*, he wrote a series of notes on what he called the *inframince*.[15] The term, he declared, could not be defined; one could only give examples of it. I provide a list of Duchamp's most telling examples elsewhere;[16] here let me cite just a few:

The warmth of a seat (which has just been left) is infra-thin. (no. 4)

Infra thin separation between/the *detonation* noise of a gun/(very close) *and* the *apparition* of the bullet / hole in the target . . . (no. 12 verso)

2 forms cast in/the same mold (?) differ/from each other/by an infra thin separative/amount—

just touching. While trying to place 1 plane surface/precisely on another plane surface/you pass through some *infra thin moments*— (no. 45).

Those infrathin moments or qualities are related, in a slightly later note, to Duchamp's definition of "*Nominalism* [literal]":

No more generic/specific/numeric/distinction between words (tables is/not the plural of table, ate has nothing in common with eat). No more physical/adaptation of concrete words; no more/conceptual value of abstract words. (no. 185)

Comic as some of these distinctions sound, Duchamp took them quite seriously: indeed, no two of his famous boxes, no two of his readymades or scraps of paper are identical: for him, "ate" is not the same as "eat," "table" as "tables," and "identity" a meaningless concept.

More than thirty years after Duchamp coined the term *infrathin*, the philosopher Gilles Deleuze declared, "Modern life is such that, confronted with the most mechanical, the most stereotypical repetitions, inside and outside ourselves, we endlessly extract from them little differences, variations and modifications." Those "little differences" are crucial in that:

> I make, remake and unmake my concepts along a moving horizon, from an always decentred centre, from an always displaced periphery which repeats and differenciates them. The task of modern philosophy is to overcome the alternatives temporal/non-temporal, historical/eternal and particular/universal. . . . Neither empirical particularities nor abstract universal: a *Cogito* for a dissolved self.[17]

"But isn't *the same* at least the same?" Wittgenstein asks sardonically in proposition §215 of *Philosophical Investigations*, answering his own question as follows:

> We seem to have an infallible paradigm of identity in the identity of a thing with itself. I feel like saying: "here at any rate there can't be a variety of interpretations. If you are seeing a thing you are seeing identity too."
>
> Then are two things the same when they are what *one* thing is? And how am I to apply what the *one* thing shows me to the case of two things?
>
> §216. "A thing is identical with itself."—There is no finer example of a useless proposition, which yet is connected with a certain play of the imagination. It is as if in imagination we put a thing into its own shape and saw that it fitted.[18]

In Duchamp's words above, "2 forms cast in / the same mold (?) differ / from each other / by an infra thin separative / amount." The ordinary observer may not notice this difference, which is perhaps best understood as the artist's domain. Deleuze cites the aesthetician Pius Servien as follows:

Pius Servien rightly distinguished two languages: the language of science, dominated by the symbol of Equality, in which each term may be replaced by others, and lyrical language, in which every term is irreplaceable and can only be repeated. Repetition can always be "represented" as extreme resemblance or perfect equivalence, but the fact that one can pass by degrees from one thing to another does not prevent their being different in kind. (*Difference and Repetition* 2)

"Lyrical language [is that] in which every term is irreplaceable and can only be repeated": if this sounds like Archibald MacLeish's notorious *Ars Poetica*, with its injunction that "A poem should not mean, / but be," or like Cleanth Brooks's "heresy of paraphrase," perhaps it is time for some differential reading of the critics as well as the poets.

Academic criticism today, unfamiliar as it generally is with the actual practice of the scorned and fabled New Criticism, has often taken the position that the emphasis on the materiality of the text—its actual language, syntax, use of white space, and typographical elements, as theorized by such poet-theorists as Charles Bernstein and Steve McCaffery—is no more than an updated version of the old Brooks-and-Warren poetic. Thus Jennifer Ashton, in a review essay on recent studies of modernism, cites Charles Bernstein's statement that "the poem said any other way is not the poem" as a signal instance of "the New Critical heresy," for, so she claims, Bernstein's view, like Lyn Hejinian's rejection of closure, makes it impossible to interpret a given poem; one can only "experience" it.[19]

Such critique—and it persists in English departments—cries out for a bit of differential reading. For one thing, those big words—*experience* and *interpretation*, like *autonomy* and *materiality*—are never defined. Ashton refers briefly to Fredric Jameson's diagnosis of the "failure" of "postmodernism" to practice "historical critique" ("Modernism's 'New' Literalism" 382), but then again, what is the difference between their "postmodernism" and, say, Charles Olson's or Frank O'Hara's—the poetic mode of an earlier generation to be found in such anthologies as Donald Allen's *The Postmoderns*?[20]

Indeed, Bernstein's "The poem said any other way is not the poem" is not, in fact, a Brooksian formulation. For Brooks, as I noted earlier, the language of poetry is equivalent to the language of paradox, and a given poem's central paradox, expressed metaphorically, must permeate the entire poem and give it an ordered, centered structure. The role of sound, syntax, visual layout—these are aspects of the "saying another way" that Brooks didn't especially consider. Indeed, the very anthologizing of, say, Andrew Marvell's

"The Garden" or Robert Frost's "Once by the Pacific" prevented attention to textual and materialist poetics.

Ce que dit la poésie ne peut être dit autrement. ("That which poetry says cannot be said otherwise.")[21] These are the words not of a New Critic but of the French poet-mathematician-theorist Jacques Roubaud, one of the founders and most active members of the Oulipo,[22] and they were written for a roundtable on poetics in 2002. It would be pedantic to detail here the history of this theory of poetry; suffice it to say that it has its ancestry in Plato and Longinus, the medieval rhetoricians, the troubadour poets, in Baudelaire and especially Stephane Mallarmé, whose *Crise de vers* is perhaps its central document. In our century, the key figures are Roman Jakobson, himself a Russian Futurist poet, and his Formalist circle, whose studies of the "orientation toward the neighboring word" have given us some of the most intriguing essays on poetics we have.

"Art," declared Hugh Kenner, a critic no one has ever tried to place in the New Critical camp, "lifts the saying out of the zone of things said." The reference is to Williams (whom the New Critics studiously ignored, their British counterparts referring to him dismissively as Carlos Williams) in Kenner's well-known essay "Something to Say." And to make his point, he reformats "The Red Wheel Barrow" in prose:

So much depends upon a red wheelbarrow glazed with rainwater beside the white chickens.

"Try it over in any voice you like," notes Kenner, "it is impossible. . . . To whom might the sentence be spoken, for what purpose? . . . Not only is what the sentence says banal, if you heard someone say it you'd wince. But hammered on the typewriter into a *thing made,* and this without displacing a single word except typographically, the sixteen words exist in a different zone altogether, a zone remote from the world of sayers and sayings" (*Homemade World* 60). Or in Charles Bernstein's words in *Artifice of Absorption,* "the poem said any other way is not the poem."

"While trying to place 1 plane surface / precisely on another plane surface / you pass through some *infra thin moments.*" Duchamp, one imagines, would have understood perfectly Deleuze's declaration that "on every occasion *these concepts of a pure difference and a complex repetition* seemed to connect and coalesce. The divergence and decentering of difference corresponded closely to a displacement and a disguising within repetition" (*Difference and Repetition* xx, emphasis Deleuze's). Thus there are numbers of versions of Du-

champ's famous French window called *Fresh Widow,* and the readymade is
further replicated in Duchamp's various boxes and *boîtes en valises,* but it
could never have any other name than *Fresh Widow.*

While I was contemplating these issues, I received a copy of Susan Howe's
new book, *The Midnight* (2003), her extraordinary intricate verbal/visual/
"textile" collage memoir of her mother, Mary Manning, who died in 1999.
The notion of "difference in repetition" governs the whole book, whose "Bed
Hangings" are themselves textiles, whose stitchings and unstitchings reveal the most infrathin changes. Examples abound, but here let me mention just one such infrathin moment, which occurs on page 119, following,
on the facing page, Howe's witty and malicious biographical sketch of the
Irish actor and director Michael Mac Liammóir (born Alfred Willmore in
1890 in Kensal Green, London)—an actor-director whose memoir "Some
Talented Women," published in Sean O'Faoláin's magazine *The Bell* (1944),
commented cattily on Mary Manning's "caustic tongue" and remarked:

> Her ruling passion was ambition. She worshipped success. It was the
> most natural reaction of a temperament set in the major key against
> the country in which she had lived all her life and where everything
> had failed; and it was inevitable that she should later have married an
> American and gone to live in Boston.[23]

Howe never comments on the justice or injustice of this assessment: it
awaits the adjudication of myriad collage fragments. Conflicting images and
references to Manning both precede and follow the Mac Liammóir passage. But on page 119 (see figure 1), the poet reproduces a facsimile of the first
or "A" page of Mary Manning's address book, the last such she owned, in
which she was jotting down phone numbers at the time of her death. The
facsimile page is separated by a block of print (Howe's account of her mother's comings and goings between Ireland and Boston, finally settling in the
latter) from a rather muzzy photograph of a young girl, pasted at an angle
into its frame, reproduced at the top of the page. Howe's note for this image
reads "Photograph of Mary Manning, circa 1913. Caption reads: 'Watching
an aeroplane / Mary Manning.'" But the caption is not reproduced here.

Watching an aeroplane in 1913? The page from the address book has been
cropped and angled so that only two numbers are legible: Aer Lingus (800–
223-6537) and Audio-Ears (484-8700). What do these signify? Was Mary
Manning Howe planning a trip to Ireland when she died? Did she want to
die in her home country? Or is it merely a useful phone number to have when
Irish visitors come to Cambridge? Again, if this very old lady wanted to call

Audio-Ears, perhaps for a new hearing aid or repair of an old one, what does that signify vis-à-vis thoughts of death and Ireland? Mary Manning's purpose remains mysterious. But *The Midnight* itself lifts the saying out of the zone of things said. For can it be a coincidence that *Aer* is an anagram for *Ear(s)*? Or that *Lingus* contains the root that gives us *linguistic*? Then, too, *Aer* is a synonym for "air" or song—a language air, so to speak—and as such it depends, of course, on "Audio Ears." Maybe Mary Manning Howe's life wasn't such a failure after all. In any case, Howe's intricate differentials testify to the Deleuzian "displacement and disguising within repetition" that make poetic language what it is.

Close reading, especially of the radical differential texts of our time, provides, we have seen, fewer answers than questions—questions I try to deal with in the essays in this collection. Why is Eliot's "Gerontion" such a brilliant poem, despite its inclusion of unpleasant anti-Semitic passages, and what does sound structure have to do with it? How do Pound's catalogues of proper names function in *The Cantos,* and what does it mean to write a long poem that is so oddly nominalist? Is Pound's in fact, as is usually thought, an "ideogrammic" mode of writing? How does Eugene Jolas's multilingualism work, and what developments in later poetry does it anticipate? How does Haroldo de Campos adapt the lessons of Concrete poetry to the writing of prose, and how does Joyce's example in the *Wake* help to create a "concrete prose" that many contemporary poets are now using? Or again, what happens when Concrete poetry is related to musical form as in the early work of Ronald Johnson? Why did Beckett begin to write radio plays in the sixties, and how do these relate to his work in the theatre on the one hand, and to the evolution of *Hörspiel* on the other? What happens when Beckett collaborates with a composer like Morton Feldman? Does the inclusion of music detract from the power of the language itself? Or enhance it?

The essays on contemporaries raise somewhat broader issues. How do Language poets, ostensibly committed to the removal of the lyric voice, re-inscribe the subjectivity of the poet? How does the second generation of Language poets adapt the lessons of the first? And how does a "difficult" Language poet like Rae Armantrout relate to another "difficult"—but much more celebrated and evidently accessible—poet like Jorie Graham? How does an epistolary memoir like Tom Raworth's *Letters from Yaddo* relate to more conventional prose poems? How has the example of Oulipo, with its elaborate rules for a poetry of constraints, become prominent in the writing of younger poet-performers like Christian Bök and Caroline Bergvall? How does the adoption of constraint differ from the use of conventional metrical

Mary Manning had crossed the Irish Sea several times, though never the English Channel, and had crossed the Atlantic Ocean both ways twice (third class). Economic survival tactics during a time of war, revolution, counter-revolution, and the traumatic birth of a nation, meant setting out as a poor relation. So, after being an actress, a theatre critic, a magazine editor, the author of two plays and a novel, she arrived in Cambridge, Massachusetts in 1934 at the home of her Aunt Muriel where she met my father and became a faculty wife and a mother.

Even into her nineties she kept leaving in order to arrive one place or another as the first step in a never ending process somewhere else.

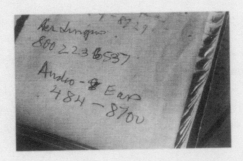

119

Fig. 1. Page 119 from *The Midnight* by Susan Howe (Copyright © 2003 Susan Howe. Used by permission)

form, and why, in this connection, is so much latter-day free verse so indifferent to the use of sound?

All of the essays in *Differentials* have been written within the past five years, all of them for specific occasions. Some have appeared in major journals or book collections, others in obscure "little magazines." A number have never been published before, and many are extensively revised. Since in most cases the occasion dictated, at least in part, a given argument or topic, I describe these occasions in brief headnotes. The collection is framed by two broader essays—the first, "Crisis in the Humanities?" is pedagogical, the second, "Writing Poetry/Writing about Poetry: Some Problems of Affiliation" both pedagogical and personal. When I reread the fourteen essays in sequence, I was surprised to find that they do in fact have a larger rationale and, I hope, a particular urgency.

This collection would not exist were it not for the many conference organizers, lecture coordinators, and editors of various journals and book collections, whose generous invitations prompted me to write (or rewrite) this or that essay: H. Porter Abbott, Helène Aji, Louis Armand, Rae Armantrout, Shyamal Bagchee, Mary Jo Bang, Ralph Berry, Sergio Bessa, Joel Bettridge, Regis Bonvicino, Graçia Capinha, Brian Caraher, Laura Cowan, Joshua Cohen, Thomas Cousineau, Jeffrey Di Leo, Joseph Donahue, Nate Dorward, Susan Dunn, Edward Foster, Ruben Gallo, Thomas Gardner, Fanny Howe, Wolfgang Huemer, David Jackson, Lynn Keller, John Kinsella, Peter Nicholls, Lois Oppenheim, Peter Quartermain, Claudia Rankine, David Rudrum, Rainer Rumold, Jean-Michel Rabaté, Lyle Shlesinger, John Tranter, Robert Von Hallberg, and John Watkins.

A number of the poets whose work is discussed in specific essays provided indispensable information: Rae Armantrout, Caroline Bergvall, Christian Bök, Kenneth Goldsmith, Susan Howe, Tom Raworth, and Rosmarie Waldrop. The late Haroldo de Campos, whose untimely death came just as I was putting the final touches on this manuscript, sent me many useful little magazines and broadsides, as did his brother, Augusto de Campos. And another poet who is also a scholar-critic, Craig Dworkin (whom I had the privilege of teaching when he was a Stanford undergraduate), read every essay here and made trenchant comments and suggestions.

But my greatest debt is to the two editors of the Contemporary Poetics Series at the University of Alabama Press—Charles Bernstein and Hank Lazer. It was Charles who first suggested to me that these essays might make an interesting book and who helped me conceptualize the volume. And Hank played the role of hands-on *editor extraordinaire,* going through what was originally a much longer manuscript, pruning and rearranging individual items so that they began to take shape. Hank's long and totally informed critique raised those hard questions that provided me with the challenge to undertake revision, essay by essay. In the few cases when I did not take his advice and preferred to include essay X rather than Y, I felt that I was carrying on a dialogue with a highly trusted mentor. This book obviously would not exist without his and Charles's initiative and guidance.

Differentials

This essay was written for a 1999 symposium at the Stanford Humanities Center on the question "Have the Humanistic Disciplines Collapsed?" It was subsequently published in the Boston Review *and revised in 2003 in response to more recent developments in the arts and humanities, especially the Internet revolution.*

I

Crisis in the Humanities?

Reconfiguring Literary Study for the Twenty-first Century

One of our most common genres today is the epitaph for the humanities. A few years ago, for example, Robert Weisbuch, the president of the Woodrow Wilson National Fellowship Foundation, declared:

> Today's consensus about the state of the humanities—it's bad, it's getting worse, and no one is doing much about it—is supported by dismal facts. The percentage of undergraduates majoring in humanities fields has been halved over the past three decades. Financing for faculty research has decreased. The salary gap between full-time scholars in the humanities and in other fields has widened, and more and more humanists are employed part time and paid ridiculously low salaries. . . . As doctoral programs in the humanities proliferate irresponsibly, turning out more and more graduates who cannot find jobs, the waste of human talent becomes enormous, intolerable.
>
> More broadly, the humanities, like the liberal arts generally, appear far less surely at the center of higher education than they once did. We have lost the respect of our colleagues in other fields, as well as the attention of an intelligent public. The action is elsewhere. We're living

through a time when outrage with the newfangled in the humanities—
with deconstruction or Marxism or whatever—has become plain lack
of interest. No one's even angry with us now, just bored.[1]

Devastating as that last comment is, I'm afraid it is all too accurate; for consider one further fact that Weisbuch didn't mention: the economy that could
not accommodate even the best of our new humanities PhDs in 1999 was still
a boom economy, with unemployment at a forty-year low of 4.2 percent. The
subsequent recession has of course exacerbated the situation, as statistics in
the *Chronicle of Higher Education* and *PMLA* confirm. The most recent MLA
census, in any case, reveals that less than half of new English and 38 percent
of Modern Language PhDs now obtain tenure-track positions.

Weisbuch's own "solutions" for this dismal state of affairs—he calls them
"Six Proposals to Revive the Humanities"—are the following: (1) to gather
data on our departments, finding out where our graduates get jobs so as
to ensure better planning, (2) to "practice doctoral birth control," using
Draconian means to cut down the number of entering graduate students,
(3) to "reclaim the curriculum" by having all courses taught by full-time faculty members rather than adjuncts, (4) to "create jobs beyond academe for
humanities graduates," (5) to "redesign graduate programs so as to accommodate the new community college market where teaching skills are more
important than scholarly expertise," and (6) "to become newly public"—that
is, to make better contacts with the so-called outside world.[2]

The trouble with such practical solutions is that they assume we have a
clear sense of what the humanities do and what makes them valuable: it is
just a matter of convincing those crass others, whether within the university
or outside its walls, that they really need us and can use our products. But
the more we probe the "humanities" question, the more apparent it becomes
that whereas schools of engineering or departments of economics have a
specific curriculum and mandate, the "humanities" umbrella—at my own
university, Stanford, the disciplines included are history, philosophy, religion,
the various language and literature departments, art history, drama, and
musicology—remains amorphous.

What *does* the term *humanities* mean today? The mission statement of
the National Endowment for the Humanities (NEH), found on its Web site
(www.neh.fed.us), reads as follows:

What are the Humanities?
The humanities are not any one thing. They are all around us and evident in our daily lives. When you visit an exhibition on "The Many

Realms of King Arthur" at your local library, that is the humanities. When you read the diary of a seventeenth-century New England midwife, that is the humanities. When you watch an episode of *The Civil War,* that is the humanities too.

Note that in all of these examples, the recipient of the humanistic "knowledge" proffered is merely passive, the exhibitions and TV programs designed, of necessity, for an audience that has no prior knowledge of King Arthur or the Civil War. In the hope that the more-or-less vacuous NEH statement was merely an aberration, I turned to the "National Foundation on the Arts and Humanities Act of 1965," which brought the NEH and NEA (National Endowment for the Arts) into being:

(1) The arts and humanities belong to all the people of the United States.

What can "belong" possibly mean here? As a citizen, I do not "own" specific artworks and philosophical treatises the way I might own stock or real estate. And how does this compare with the sciences? Does microbiology—or protein chemistry—"belong" to all the people of the United States?

(2) An advanced civilization must not limit its efforts to science and technology alone, but must give full value and support to the other great branches of scholarly and cultural activity in order to achieve a better understanding of the past, a better analysis of the present, and a better view of the future.

At best, this statement is blandly patronizing. Imagine someone claiming that "An advanced civilization must not limit its efforts to the humanities alone, but must give full value and support to those great branches, the sciences and social sciences"? But further, the assertion that arts and humanities somehow make us better persons and citizens is, to say the least, questionable. For as we learned in World War II (and of course we had always known it), "culture" by no means ensures ethical behavior; Hitler, let's remember, was so enraptured by Wagner that he attended performances of *Lohengrin* at the Vienna Opera House ten times in the course of the 1908 five-month season.[3]

(3) The arts and the humanities reflect the high place accorded by the American people to the nation's rich cultural heritage and to the fos-

tering of mutual respect for the diverse beliefs and values of all persons and groups.

Do the arts and humanities foster diversity? I know of no evidence for this proposition. Heidegger's essays on Hölderlin are generally held to be classics of twentieth-century philosophy and literature. They aim to define the poet's unique genius, but the last thing they foster is "respect for the diverse beliefs and values of all persons and groups."

But if the NEH's claims for the humanities are dubious, they are also quite typical. At Stanford University, for example, the official *Bulletin* contains this description:

> The School of Humanities and Sciences, with over 40 departments and interdepartmental degree programs, is the primary locus for the superior liberal arts education offered by Stanford University. Through exposure to the humanities, undergraduates study the ethical, aesthetic, and intellectual dimensions of the human experience, past and present, and so are prepared to make thoughtful and imaginative contributions to the culture of the future.

The language used here is revealing. Whereas the social sciences (according to the *Bulletin*) teach "theories and techniques for the analysis of specific societal issues," and the "hard" sciences prepare students to become the "leaders" in our increasingly technological society, the humanities "expose" students to the "ethical, aesthetic, and intellectual dimensions of the human experience." Exposure is nice enough—but also perfectly dispensable when leadership and expertise are at stake. Indeed, the humanities, as now understood and taught in our universities, no longer possess what Pierre Bourdieu calls "symbolic capital": an "accumulated prestige, celebrity, consecration or honour" founded on the "dialectic of knowledge (*connaissance*) and recognition (*reconnaissance*)."[4] In the capitalist and multicultural democracy of late-twentieth-century America, based as it is on money rather than on social class, "exposure" to the "intellectual dimensions of the human experience" is no longer a sine qua non of success or even of the Good Life. Our recent presidents, from Jimmy Carter and Ronald Reagan to the two George Bushes and even the Rhodes scholar Bill Clinton, are a case in point.

Consider the controversy about the NEH's invitation to Bill Clinton to deliver the 2000 Jefferson Lecture in the Humanities, an invitation Clinton declined in response to strong protest from the scholarly community. The annual Jefferson Lecture, inaugurated in 1972 by Lionel Trilling, has been given by the likes of Jaroslav Pelikan, C. Vann Woodward, Vincent Scully, Caroline Walker Bynum, and Emily T. Vermeule—all of them serious scholars and outstanding intellectuals in their respective disciplines, ranging from architecture (Scully) to history (Woodward) to classics (Vermeule). Accordingly, when William Ferris, the chairman of the NEH, explained his hope was that in making the Jefferson Lecture a presidential event, "the humanities" would be brought "into the lives of millions of Americans who don't know what the humanities are and have no sense of the great work we do [at the NEH],"[5] what he was really saying was that the term *humanities* no longer means anything. At best, it seems, the term has a negative function, specifically, in the case of the Jefferson Lecture, giving the president a chance to make a speech that would not be overtly political but would deal with what are vaguely conceived as "humanistic" values. And of course this "lecture" would be written by the president's speechwriters—a situation that in the scholarly community would be classified as simple plagiarism.

Given this climate, perhaps we can think more seriously about the state of the "humanities" if we begin by getting rid of the word "humanities"—a word, incidentally, of surprisingly recent vintage. The first edition of the *Oxford English Dictionary* (*OED*), whose supplement appears in 1933, does not include it at all. *Humane, humanism, humanist, humanity, humanitarian:* these are familiar cognates of the word *human,* but *humanities* was not the term of choice for an area of knowledge and set of fields of study until after World War II. The more usual (and broader) rubric was Liberal Arts; Arts and Sciences; or Arts, Letters, and Sciences. The shift in terminology, reflected in the now-ubiquitous humanities centers, humanities special programs, and humanities fellowships, testifies, paradoxically, to an increasing perplexity about what these designations might mean.

When we study the roster of fellows at the various humanities centers and institutes in the United States, a clear trend emerges: anthropology and history have taken over the humanities field. In 2003 I served on the selection committee for internal fellows at the humanities center of a leading Midwestern university, and although the staff very much hoped to attract candidates in art history, literature, musicology, and philosophy, the competitive applications came from what we might call the proto-social sciences, like environmental studies or human biology. Indeed, the top candidate in the pool was a professor from the law school.

How did we get into this bind? As someone trained in the discipline of English and Comparative Literature, I want to take a look at what traditionally has been one of the central branches of the humanities: the study of literature or, as I prefer to call it, *poetics.* "Literature" is an imprecise designator that came into use only in the eighteenth century,[6] whereas discussions of the poetic have a much more ancient and cross-cultural lineage. The discipline of poetics (which, from Plato through the nineteenth century, comprised narrative and drama as well as lyric) has been classified in four basic ways:

(1) The poetic may be understood as a branch of rhetoric. From Aristotle's profound understanding of *rhetoric* as the art (*techné*) of finding the available means of persuasion, to Cicero and Quintilian's division of rhetoric into three tasks—*docere* (to teach), *delectare* (to delight), and *movere* (to move)—and three faculties—*inventio* (the finding of arguments), *dispositio* (the arrangement into parts), and *elocutio* (style)[7]—to the handbooks of the medieval rhetoricians like Geoffrey of Vinsauf, to the late-eighteenth-century manuals of Hugh Blair and George Campbell, to the rhetorical hermeneutics of the contemporary Groupe Mu,[8] *rhetoric* has flourished as the study of *how* a piece of writing is put together. It has gradually evolved from its early prescriptive character (the description of rhetorical devices and strategies necessary to teach, delight, or move a given audience) to the more empirical study of what figures and devices actually *are* used in literary and nonliterary composition. Rhetoric thus means primarily *practical criticism*—the examination of diction and syntax, rhythm and repetition, and the various figures of speech.

But effective rhetoric, as Aristotle first demonstrated in what is still the great treatment of the subject, is no mere "ornament," as the tropes and rhetorical figures used to be called, but a matter of *ethos* and *pathos:* the artful presentation of a self designed to be persuasive to its audience, and the construction of an audience that will empathize with that self. To take some Renaissance examples, if Philip Sidney provides us with an excellent example of the ethical argument (in his case, the *sprezzatura* that makes us sympathize with Astrophel in the sonnet sequence *Astrophel and Stella,* as with the charmingly modest speaker of *The Defense of Poetry*), John Donne is the master of the pathetic argument: the urgent and passionate appeal to the poet's (and preacher's) fellow sinners to be at one with his suffering.

As such, rhetoric is at the very center of our discipline as literary scholars. No other discipline, after all, has as its central focus the issue as to how language actually works and what it does, whether in newspaper editorials or poems or the weather report. Conversely, inattention to rhetoric, as in Harold Bloom's otherwise powerful poetry criticism, downgrades the materiality of the text at the expense of its dominant myths and ideas, thus occluding the significant differences between, say, a Wallace Stevens poem and an Emerson essay. At the same time, the focus on the rhetorical dimension of a given text inevitably downplays the cognitive import of the poetic construct. Rhetoric, Michel Meyer argues in an interesting study, flourishes where ideologies fail, or, in Nancy S. Struever's words, it "reveals a deep commitment to question/response formations as more fundamental than concepts of referentiality in discursive exchange."[9] This points the way to the second frame for literary study.

(2) From Plato to Heidegger and Levinas, the *poetic* has often been understood as a branch of philosophy, and hence as a potential expression of truth and knowledge. Because poetry couldn't pass Plato's truth test—even Homer told false and salacious stories about the gods—the poets were ostensibly banished from the Republic. I will have more to say of this below, but for the moment, I note only that this conception of poetry is antithetical to the first. If the main purpose of a literary text is to convey knowledge or formulate truths, questions of form and genre take a backseat. Arthur Rimbaud's abandonment of the alexandrine, for example, in favor of free verse and then prose poetry would matter much less than the visionary content of those dense and oblique Rimbaldian texts, verse, or prose. Again, if theories of poetry-as-rhetoric regard James Joyce and Ezra Pound as key modernists, the theory of poetry-as-philosophy would (and has) put Samuel Beckett or Paul Celan at that center.

The treatment of poetry as truth or knowledge has produced some marvelous criticism, especially in the Romantic period and again after the Second World War, when Heidegger came to prominence; but it has its own problems, perhaps most notably that it favors a limited corpus of literature at the expense of all others—the lyric of Wordsworth and Shelley, for example, at the expense of, say, a Jane Austen novel, which doesn't lend itself to comparable philosophical reflection. Then, too—and I will have more to say on this below—the equation of poetry and philosophy tends to shortchange the former: when a given artwork is seen to exemplify or illustrate, say, Adorno's aesthetic theory or Althusser's theory of interpellation, its heterogeneity is ignored, the pedagogical aim being one of exemplification rather than respect for the poem's own ontology.

(3) From antiquity to the present, poetry has also been classified as one of the arts (this time Aristotle is more important than Plato). In this configuration, poetry is placed in the context of the visual arts, music, dance, architecture, and so on. In the *Ion*, Plato argued that the practice of poetry involves *techné kai episteme. Techné* was the standard Greek word both for a

practical skill and for the systematic knowledge or experience that underlies it. "The resulting range of application," Stephen Halliwell points out, "is extensive, covering at one end of the spectrum the activity of a carpenter, builder, smith, sculptor, similar manual craftsman, and, at the other, at least from the fifth century onwards, the ability and practices of rhetoricians and sophists." [10] So *techné,* meaning "craft," "skill," "technique," "method," "art," coupled with *episteme,* meaning "knowledge," is the domain of the arts. But the discourse about poetry, Plato concludes in the *Ion,* doesn't seem to have sufficient *techné kai episteme:* unlike the shipbuilder or carpenter, the rhapsode demonstrates no special skill in speaking about Homer, and hence his ability to do so must be purely a matter of inspiration—in other words, an instinctive ability to interpret Homer that cannot be taught or learned—it simply *is.*

Criticism, by this account, is no more than a second-order discourse, a repetition, in diluted form, of what a given poem or artwork "says." Scientists and social scientists often hold this view of poetics: witness the NEH commentary cited above. But the theory that poetry is a branch of the arts need not lead to such impressionism. On the contrary, to conceive of poetry as an art also implies that it is a form of discourse inherently *other,* that poetic language is to be distinguished from ordinary speaking and writing. This is the Aristotelian view: a tragedy or epic will be read less for its potential truth value or its specific rhetorical properties than as a unique aesthetic construct, whose "plot" or structure (*ton pragmaton systasis*) is coherent and characterized by what Aristotle called *to prepon* (fitness). The "formalist" analysis that such structures prompt is often associated with the New Critics, although their interest was primarily in thematic, rather than in formal or structural, coherence.

For real Formalist criticism in our time, we must look less to the New Critics than to the Russian Formalists, whose object was to define *poeticity* not in the individual poem but as a recurrent feature in poems across a wide spectrum. Indeed, the Russian Formalists studied the poetic function in a variety of genres and media, from the folk epic to the personal letter. A showpiece would be Roman Jakobson's "Marginal Notes on the Prose of Boris Pasternak," which analyzes the role of passive verb constructions in creating the particular tone of a Pasternak short story, Jakobson's point being that "prose" can be just as "artistic" as "poetry." [11] The Formalist division between "literary" and "ordinary" language has been challenged from many quarters: for example, in Stanley Fish's famous essay "How Ordinary Is Ordinary Language?" (1973), which argues that so-called poetic devices can be found in newspaper editorials as easily as in lyric poems. [12] But although most critics in the Formalist tradition would today concede that the distinction between literary and ordinary language is not hard and fast, they would argue that it is useful to concentrate on difference rather than similarity. "Do not forget," as Wittgenstein put it in his box of notes called *Zettel,* "that a poem, although it is composed in the language of information, is not used in the language-game of giving information."[13]

(4) Formalist theory has often been accused of excessive technicality and aridity: in the politicized post-Vietnam era, it came under sharp attack from those who take poetics to be essentially a historical or cultural formation. Indeed in this fourth paradigm, formalism becomes a dirty word, a smokescreen for ignoring the ideology and political ethos of a given work. For the cultural critic, the only real justification for literary study is the concession that poems and novels can do "cultural work." From this perspective, a poetic text is primarily to be understood as a symptom of the larger culture to which it belongs and as an index to particular historical or cultural markers. Literary practices, moreover, are taken to be no different in kind from other social or cultural practices. A poem or novel or film is discussed not for its intrinsic merits or as the expression of individual genius, nor for its expression of essential truths, nor for its powers of persuasion, but for its political role, its exposure of the state of a given society. In this scheme of things, questions of value inevitably take the backseat, there being in fact no reason why Henry James's novels are a better index to or symptom of the cultural aporias of turn-of-the-century America than are the best sellers of the period—or, for that matter, early-twentieth-century domestic architecture, popular periodicals, or medical treatises. Read the list of topics currently being studied in university courses or at humanities centers and you will find that "literature" functions almost exclusively in this way.

Poetry as rhetoric, poetry as philosophy, poetry as an art, poetry as cultural production—what is at stake in adopting one of these classifications to the exclusion of the others? Interestingly, the first three inevitably incorporate the fourth into the discipline, in that they examine the history and cultural position of the different poetic, rhetorical, philosophical, and generic forms as well as the history and culture of their philosophical reception. But *history of* is very different from the transposition that views literature itself *as history*—the position of contemporary cultural studies, which is committed to the demolition of such "obsolete" categories as poetic autonomy, poetic truth, and formal and rhetorical value. Since cultural studies currently dominate the arena of literary study, I want to focus here on this particular approach.

We might begin by noting that the treatment of poetry as a branch of history or culture is based on the assumption that the poetry of a period is a reliable index to that period's larger intellectual and ideological currents. Beckett's *Endgame,* for example, testifies to the meaninglessness and horror of a post-Auschwitz, nuclear world. But as critics from Aristotle to Adorno have understood, the theory that imaginative writing is an index to its time ignores what is specific to a work of art, along with its powers of invention, transformation, and resistance. This is Aristotle's point in the ninth chapter of the *Poetics:*

> The difference between a historian and poet is not that one writes in prose and the other in verse. . . . The real difference is this, that one tells what happened and the other what might happen. For this reason poetry is something more philosophical and serious (*kai philosophoteron kai spoudaioteron*) than history, because poetry tends to give general truths while history gives particular facts.
>
> By a "general truth" I mean the sort of thing that a certain type of man will do or say either probably or necessarily. . . . A "particular fact" is what Alcibiades did or what was done to him.
>
> It is clear, then . . . that the poet must be a "maker" (*poietes*) not of verses but of stories, since he is a poet in virtue of his "representation," and what he represents is action. (#1451b)[14]

The meaning of the possible ("what might happen") is made clearer by Aristotle's response to Plato's complaint that poets are dangerous to the state because they tell lies. "The standard of what is correct," writes Aristotle, "is not the same in the art of poetry as it is in the art of social conduct or any other art. . . . It is less of an error not to know that a female stag has no horns than to make a picture that is unrecognizable" (#1461).

But of course Plato understood this distinction perfectly. The danger of poetry to the ideal republic, after all, is in direct proportion to its power, its charm, its magic: "We will beg Homer and other poets not to be angry if we cancel those and all similar passages [e.g., "false" stories about the gods], not that they are not poetic and pleasing to most hearers, but because the more poetic they are the less are they suited to the ears of boys and men who are destined to be free."[15] One could hardly endow the poetic with more power. And indeed, when in Book X of the *Republic* Plato takes up the ancient "quarrel between philosophy and poetry" so as to dismiss the latter from the well-governed state, he admits that "we ourselves are very conscious of her spell," "her magic." That magic reappears at the conclusion of the *Republic* with the poetic myth of Er, as if to let us know that despite all the good reasons to the contrary, for Plato, poetry is finally the highest calling.

In distinguishing mimesis (representation) from diegesis (straightforward exposition or narrative in the author's own person), Plato, and Aristotle after him, isolate the *fictive* as the essential characteristic of the poetic construct: not what *has happened* but what *might happen* either possibly or probably. In his celebrated *Metahistory*, Hayden White taught us that, contra Aristotle, historical writing, even the "simplest" chronicle, also has a fictive element.[16] White places nineteenth-century historiography from Hegel and Michelet to Nietzsche and Croce within the larger tradition of narrative fiction. But *Metahistory* was published thirty years ago (1973), and since then a major reversal has set in. For even as the notion of text as representation continues to be operative (there being no "reality" outside textual representation that one can access), in practice the emphasis on representation has created, ironically enough, a situation where the *what* of mimesis has become much more important than the *how*. Subject matter—whether divine-right kingship in Renaissance England or the culture of condoms in early-twentieth-century America—becomes all.

At its best, the alignment of poetic and cultural practices has given literary study a new life. *Ulysses,* for example, was originally read as a parodic modern-day *Odyssey* or as an elaborate experiment in which plot and character are subordinated to the investigation of the possibilities of language. The structure of the novel, with its astonishing network of leitmotifs, allusions, cross-references, and symbolic threads, was examined from every possible angle. From the perspective of the new cultural studies, however, *Ulysses* is more properly read as an examination of the dynamics of race, power, and empire as these play themselves out in the colonial Ireland of the early twentieth century—an Ireland whose very consciousness has been created by its subaltern position vis-à-vis its English oppressors. As such, Joyce's novel provides us with rich material about nationalism, colonialism, and imperialism as well as specific gender and racial inequities: for example, the Joycean dialectic that regards woman as either virgin or whore. In the same vein, Joseph Conrad's *Heart of Darkness* and *Nostromo* are now read primarily as depictions of the horrors of colonial oppression under capitalist expansion, this time with respect to race in Africa and Central America; and here too the representation of gender (e.g., Kurtz's African woman versus his "Intended") has become the subject of interesting and useful critique.

The past decade has witnessed dozens of books on these subjects, there being plenty of room within cultural studies for debate on such issues as the relative complicity of Joyce himself with his colonial oppressors or the iden-

tification between Conrad and the notorious Kurtz. But in its zeal to unmask the hidden ideologies of these and related novels, critics seem to have
forgotten what brought them to *Ulysses* or *Heart of Darkness* in the first
place—namely, the uniqueness of these novels as works of art. Plenty of novels, poems, and plays deal with Irish nationalism and British oppression, but
they have little of Joyce's appeal. Indeed, *Ulysses,* read as it is around the
world by a steadily growing audience, is admired first and foremost for the
brilliance, inventiveness, and power of its language and rhetoric, beginning
with those absurd advertising jingles that go through Bloom's mind as he
wanders the Dublin streets—jingles like "What is home without Plumtree's
potted meat? Incomplete." And these slogans are never merely fortuitous:
Bloom's own home, after all, is "incomplete" without Molly's "plums" and
"potted meat." And the rhyme echo relates to the musical motifs associated
with Molly and her lover, Blazes Boylan.

Then, too, despite all the "newness" of postcolonial theory, it is a question whether most discussions of nationalism and imperialism in *Ulysses* are
really all that different from such early Joyce studies as William T. Noon's
Joyce and Aquinas or Kevin Sullivan's *Joyce Among the Jesuits.* Of the former,
a recent reviewer, Cary Makinson, for Amazon.com writes:

> This book has been a classic in Joyce studies for many years. Joyce had
> said famously that if you wanted to understand his writing, you first
> had to understand Aquinas. Jumping off from this typically Joycean
> hyperbole, Noon explicates Joyce's Catholicism from the angle of Tho-
> mistic Aesthetics. A technical/theological subject made very readable.
> A must for any wannabe Joyce scholar.

Joyce and Aquinas was published in 1957, a time when it was still assumed
that to understand a novel meant to understand its author's "ideas." In the
wake of structuralist and then post-structuralist theory, such notions went
out the window: after all, it is argued, we cannot trust the author to understand the ideological formations that have shaped his consciousness, and it
is hence up to the critic to unmask these. Yet, in the long run, the Thomis-
tic philosophy on which Joyce was raised probably figures just as largely in
his verbal universe as do his representations of nationalism or imperialism.
Ulysses is, in any case, sui generis in its fusion of particular motifs and ideological markers. Even *Finnegans Wake* has a different radius of discourse.

It is this uniqueness of the artwork that cultural studies downplays. Indeed, in its more extreme incarnation, cultural theory can dispense with

poetics altogether. Studies of consumerism, for example, can be based on the analysis of shopping malls or Home Depot layouts; no literary texts are required. Racial stereotyping manifests itself as readily in the newspapers or cartoons of a given period than in novels or plays. Teen culture can be explored through music, film, and computer games. The ideologies of globalization and nationalism can be profitably studied by examining network television and Internet discourse. And popular film is much more telling, so far as cultural theory is concerned, than are the art films of Federico Fellini or Jean-Luc Godard.

By the early nineties, in any case, English (and foreign language) departments found themselves in the odd position of teaching anything but literature. Indeed, I have seen job candidates who are vying for the precious few tenure-track positions available actually apologize for discussing a novel or poem and hurrying through these same discussions so as to get on to some important theoretical point relating to postcolonialism or queer theory or globalization. In this context, humanities centers inevitably find that the applications coming in from the anthropology department or the law school are more interesting than those from English or such related fields as musicology and art history. Inadvertently, but surely, humanities has become social science without the statistics. No wonder, then, that foundation directors like Robert Weisbuch see the humanities—and especially literary study—as an embattled area, a field in crisis. No wonder that provosts and deans, having to make difficult budget decisions, cut positions that seem to be expendable.

But the crisis is not quite what we think it is. Poetics, we might say, abhors a vacuum: if the university doesn't offer courses on William Blake or Dante Gabriel Rossetti, on Ezra Pound or Samuel Beckett, the action moves elsewhere.[17] And here the impact of the Internet comes in. There are currently at least three Samuel Beckett Web sites, beginning with the *Samuel Beckett On-line Resources and Links Page,* which contains the texts of almost all of Beckett's works and a comprehensive set of secondary sources, including articles, reviews, commentaries, videos of the major plays, interviews—in short, an astonishing set of documents by and about Beckett. The site even produces seven parodies of *Waiting for Godot* written over the years. Then, too, the site is interactive, allowing for discussion about the varying and constantly growing set of entries. A second Web site is *The Samuel Beckett Endpage,* founded by Porter Abbott at the University of California–Santa Barbara in 1996; this scholarly site contains recent Beckett news, scholarly notes from around the world, biographical material, thorough bibliographies of Beckett scholarship, and a good selection of the texts themselves online. And a third Beckett site—this one devoted to the scholarship—may be found at LiteraryHistory.com.[18]

Who is accessing these sites? Students, surely, but not only students or their professors. It seems that there are actually thousands of people "out there" who want to learn more about Beckett's work and share their interpretations of and enthusiasm for that work. And the same is true of Web sites devoted to Rossetti and Blake, to John Cage and Gertrude Stein, and to movements such as Futurism or Dada. Futurist texts (e.g., F. T. Marinetti's manifestos), often out of print and unavailable, can be viewed on a beautiful British site called *Futurism and Futurists,* owned by the independent scholar Bob Osborn. This site features all the major manifestos, artworks, photographs, the key writings, as well as a glossary of Futurist terms. There are also related Dada sites (for example, the Marcel Duchamp site *tout-fait*) and, perhaps above all, Kenneth Goldsmith's *UbuWeb.*[19] This latter Web site is a work of art in itself. Goldsmith, trained as a visual artist and now a word artist and poet as well, has designed *UbuWeb* so as to please the eye as well as to provide information: it features sound and visual poetry that is unavailable even in most research libraries. There are portfolios on subjects like conceptual art, radio, and ethnopoetics; scholarly essays on different poets and artists; and best of all, the primary materials themselves. On *UbuWeb* you can hear various renditions of Kurt Schwitters's *Ursonate,* including Schwitters's own. Or you can hear Marinetti reciting *Zang Tuum Tumb,* examine the Concrete poems of Haroldo de Campos, and read the out-of-print issues of the great seventies avant-garde magazine *Aspen.*

Goldsmith is not himself an academic, and he does not apply for funding from the NEA or NEH, so he need not compromise his values. Yet, within a five-year period or so, he has made *UbuWeb* an indispensable site for artists, poets, art historians, and literary scholars. As such, poetics is attracting a new generation of students who are coming to aesthetic discourses by the circuitous channels of the digital media. I use the word "aesthetic" advisedly here, for the audience in question is primarily interested in how Beckett's radio plays or Apollinaire's *calligrammes* actually function and what younger artists and poets can learn from these examples. In the context of actual art making, the relationship between poetry and its audience (the rhetorical) and the examination of the poem as formal, material construct will once again predominate. At the same time, as anyone who has used the *Wittgenstein Archives* (http://www.hit.uib.no/wab) at the University of Bergen in Norway knows, the relation of poetry to its philosophic analogues has never received as much attention as it is getting today.

What, then, of the "crisis" in the humanities? Given the astonishing interest in artworks and poetries manifested on the Internet, is the crisis perhaps more apparent than real? Yes and no. Within the academy, and especially in literature departments, it is real enough, as the shrinking enrollments and depressed job market indicate. But these phenomena may well be symptoms of something else—a bad fit between an outmoded curriculum and the actual interests of potential students. The main thrust of curriculum changes in English courses over the past few decades has been the shift in attention from major writers to minority ones and hence to include many more poems and fictions by underrepresented racial and ethnic groups as well as by women. But without clear-cut notions of *why* it is worthwhile to read literary texts, whether by established or marginalized writers, in the first place, the study of "literature" becomes no more than a chore, a way of satisfying distribution requirements.

"Theory" courses, as currently taught, exacerbate this problem. Suppose, for example, a class is assigned Peter Bürger's now-classic *Theory of the Avant-Garde*, along with some Marxist theory that provides background for Bürger's argument. The book posits that the early-twentieth-century avant-garde was a brave attempt to transform art but that it failed because it did not succeed in overturning the bourgeois institution of art as autonomous. But Bürger seems to equate the avant-garde with a few Dada and Surrealist works, for instance Duchamp's *Fountain,* and makes no mention of the Russian avant-garde that is arguably the very core of avant-gardism in the early twentieth century, the one avant-garde that fused, at least briefly, the radical aesthetic and the political critique that Bürger takes as a requisite for genuine avant-garde activity.[20] The narrowness of Bürger's definition puts his theory into serious question. But the student who has yet to be exposed to the works themselves (French or Russian or otherwise) cannot possibly make a reasoned critique of Bürger's thesis.

Or take the current cult of Adorno, as presented to students who have no way of contextualizing his dense theoretical and critical commentary. When, for example, we read in Adorno's "On Lyric Poetry and Society," "My thesis is that the lyric work is always the subjective expression of a social antagonism," and "the objective world that produces the lyric is an inherently antagonistic world," we should be aware that Adorno's is a wholly Eurocentric position and that he takes nineteenth-century German poetry and philosophy as normative.[21] But was the classical Chinese poem "the subjective expression of a social antagonism"? Are the lyrics in George Herbert's *The Temple* such an expression? And is it necessarily true that Heinrich Heine was not Baudelaire's equal because the former "surrendered more willingly to the flow of things; he took a poetic technique of reproduction, as it were, that corresponded to the industrial age and applied it to the conventional romantic archetypes, but he did not find archetypes of modernity"?[22] How can the student, who has probably never read either Heine or Baudelaire, tell?

Thus, the dominant cultural studies paradigm, combining, as it does, heavy doses of undigested European theory with American "minority" exemplars, can do little but confuse the student who would like to understand specific artworks and their relationship to one another. What is urgently needed—and here again Internet possibilities may lead the way—is a more "differential" and inductive approach to literary study, indeed to the humanities in general. This does not mean "covering" all periods of English (or whatever) literature or making one's way through as many canonical works as possible. But the wider one's reading in a specified area, the greater the pleasure of a given text and the greater the ability to make connections between texts.

It is interesting in this regard to see how pragmatic the premises of classical theory were. Plato's notion of what poetry does to move its audience was based on all the examples available to him, especially the example of Homer, who, so Plato thought, represented quintessential poetry more fully than any of his rival poets. Similarly, Aristotle's famous definition of tragedy in the *Poetics* ("A tragedy is the imitation of an action that is heroic, complete, and of a certain magnitude") is based on the examination of virtually dozens of compositions calling themselves "tragedies," which exhibited particular features. It is, for example, because Greek tragedy did invariably include music and dance that Aristotle listed *melos* and *opsis* among its six elements and believed he had to examine their function.

I am well aware that Plato and Aristotle, Longinus and Horace had a much smaller corpus to deal with than does the Adorno of "On Lyric Poetry and Society." And indeed the literary field is now so vast, heterogenous, and eclectic that it is obviously impossible to make universal choices as to which artworks to examine and how to organize meaningful curricula. But students can be taught—and here the question of expertise comes in—what the issues of analyzing poetry are; they can be taught narrative modes and lyric genres, the tropes and rhetorical figures to be found in any written text, the possibilities for rhythm and meter, "poetry" and "prose." In musicology and art history such study is taken for granted: no one who cannot read a score or know the parts of the orchestra is likely to make pronouncements about a particular symphony. But in poetics we tend to assume that there is no vocabulary to master, that anyone can—and does—*read*.

The first step, then, would be to teach the student that *reading,* whether of a legal brief or the newspaper or even of an Internet ad, takes training. And that the methods learned, applied to one's own literature for starters and then to the really exciting literature of the past—allowing that past to be flexible, not confined to a narrow canon—will make the student see how language works in a given poem or play or novel. For language—which is, after all, the *material* of literature as well as the means to its *fictiveness*—will be the central object of study, a study that involves all four of the paradigms outlined above. Such study, I believe, will come back into favor for the simple reason that, try as one may, one cannot eliminate the sheer jouissance or pleasure of the text. Thus, just at the moment when the common wisdom was that Marcel Proust was passé, what with his *longeurs,* his irritating snobbery and elitism, two new monumental biographies (by Jean-Yves Tadié [1997] and William H. Carter [2000]) appeared. Proust study groups sprang up in various cities. Newspapers talked of a Proust "revival," but of course it is more properly a Proust "survival." Proust won't go away, because *A La Recherche du temps perdu* is an encyclopedia of narrative forms, of complex language constructions, of historical and cultural ironies, as well as a psychological analysis of love and jealousy incomparable in its richness and passion. There may be little blips on the Proust radar screen—now he is up, now down—but the oeuvre is there, continuing to challenge and fascinate readers.

In chapter 4 of the *Poetics,* Aristotle discusses aesthetic pleasure, specifically the two pleasures he takes to be associated with artworks in whatever medium—the "pleasure of representation" and the "pleasure of recognition":

> Speaking generally, poetry seems to owe its origin to two particular causes, both natural. From childhood men have an instinct for representation, and in this respect man differs from the other animals in that he is far more imitative and learns his first lessons by representing things. And then there is the enjoyment people always get from representations. (#1448b)

The pleasure of representation is the basic human instinct one can observe most directly in young children who "play" at being someone else, who make up a story and pass it off as "true." It is the pleasure of invention, of fictiveness. The twin pleasure, that of recognition, is its mirror image, the pleasure of taking in the impersonations, fictions, and language creations of others and recognizing their justice. When, for example, Prufrock concludes his "love song" with the line, "Till human voices wake us and we drown," the most un-Prufrockian of us will recognize the aptness of the metaphor.

Pleasure was paramount for Aristotle, as it was for Plato, who banished the poets from the Republic because their work produced too much pleasure and passion in its audience. But of course the pleasure calculus is complex: "one should not seek," we read in *Poetics* XIV, "from tragedy all kinds of pleasure but that which is peculiar to tragedy, and since the poet must by 'representation' produce the pleasure which comes from feeling pity and fear, obviously this quality must be embodied in the incidents" (#1453b). *Catharsis,* the purgation of pity and fear, is not an end in itself; it is a particular kind of poetic pleasure. And so on.

It is, I would argue, the contemporary fear of the pleasures of representation and recognition—the pleasures of the *fictive,* the *what might happen*—and its subordination to the *what has happened*—the *historical/cultural*—that has trivialized the status of literary study in the contemporary academy and shrunk the corresponding departments. Indeed, the neo-Puritan notion that literature and the other arts must be somehow "useful," and only useful, that the Ciceronian triad—*docere, movere, delectare*—should renounce its third element ("delight") and even the original meaning of its second element, so that *to move* means only to move readers to some kind of specific action, has produced a climate in which it has become increasingly difficult to justify the study of English or Comparative Literature at all.

Given this climate, we are now witnessing a deep pessimism, expressed in various jeremiads as to the death of humanistic studies in our time. In a recent essay, "The Humanities—At Twilight?" George Steiner argues that in contemporary technocratic mass culture, there may, alas, be no room at all for the humanities:

> Democracy and economic-distributive justice on a democratic plane are no friend to the autistic, often arcane, always demanding enterprise of "high culture." . . . Add to this the failures, the collaborative treasons of the clerics, of the arts, of the humanities in the fullest sense, during the long night of this century in Europe and Russia. Add to this the fundamental doubt . . . as to whether the humanities humanize, and the thrust of the crisis is inescapable.[23]

Interestingly, Steiner's elegiac essay never refers to a single work of art written since World War II: Adorno's adage that there can be no poetry after Auschwitz seems to be taken as a given. Again, Steiner seems to be wholly unaware of the digital media and their particular kinds of cultural production and dissemination of literature. This *retro Kulturdrang* strikes me as just as problematic as Weisbuch's "how-to" practicalities. For one cannot kill the basic human instinct to make poetry—the German verb *Dichten* is apposite here—and to enjoy the poetry making of others: indeed, the study of poetry has been with us much longer than any of the academic orthodoxies or philistine practices Steiner deplores. Some things, it seems, never quite collapse. Let me conclude with a little Frank O'Hara poem that is nicely apropos:

> Lana Turner has collapsed!
> I was trotting along and suddenly
> it started raining and snowing
> and you said it was hailing
> but hailing hits you on the head
> hard so it was really snowing and
> raining and I was in such a hurry
> to meet you but the traffic
> was acting exactly like the sky
> and suddenly I see a headline
> LANA TURNER HAS COLLAPSED!
> there is no snow in Hollywood
> there is no rain in California
> I have been to lots of parties
> and acted perfectly disgraceful
> but I never actually collapsed
> oh Lana Turner we love you get up[24]

In 2002 Professor Shyamal Bagchee invited me to give the annual T. S. Eliot Memorial Lecture for the Eliot Society, which meets annually in St. Louis, the place of the poet's birth. For the occasion, I thought it would be valuable to reconsider one of Eliot's most well-known but still highly controversial poems.

2

Cunning Passages and Contrived Corridors

Rereading Eliot's "Gerontion"

Ce que dit la poésie ne peut être dit autrement.
          Jacques Roubaud, "Poésie et Pensée: quelques remarques"

"Gerontion," written in the summer of 1919 and originally intended as the prelude to *The Waste Land*,[1] was first published in T. S. Eliot's 1920 volume *Ara Vos Prec* (London: Ovid Press).[2] It did not have a good press. The anonymous reviewer for the *Times Literary Supplement* complained that the poet's world-weariness was no more than a "habit, an anti-romantic reaction, a new Byronism," while Desmond MacCarthy in the *New Statesman* describes "Gerontion" as follows:

> The whole poem is a description at once of an old man's mind, and of a mood which recurs often in Mr. Eliot's poems, namely, that of one to whom life is largely a process of being stifled, slowly hemmed in and confused. . . . His problem as a poet is the problem of the adjustment of his sense of beauty to these sorry facts.[3]

MacCarthy goes on to say that the symbolism of the first verse of "Gerontion" is "obvious": "When the old man says he has not fought in the salt marshes, etc., we know that means that he has not tasted the violent romance of life. We must not dwell too literally on the phrases by which he builds up the impression of sinister dilapidation and decay." And these reservations about Eliot's language lead MacCarthy to the conclusion that "He belongs to that class of poets whose interest is in making a work of art, not in expressing themselves" (*Critical Heritage* 116).

Imagine criticizing a poet for his desire to make a work of art rather than "expressing" himself! If MacCarthy's distinction sounds naïve, we should bear in mind that the expressivist theory that animates it is still very much with us. Indeed, the assumption that a poem's language is no more than a vehicle that points to a reality outside it—in this case, "the description of an old man's mind and mood"—still animates most criticism. In this regard I am particularly intrigued by MacCarthy's "etc." in the sentence "When the old man says he has not fought in the salt marshes, etc., we know that means that he has not tasted the violent romance of life." The phrases "heaving a cutlass" and "Bitten by flies" are presumably part of this etcetera, as if to say that, well, these are just more of the same. "Fought," moreover, despite its chiastic use in the first six lines—

Nor *fought* in the warm rain
Nor knee deep in the salt marsh, heaving a cutlass,
Bitten by flies, *fought*[4]—

doesn't really mean "fought"; the verb must be understood as a metaphor for "lived" or "had intense experiences." "In reading Mr. Eliot," says MacCarthy, "an undue literalness must at all costs be avoided" (*Critical Heritage* 115).

Such reservations about the role played by a poem's actual language stand behind many of the critiques of "Gerontion." The most common charge has been that, brilliant as "Gerontion" is at the local level, it is finally not a coherent poem. "'Gerontion,'" writes Bernard Bergonzi, "is Eliot's one poem where the language itself forms a barrier or smoke screen between the reader and the essential experience of the poem. . . . it fails because of the slipperiness of its language: the desire to preserve a maximum openness to verbal suggestiveness makes 'Gerontion' an echo chamber where there is much interesting noise but nothing can be clearly distinguished."[5] And the case is made even more forcefully by Stephen Spender:

If the second half of "Gerontion" doesn't really convince, either on the level of imagination or of intellectual argument, this is because the attempt to draw a parallel between the poetry of the Jacobean playwrights about political intrigues at small Italian courts with the situation of Europe at the time of the signing of the Treaty of Versailles doesn't work. The modern political theme, which affects the whole world, is being forced through too narrow a channel.

And Spender concludes: "After the strong first part of 'Gerontion,' the poem becomes lost in its own corridors and dark passages. It is not so much obscure as cryptic. . . . The last part of 'Gerontion' hovers ambiguously between tragic statement and black farce, with 'high camp' thrown in at the end."[6]

A telling contrast, Spender argues, is with another great poem of the very same moment: Yeats's "The Second Coming." Citing the passage beginning with "Things fall apart; the centre cannot hold," Spender remarks that "Yeats states in six lines what Eliot conveys indirectly through his long passage of Jacobean pastiche. . . . The tone of these lines is Biblical, apocalyptic and Aeschylean, and it is this which Eliot was to adopt in *The Waste Land*." And Spender cites the lines in "The Burial of the Dead" based on Ezekiel 2, "What are the roots that clutch, what branches grow / Out of this stony rubbish?" But this particular vocal register is only one of many in *The Waste Land*, with its collage of contrasting voices, and as for "Gerontion," the monologue we read, far from being that of the prophet or visionary, projects the voice of an introspective, self-searching and self-conscious being, who does not necessarily trust his own eyes. The Yeats of "The Second Coming" *knows* what has happened in a world where "The best lack all conviction, while the worst / Are full of passionate intensity." The vision of the "blood-dimmed tide," which prepares us for the image of the "rough beast, Slouch[ing] toward Bethlehem to be born," is conveyed as a larger mythic construct, available to all who open their eyes to see it. In "Gerontion," by contrast, there is no such visionary truth, only a series of tentative gropings—those "Tenants of the house / Thoughts of a dry brain in a dry season." "Thoughts," in this context, are inseparable from the meanings conveyed by verbal, rhythmic, and syntactic units. At each point in Eliot's resonant echo chamber, meanings that are multiplex are arraigned, the poem generally moving simultaneously on at least three planes—the sexual, the sociocultural, and the religious.

In recent years, however, discussion of what "Gerontion" "says" has focused less on the issue of structural coherence than on the poem's purported anti-Semitism, although the two are, as we shall see, not unrelated. The fullest case against Eliot on this score was made by Anthony Julius in his *T. S. Eliot: Anti-Semitism, and Literary Form* (1995). Julius's second chapter, devoted to "Gerontion," makes much of the three lines:

And the Jew squats on the window sill, the owner,
Spawned in some estaminet of Antwerp,
Blistered in Brussels, patched and peeled in London.[7]

This passage, says Julius, "breathes hate, the sibilants hissing scorn" (45). The word "spawned" prompts Julius to expatiate on swamps and slime as breeding ground for the subhuman Jewish race. "Blistered" is a reference to the pustular skin diseases associated with Jews, especially smallpox (46). But the truly offensive word in the passage is "squats." "The squatting Jew," writes Julius, "his posture defecatory, becomes what he expels, just as his own motion enacts what must be done to him." And he reminds us that anti-Semites have commonly referred to the Jew as a form of "social excrement" (134).

That verbs like "spawned" and "squats" are insulting and disparaging—a point taken up in a recent study by Rachel Blau DuPlessis, who calls her methodology in tracing the meanings of these words "social philology"[8]— is obvious enough, the question being what the poem does with this "offensive" material. Julius is forced to admit that the "horror picture" of the passage in question is not carried further in Gerontion's monologue. Why? His own explanation is that "Gerontion resists all consoling visions, including the consolations of anti-Semitism, which is a casualty of its relentless negativity" (59). Since Gerontion believes in nothing—neither God nor History nor Progress of any sort—he rejects all frameworks; and even anti-Semitism, Julius posits, is, after all, a framework. Thus the poem rejects form; it "sets its face against the tradition of the dramatic monologue," which is its chosen genre. And since it refuses even anti-Semitism as an "organizing principle," the poem "lacks coherence" (61).

Again, then, the charge against "Gerontion" is that it is incoherent. Coherence, according to this view of poetry, must involve consistency of voice and narrative, of imagery and mythological frame. For Julius, "Gerontion" is not sufficiently Browningesque; it does not carry through the fiction of an individual dramatized subject, whose speech is determined by the control of a silent addressee. Ironically, although Julius's subject is such an important one—Eliot's anti-Semitism and how Eliot's readers have managed to rationalize it away—his reading of "Gerontion" is written under the sign of the New Criticism he ostensibly scorns, for it treats the poem as an autonomous artifact, whose words express certain sentiments about the Jews. But what happens if we look not at genre or external reference but at the poem's actual language, syntax, and rhythm as Eliot's poem took shape in the winter of 1919?

"Language," as Eliot's contemporary Wittgenstein reminds us, "is *not contiguous* to anything else."[9] And further: "to imagine a language means to imagine a form of life."[10] Julius sees "Gerontion" as a "querulous poem" in which "there is no bitterness because there is no loss" (43). To make this assertion, he must take out of context Gerontion's insistence that he is "A dull head among windy spaces" (line 16), and that he has "no ghosts" (line 33), that he has, accordingly, never properly suffered, being no more than an empty vessel.

But does this interpretation really account for the poem? I propose here to look closely at its linguistic and sonic substructure, especially in the first two movements, which comprise lines 1–33. My assumption as we proceed is that there are no "etceteras" here, that every word, and indeed every sound and rhythmic movement, makes a difference. Consider the opening:

Here I am, an old man in a dry month,
Being read to by a boy, waiting for rain.
I was neither at the hot gates
Nor fought in the warm rain
Nor knee deep in the salt marsh, heaving a cutlass,
Bitten by flies, fought.

These lines have received more than their share of explication, beginning with their relationship to the epigraph from *Measure for Measure* and their appropriation of the passage in A. C. Benson's biography of Edward Fitzgerald (1905): "Here he sits, in a dry month, old and blind, being read to by a country boy, longing for rain." The phrase "hot gates" is a literal translation of the Greek proper name *Thermopylae*—thus a reference to the decisive battle (480BC) of the Persian Wars, in which the Spartans defeated the Greeks at the narrow pass by that name. Also Greek is the title "Gerontion," meaning "little old man" and signaling (or seeming to signal) that this, like "The Love Song of J. Alfred Prufrock," is a monologue spoken by an invented persona.[11]

But such source study can do little to account for the passage's peculiar power and passion, for the sense that something terribly important, both to the poet and the reader, is at stake here. Indeed, the "little old man" cover recedes almost immediately, and by line 17 ("Signs are taken for wonders") the vocal urgency is clearly the poet's own, even if it is an abstracted version, or "auditory illusion" to use Hugh Kenner's phrase,[12] of that personal presence. The subject may *feel* like an old man because he has not *fought*, because he has made the Dantean "grand refusal" in his rejection of Christ, and because, as we learn later in the poem, his moral and sexual failures have made him lose his "sight, smell, hearing, taste, and touch" (line 60). But physical age has no more to do with the things that count in this poem than it does in "Prufrock," another poem in which the young male speaker feels old. Indeed, as Denis Donoghue points out, the first title Eliot tried out was *Gerousia*, "Greek for a consultative body or council of elders in Sparta" (*Words Alone* 77). Eliot's original intention, it seems from this, was to produce an anatomy of the modern condition by presenting us with a "council," sitting in judgment of those the Tiger devours. Such an anatomy would, of course, accord with *The Waste Land*.

The epigraph, in this regard, is something of a diversion. The Duke's words to Claudio, who has been falsely sentenced to death—"Thou hast not youth nor age / But as it were an after dinner sleep / Dreaming of both"— with their reference to the limbo in which Claudio finds himself as he prepares to meet his Maker, are not really very relevant to Gerontion's state. For unlike Claudio, Gerontion is not "dreaming of both" but is quite aware of his condition, *now*, and what has brought him to it. Indeed, one could easily dispense with this epigraph, which was originally the first of two, the other, from *Inferno* xxxiii, 121–22, was *Come il mi corpo stea / Nel mondo su, nulla scienza porto* ("How it stands with my body in the world above, I have no knowledge"). This epigraph was excised in the poem's second draft (see Ricks, *Invention of the March Hare* 351), perhaps because Gerontion's real concern is with the state not of his body in the world above but of his soul in the world below.

Early readers, not understanding the use of found text, which is now such a common technique in poetic composition, thought the "stealing" of lines from A. C. Benson indicated a lack of originality on Eliot's part. But what is, on the contrary, so remarkable is that Eliot could take a fairly neutral passage like Benson's, delete the words "blind" and "country" as redundant, and change "he sits" to the immediacy of "Here I am." He also transforms the sound structure of Benson's fairly labored prose sentence:

> / /\ / ||　 /　/ |　　/　/
> Here I am,　an old man　in a dry month,
> /　　/　 | /\ / || /　　　/
> Being read to　*by a boy*,　*wai*ting for *rain*.[13]

These lines are so familiar that we sometimes forget just how strange they are. The opening announcement "Here I am," for example, is intentionally misleading, for we never learn where "here" is or indeed who it is that is declaring "I am."[14] Is the voice of line 1 the same who says in line 55, "I would meet you upon this honestly"? And what is the relation of rhythm to the speaker's identity? To note, as have most of the commentaries, that in "Gerontion" Eliot is adapting Jacobean blank verse,[15] doesn't take us very far. In dramas like Thomas Middleton's *Changeling,* the major source for lines 55–61 of "Gerontion," the line, however irregular, has ten syllables and an iambic base, as in

          /   /   /   / /\   /
    But cast it to the ground regardlessly

or

          /   /   /   /   /
    Was prophet to the rest, but ne'er believed.

But although the first line of "Gerontion" has ten syllables, it breaks into three rhythmic units, and its ten monosyllables, all of them basic English words, contain seven stresses broken by a caesura, so that any potential forward thrust the line might have gives way to near-gridlock, in keeping with the "Thoughts of a dry brain in a dry season" of the poem's ending.

The second line, again a pentameter, this time with an extra syllable, again breaks into three groups, but it is more lightly stressed and foregrounds both alliteration and assonance. *Being* and *waiting:* the two present participles stress the suspension of Gerontion's state of consciousness, its activity in a continuous present in which all roles are reversed, boys reading to old men rather than vice versa. The spiritual dryness of Gerontion is stressed throughout the poem, but the reference to "month," rather than "day" or "week" or "year," is by no means arbitrary. Like "depraved May" in line 21 or "April is the cruelest month" in *The Waste Land,* the time reference, as in Yeats's *A Vision,* is to the lunar cycle, the repeat in history. In its tension between linear and cyclical time, between the linear life span and the possibility of cyclical renewal, "Gerontion" also looks ahead to the *Four Quartets.*

In lines 3–6, even the ghost of pentameter gives way to a heavily stressed free verse:

       /   / /
    I was neither at the hot gates
       /   / /
    Nor fought in the warm rain
       / /   /   / \ /   /
    Nor knee deep in the salt marsh,   heaving a cutlass, >

/   /   ‖   /
Bitten by flies,   fought.

Lines 3 and 4, with their matched stresses on "hot gates" and "warm rain," are curiously resonant. "Hot gates" (*Thermopylae*) is an allusion to the battle-fields of World War I, where Eliot longed to serve, especially after the United States entered the war in 1917. In a letter to his father (4 November 1918), the poet, who had been disqualified for active duty because of physical disabili-ties, including a hernia,[16] relates the strenuous—almost comic—efforts he made to get a commission in Naval Intelligence or in the Interpreter's Corps, commissions for which he was rejected despite a string of recommendations from men in high places (see ll. 246–49). This was evidently a great blow to the poet, who was anxious to persuade his father of his patriotism and will-ingness to engage in action. When Henry Ware Eliot died suddenly two months later (7 January 1919), without having any sense that his son would become a famous poet, the young Eliot was literally distraught (see ll. 267ff.). "Gerontion" was begun shortly afterward and takes into account that the poet quite literally missed out on the "hot gates" as well as the "warm" or life-giving rain that would have signified his baptism into a true manhood, an engagement with the trials of wading "knee deep in the salt marsh." Nor has the speaker come to terms with sexual maturity: "I was neither at the hot gates" refers not only to war but also to the disaster of Eliot's marriage to Vivien, in which no "heat" was ever generated.

But what is perceived in life as a painful failure becomes the occasion for a poetic, especially a rhythmic, triumph. The impact of the word "fought," put forward rather quietly in line 4—"Nor fought in the warm rain"—is held in suspension in the progress of the long irregular alexandrine of line 5— "Nor knee deep in the salt marsh, heaving a cutlass," a line enjambed so that the reader pushes on for another four strongly accented syllables—"Bitten by flies"—only to come to the caesura, followed by the reappearance of the iso-lated verb *fought.* The alliterative "*flies* ‖ *fought*" is something of a tongue twister; the verb, moreover, is now intransitive: it's not just that Gerontion refused to "fight" at one time or that he refused to fight someone specific; rather, *refusal* seems to be his general condition. The self-reproach is inten-sified by the harsh fricative and voiceless stop that frame the long dipthong of *fought*: the word is almost spit out.

To appreciate Eliot's manipulation of sound, we might look at the opening of "Gerontion" in the French translation of Pierre Leyris:

Me voici, un viellard dans un mois de sécheresse,
Écoutant ce garçon me lire, attendant la pluie.

Je n'étais pas au brûlant defile
Je n'ai pas combattu dans la pluie chaude
Ni embourbé dans la saline jusqu'au genou,
Levant un glaive, mordu par les mouches, combattu.[17]

This follows faithfully Eliot's phrasing, imagery, and syntax, from *attendant la pluie* ("waiting for rain") to *combattu dans la pluie chaude* ("fought in the warm rain"), and the final *mordu par les mouches, combattu* ("bitten by flies, fought"). It is difficult to think of a more skillful way of rendering Eliot's poem in French, and yet one feels that in Leyris's text most of "Gerontion's" force has been lost. First, the heavy double stressing on "old man" "dry month," "hot gates," "warm rain," "knee deep," "salt marsh." And more important, the harsh stops, spirants, and fricatives of "heaving a cutlass" and "bitten by flies, fought" are wholly lost in the gentle, harmonious sounds of *Levant un glaive* (note the internal rhyme, open vowels, and soft *l*'s), *mordu par les mouches* (alliteration of *m*'s, soft *o* and *u*), and *combattu,* which all but rhymes with *mordu.* In French translation, then, Gerontion's voice, so agitated in the original, sounds almost steady.

It is in the context of Gerontion's extreme agitation—an agitation contained in sound and rhythm of the passage rather than in the words themselves—that we must consider the lines that follow:

My house is a decayed house,
And the Jew squats on the window sill, the owner,
Spawned in some estaminet of Antwerp,
Blistered in Brussels, patched and peeled in London.
The goat coughs at night in the field overhead;
Rock, moss, stonecrop, iron, merds.
The woman keeps the kitchen, makes tea,
Sneezes at evening, poking the peevish gutter.

           I an old man,
A dull head among windy spaces.

Those who defend this passage against the charges Julius and others have made usually do so on the grounds that "Gerontion" is, after all, not Eliot's own meditation but the monologue of a diseased mind. "Gerontion's mind," writes Jewel Spears Brooker, "is a metaphor for the mind of Europe, a collapsing mind with which Eliot had little sympathy. . . . [The poem's] characters—whether Greek, Christian, or Jewish—exist in Gerontion's demented mind, and all, including himself are represented as withered and repulsive remnants." [18] And Christopher Ricks remarks, "The consciousness in 'Gerontion,' is not offered as healthy, sane and wise; who would wish to be he, and what endorsement then is being asked for the thoughts of his dry brain in its dry season?" And Ricks adds, "Some of the queasy resentful feelings are bent upon a different Jew who may indeed be the owner, Christ." [19]

The argument for Gerontion as fictional persona is never quite convincing. For one thing, as in the case of "Prufrock," Gerontion is too perceptive, too aphoristic and definitive in his judgments to be dismissed as some sort of mental case. In the course of the poem, moreover, Gerontion asks questions—"After such knowledge, what forgiveness?" "What will the spider do, / Suspend its operations . . . ?"—or makes revelatory statements—"I that was near your heart was removed therefrom," "I have lost my passion"—that look straight ahead to related passages in *The Waste Land,* a poem of multiple, often contradictory voices.

But if the portrait of the squatting Jew is not just a projection of Gerontion's diseased mind, how then *are* we to take it? Perhaps a brief biographical excursus will be helpful here. After the war Eliot knew that he would not be returning to the United States to live. In England his poetry had at least found some acclaim, he had a foothold in the literary press, and he could eke out a living and take care of Vivien, with the help of her family and their friends. Yet he was by no means reconciled to British life. On 2 July 1919 he wrote to his brother Henry:

> Don't think that I find it easy to live over here. It is damned hard work to live with a foreign nation and cope with them—one is always coming up against differences of feeling that make one feel humiliated and lonely. *One remains always a foreigner. . . .* It is like being always on dress parade—one can never relax. It is a *great strain. . . .* People are more aware of you, more critical, and they have no pity for one's mistakes or stupidities. . . . They seek your company because they expect something particular from you, and if they don't get it, they drop you. They are always intriguing and caballing; one must be very alert. . . . *London is something one has to fight very hard in, in order to survive.* [20]

This was written just a week before Eliot wrote John Rodker that he had completed "the new poem I spoke of—about seventy-five lines" (*Letters* 312), which was "Gerontion." And a day or two later he remarked to Mary Hutchinson: "But remember that I am a *metic*—a foreigner" (318).

Remaining "always a foreigner" was especially painful in view of Eliot's circumstances in 1919. In May 1915 he had lost the man he may have loved more than any other—Jean Verdenal—who had been the friend of his youth in Paris and was killed in action in the Dardanelles. Eliot's impulsive marriage to Vivien Haigh-Wood, a month later—perhaps on the rebound from the sorrow of Verdenal's death—had revealed itself as a nightmare, even as Bertrand Russell, once Eliot's mentor, was having an affair with Vivien right under Eliot's nose and partly with his collusion.[21] And then, having failed to get a military commission or to reconcile with his parents, who had disapproved strongly of his marriage, he received the news of his father's sudden death. Clearly, the poet's personal troubles—his almost visceral revulsion from both Vivien and Russell as well as his alienation from the Bloomsbury of the Stephens sisters, Vanessa and Virginia, and the Garsington circle of Lady Ottoline Morrell—demanded an outlet in his writing.

Ironically, none of the above had even the slightest amount of Jewish or foreign blood; they were, on the contrary, of pure English stock, and Lord Russell was a member of the high English aristocracy. In this context the venom directed against the Jew "spawned in some estaminet in Antwerp," like the venom displayed vis-à-vis women, especially in *The Waste Land*, must be understood as a psychic displacement: all of Eliot's hatred and resentment for Russell and Vivien, like his guilt feelings toward his parents, were displaced onto nightmare figures with labels like "the Jew," or, later in the poem, "Mr. Silvero / With caressing hands" and "De Bailhache, Fresca, [and] Mrs. Cammel." Reluctant to write openly about evils he could not quite put his finger on, he invented an elaborate objective correlative based on stereotypes of Jewish or "Oriental" or female behavior. The closest Eliot came to "direct treatment of the thing" was in *The Waste Land*, where the twenty-eight-line passage in "The Game of Chess" that begins with line 111— " 'My nerves are bad to-night. Yes, bad. Stay with me. / 'Speak to me. Why do you never speak. Speak' "—and culminates in the "Shakespeherian Rag," with its assertion that " 'I shall rush out as I am, and walk the street / With my hair down, so' "—has been shown to be closely modeled on Vivien's own speech habits; indeed, it was she who added the devastating line "What you get married for if you don't want children?" found in the pub sequence.[22] In "Gerontion," however, the hostility is deflected onto "acceptable" targets like the Jews.

But isn't this precisely what anti-Semitism is? Isn't it inherently *ressentiment* or displacement of hostility and self-hatred onto a scapegoat? Of course, if we add the proviso that the self-disgust and suffering displayed in Eliot's "objective correlative" is what makes "Gerontion" such a powerful and, quite literally, memorable poem. We see the speaker threatened by a "Jew" who, far from being a successful grasping landlord, squeezing money out of poor old Gerontion, is himself a squatter, a victim of poverty, misery, and disease, a figure who, in Julius's words, "becomes what he expels." Squatting on the window sill, he belongs neither inside the "decayed house," nor can he escape its precincts. In a similar vein, Eliot's misogyny, which will be more openly declared in *The Waste Land,* is here displaced onto a nameless, faceless, generic old woman, who "Sneezes at evening, poking the peevish gutter" (note the remarkable use of the long *e* phoneme)—a sexless figure who is no more of a threat than the goat that "coughs at night in the field overhead." Note that there is no flock of goats in this field but only "the" goat, on the analogy of "the" Jew and "the" woman. And this goat, a far cry from Pan the goat god or the satyr of Greek mythology, does nothing but "cough," even as the woman does nothing but sneeze and poke. As the *scapegoat* of Jewish mythology,[23] it is a fitting companion for Gerontion.

The key to this proto-surreal nightmare landscape, peopled by characters devoid of humanity, is found in line 12—

$$/ \quad \| \quad / \quad \| \quad / \quad /\backslash \quad \| \quad /\backslash \quad \| \quad /$$
Rocks,   moss,   stonecrop,   iron,   merds—

where each noun in the poet's catalogue is separate and emphatically sounded, as in a roll call. The first four nouns, moreover, are phonemic variations on the same *o, r,* and *s* sounds: *stonecrop* echoes *rocks* and *moss,* as does the second syllable of *iron.*[24] But then comes a new vowel sound (*e*) and an even nastier reference, this time to the shit (*merds,* from the French *merde,* here rhyming with *turds*) that dominates the scene. By the time we come to the refrain, "I an old man / A dull head among windy spaces,"[25] the various occupants of this arid stonecrop seem no more than a projection of the poet's own self-hatred and despair: Gerontion, the goat, the Jew, the woman who "keeps the kitchen" and "sneezes at evening," even the gutter, described in a transferred epithet as "peevish"—all are interchangeable. The woman "makes tea," the Jew "squats," but the poet himself does nothing at all; he merely exists, verbless, "a dull head among windy spaces." Eliot's winds have been read as allusions to Dante's ceaseless and aimless winds, to the biblical wind that bloweth where it listeth and even, by Genesius Jones, to the Holy Spirit, but I want to note here that contrary to Desmond MacCarthy's caution that we mustn't take Eliot too literally, these windy spaces really *are,* first and foremost, just that—the winds blowing in the empty spaces of the infinite sky over the "Rocks, moss, stonecrop, iron, merds" of Gerontion's—more accurately, the poet's—mental landscape.

If the poem continued in this despairing vein, the scene might become

too oppressive. But Eliot, a master of vocal registers, now suddenly shifts
tone:

> Signs are taken for wonders. "We would see a sign!"
> The word within a word unable to speak a word,
> Swaddled with darkness. In the juvescence of the year
> Came Christ the tiger

The shift to the cry of the unbelieving Pharisees (who are, of course, Jews),
calling upon Christ to prove his divinity by performing a sign (Matthew
12:38), modulates, in turn, into the words of Lancelot Andrewes's Christmas
sermon, adapting the Gospel of St. John ("The word without a word; the
eternal Word not able to speak a word"), a phrase that is given an Eliotic twist
in the substitution of "within" for "without" to refer to the difficulty of receiving the Logos. The springtime ritual looks ahead to "April is the cruelest
month": "juvescence" is not, I think, an incorrect version of "juvenescence,"
as is often suggested, but a neologism, based on its opposite—"senescence."
The tiger is of course Blake's tiger, but John Crowe Ransom, in one of the
first and most detailed explications of "Gerontion," is right to note that "the
lamb who came to be devoured turns into the tiger when Gerontion has forgotten the lamb."[26]

But beyond its allusive texture, this is a highly complex passage. Take the
opening alexandrine:

>   /   /   /   ‖   /   /   /
> Signs are taken for wonders.   "We would see a sign!"

The first sentence, with its trochaic/dactylic rhythm, is a summarizing commentary, no doubt spoken by the poet whose voice now merges wholly with
Gerontion's, whereas the second sentence, a direct citation from Matthew, is
iambic. Eliot's Imagist contemporaries would no doubt have given each sentence its own line:

> Signs are taken for wonders.
> "We would see a sign!"

In joining both sentences in one line, Eliot obscures the distinction between commentary and citation, the voice of the narrator and the voice
of the Pharisee addressing Christ. And this is obviously intentional: for the

"dull head among windy spaces" that has been our guide thus far, there is no real distinction between these voices. Indeed, the poet himself is a Pharisee, whose passivity and inability to act or even think ("Think now" will become a major motif in this poem) causes "Signs" to become so essential. Meanwhile "the word within a word, unable to speak a word" remains unheard, "Swaddled in darkness." The long thirteen-syllable line, run over into the next foreshortened one, creates the explosion of

> /   /   /
> Came Christ the tiger

where the alliteration of the *k* sound yields to the assonance of "Christ" and "tiger"—the two becoming immediately seen as one.

And now, without transition, the poem shifts from the image of Gerontion's general condition and the Christian admonition that follows to a particular surreal scene:

> In depraved May, dogwood and chestnut, flowering judas,
> To be eaten, to be divided, to be drunk
> Among whispers; by Mr. Silvero
> With caressing hands, at Limoges
> Who walked all night in the next room;
> By Hakagawa, bowing among the Titians;
> By Madame de Tornquist, in the dark room
> Shifting the candles; Fräulein von Kulp
> Who turned in the hall, one hand on the door.
>   Vacant shuttles
> Weave the wind. I have no ghosts,
> An old man in a draughty house
> Under a windy knob.

In the passage from *The Education of Henry Adams* to which the first line alludes (see Southam 44), "dogwood and chestnut, flowering judas" represent the lush, sensual vegetation of the Washington-area landscape so unfamiliar to a New Englander. Eliot, it is generally assumed, parodied Adams's ecstatic description so as to set the scene for the ghostly parody of the sacrament in the modern world—a kind of Black Mass. The "dry month" of line 1 is now a "depraved May," and the reference to "judas" points back, of course, to the betrayal of Christ.

Yet this obvious contrast between contemporary debasement and the Christian Word is hardly the whole story. Indeed, when we read Adams's own account, it seems to point elsewhere. "No European spring," writes Adams, "had shown him the same intermixture of delicate grace and passionate depravity that marked the Maryland May. He loved it too much as if it were Greek and half human" (see Southam 44). It is the Greek connection and the "lov[ing] it too much" that makes the reader of "Gerontion" pause; for like Adams, Eliot longed for the "delicate grace and passionate depravity" associated with things "Greek and half human." Gerontion, after all, is himself Greek, and the denizens of the poem are certainly presented as only "half human." In this context, the memory of "depraved May, dogwood and chestnut, flowering judas" may not be primarily negative after all. On the contrary, the suggestion is that "depraved May" was the "month" in which Gerontion flourished—as lush and wet as that other month has been "dry." One thinks of the Hyacinth Girl in *The Waste Land*, "Your arms full, and your hair wet" (*Collected Poems* 54). When Adams says he associates "passionate depravity" with the Greeks, he is thinking not of the actual Greek landscape, which is dry and rocky ("Rocks, moss, stonecrop, iron, merds"), but of the Greek deities, half-human, half-animal, sporting in the shade. "Judas," however much an emblem of betrayal, is, after all, depicted as "flowering." So, the poem implies, the pagan sacrament ("To be eaten, to be divided, to be drunk") was seductive enough to attract Gerontion and his friends until it was received "Among whispers" by a particular arty coterie. The nymphs and satyrs have departed, and instead we get sophisticated city dwellers like Mr. Silvero, Hakagawa, Madame de Tornquist, Fräulein von Kulp.

Like "the Jew [who] squats on the window sill," these participants in what seems to be a sinister rite are less characters than caricatures, their mongrelized names testifying to their dubious pedigrees. *Silvero* (a silver alloy of some sort, a silver cover for *vero*, true), *Hakagawa* (whose affix, as Pound remarked when Eliot sent him the poem, means "river" in Japanese), the Blavatsky-clone *Madame de Tornquist* ("turncoat"?), who is soon to metamorphose into the Madame Sosostris of *The Waste Land*, and Madame de Tornquist's German accomplice Fräulein von Kulp (*culpa*). In the cartoon metropolis where these figures operate, there are no actions, merely gestures. What objects (or is it people?) have come under the touch of Mr. Silvero's "caressing hands"? And if he "walked all night in the next room," next to what was it? Or is the room in question next in line? Silvero is "caressing," Hakagawa—an inveterate art groupie, no doubt, or a gallery owner or art collector—is "bowing among the Titians," and Madame de Tornquist "shifting the candles," not, as one might expect, at the church altar, but in "the dark room." Is it a séance? And who is to be raised from the dead instead of Christ? Fräulein von Kulp's movements are especially mysterious: she only "turned in the hall, one hand on the door." Will she run into Mr. Silvero in this "cunning passage"? Is she leaving the séance or about to participate in one? We never find out, for now Eliot gives us the biblical statement: "Vacant shuttles / Weave the wind" (an allusion to Job's "My days are swifter than a weaver's shuttle, and are spent without hope. Oh remember that my life is wind" [Job 7:6–7]), followed by the curious confession that "I have no ghosts," and then the refrain "An old man in a draughty house / Under a windy knob."

The passage leads up to the dramatic question that has since taken on a life of its own: "After such knowledge, what forgiveness?" Ironically, the immediate question these words evoke is not about forgiveness but about knowledge. For what can the knowledge be that has produced such a conundrum? What is it Gerontion *knows* that demands forgiveness? I believe that the "Depraved May" passage contains many hints, buried in the very fabric of the language. "Depraved," for starters, contains the paragram *pray*. It is the refusal to pray, the absence of prayer in this remembered scene, that has made the poet's May so "depraved." "Judas" contains the syllable "jew," which is to say that the eating, dividing, and drinking going on here might have been the real sacrament rather than its debasement into "flowering judas." The "whispers" in line 23 are literally enacted in the sequence "*whispers*" / "*Mister*" / "*Silvero*," and the hissing *s* is carried over into "caressing." Because Gerontion's story has never been inscribed on the loom of history, because the shuttles remain vacant, there is little to go by. The poet, moreover, doesn't want exposure, and so he avoids all lessons the past might provide. And the "draughty" house is also the house of "drought."

But of course Gerontion does have his ghosts. Consider this passage:

After such knowledge, what forgiveness? Think now
History has many cunning passages, contrived corridors
And issues, deceives with whispering ambitions,
Guides us by vanities. Think now
(ll. 34–37)

Again, let us ask: what does Gerontion *know* that makes it so difficult for him to forgive himself? To begin with, he had a chance to know Christ, to partake of His body and blood, to take Communion, but somehow he refused. Accordingly, "The tiger springs in the new year. Us he devours." But there are other forms of knowledge the poet refused. "Gerontion" was supposed to be the prelude to *The Waste Land,* and there we read:

> *Datta:* what have we given?
> My friend, blood shaking my heart
> The awful daring of a moment's surrender
> Which an age of prudence can never retract
> By this, and this only, we have existed
>   (*Collected Poems* 68)

This passage is nicely glossed by the lines in "Gerontion," "Gives too soon / Into weak hands, what's thought can be dispensed with / Till the refusal propagates a fear." And again, the admonition is "Think."

After such knowledge, what forgiveness? After having known what "blood shaking my heart" could be, how could the poet have rejected love in the interest of prudence? How could he have been so weak as to think he could dispense with love, only to find himself a potential "old man" whose "refusal propagates a fear"? Thinking, unfortunately, won't change anything.

These are the "ghosts" that haunt the Gerontion who tries to tell himself that he has no ghosts:

> I that was near your heart was removed therefrom
> To lose beauty in terror, terror in inquisition.
> I have lost my passion: why should I need to keep it
> Since what is kept must be adulterated?
> I have lost my sight, smell, hearing, taste and touch:
> How should I use them for your closer contact?
>   (ll. 55–61)

These "Jacobean" lines make sense only if we take them to be both about secular and spiritual love. What a poem says, as Jacques Roubaud puts it, cannot be said any other way. The loss of the five senses in line 50 takes us back to that earlier catalogue, "Rocks, moss, stonecrop, iron, merds"—items threatening to the touch, to smell, taste, sight, and hearing—that constitute the landscape when all that matters has been lost.

What is left is no more than a "wilderness of mirrors," in which some further humanoids—De Bailhache, Fresca, Mrs. Cammel—are "whirled / Beyond the circuit of the shuddering Bear / in fractured atoms." In this ghostly frozen landscape, the little white gull cannot fight the wind and collapses in a mass of "white feathers" in the snow. All that is finally left, as the poem's speaker knows, is

/   /

Tenants of the house,

/   / /   / /

Thoughts of a dry brain in a dry season.

What is striking here is that the stress clusters, reminiscent of the poem's opening, are now unbroken by midline caesurae. The rhythm merely *flows*, weakly alluding to the agitated pace of "Here I am, ‖ an old man | in a dry month." The game, Eliot suggests, is over.

Is "Gerontion" incoherent? Certainly not at the level of language and rhythm, where every word and phrase has its echo in the "wilderness of mirrors" of earlier or later strophes. Eliot moves easily between the concrete of "Hakagawa, bowing among the Titians" and the abstract of "Gives too late / What's not believed in." The tension between the two, which has bothered numerous critics, seems quite intentional: only by exploring the tension between abstract/concrete, conceptual/perceptual, general/particular, can the Voice of the poem come to terms with the reality of its situation.

What is that situation? At one pole, the poet who might have known the mercy and grace of God, the Christian dispensation, has rejected it and must hence live in a secular realm in which redemption is precluded. At the other, more personal pole, Eliot presents himself as one who, having neither been "at the hot gates / Nor fought in the warm rain," turned to the literary life of London and country houses, the life of English upper-class society, which, as I remarked earlier, was hardly the society of "the Jew," "Patched and peeled in London"; or the society of Mr. Silvero with his cult of Limoges, or Fräulein von Kulp, "one hand on the door"; or certainly not the oddly named Fresca, who seems to have no family name at all and keeps company with Mrs. Cammel, whose name sounds suspiciously Jewish. No, the society Eliot frequented during the war years and their aftermath was the best "literary" society England had to offer. It was the bisexual "enlightened" society of Bloomsbury, perhaps, that sullied the memory of the poet's own private savior, the romantic young Frenchman named Jean Verdenal and all he stood for. And it was further a society that all too offhandedly rejected the Christ of the Gospels. Bertrand Russell, for example, was a confirmed atheist, and Bloomsbury generally made fun of Christian faith as hopelessly childish

and antiquated. In this religious void, only "vacant shuttles weave the wind."
And since Eliot can never reveal his real secret about Verdenal, he can only
turn to Christ, who will forgive all sins.

One of the wonders of "Gerontion" is thus how a deeply personal situation finds its objective correlative so that the poem appears to be, in its later
passages, a disquisition about larger, impersonal issues, questions of history
and memory, sin and redemption. It is a matter of charging language with
meaning so that "depraved May" will readily reveal the power of what it
means to *pray*. Is "Gerontion" an anti-Semitic poem? No one could deny that
the three lines in question have a nasty, anti-Semitic cast. But does this mean
that the thrust of Eliot's complex monologue is a slur on the Jews? Hardly.
For it is finally a meditation in which critique is pointed inward. There is no
forgiveness, only the knowledge of how one has come to such a pass.

Like all good poems, "Gerontion" cannot be paraphrased; it cannot be described as "about" an old man's confused mind or "about" the refusal to take
Communion, or about the decay of religion in a secular world. All these motifs enter in, but the force of the poem depends on its extraordinary language. Take the name De Bailhache in the last section, De Bailhache being one of those "whirled / Beyond the circuit of the shuddering Bear / In
fractured atoms." De Bailhache is not a "proper" French surname; its parts
don't cohere. But literally the name gives us the first syllable of *bailler* (to
yawn) plus *hache* (axe). An *hache de guerre* is a battle-axe or tomahawk; *haché*
means "minced" or "crushed," as in *bifteck haché*, which is hamburger.

Bailhache as yawner looks ahead to the "sleepy corner" to which this person and his friends will soon be driven. Bailhache as "battle-axe" or "tomahawk" is a variant on the cutlass the poet wishes he had heaved in the salt
marsh. Bailhache represents the hamburger one becomes when one's proper
names seem to be at odds. And finally the "De" is the most common of af-
fectations: the prefix designating an aristocratic connection.

All of these connotations obtain. But in line 68, De Bailhache is also an
anagram on the word *delay* that precedes it. And that is perhaps the most
intriguing suggestion of the proper name. Would that there were a delay for
De Bailhache, Fresca, and Mrs. Cammell, "whirled beyond the circuit of
the shuddering Bear / In fractured atoms"! Gerontion may tell us he has
no ghosts, but the poem knows better. In Eliot's great phantasmagoria, the
ghosts are everywhere.

In July 2001 I was invited to give a plenary address at the biennial interna-
tional Ezra Pound Conference in Paris. It was a pleasure to reread Pound
from the perspective of the seemingly so different Marcel Duchamp, with
whose work I was then preoccupied. The essay that resulted profited from
the comments of an audience of poets and artists at the lecture series curated
by Sergio Bessa for the White Box Gallery in Chelsea. It was published in the
inaugural issue (2003) of Paideuma.

3
The Search for "Prime Words"
Pound, Duchamp, and the Nominalist Ethos

> but Wanjina is, shall we say, Ouan Jin
> or the man with an education
> and whose mouth was removed by his father
>   because he made too many *things*
> whereby cluttered the bushman's baggage. . . .
> Ouan Jim spoke and thereby created the named
>   thereby making clutter
>   Ezra Pound, Canto 74

In a pioneer study of Ezra Pound's translations of the Chinese poems found
in Japanese transcription in Ernest Fenollosa's notebooks, Sanehide Kodama
discusses the specific changes Pound made in the "Song of Ch'ang-kan" by
Li Po (Rihaku in Japanese), translated as "The River-Merchant's Wife: A Letter."[1] The original, writes Kodama, has the rigid form of *gogon zekku:* "eight
lines, with five characters in each line in a strict structural and rhyming pattern" (220). And he goes on to describe the difference in tone as well as verse
form between Li Po's original and Pound's dramatic monologue, commenting, as have Ronald Bush and others, on the greater subtlety and complexity
of Pound's portrait, in his version the wife becoming much less submissive,
indeed somewhat rebellious.[2]

But the difficulty in assessing the speaker's psychology—is she voicing her
willingness to go to great lengths to meet her husband, or threatening, as
Ronald Bush believes, to come "as far as Cho-fu-Sa but no farther"? ("Pound

and Li Po" 42)—is surely compounded by a facet of Pound's poetry rarely discussed, namely, his curious use of proper names. Consider the poem's last four lines:

> If you are coming down through the narrows of the river Kiang,
> Please let me know beforehand,
> And I will come out to meet you
>   As far as Cho-fu-Sa.

In the Fenollosa transcription, which gives the Japanese sound equivalent for each Chinese character, followed by their literal English translation and then a syntactically normalized version, we read:

So	*ban*	*ka*	*sam*	*pa*
Sooner or later	descend	three	whirls	(name of spot on Yangtse Kiang where waters whirl)

> If you be coming down as far as the Three Narrows sooner or later

Yo	*sho*	*sho*	*ho*	*ka*
Beforehand	with	letter	report	family-home

> Please let me know by writing

Sho	*gei*	*fu*	*do*	*yen*
Mutually	meeting	not	say	far

> For I will go out to meet [you], not saying that the way be far

Choku	*chi*	*cho*	*fu*	*sa*
Directly	arrive	long	wind	sand
			(a port on the Yangtse)	

> And will directly come to Chofusa.
>   (Kodama 228–29)

The poet and Sinologist Wai-Lim Yip translates the lines:

> When eventually you would come down from the Three Gorges,
> Please let me know ahead of time,
> I will meet you, no matter how far,
> Even all the way to Long Wind Sand. (194)

And another translator, Arthur Cooper:

Late or early coming from Sam-pa,
Before you come, write me a letter:
To welcome you, don't talk of distance,
I'll go as far as the Long Wind Sands!

(Kern 199)

Both Cooper and Yip follow Fenollosa in rendering the Yangtse port *Chofusa* as "Long Wind Sand[s]."[3] But Pound, here and frequently in *Cathay,* insists on retaining the Chinese name, even if he often has to make it up, as is the case in the poem "Separation on the River Kiang," where the phrase *ko jin* ("old acquaintance") is turned into a proper name, "Ko-jin" ("Ko jin goes west from Ko-kaku-ro").[4] The "river Kiang" is a related example of what we might call Pound's hyper-naming project. In colloquial Chinese, as Yunte Huang observes, *Kiang* ("river") usually refers to a particular *Kiang*—the Yangtse—just as suburbanites in the New York area will talk of going "into the city" when they mean "New York City."[5] Thus, when Pound's river merchant's wife suggests to her husband, "If you are coming down through the narrows of the river Kiang," she is, so to speak, repeating herself.

Such overdetermination of nouns and noun phrases is typically Poundian. In *Cathay,* as in "Near Perigord," "Provincia Deserta," and especially in *The Cantos,* Pound's is a poetry studded with proper names, whether of fictional or real persons and places: the names of Greek deities, Chinese emperors, or Roman poets, or of actual persons and places from his own acquaintance, ranging from local restaurants in the Tyrol to London acquaintances—all of these rendered by formal names, nicknames, pet names, and names in various American or foreign dialects. The later Cantos embed such proper names in a structure of Chinese ideograms (which themselves function as names) as well as passages of found text, so that citation, used sparingly by Pound's fellow modernist poets, becomes the preferred poetic material. But the question is *why.* Why this longing to turn words that have specific meanings into proper names—names that designate a particular person or place and hence restrict the possibilities of reference? Why is "Cho-fu-sa" preferable to "Long Wind Sands"?

The usual answer is that the proper name is a form of concrete image, that the title "Separation on the River Kiang" has a specificity that would be missing if the title were merely "Separation on the River." Proper names, by this account, are part and parcel of Pound's Imagist, and later Vorticist, doctrine, with its call for "direct treatment of the thing" and the "new method" of "luminous detail."[6] The Image, we read in *Gaudier-Brzeska,* is "the point of maximum energy," the "primary pigment"; it is "a radiant node or cluster . . . A VORTEX, from which, and through which, and into which ideas are constantly rushing."[7] If, as Pound says in "A Retrospect," "the natural object is always the *adequate* symbol" (*Literary Essays* 4), if, as he puts it later in the *ABC of Reading,* the Chinese ideogram is the touchstone for poets because, unlike the letter unit of the Western alphabet, the ideogram provides us with "the picture of a thing,"[8] then the proper name is essential to a poetics of "constatation of fact," of "accuracy of sentiment."[9] Indeed, so "accurate" and specific are Pound's images and proper names that critics like Hugh Kenner and Richard Sieburth have remarked on their documentary realism: one can, it is often said, find a particular fresco in a given Romanesque church, by following the "directions" in *The Cantos.* Pound's, says Kenner, is a "Michelin map [that] will guide you, perhaps two hours by car from Montségur. A system of words denotes that verifiable landscape. . . . The words point, and the arranger of the words works in trust that we shall find their connections validated outside the poem."[10]

In Pound's later work, Imagist "constatation of fact" is increasingly associated with Confucianism—specifically, the doctrine in the *Analects* cited by Pound at the opening of *Guide to Kulchur:*

> Tseu-Lou asked: *If the Prince of Mei appointed you head of the government, to what wd. you first set your mind?*
>
> Kung: *To call people and things by their names, that is by the correct denominations, to see that the terminology was exact. . . .*
>
> *If the terminology be not exact, if it fit not the thing, the governmental instructions will not be explicit, if the instructions aren't clear and the names don't fit, you can not conduct business properly.*[11]

The **chêng ming,** as the "rectification of names" is called, is essential to a well-ordered society. Things in actual fact, Confucius believed, should be made to accord with the implication attached to them by names. Indeed, as Fung Yu-Lan puts it in his history of Chinese philosophy, "every name contains certain implications which constitute the essence of that class of things to which this name applies. Such things, therefore, should agree with this ideal essence. The essence of a ruler is what the ruler ideally ought to be. . . . There is an agreement between name and actuality."[12]

No doubt Pound yearned for such a perfect fit, for the hierarchical order first celebrated in Canto 13 ("Kung walked in the temple . . . ") and amplified by Pound in his translation of Confucian writings called *The Unwobbling Pivot & the Great Digesty* (1947). In theory, the Confucian *Ch'I* ("air" or "breath"), which Pound derived from Mencius, is regularly invoked in *The*

Cantos, where it is regularly associated with the neo-Platonic "great ball of crystal" (see esp. Cantos 100, 116), the Plotinian *nous* celebrated by Pound's favorite medieval philosophers and poets. Canto 51, for example, opens with a citation from Guido Guinicelli's *Al cor gentil:* "Shines / in the mind of heaven God / who made it / more than the sun / in our eye" and in Canto 55, we read:

> Honour to CHIN-TSONG the modest
> Lux enim per se omnem in partem
> Reason from heaven, saith Tcheou Ton-y
>   enlighteneth all things
> seipsum seipsum diffundit, risplende[13]

Michael André Bernstein comments:

> Chin-song (Shên-Tsung) was one of the Chinese Emperors . . . of whom Pound approved because of his able administration and adherence to the Confucian ideal of the just ruler.
>
> The next line as well as part of the last one is a variation of Robert Grosseteste's (c. 1175–1253) statement in his treatise *De Luce,* "Lux enim per se in omnem partem se ipsum diffundit," and means, "For light, of its nature shines (diffuses itself) in all directions." . . . Tcheou Ton-y (Chou Tun-I) was a noted Confucian scholar and philosopher (1017–1073) who wrote a commentary on the *I Ching.* The theory here attributed to [him] is one dear to Pound, neo-Platonism, and Confucianism: the natural relationship between heaven and earth is one of essential harmony; the cosmos is governed by a divine reason. . . . The repetition of "seipipsum, seipsum" (itself, itself) suggests a cry of joy.[14]

The light shines forth. *Risplende.*

But the fact is that even ardent expositors of Pound's Confucianism and neo-Platonism have had to concede that the privileged moments in *The Cantos* when the poet is able to celebrate the *chêng ming* and invoke the "great acorn of light" (116/813) are largely offset—indeed, contradicted—by the actual verbal texture of Pound's "epic including history." For Bernstein, this contradiction suggests a "chronic limitation" of Pound's ideogrammic technique. When, for example, in Canto 54, the line "and HAN was after 43 years of TSIN dynasty," is juxtaposed to the lines, "some cook, some do not cook, / some things can not be changed" (54/275), with their reference to the friction between Pound's wife, Dorothy, and mistress, Olga, in their ménage à trois days during the war, Bernstein complains that the personal reference trivializes rather than intensifies the Confucian historiography that precedes it (*Tale of the Tribe* 45–46).

But there is another way of regarding Pound's seeming failure to sustain his vision. My own sense is that however much Pound yearned to *believe* in Confucian and neo-Platonic doctrine, his own bent was toward a *nominalism* that ironically nourished his long poem much more successfully than he himself might have imagined. Indeed, whereas the invocation of the resplendent light could yield brief epiphanic moments of lyric intensity, they could hardly sustain an encyclopedic poem, written over half a century, as could Pound's particular brand of nominalism.

For the medieval Scholastics, nominalism was the doctrine that "denies the existence of abstract objects and universals, holding that these are not required to explain the significance of words apparently referring to them. Nominalism holds that all that really exists are particular, usually physical objects, and that properties, numbers, and sets (for instance) are not further things in the world, but merely features of our way of thinking or speaking about those things that do exist."[15] Thus defined, nominalism is not simply equivalent to empiricism, for it takes the particulars in question not as so much material data but as discrete and unique bearers of meaning. It is the relation of particular to the "essence" beyond it that is questioned. What makes Pound a nominalist is his peculiar fixation on the uniqueness of a given word or object, its *haeccitas,* its *difference* from all other words or objects. Such "thisness," we should note, is not necessarily a matter of the concrete image. Indeed, the language of *The Cantos* is hardly "concrete" in the sense of "visual" or "descriptive." There is, for example, nothing in Pound to match William Carlos Williams's graphic tactility in "Queen Anne's Lace" and "Young Sycamore," or Wallace Stevens's color imagery in "Sea Surface Full of Clouds." Indeed, in Jean-Michel Rabaté's words, Pound's "montage of quotations forces a whirl of details, particular objects, points of interest, clashes of utterances onto the reader," so that direct reference is curiously undercut. "The real is not given 'in' the text—it remains outside. . . . it withholds itself as sign, the transparency looked for vanishes as soon as the operation of reading and of writing has begun."[16]

It is this subtle oscillation between "reference and reverence" (Rabaté's phrase) that gives *The Cantos* their distinctive cast. The drive to turn the signifier—the found object, citation, or proper name—into that which it signifies relates Pound's work to that of a fellow artist who, on the face of it, would seem to have precious little in common with him except that he was Pound's exact contemporary—namely, Marcel Duchamp.[17] The two were casual acquaintances—first through their mutual friendship with François

Picabia and his circle, later perhaps through the artist Mary Reynolds, who was Pound's friend and Duchamp's longtime mistress—but Pound's aestheticism was a far cry from Duchamp's cultivated indifference, his persistent question whether, as he put it in a youthful notebook entry, one couldn't perhaps "make works that are not works of 'art'," which stands behind his "readymades" and boxes.[18] In Duchamp's lexicon, each word, number, or material object bears a distinct name—a name not to be confused with any other and pointing to no universal concept outside itself. The term *nominalism* itself comes up in a number of notebook entries. Here is one from 1914:

Nominalism [literal] = No more generic, specific numeric distinction between words (tables is not the plural of table, ate has nothing in common with eat). No more physical adaptation of concrete words; no more conceptual value of abstract words. The word also loses its musical value. It is only readable (due to being made up of consonants and vowels), it is readable by eye and little by little takes on a form of plastic significance. . . .

    This *plastic* being of the word (by literal nominalism) differs from the *plastic being* of any form whatever . . . in that the grouping of several words without significance, reduced to literal nominalism, is *independent of the interpretation*.[19]

"This nominalism," says Thierry de Duve, in his important study of Duchamp (called, after a related note, *Pictorial Nominalism*), "is literal: it turns back on metaphor and takes things literally. Duchamp intends to specify those conditions that in his eyes allow the word to remain in is zero degree, force it into the realm of nonlanguage."[20]

Duchamp understood, of course, that such "zero degree" nominalism could not exist, that the plural form cannot "forget" that it derives from the singular, the feminine from the masculine, and so on. In wanting to endow the word with "a form of plastic significance" that would be "independent of interpretation," he hoped to heighten the reader/viewer's sensitivity to *difference*, to what Duchamp called, in his posthumously published notes, the *inframince*. This word—in English, *infrathin*—defies definition. "One can only give examples of it," Duchamp declared (*Notes* #5). Here are a few:

The warmth of a seat (which has just been left) is infra-thin (#4)

In time the same object is not the / same after a 1 second interval— what / relations with the identity principle? (#7)

Subway gates—The people / who go through at the very last moment / infra thin—(#9 recto)

Velvet trousers- / their whistling sound (in walking) by / brushing of the 2 legs is an / infra thin separation signaled / by sound. (it is *not?* an infra thin sound) (#9)

When the tobacco smoke smells also of the / mouth which exhales it, the 2 odors / marry by infra thin (olfactory / in thin). (#11)

Infra thin separation between / the *detonation* noise of a gun / (very close) *and* the *apparition* of the bullet / hole in the target. . . . (#12)

Difference between *the contact* / of water and *that* of / molten lead for ex, / or of cream. / with the walls of its / own container. . . . this difference between two contacts is infra thin. (#14)

2 Forms cast in / the same mold (?) differ / from each other / by an infra thin separative / difference. Two men are not / an example of identicality / and to the contrary / move away / from a determinable / infra thin difference—but (#35)

just touching. While trying to place 1 plane surface / precisely on another plane surface / you pass through some *infra thin moments*—(#46)

The role of the artist, Duchamp implies with these witty examples, is to be attentive precisely to such all but imperceptible difference. As he put it in another 1914 note, this one later placed in the *Green Box* of 1934:

Conditions of a language:
The search for "*prime words*" ("divisible" only by themselves and by unity). Take a Larousse dict. and copy all the so-called "abstract" words. i.e., those which have no concrete reference.

Compose a schematic sign designating each of these words. (this sign can be composed with the standard stops)

These signs must be thought of as the letters of the new alphabet . . .

Necessity for *ideal continuity,* i.e.: each grouping will be connected with the other grouping by a *strict meaning* (a sort of grammar, no longer requiring a pedagogical sentence construction. (*Essential Writings* 31–32)

But why are *prime words*—words divisible only by themselves—so desirable? Here we might come back for a moment to the lines from Pound's "River-Merchant's Wife," "And I shall come out to meet you / As far as Cho-fu-sa." Why, to repeat my earlier question, is this designation preferable to the "Warm Wind Sands" of Yip and Cooper? Perhaps because the signifier *Cho-fu-sa*, real place though it is, gives us so little information to go on. For the Anglophone reader—and that, of course, is the reader for whom Pound is writing—*Cho-fu-sa* is suggestively exotic but withholds any further meaning. How far *is* Cho-fu-sa? How long would it take to get there? We cannot tell any more than we can recognize, earlier in this same poem, the location of *Ku-to-yen*, a Poundian neologism based on the amalgam of two words: *Kuto* (the locality) and *Enyotai*, designated by Fenollosa as the huge rock in the river at the entrance of the narrows at Kuto (see Kodama, "Cathay and Fenollosa's Notebooks" 223).

Names like *Cho-fu-sa* and the fictional *Ku-to-yen* draw the reader into the poet's confidence: of course you know, the poet seems to be telling us, what it is I'm talking about. You too have been there. The specific name, in other words, takes on an aura despite the emptiness of the signifiers in question, their lack of semantic density. In *The Cantos* such naming becomes much more elaborate: names are often piled on unrelated names in various metonymic configurations. Given that Pound was, after all, wedded to the notion that "Dichten = condensare" (*ABC of Reading* 36), that "It is better to present one Image in a lifetime than to produce voluminous works" (*Literary Essays* 4), why the Gargantuan excess, the immoderate roll call of names?

Before we turn to *The Cantos* themselves, it is interesting to note that even in his brief Paris phase (1920–1923), when he flirted with Dada, Pound produced texts quite unlike, say, Tristan Tzara's in their inclusion of documentation. Consider, in this regard, his little-known poem called *Kongo Roux*, written for Picabia's special issue of *391* called by the nonsense name *Le Pilhaou thibaou* (10 July 1921). *Kongo Roux*, printed on the verso of Picabia's letter to "Mon cher Confucious" [*sic*] is reproduced by Andrew Clearfield in an essay for *Paideuma*,[21] which describes the piece as a "typical Dada *jeu d'esprit*" (120, see figure 2). Richard Sieburth, who discusses it more fully in his essay "Dada Pound," calls it "as close to the real Dada thing as [Pound] would ever get," observing:

> [T]he piece is a deliberately incoherent farrago of slogans and ramblings whose zany truculence and typographical hijinks combine Vorticist polemic with Picabian put-on. The title pun (Kangaroo/Red Congo) refers to the name of a Utopian "denationalist" city which

KONGO ROUX

Femme, moyen nécessaire pour la reproduction.
Disciple, moyen (pas nécessaire) pour la reproduction.
Reproduction, pas nécessaire.

Réformateur

Dit le cochon : « O que le monde soit porcin.

Souscrivez (naturellement) à l'emprunt Papal!   SOUVENIR
Pour la patrie, tant que vous voulez, Mais pour   Dernier auto-da-fé.
une Société anonyme de Pétrole, Mourir... Pourquoi ?   Espagne a. d. 1759
           Mourir.   Inquisition rétablie
           Portugal a.d. 1824
           Souscrivez à l'

Historique

A Vérone on voit, voit encore, un orifice de boîte,
c'est au Piazza dei Signori, un petit trou dans une
tablette de marbre, avec l'inscription : Cette boîte est
pour les dénonciations des usuriers et des contrats
injustes d'usure. 1320-1921, on appelle ça le PROGRÈS.

Crédit

Croyance que l'autre va payer.
Crédit solide, croyance raisonnable que l'autre va payer.
Ça... dépend de la conduite de tous ;
Tous doivent avoir suffrage en tout ce qui concerne
l'allocation des crédits... Ah ben oui.
C'est à vous, un tel, à 5 o/o
C'est à vous, Fulano, à 30 o/o. Fiche-moi la paix.
Paixtrole.
On veut les marchés de la lune. (O Jules unanime et Laforgue.)
Tout de même c'est l'Allemagne qui doit commencer,
      vu
vu que la France est fichue le jour où elle retire ses troupes des bords du Rhin.
      (ben oui iou oui mong vieux, j'arrive de loing, pas d'illusion.)
vu que la France sera foutue, et que le Rhin était internationalisé par le traité d'il y a cent ans. C'est l'Allemagne qui doit commencer
en nous donnant un tout petit coin, un tout petit Heidelberg, ou un tout petit Schaffausen pour ville DÉNATIONALISTE, ville
dénationaliste sans troupes, sans armée, sans aucune importance militaire, sans aucun gouvernement sauf pour balayer les rues,
et pompe: le gaz et l'électricité (pouvoir de la houille blanche, le Rhin coule toujours).

On appellera
ça KONGO,
ou Venusberg
ou la nouvelle
Athènes selon

Les révolutions ont été beaucoup moins coûteuses qu'on ne le suppose. Lisez Goncourt (qui n'aimait pas Mme Récamier) il dénonce le
mauvais goût du Directoire (ayant supporté plusieurs sortes de mauvais goût dans son temps) — et quand il veut dénigrer les sans-
culottes il trouve : LA NOTE, addition : plusieurs églises, plusieurs villas (très chics) et le mobilier — non détruit en masse, mais
plutôt vendu aux enchères, mis en vente sur les quais.
JE NE VEUX PAS, non, je ne veux pas de révolution, *seulement* vu que nous sommes gouvernés par la finance, vu que la cause
des guerres est connue - aussi bien et clairement que la cause de la syphilis », c'est-à-dire la compétition pour vendre des « surplus »
dans un marché qui rétrécit...
     e voudrais, oui, je préférerais que les financiers gouvernassent directement qu'ils fussent responsables vis-à-vis des peuples ;
au lieu de gouverner par une quantité de sales types, choisis par eux (les financiers) responsables vis-à-vis des financiers et « élus »
par le peuple.
Christianisme : malgré qu'il ne soit plus la croyance de l'homme pensant européen, il n'y a pas une seule coutume, loi, convention ni
de l'Europe, ni de l'Amérique qui ne soit pourrie à cause de cette base — totem de tribu SHEENY, Yid, taboo, pourriture
— Moïse habile politique — pourriture monothéos.
MONOtheism, l'idée la plus crûment et immaturément idéologue, intellectuelle, maladivement cérébraliste, idée la moins fondée, la
moins prouvée qui ait jamais été avalée par 3/8 de la race humaine.

« Jésus-Christ était nègre. » (Voir les écrits
         de Marcus Garvey.
         un noir.)

         Ainsi San Zeno.
         Bravo Marcus !

SOMMAIRE

Femelle, chaos.
Mâle, point fixe de stupidité.
Femme, boulotte roulante sur quatre totems.... taboo et beretta.
Homme, particule imbécile magnétisée par l'inconnu.

$$\frac{\text{Le contrôle des crédits internationaux}}{\text{masque à gaz muselière}} = \frac{X}{\text{jeune homme}}$$

Etats-Unis d'Amérique, Diabetics'Union for the suppression of sugar.
    (Union des diabétiques pour la suppression du sucre)

Ezra POUND.

(left margin) E. P.   Ce sont les singes qui font les lieux-communs.

(right margin) il y a deux infinis : Dieu et la bêtise. Edgard VARÈSE.

Fig. 2. *Kongo Roux* by Ezra Pound (reproduced from Andrew Clearfield, "Pound, Paris, and Dada," *Paideuma* 7, no. 1 & 2 [spring and fall 1978])

Pound suggests should be founded on the demilitarized banks of the Rhine—a city "sans armée, sans aucune importance militaire, sans aucune gouvernement sauf pour balayer les rues."[22]

A note in Pound's margin, Sieburth points out, relates *Kongo Roux* to "la nouvelle Athènes" and thus indirectly to Pound's ideal city, Dioce. Such idealization, we might note, is hardly Dadaesque; neither, as Sieburth himself notes, is the poem's explicitly political tone and *Blast*-like diatribe against the conspiracy of financiers and usurers. But more important: here, quite atypically for Picabia or Tristan Tzara or Hugo Ball, is a panoply of historical references—for example, "Souvenir / Dernier auto-da-fé, / Espagne a.d. 1759," "Inquisition retablie Portugal a.d. 1824," and "Piazza dei Signori"; or again, the iniquities of "des contrats / Injuste d'usure 1320–1921," "Jules unanime et Laforgue," to "Goncourt (qui n'aimait pas Mme Récamier)," and even the note "'Jesus-Christ était nègre' (Voir les écrits / de Marcus Garvey, / un noir" (Clearfield, "Pound, Paris, and Dada" 135).

From Marinetti to Tzara's M. Antipyrine, avant-gardists scorned such musty dates and references to historical persons and places as hopelessly retro. But Duchamp, who remained aloof from Paris Dada as from all the contemporary movements that tried to absorb him (his readymades, for that matter, well preceded Dada),[23] would have understood, although his own names like the *Tzanck Check*, drawn on "The Teeth's Loan & Trust Company Consolidated" and made out to Duchamp's dentist, Dr. Daniel Tzanck (see figure 3), are, of course, more fanciful, punning, and less directly referential than Pound's. But such punning names as "Jules unanime," which substitutes the movement Jules Romains founded for his last name and then lines him up, inappropriately, with the poet Jules Laforgue, could be understood as *infrathin* variations on such titles as *L. H. O. O. Q.* for the moustached Mona Lisa. "Ate" is not "eat," "tables" not "table."

The *Kongo Roux* technique, in any case, is perfected in *The Cantos*, especially in the Pisan sequence, in which Pound relies so heavily on memory to provide him with narrative and image. Here is a typical passage from Canto 78:

> Be welcome, O cricket my grillo, but you must not
>   sing after taps.
> Guard's cap quattrocento
>   o-hon dit que'ke fois au vi'age
> 5   qu'une casque ne sert pour rien
>   'hien de tout

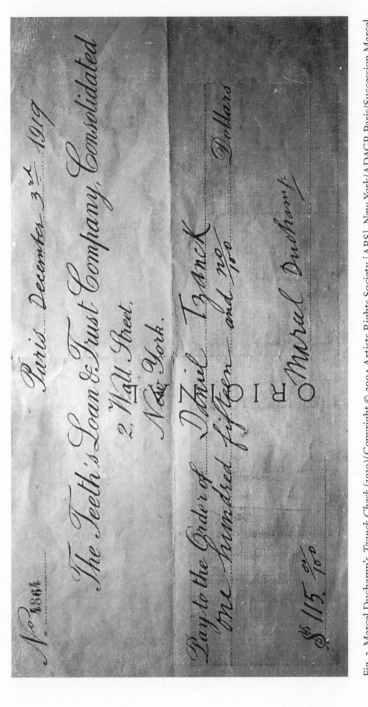

Fig. 3. Marcel Duchamp's *Tzanck Check* (1919)(Copyright © 2004 Artists Rights Society [ARS], New York/ADAGP, Paris/Succession Marcel Duchamp. Used by permission.)

> Cela ne sert que pour donner courage
> à ceux qui n'en ont pas de tout
> So Salzburg reopens
> 10   Qui suona Wolfgang grillo
> P° viola da gamba
> one might do worse than open a pub on Lake Garda
> so one thinks of
> Tailhade and "Willy" (Gauthier-Villars)
> 15   and of Mockel and La Wallonie . . . en casque
> de crystal rose les baladines
>
> with the cakeshops in the Nevsky
> and Sirdar, Armenonville or the Kashmiri house-boats
> en casque de crystal rose les baladines
> 20 messed up Monsieur Mozart's house
> but left the door of the new concert hall
> So he said, looking at the signed columns in San Zeno
> "how the hell can we get any architecture
> when we order our columns by the gross?"
> 25 red marble with a stone loop cast round it, four shafts,
> and Farinata, kneeling in the cortile,
> built like Ubaldo, that's race,
> Can Grande's grin like Tommy Cochran's
> "E fa di clarità l'aer tremare"
> 30   thus writ, and conserved (or was) in Verona
> So we sat there by the arena,
> outside, Thiy and il decaduto
> the lace cuff fallen over his knuckles
> considering Rochefoucauld
> 35 but the   program   (Café Dante) a literary program 1920 or
> thereabouts was neither published nor followed   [24]

Perhaps the first thing to observe is that although the *point de repère* for this passage, as is the case for the *Pisan Cantos* in general, is the poet's actual situation at war's end in the prison camp in the hills above Pisa—its location, situation, inmates, and guards—direct treatment of the thing never occurs. The first line, with its gently comic prosopoeia, chiding the cricket, as the guards have presumably chided the poet, not to "sing after taps," is complicated by the introduction of the Italian word for cricket, *grillo*. The words have the same referent, but their meaning is not simply identical, because the sounds of *grillo* have different connotations. The use of the foreign tag is, as usual in Pound, both an authenticating and a distancing device. *Grillo:* the Italian sets the Pisan stage even as it undercuts the mimesis of the address to the cricket, reminding us that what we have before us is not the real thing but, after all, a form of *writing*. The next line, "Guard's cap quattrocento" works the same way. Pound could have written "Guard's cap was a plain round one, the kind that Italians have been wearing for centuries, as you can see in their early Renaissance painting." The Italian tag *quattrocento* is not only a form of shorthand, making the point in highly condensed form; it functions here as a kind of cheering-up device. How bad, after all, can prison be if its guards look so quattrocento?

The words "Guard's cap quattrocento" are now punctuated by a little stanza, rendered in a simulation of colloquial French (*"o-hon dit que'ke fois au vi'age,"* which means "On dit quelquefois au village"), about the uselessness of helmets, designed, as they evidently were, less for actual than for psychological protection.[25] Again, the quotation is a way of undermining lyric norms whereby at this juncture in the poem the poet might express his fears for the future, his need for courage to bear his situation. As it stands, we cannot be certain whether the little adage refers to the poet himself or, on the contrary, is designed as an ironic contrast to his own will to go on, given that he has no helmet, not even a "casque de crystal rose," as in Stuart Merrill's poem (cited in line 16), to protect him.

Found text in a foreign language thus plays the same role as the proper names that follow: its hyperspecificity leaves its meaning open. In the passage that follows, every proper name seems to be autobiographical, and yet there are curious conundrums. Why, for example, "So Salzburg reopens / Qui suona Wolfgang grillo / P° viola da gamba" (line 9)? Salzburg is hardly one of Pound's sacred places—it is not even in his beloved Tyrol—and yet he remarks on the reopening after the war of the Salzburg Festival, perhaps because Mozart's chamber music and the "viola da gamba" played "piano" (softly) allow him to invoke the presence of Olga Rudge without so much as mentioning her name. To be aware of the reopening of the Salzburg Festival, moreover, may well give the poet the sense of being up on things, part of the world, as does his conversational remark that "one might do worse than open a pub on Lake Garda," as if anyone in his immediate circle were contemplating such a thing. As for the French *Symboliste* poets whose names follow—"[Laurent] Tailhade," "[Henri] Gauthier-Villars," the Belgian "[Albert Henri] Mockel," and the French American Stuart Merrill, whose line "en casque de crystal rose les baladines" is quoted twice in the passage—these poets, like Salzburg, are hardly in Pound's poetic pantheon,

Symbolisme being regularly associated, in his essays and manifestos, with romantic "slush."

Why then invoke these particular names? Before we can answer this question, we must deal with the even trickier case of the lines:

> with the cakeshops in the Nevsky,
> And Sirdar, Armenonville or the Kashmiri house-boats

The "cakeshops in the Nevsky"—that is, along the main boulevard of Petersburg, with its architectural splendors—have already appeared in earlier Pisan Cantos. The first citation of the Nevsky Prospect itself is in Canto 16, written some twenty years prior to Pound's incarceration at Pisa. Canto 16 is the third of the Hell Cantos; it juxtaposes World War I scenes with a dialogue in imitation Russian and German accents based on the account of the Russian Revolution in Lincoln Steffens's *Autobiography,* arranged by Pound in paratactic sentence units:

> And then a lieutenant of infantry
> Ordered 'em to fire into the crowd,
>   in the square at the end of the Nevsky
> In front of the Moscow station,
> And they wouldn't . . .
>   (16/75)

The next appearance of the Nevsky, this time the site not of Revolution but of cake shops, is in Canto 19 and occurs in the pre–World War I conversation of the Austro-Hungarian ambassador to London, who is reminiscing about the Good Old Days:

> That was in the old days, all sitting around in arm-chairs,
> And that's gone, like the cake shops in the Nevsky
>   (19/86)

The reference reappears, some twenty years later, in the first Pisan Canto:

> Sirdar, Bouiller and Les Lilas
>   or Dieudonné London, or Voisin's
> Uncle George stood like a statesman "REI ΠΑΝΤΑ
> fills up every hollow

> the cake shops in the Nevsky, and Schöners
> not to mention der Greif at Bolsano   la patronne getting older
> (74/453)

Both *Sirdar* on the Champs Elysées and *Voisin's* on the Rue St. Honoré, were, according to the *Companion to the Cantos* (II, 372), fashionable Paris restaurants. *Bouiller* refers to the dance hall (*Le Bal Bouillier*) on the Boulevard Saint-Michel, which we might recognize from its appearance in a number of Impressionist paintings. And *Les Lilas* is the Closerie des Lilas, a large brasserie at the intersection of the Boulevards Montparnasse and Saint-Michel, which makes frequent appearances in Hemingway and Fitzgerald. As for *Dieudonné*, the *Companion* tells us (II, 372) that it was a London restaurant at 11 Ryder Street, St. James, where the first number of *Blast* was celebrated on 15 July 1914 and where later Amy Lowell gave an Imagiste dinner that Richard Aldington called her Boston Tea Party for Ezra. The next line juxtaposes these restaurants with "Uncle George"—a reference to the isolationist congressman from Massachusetts, George Holden Tinkham, whom Pound had met in Venice. The allusions in line 181 to Mencius's Confucian commentary ("[water] fills up every hole, and then advances, flowing up to the four seas") and to Heracleitus (REI PANTA, "all things flow") suggest that unlike those senators who caved in, Tinkham, like the water "advancing," behaved like a true statesman (*Companion* II, 373). And now come more fine restaurants: *Schöners* in Vienna (where Pound may have encountered George Antheil) and *Der Greif* at Bolzano in the Tyrol.

But why the "cakeshops in the Nevsky," which reappear in Canto 78, again together with *Sirdar* and, this time, with *Armenonville*, the elegant pavilion restaurant in the Bois de Boulogne, with which it has already been coupled in 74 (456)? And what about those "Kashmiri house-boats"—an echo, like the cakeshops, of Canto 19, although Kashmir is not juxtaposed to the Nevsky but appears at the end of the Canto, where an elderly Englishman, reminiscing about his "ten years in the Indian army," recalls with pleasure those "healthy but verminous" girls to be had "at a bargain / For ten bobs' worth of turquoise" in Kashmir "in the houseboats" (19/87–88).

Canto 76 opens famously with the lines:

> And the sun high over horizon hidden in cloud bank
> lit saffron the cloud ridge
>   dove sta memoria (472)

the Italian words repeated some five pages later in another famous passage:

> nothing matters but the quality
> of the affection—
> in the end—that has carved the trace in the mind
> dove sta memoria (477)

These lines, unusually straightforward for *The Cantos,* suggest that through-out the sequence Pound is recalling his past, both of childhood and youth as well as the more recent and immediate past. But the clinamen represented by the Nevsky passages I have been citing is that the names invoked do not recall the poet's own past but, by a curious sleight of hand, a past he himself never had. For Pound never saw those cake shops in the Nevsky; he never visited Russia and indeed never expressed any real interest in things Russian, neither in Russian literature from Pushkin and Tolstoy to Chekhov and Mayakovsky, nor in Russian history or religion or art. The cake shops in the Nevsky are here, as are the houseboats of Kashmir, as ciphers of someone else's Good Old Days. The Austrian ambassador to London of Canto 16, the English ex-army officer of 19: these were hardly members of Pound's London social circle. And further, it is doubtful that the impecunious poet, living as he was in very modest lodgings during his Paris years, frequented *Sirdar* or *Dieudonné* or the elegant *Armenonville* pavilion in the *Bois.* Perhaps a rich friend like Nancy Cunard brought him to one of these places on rare occa-sions, but these restaurants were no more Pound's habitat than was *Schöners* in Vienna or Bolzano's elegant *Der Greif.*

How, then, does Pound relate these names to his sacred places: the Church of San Zeno in Verona (a frequent *point de repère* in *The Cantos* and here visited with William Carlos Williams's brother Edgar), to the sacred poetic characters like Dante's Farinata and Can Grande, or to the revered poetry ("*E fa di clarità l'aer tremare*") of Guido Cavalcanti?[26] In the lines in question (26–28), it makes sense to link Farinata to "Ubaldo," that is, Pound's good friend Ubaldo degli Uberti, an admiral in the Italian navy, who was ostensi-bly a descendant of Farinata's (see *Companion* II, 419); but the reference to "Tommy Cochran," the name of a Wyncote boy, with whom the young Ezra attended the Cheltenham Military Academy, is largely deflationary: no hero-ics for young Tommy, and not even the smile of the statue, at least not in the school pictures that depict the young cadets, of whom Ezra was one.[27] In-deed, it is only after this playful conjunction that we come to a more serious and coherent autobiographical passage—the memory of conversations with his dear old friend Bride Scratton ("Thiy") and T. S. Eliot ("il decaduto"), first in the Roman Arena in Verona and then nearby at the Café Dante in 1920, where the two poets were evidently drawing up "a literary program" that "was neither [to be] published nor followed."

Throughout the passage, the names invoked point to a more innocent time, a prewar era when the poet's life was still in the future, when Italy stood for the pleasures of tourism: great Romanesque and Renaissance art to be contemplated with one's closest friends strolling through the ruins and chatting about Dante or Cavalcanti or the French *Symboliste* poets in the local cafés and restaurants. "War," Pound was to remark many years later in Canto 110, where *Dieudonné* and *Voisin* are again cited, "is the destruction of restaurants" (800). That golden past would seem still to be alive—after all, Salzburg is reopening, Mozart being played, and the cricket song at Pisa can trigger positive and happy thoughts. But—and this is the curious modernity of *The Cantos*—the names invoked fail to cohere into a larger image-complex. The cake shops in the Nevsky, the legendary sexploits of Indian army officers in Kashmir—these are embedded into the texture of *The Cantos* precisely so as to "thicken the plot," to use John Cage's Zen term. Their "irrelevant" introjection in what is already an excess of proper names is analogous to the Duchampian demand for "prime words," for the *infrathin*.

And here Pound and Duchamp's reaction to Impressionism is important. Both came of age at the height of Impressionist pictorialism: the line from Monet to Cézanne to the Cubists and Abstractionists was a perfectly logical one, so Duchamp maintained, since in all these cases painting remained *retinal*, its colors, even in the case of abstraction, endowed with expressive value.[28] Wanting an art that might be cerebral rather than sensuous, conceptual rather than imagistic, Duchamp was assembling his readymades, boxes, and especially the *Large Glass* (*The Bride Stripped Bare by Her Bachelors, Even*), whose individual parts are identified less by their visual appearance, which is less than striking, than by their wholly distinct names: *Nine Malic Molds, Milky Way, Oculist Witnesses, Capillary Tubes*, and so on.

Pound's proper names are of course much more literal, more referential than Duchamp's punning titles,[29] but like Duchamp's, theirs is a reaction to Impressionism as a "soft" form of mimetic art. In his essay on Joyce, for example, Pound differentiates between the "clear hard prose" of Flaubert and Joyce and an impressionism that smacks of "mushy technique" (*Gaudier-Brzeska* 85):

These "impressionists" who write in imitation of Monet's softness instead of writing in imitation of Flaubert's definiteness, are a bore, a grimy, or perhaps I should say, a rosy, floribund bore. (*Literary Essays* 400)

And again, this time in his essay on the musician Arnold Dolmetsch:

What I call emotional, or impressionist music, starts with being emotion or impression and then becomes only approximately music. It is, that is to say, something in terms of something else. (*Literary Essays* 434)

Something in terms of something else: Impressionism, Pound suggests, is a mode still wedded to metaphor; the artists and poets in question failed to realize that the natural object is always the adequate symbol, that, for example, "a hawk is a hawk" (*Literary Essays* 9). Just as Duchamp wanted to escape from the discourse of painting, where *color* always "stood for" something else, so Pound came to rely on the juxtaposition of proper names—names that were almost but never quite the same. "The infra-thin separation," writes Thierry de Duve apropos of Duchamp, "is working at its maximum when it distinguishes the same from the same, when it is an indifferent difference, or a differential identity" (*Pictorial Nominalism* 160). And he cites Duchamp's note: "The difference (dimensional) between 2 mass-produced objects [from the same mold] is an infra thin when the maximum (?) precision is obtained" (Matisse, *Notes* #18).

This "maximum precision" is what Pound has in mind in *The Cantos* when he specifies those Paris restaurants, Verona churches, and characters from Dante's *Purgatorio,* placing these names and those of old friends in juxtaposition with the "cakeshops on the Nevsky." Indeed, it is the "infra-thin difference between . . . objects from the same mold" that gives Pound's properties their curious authenticity, their sense of *being there.* Like the citizens of the *Large Glass,* they take on a life of their own—"prime words divisible only by themselves."

Such nominalism, we should note, creates its own distortions. Pound may well have believed that his naming was in accord with the *chêng ming,* the "rectification of names" advocated by Confucius, but the fact is that he nominalizes concepts and categories when it suits his design. Take the lines from Canto 74, which serves as my epigraph:

but Wanjina is, shall we say, Ouan Jin
or the man with an education

Wanjina, we know, *is* a proper name, but Ouan Jin (*wen ren* in contemporary Chinese) is, as Yunte Huang has pointed out to me, nobody's name, only a category. The two-character phrase means "literatus" (or "literata," depending on the context). So Pound's lines actually say, "but Wanjina is, shall we say, a literatus / or the man with an education." But in calling Wanjina "Ouan Jin" and then adding "*the* man with an education" (where we would expect "*a* man"), Pound, as Huang observes, "makes Ouan Jin sound like someone's name, a character in Chinese history, a counterpart of Australia's Wanjina. . . . What is originally a category is now made a proper name. The verbal trick is actually quite astounding."[29]

Perhaps this is why Pound, again like Duchamp, whose readymades have remained sui generis, has proved to be so difficult to imitate. Pound's heirs from Louis Zukofsky to Black Mountain and beyond have not quite been able to reproduce his modes of naming. I have sometimes tried, as a classroom experiment, to allow students to substitute for the requisite term paper a sample Canto. It is invariably the popular choice because it seems so easy. Take *X* number of Greek and Latin names and phrases, then interlard the "right" Chinese ideograms, references to Italian Renaissance history and art, Provençal poetry, Jefferson and Adams in correspondence, contemporary references, jokes, dialogue in different accents, and anti-Semitic slurs, and presto—a Canto!

But what such exercises cannot reproduce, so subtle is Pound's nominalist technique, is the infrathin distinction that separates the singing *grillo* of the Pisa prison camp from all other insects, beginning with its English counterpart, the cricket. Such discrimination underscores the intense mobility of the poetic construct and calls for intense reader participation: in Canto 80, for example, still more restaurants are introduced—the WIENER CAFÉ (*Cantos* 526), "which died into banking" (i.e., a bank was built on its site), Florian's on the Piazza San Marco in Venice, Claridge's in London, the "bar of the Follies / as Manet saw it" (the reference is to Manet's famous mirror portrait of a young woman called *Bar at the Follies Bergère*). Each of these adds yet another dimension or differential to Pound's memorial: the Wiener Café, for example, was not far from Dieudonné's, but their respective clientele (the former pro-German, the latter pro-French) is not to be confused. The Wiener Café belongs with Wörgl (the Austrian village that tried the stamp-scripp experiment), whereas Dieudonné, although in London, brings to mind Pound's Paris years.

"But isn't the same at least the same?" asks Wittgenstein in the *Investigations*. On the same page as the "WIENER CAFÉ," we find the line "(o-hon dit queque fois au vi'age)" that we met in Canto 78 (500) as a reference to the war and the fear of violence. But here the song line functions parenthetically and ironically in a very different context, the reference being to the succession of Salon painters from Puvis de Chavannes to Eugene Carrière in a time "before the world was given over to wars" (78/526), when "near the museum" [the British Museum] "they served it mit Schlag" (526). The WIENER CAFÉ is not to be confused with any other.

The seeming excess of Poundian names—the multiplication of restaurants, cafés, and those who people them—is thus offset by the recycling of a given unit in a context that changes its thrust in what is in fact a dense economy of meanings. The acute awareness of difference is accompanied by the concomitant play of likeness—a linking of items that seem quite unrelated. In this sense, nominalism Pound-style can be understood as an instance of what Gertrude Stein called *using everything*. But then what are *The Cantos* but—to take another Stein adage—a mode of *beginning again and again*? Of citing more and more names that spill out of the Duchampian *boîte en valise* for the reader to organize, not because Pound couldn't "make it cohere," as he was wont to declare in moments of depression, but because in the poet's scheme of things, as in the case of Duchamp's readymades, art had become the process of discriminating the *infrathin*. Is the natural object always the adequate symbol? Yes, and so is the unnatural object, provided of course, that it is given its "right" name—a name that belongs to it alone.

In the spring of 2001 I was invited to the Centre international de poésie in Marseille for a conference on Wittgenstein vis-à-vis contemporary poets. In pondering the relationship, the question of poetry and translatability loomed large. The paper was well received by the attending French poets, but when I gave it again at a Wittgenstein conference at the University of London a few weeks later, this time to a group of philosophers, there was much controversy. It has since been recast a few more times for its publication in the Routledge collection Literature after Wittgenstein.

4
"But isn't *the same* at least the same?"
Wittgenstein on Translation

> Poetry is a sort of inspired mathematics.
> Ezra Pound, *The Spirit of Romance*

We usually think of the "poetic" as that which cannot fully translate, that which is uniquely embedded in its particular language. The poetry of Rainer Marie Rilke is a case in point. The opening line of the *Duino Elegies—Wer, wenn ich schriee, hörte mich denn aus den Engel Ordnungen?*—has been translated into English literally dozens of times, but as William Gass points out in his recent *Reading Rilke: Reflections on the Problems of Translation,* none of the translations seem satisfactory. Here are a few examples:

J. B. Leishman (1930)	Who, if I cried, would hear me among the angelic orders?
A. J. Poulin (1977)	And if I cried, who'd listen to me in those angelic orders?
Stephen Cohn (1989)	Who, if I cried out, would hear me—among the ranked angels?

Gass is very critical of these translations, but to my ear his own is no better: "Who if I cried, would hear me among the Dominions of Angels?"[1] The difficulty, as I have suggested elsewhere,[2] is that English syntax does not allow for the dramatic suspension of *Wer, wenn ich schriee . . .* and that the noun phrase *Engel Ordnungen,* which in German puts the stress, both phonically and semantically, on the angels themselves rather than on their orders or hierarchies or dominions, defies effective translation. Moreover, Rilke's line contains the crucial and heavily stressed word *denn* (literally "then"), which here has the force of "Well, then," or in contemporary idiom "So," as in "So, who would hear me if I cried out . . . ?" But "So" sounds too casual in the context of Rilke's urgent meditation, and translators have accordingly tended to elide the word *denn* completely, thus losing the immediacy of the question. Further, *denn* rhymes with *wenn* as well as with the first two syllables of *den En-gel,* the rhyme offsetting the intentionally contorted sound of the verb sequence *schriee, hörte* so as to create a dense sonic network that is inevitably lost in translation.

The same holds true when the German-into-English process is reversed. Consider the famous fifth stanza of Robert Lowell's *Skunk Hour:*

One dark night,
my Tudor Ford climbed the hill's skull;
I watched for love-cars. Lights turned down,
they lay together, hull to hull,
where the graveyard shelves on the town . . .
My mind's not right.

Manuel Pfister translates this as follows:

In einer dunklen Nacht
erklomm mein Tudor-Ford des Hügels Schädel;
ich hielt Ausschau nach Liebesautos. Scheinwerfer ausgeschaltet,
lagen sie beieinander, Rumpf bei Rumpf,
wo der Friedhof such zur Stadt neigt . . .
Mein Geist ist wirr.[3]

This strikes me as a perfectly intelligent translation, without any of the obvious glitches we find in, say, William Gass's rendering of Rilke's *Ich verginge von seinem stärkeren Dasein* as "I would fade in the grip of that completer existence," or Stephen Cohn's, "I would die of the force of his being" (*Read-*

ing Rilke 62–63). But what eludes Pfister is Lowell's particular tone. "One dark night," for starters, has a fairy-tale quality (as in "Once upon a time") that gives an ironic edge to the reference to Saint John of the Cross's "Dark Night of the Soul"—a quality lost in the German *In einer dunklen Nacht*. In line 2, the pun on "Tudor ('two-door') Ford" disappears even though Pfister retains the absurdly pretentious brand name. And his rendition of the third line is at once too specific and too long-winded: Lowell's casual "I watched" becomes the emphatic *Ich hielt Ausschau*, and *Scheinwerfer ausgeschaltet* ("headlights turned off") does not allow for the resonance of "lights" or of "turned down," which here connotes beds as well as the lights themselves. In the next line, the image of "love-cars" lying together *Rumpf bei Rumpf* is that of the trunks of two bodies or torsos locked together. But the punning "Hull to hull," is more sinister, referring as it does to empty vessels as well as to empty plant husks. Lovemaking, in this context, is itself a form of death. And the death motif is underscored in the next line, where the verb "shelves" suggests that the graveyard is emptying its contents (the dead) on the town itself. The force of "shelves" is dissipated in the German *neigt*, which means "inclines" or "bends." Finally, "My mind's not right" is not just the poet's *cri de coeur* but also an allusion to Satan's jealous response when he spies Adam and Eve in *Paradise Lost*. Thus, although Pfister's translation—*Mein Geist ist wirr*—is accurate enough, the ironic self-deprecation of the poet-voyeur is absent. Then, too, Lowell's semantically charged rhyming lines—"One dark night" / my mind's not right," or again, the rhyme "hill's skull" / "hull to hull"— have no counterpart in Pfister's unrhymed version.

Translation, it seems, inevitably involves such slippage of meaning, especially in the case of poetry. Why is it, then, that the modernist philosopher perhaps most sensitive to such slippage, the philosopher who insisted that "*The limits of my language* mean the limits of my world," that indeed "Language is not *contiguous* to anything else,"[4] is read around the world in dozens of different languages, without much concern as to the translatability of his propositions? I am speaking, of course, of Wittgenstein, whose writings on how words mean are not only judged to be reasonably translatable but were originally known—indeed largely continue to be known—not in the author's own German but in the English of his Cambridge translators, G. H. von Wright, G. E. M. Anscombe, Alice Ambrose, Rush Rhees, years before his native Austria took him quite seriously. Then, too, most of these "writings" were not "writings" at all but transcriptions of Wittgenstein's Cambridge lectures as recorded by his students, lectures—or, rather, "remarks"— delivered in Wittgenstein's somewhat awkward, nonidiomatic English. Yet volumes of analysis have been based on such sentences as "A picture held us

captive," where "picture" is not the only (or even necessarily the most adequate) translation of the German word *Bild*. Do the "limits of language,"
as Wittgenstein construed them, then have nothing to do with the actual
language being used?

The answer is perhaps so obvious that we don't usually take it into account. In formulating his aphoristic propositions, Wittgenstein is not interested in the subtleties of figurative language but, on the contrary, in the
difficulty of determining the *denotative* meanings of ordinary words and
phrases placed in particular syntactic constructions. Hence, although, as in
the case of any discourse, there are more and less adequate translations—
translations that render as fully as possible the author's *intended* meaning—
Wittgenstein's propositions are by no means *untranslatable* in the sense that
Rilke's *Duino Elegies* or Lowell's "Skunk Hour" are untranslatable.

Consider the following from the facing pages (German-English) of *Philosophical Investigations,* translated by G. E. M. Anscombe in 1958:

*Warum kann ein Hund nicht Schmerzen heucheln? Ist er zu ehrlich?
Könnte man einen Hund Schmerzen heucheln lehren? (§250)*

Why can't a dog simulate pain? Is he too honest? Could one teach a dog
to simulate pain? (§250)

Or again:

*Warum kann meine rechte Hand nicht meiner linken Geld schenken?—
Meine rechte Hand kann es in meine linke geben. Meine rechte Hand kann
eine Schenkungsurkunde schreiben und meine linke eine Quittung.—
Aber die weitern praktischen Folgen wären nicht die einer Schenkung
(§268)*

Why can't my right hand give my left hand money?—My right hand
can put it into my left hand. My right hand can write a deed of gift
and my left hand a receipt.—But the further practical consequences
would not be those of a gift. (§268)[5]

And for good measure, here is §268 in French, as translated by Jacques Bouveresse:

*Pourquoi ma main droite ne peut-elle pas faire don d'une somme d'argent
à ma main gauche?—Ma main droite peut rédiger un acte de donation et*

*ma main gauche un reçu.—Mais les conséquences partiques ultérieures
ne seraient pas celles d'une donation.*[6]

In such cases, the issue is neither the connotative power of synonymous
words (the difference between "orders of angels," "hierarchies of angels," or
"angel dominions"), nor syntactic suspension, as in Rilke's opening construction *Wer, wenn ich schriee . . . ,*" nor punning, as in Lowell's "they lay
together hull to hull." Rather, Wittgenstein is demonstrating the difficulties of pinning down the meanings of even the most ordinary, everyday
words, such as *believe, hope, give, pain, right,* and *left.* If, as the central Wittgensteinian aphorism would have it, *Die Bedeutung eines Wortes ist sein
Gebrauch in der Sprache* ("The meaning of a word is its use in the language,"
Philosophical Investigations §43), then these words have no fixed denotative
meaning but depend largely on the context in which they appear. If my right
hand puts money into your left hand, I am *giving* you something. But if
the left hand is my own, the act of putting money into it may be no more
than a nervous habit, rather like playing with rubber bands. For both hands
are mine, and so the verb "to give" (*schenken, faire don*) does not seem applicable. Again, the word "pain" (*Schmerzen*) is one we all use regularly, but
its simulation—perfectly understandable to a young child, who may well
simulate pain so as to get attention or avoid having to do something—cannot
be performed by a dog. And this is the case whether the language in question
is German, English, French, or Chinese.

The logical implication of the distinction I have been drawing is that *poetry* is that which deals with the connotative and tropical power of words
and the rhythmic and sonic quality of phrases and sentences, whereas *philosophy* (literally "the love of wisdom") involves the conceptual and abstract
language of making meaningful propositions. What, then—and this is my
subject here—can Wittgenstein possibly have meant by the following entry
(1933–1934) in *Culture and Value*?

> *Ich glaube meine Stellung zur Philosophie dadurch zusammengefaßt zu
> haben, indem ich sagte: Philosophie dürfte man eigentlich nur dichten.
> Daraus muß sich, scheint mir, ergeben, wie weit mein Denken der Ge-
> genwart, Zukunft, oder der Vergangenheit angehört. Denn ich habe mich
> damit auch als einen bekannt, der nicht ganz kann, was er zu können
> wünscht.*

I think I summed up my position on philosophy when I said: One
should really only do philosophy as *poetry.* From this it seems to me it

must be clear to what extent my thought belongs to the present, to the future, or to the past. For with this I have also revealed myself to be someone who cannot quite do what he wishes he could do.[7]

What does this enigmatic statement mean? If we note that the cognate noun *Dichtung* also refers to *fictionality,* as in Goethe's title *Dichtung und Wahrheit,* where *Dichtung* ("Fiction") is opposed to "Truth," why should philosophy, traditionally the search for truth, be presented as poetic fiction? Given Wittgenstein's concern for "meaningful" statement, aren't the two discourses antithetical? And why should as rigorous a thinker as Wittgenstein declare that he himself is not quite up to the task of formulating this new role for philosophy?

Wittgenstein's overt commentary on poetry sheds little light on this question. His impatience with aesthetic theory is legendary: in the *Lectures on Aesthetics,* for example, he declares, "One might think Aesthetics is a science that tells us what's beautiful—it's almost too ridiculous for words. I suppose this science would also be able to tell us what sort of coffee tastes good."[8] And the notebook entries collected in *Culture and Value* are given to statements like the following:

> If I say A has beautiful eyes someone may ask me: what do you find beautiful about his eyes, and perhaps I shall reply: the almond shape, long eye-lashes, delicate lids. What do these eyes have in common with a Gothic church that I find beautiful too? Should I say they make a similar impression on me?" (24)

"The concept of 'the beautiful,'" says Wittgenstein, "has caused a lot of mischief" (55). And again, "Am I to make the inane statement, 'It [the musical theme] just sounds more beautiful when it is repeated'? (There you can see by the way what a silly role the word 'beautiful' plays in aesthetics.) And yet there *is* just no paradigm other than the theme itself" (52).

At the same time, the Wittgenstein who refused to theorize about art was quite ready, in his letters, journals, and conversations, to pronounce on a given work with great conviction. The words *großartig* and *herrlich* appear again and again with reference to a Mozart symphony, a Mörike poem, to Lessing's *Nathan the Wise,* or Dostoyevsky's *Brothers Karamazov.* Schubert's Quintet in C Sharp, op. 163, is *von phantastischer Großartigkeit* ("exhibits fantastic brilliance"), Mozart and Beethoven are called *die wahren Göttersöhne* ("the true sons of God"), the second movement of Beethoven's *Eroica* is *unglaublich* ("unbelievable," "fabulous"), Brahms's "Handel-variationen," *un-*

heimlich ("uncanny," "sublime").[9] Negative judgments are just as emphatic: Alfred Ehrenstein's poetry is *ein Hundedreck* ("dog shit"), Mahler's music is *nichts wert* ("worthless"), "the characters in the second part of 'Faust' *erregen unsere Teilnahme gar nicht*" ("are ones with whom we can't identify at all").[10] The recitation of a fellow officer at Monte Cassino was so unbearable in its "false pathos" that it was like "receiving an electric shock."[11] And so on.

The almost comic vehemence of these extreme aesthetic judgments is a function of what we might call *le côté Viennoise* of Wittgenstein—the social code of his time whereby those who are *gebildet* (cultured, well educated) took it to be incumbent upon them to pronounce on the given artwork or performance or concert as *großartig* or *schrecklich*, and so on. In this respect, as in his actual tastes for classical music and literature, Wittgenstein was very much of his time and place. To understand what he meant by the proposition that "One should only do philosophy as a form of *poetry*," we must, accordingly, look elsewhere—not at what Wittgenstein *said* about the poetic but at the example his own writing provides. In the preface to what was, with the exception of the *Tractatus*, his one consciously designed book, the *Philosophical Investigations* (1953), he notes:

> I have written down all these thoughts as *remarks* [*Bemerkungen*], short paragraphs, of which there is sometimes a fairly long chain about the same subject, while I sometimes make a sudden change, jumping from one topic to another . . . the essential thing was that the thoughts should proceed from one subject to another in a natural order and without breaks.
>
> After several unsuccessful attempts to weld my results together into such a whole, I realized that I should never succeed. The best that I could write would never be more *than philosophical remarks*. . . . And this was, of course, connected with the very nature of the investigation. For this compels us to travel over a wide field of thought, *criss-cross in every direction*. . . . Thus this book is really only an album. (v, my emphasis)

Such commentary cleared the way for the publication of the many fragments found after Wittgenstein's death, some in notebooks, some on separate scraps of paper or *Zettel*, as a further assortment of Wittgenstein's remarks—this one left in a single box file—is called. As G. H. von Wright, the editor of the *Vermischte Bemerkungen* ("Assorted Remarks," which came to be translated under the misleading title *Culture and Value*), explains:

In the manuscript material left by Wittgenstein there are numerous notes which do not belong directly with his philosophical works although they are scattered amongst the philosophical texts. Some of these notes are autobiographical, some are about the nature of philosophical activity, and some concern subjects of a general sort, such as questions about art or about religion. *It is not always possible to separate them sharply from the philosophical text. . . .*

Some of these notes are ephemeral; others on the other hand—the majority—are of great interest. *Sometimes they are strikingly beautiful and profound.* (*Culture and Value,* Foreword, my emphasis)

Here von Wright seems to be following Wittgenstein's own lead that "philosophy" shades into "poetry" and vice versa. But how and why? Some early entries in *Culture and Value* (see 2–7) may be apropos:

Each morning you have to break through the dead rubble afresh so as to reach the living warm seed.

A new word is like a fresh seed sewn on the ground of the discussion.

When we think of the world's future, we always mean the destination it will reach if it keeps going in the direction we can see it going in now; it does not occur to us that its path is not a straight line but a curve, constantly changing direction.

Each of the sentences I write is trying to say the whole thing, i.e. the same thing over and over again; it is as though they were all simply views of one object seen from different angles.

The thread that runs through these aphorisms and propositions is on the need for what Gertrude Stein had already called, in her "Composition as Explanation" (1926), *beginning again and again.* Truth is not something that can be uncovered; it can only be *rediscovered,* day after day. The value of breaking through the dead rubble each morning and in viewing each object from as many angles as possible is that one keeps one's mind *open,* that conclusions are always tentative, and that the process of discovery is always more important than any particular end result.

Not a straight line but a curve, constantly changing direction. Theoretical formulation, generalization, moral injunction: these, for Wittgenstein, are dangerous. "Philosophy," we read in his *Lectures, Cambridge 1930–1931*, "is not a choice between different 'theories.' It is wrong to say that there is any one theory of truth, for truth is not a concept" (75). At the same time, the *process* of investigation is itself of value, provided one is able and willing to *revise* one's ideas and suppositions when necessary. "I find it important in philosophizing," says Wittgenstein, "to keep changing my posture, not to stand for too long on *one* leg, so as not to get stiff. Like someone on a long up-hill climb who walks backwards for a while so as to refresh himself and stretch some different muscles" (*Culture and Value* 27). And further:

> If I am thinking just for myself, not with a view to writing a book, I jump all around the subject; this is the only natural way of thinking for me. With my thoughts forced into line, to think further is torture to me. Should I even try it? (28)

This is, on the face of it, a very odd statement, for why should it be "torture" (*eine Qual*) simply to organize one's thoughts, to produce a coherent linear discourse? Isn't this precisely what we expect an "investigation," especially a philosophical investigation, to do?

Here we must come back to the 1933 statement about philosophy's link to poetry, in which Wittgenstein "reveals" himself as "someone who cannot quite do what he wishes he could do" (*Culture and Value* 25). If we read this mysterious paragraph biographically, it would seem that the student of Bertrand Russell, who had set out to become the mathematical logician that we find in the opening sections of the *Tractatus* (1922)—although even here the eccentricity of the numbering is a kind of poetic clinamen[12]—had discovered, by the early thirties, that his métier was a mode of writing that depended on constant revision, a casting off of the "egg-shells of the old, sticking to" his prior formulations (*Culture and Value* 43). Such writing inevitably takes the form of short, fragmentary, and often gnomic utterance. Not the "Tractatus" or linear discourse, not even the essay in the spirit of Montaigne or the Heideggerian meditation, but a sequence of "criss-cross" aphorisms, sometimes self-canceling or even self-contradictory. Indeed, it is discourse less designed to *say* than to be *seen as* showing something. And we think of the following aphorism in *Zettel*:

> *Das Sprechen der Musik. Vergiß nicht, daß ein Gedicht, wenn auch in der Sprache der Mitteilung abgefaßt, nicht im Sprachspiel der Mitteilung verwendet wird.* (§160)

The way music speaks. Do not forget that a poem, even though it is composed in the language of information, is not used in the language-game of giving information. (§160)[13]

But although this proposition allies poetry to philosophy in that neither is characterized by the information-giving function of the sciences or social sciences, our initial question remains: how can Wittgenstein's "philosophical remarks" be taken as *poetic* when they are so markedly stripped of the usual "poetic" trappings? And further, given that Wittgenstein's propositions seem to have the same force whether we read them in the original German, or in English, French, or Japanese, what is the relation of "poetic" to "philosophical" meaning?

One possible answer—and this case is often made—is that what makes Wittgenstein's writing "poetic" is his use of homilies and proverbs animated by metaphors of charming and almost childlike simplicity: for example, "Talent is a spring from which fresh water is constantly flowing" (*Culture and Value* 10), "Ideas too sometimes fall from the tree before they are ripe" (27), or the famous lines "What is your aim in philosophy?—To shew the fly the way out of the fly-bottle" in the *Investigations* (§309). But such figurative language may well have more to do with rhetorical strategy—the ethical argument that gives Wittgenstein credence as someone we can trust—than with the enigmatic nature of Wittgenstein's real questions, which, whatever homely metaphor is used for pedagogical purposes, ultimately revolve around the *literal* meaning of everyday words. "Why can't a dog simulate pain? Is he too honest?" (§250).

A better clue to Wittgenstein's concept of the poetic is provided by the distinction he repeatedly draws between *science* and *mathematics*. "Man," we read in a 1930 entry in *Culture and Value*, "perhaps populations in general—must awaken to wonder. Science is a way of putting him back to sleep" (5). And again:

People sometimes say they cannot make any judgment about this or that because they have not studied philosophy. This is irritating nonsense, because the assumption is that philosophy is some sort of science. And it is talked about almost as if it were the study of medicine.— But what one can say is that people who have never undertaken an investigation of a philosophical kind, as have, for example, most mathematicians, are not equipped with the right visual organs for this type of investigation or scrutiny. (29)

Indeed, there is a "strange resemblance between a philosophical investigation (especially in mathematics) and an aesthetic one" (25). And in 1946, when the first part of the *Philosophical Investigations* was finished, Wittgenstein noted in his journal, "My 'achievement' is very much like that of a mathematician who invents a calculus" (*Culture and Value* 50).

Invent is the key word here. Philosophy, as Wittgenstein sees it, is a form of continual reinvention with a view to making language more functional, the ideal being the precision of numbers. Language can never, of course, approximate that precision, which is why the process of removing its false "signposts," its mistaken assumptions and usages, is so endlessly fascinating. And as in mathematics, this is the case regardless of time and place, regardless therefore of the specific language in question:

> People say again and again that philosophy doesn't really progress, that we are still occupied with the same philosophical problems as were the Greeks. But the people who say this don't understand why it has to be so. It is because our language has remained the same and keeps seducing us into asking the same questions. As long as there continues to be a verb "to be" [*sein*] that looks as if it functions in the same way as "to eat" [*essen*] and "to drink [*trinken*], as long as we still have the adjectives "identical" [*identisch*], "true" [*wahr*], "false" [*falsch*], "possible" [*möglich*], as long as we continue to talk of a river of time [*einem Fluß der Zeit*], of an expanse of space [*einer Ausdehnung des Raumes*], etc., etc., people will keep stumbling over the same puzzling difficulties and find themselves staring at something which no explanation seems capable of clearing up. (*Culture and Value* 15)

I have put in some of the German terms here so as to show that indeed language, at the level Wittgenstein studies it, has "remained the same and keeps seducing us into asking the same questions." For Wittgenstein, the *poetic,* as I remarked earlier, is not a question of heightening, of removing language from its everyday use by means of appropriate troping or rhetorical device. Rather, what makes philosophy poetic is its potential for invention, its status as what we now call *conceptual art*—the art that, in Sol LeWitt's words, "is made to engage the mind of the viewer rather than his eye"—or, more broadly speaking, his senses—the art, as it were, that tracks the process of *thinking* itself.[14]

In Wittgenstein's practice, conceptual art begins with the investigation of grammar, the description of the actual relations between words and phrases in the larger unit in which they are embedded. The surface word order, of course, will vary from language to language, according to the rules that language prescribes for the relationship between parts of speech. But the basic relationship of parts of speech—nouns, verbs, adjectives, prepositions—*to one another* will remain the same. Thus, if we take the earlier example, "Why can't a dog simulate pain? Is he too honest?" the original German, *Warum kann ein Hund nicht Schmerzen heucheln? Ist er zu ehrlich?* has a slightly different word order in English, where the noun "pain" follows the transitive verb whose object it is, and the negative ("can't") comes first in the sentence. But the basic syntax of the question-and-answer structure is perfectly clear, whichever the language. In fact, given the notion that "There are no gaps in grammar;—grammar is always complete" (*Lectures 1*, 16), the meanings of ordinary, everyday words become all the more tantalizing and a challenge to the philosopher as poet.

Take the following entry from *Culture and Value:*

Die Philosophen, welche sagen: "nach dem Tod wird ein zeitloser Zustand eintreten," oder, "mit dem Tod tritt ein zeitloser Zustand ein," und nicht merken, daß sie im zeitlichen Sinne "nach" und "mit" und "tritt ein" gesagt haben, und, daß die Zeitlichkeit in ihrer Grammatik liegt. (22)

Philosophers who say: "after death a timeless state will begin," or "at death a timeless state begins," and do not notice that they have used the words "after" and "at" and "begins" in a temporal sense, and that temporality is embedded in their grammar. (22)

In its scrutiny of something as seemingly minor as a tense shift, a shift that in English, as in German, requires such words as "after" (*nach*) and "at" (*mit*), this little fragment—not even a complete sentence—embodies Wittgenstein's repeated insistence that "Language is not *contiguous* to anything else" (*Lectures 1*, 112). For it is only *inside* language that the basic paradox in question reveals itself—the paradox that the so-called timeless state (*zeitloser Zustand*) after death can be talked about only within the language of temporality that is ours, that is all that we have. Accordingly, as Wittgenstein had put it in the *Tractatus,* "Death is not an event in life. Death is not lived through." Indeed, "If by eternity is understood not endless temporal duration but timelessness, then he lives eternally who lives in the present" (§6.4311).

To take another, very different consideration of temporality, consider the following analysis of the meaning of the word *interval* in *Wittgenstein's Lectures, Cambridge 1932–1935*.

> If we look at a river in which numbered logs are floating, we can describe events on land with reference to these, e.g., "*When* the 105th log passed, I ate dinner." Suppose the log makes a bang on passing me. We can say these bangs are separated by equal, or unequal, intervals. We could also say one set of bangs was twice as fast as another set. But the equality or inequality of intervals so measured is entirely different from that measured by a clock. The phrase "length of interval" has its sense in virtue of the way we determine it, and differs according to the method of measurement.[15] (13)

Here, Wittgenstein's investigation examines the curious shift in the meaning of a single word—*interval*—depending on the context in which it occurs. The "interval" measurable by the passage downstream of logs does not have the same status as the "interval" measured by a clock. But the mystery of the word has nothing to do with the specific language in question: in French, for example, we read, "*Aussi les critères qui déterminent l'égalité des intervalles séparant le passage des rondins sont-ils différents de ceux qui déterminent l'égalité des intervalles mesurés par une horloge.*"[16] Whether *interval, intervalle,* or the German *Abstand,* the argument as to the possible meanings of "interval" remains intact.

"But isn't *the same* at least the same?" Wittgenstein's question in the *Philosophical Investigations* (§215) elicits the "useless proposition" that, yes, "A thing is identical with itself." Useless, because, as Wittgenstein has already argued earlier in the book (§61), we still have not come to a "*general* agreement about the use of the expression 'to have the same meaning' or 'to achieve the same.' For it can be asked in what cases we say: 'These are merely two forms of the same game.'" Or consider the following from the so-called Big Typescript of the late thirties: "The man who said that one cannot step into the same river twice said something wrong; one can step into the same river twice."[17] Literally this is the case: certainly, if Wittgenstein were walking along the banks of the Thames, he could easily step into the same river twice. But then Heraclitus, whose metaphorical aphorism Wittgenstein is calling into question, could respond that the second time round, it would not be quite the "same" river. Wittgenstein knows this, but he also knows that the "same" in "same river" is not quite the same as the "same" of "I have the same pain you have." For how can I judge the intensity of your pain? How do I know, for that matter, that you're not just pretending to be in pain? What can "same" possibly mean in such verbal constructions? It is, as in the case of "interval," the inherent difference between one *same* and another that makes language so mysterious.

some thing black

An examination of Wittgenstein translations thus leads us to the understanding that, as David Antin has put it succinctly, Wittgenstein "is not a poet of the German language or the English language; he is a poet of thinking through language," "a poet of nearly pure cognition."[18] As such, the Wittgensteinian language game paves the way for some of the most interesting poetic experiments of our own moment. The French *Oulipo*, for example, seems to have exerted as powerful a force in translation as in the original, even though a lipogram like Georges Perec's *La Disparition* (1969), which excludes the most common of French letters, *e*, would seem to be entirely "untranslatable."[19] Interestingly, the English translation *A Void* (1995), rendered brilliantly by Gilbert Adair, has proved to be almost as popular as the original, the point being that the central motive and its working out are wholly translatable, whatever the surface details.

In *Oulipo*, the essential analogy, as was the case in Wittgenstein, is between literature and mathematics, specifically with respect to the concept of *configuration*. As Warren Motte puts it:

> One looks for a configuration each time one disposes of a finite number of objects, and one wishes to dispose them according to certain constraints postulated in advance; Latin squares and finite geometries are configurations, but so is the arrangement of packages of different sizes in a drawer that is too small, or the disposition of words or sentences given in advance (on the condition that the given constraints be sufficiently "crafty" for the problem to be real). . . .
> Another way of considering the Oulipian enterprise is as a sustained attack on the aleatory in literature, a crusade for the maximal motivation of the literary sign.[20]

Let us see how this works in practice. In 1986 the French Oulipo mathematician/poet/novelist Jacques Roubaud published a long poetic sequence, *Quelque chose noir*, prompted by the tragic death of his young wife, the photographer Alix Cléo Roubaud. The English translation, made by Rosmarie Waldrop, was published in 1990 as *some thing black*.[21] Formally, the sequence is based on the number nine: there are nine sections, each having nine poems, and each poem has nine strophes, ranging from a single line to a paragraph made of phrases and clauses, oddly punctuated by periods rather than commas and avoiding all initial capitals. The number scheme—9 × 9 × 9—gives us 729 sections, which, together with the final poem, *Rien*, makes 730 or precisely 2 × 365 or two calendar years. *Rien* ("Nothing") is dated 1983 and marks the event of death itself, whereas the first poem of part 1 is "Meditation of 5/12/85," evidently written two years later. The course of the painful two-year passage is noted throughout, thus fulfilling Roubaud's axiom that "A text written according to a constraint describes the constraint."[22]

But there is more. For *nine* is of course Beatrice's number in Dante's *Vita Nuova*. The first chapter opens with the sentences "Nine times the heaven of the light had revolved in its own movement since my birth and had almost returned to the same point when the woman whom my mind beholds in glory first appeared before my eyes. She was called Beatrice by many who did not know what it meant to call her this."[23] The poet first lays eyes on his *donna ideale* at the start of her ninth year and "almost at the end of his ninth." He finally meets her exactly nine years later, when he is eighteen, and she greets him for the first time on the ninth hour of that day. So it goes through a series of visions associated with the number nine until we come to chapter 29 and read:

> Now, according to the Arabic way of reckoning time, her most noble soul departed from us in the ninth hour of the ninth day of the month. . . . she departed this life in the year of our Christian era, that is of the year of Our Lord, in which the perfect number had been completed nine times in the century in which she had been placed in this world; for she was born a Christian of the thirteenth century. Why this number was so closely connected with her might be explained as follows. Since, according to Ptolemy and according to Christian truth, there are nine moving heavens, and according to common astrological opinion, these heavens affect the earth below according to their conjunctions, this number was associated with her to show at her generation of nine of the moving heavens were in perfect conjunction one with the other. This is one reason. But, thinking more deeply and guided by infallible truth, I say that she herself was this number nine; I mean this as an analogy, as I will explain. The number three is the root of nine, because, independent of any other number, multiplied by itself alone, it makes nine, as we see quite plainly when we say three threes are nine; therefore if three is the sole factor of nine, and the sole factor

of miracles is three, that is, Father, Son and Holy Ghost, who are three
and one, then this lady was accompanied by the number nine to convey
that she was a nine, that is, a miracle, of which the root, that is, of the
miracle, is nothing other than the miraculous Trinity itself. Perhaps a
more subtle mind could find a still more subtle reason for it, but this
is the one which I perceive and which pleases me the most.

Roubaud's $9 \times 9 \times 9$ structure at once pays homage to and inverts the Dantean cosmos. Like the *Vita Nuova, Quelque chose noir* memorializes the beloved dead woman, but Roubaud's love is not an idealized image of female
perfection but his actual wife, whose body he knows intimately and whose
photographic representations, both her own and those of others, are all too
"real." In Roubaud's secular cycle, there is no afterlife for "you," no vision
beyond material death. Accordingly, the number nine shifts from referent to
hidden formal principle, the two-year cycle moving to the near silence of the
coda *Rien* ("Nothing," 147–48), whose page is all but blank, its nineteen minimalist lines, justified at the right margin, representing a short-circuiting of
speech itself:

Ce morceau de ciel
désormais
t'est dévolu

où la face aveugle
de l'église
s'incurve

compliquée
d'un marrionnier,

le soleil, là
hésite
laisse

du rouge
encore,
avant que la terre
émette

tant d'absence

que tes yeux
s'approchent

de rien

Rosmarie Waldrop's translation follows the original closely, even as she can reproduce the page layout of the original to create a near match (143–44):

this patch of sky
henceforward
your inheritance

where the blind façade
of the church
curves inward

complicated
by a chestnut tree

here the sun
hesitates
leaves

some more
red

before the earth
emit

so much absence

that your eyes
approach

nothing

Lines like "tant d'absence / que tes yeux / s'approchent / de rien" can be translated quite precisely: "so much absence / that your eyes / approach /

nothing." But as in Wittgenstein's riddling propositions, Roubaud's "simple" diction is nothing if not enigmatic. How does the earth "emit / so much absence"? How do the eyes of the dead approach "nothing"? Eyes, nails with blood caked underneath them, arms, legs—these appear again and again in *Quelque chose noir* but remain elusive. In Antin's terms, Roubaud's is a poetry of cognition rather than of texture.

Or consider *Irresemblance* ("Unlikeness"), which is the fourth prose poem of part 1:

L'irresemblance:

Le résultat de l'investigation était celui-ci: le précipité des ressemblances. la toile de la ressemblance. ses fils croisés et recroisés.

Parfois la ressemblance de partout. parfois la ressemblance là.

Ensuite que toi et ta mort n'avaient aucun air de famille.

Cela semble simple.   alors: il   n'y avait plus lieu d'une réquisition difficile. d'aucune interrogation rude. simplement le bavardage douloureux, inutile. superficiel et trivial.

"Un chien ne peut pas simuler la douleur.   est-ce parce qu'il est trop honnête?"

Il faillait faire connaissance avec la description.

En quelque mots ce qui ne bougeait pas.

Car cela m'avait été renvoyé reconnu, alors que rien ne s'en déduisait de mon expérience.

Tu étais morte, et cela ne mentait pas. (17)

The result of the investigation: a deposit of likenesses. weave of likeness. threads crossed and recrossed.

Sometimes likeness from anywhere. sometimes this likeness here.

Then, that you and your death shared no family trait.

It seems simple.   hence: no grounds for difficulties or demands for rude interrogation. just painful chatter, useless. superficial and trivial.

"Why can't a dog simulate pain? Is he too honest?"

I had to make friends with description.

In so many words, what did not move.

For this I recognized. Though none of it derived from my experience.

You were dead. this was no lie. (15)

Here, Roubaud's "investigation" into the response of the living to death begins by probing *le précipité des ressemblances,* since any word or image, as Wittgenstein taught us, is part of a language game made up of family resemblances. If the body in question could only be like something familiar, it would not seem dead. But by the third sentence, the poet has recognized that *Ensuite que toi et ta mort n'avaient aucun air de famille.* There are no family resemblances between a person and a state of being or nonbeing—in this case, death. One recalls the aphorism in the *Tractatus,* "Death is not an event in life. Death is not lived through." "None of it," we read in the penultimate line, "derived from my experience" (*"rien ne s'en déduisait de mon expérience"*). And yet there is more than "painful chatter," for relationships between items do manifest themselves, even if they are negative ones. In the fifth strophe, Wittgenstein's "Why can't a dog simulate pain? Is he too honest?" which I cited earlier, is given an ironic twist. For since in this case the poet himself seems incapable of simulating feeling, for example, even the slightest pleasure, perhaps Wittgenstein's distinction between man and dog must be qualified, at least so far as human "honesty" is concerned. Given these circumstances, there can be only resignation—the recognition that *Il fallait faire connaissance avec la description* ("I had to make friends with description"). Philosophy, Wittgenstein was fond of saying, leaves everything as it is; it can only describe. The same, Roubaud suggests, may be said of poetry. And even then the poet can describe only the physical facts—the *ce qui ne bougeait pas* or "what did not move." The ninth sentence is thus the flat recitation of fact: *Tu étais morte, et cela ne mentait pas* ("You were dead.

this was no lie"). It is a statement that takes us back to the question of the dog's "honesty" above. Indeed, the beloved who has become a "black thing" is not, like Beatrice, "a nine, that is a miracle, of which the root, that is of the miracle, is solely the miraculous Trinity." She merely *is*, or rather *was*.

Here is what we might call a conceptual poetry *à la lettre*—a set of strophes, largely written in denotative language, that modulate familiar abstract nouns, personal pronouns, and adverbs of time and place (*Parfois, là*). The network of likenesses and differences, so subtly articulated in the tension between numerical base and linguistic construction creates what is a highly wrought poetic text that is nevertheless quite amenable to translation. Rosmarie Waldrop, herself an important poet who might well deviate from the original were it desirable to do so, has here produced a remarkably literal translation. But then what were her alternatives? Take the line *Tu étais morte, et cela ne mentait pas*, which Waldrop renders as "You were dead. this was no lie." Grammatically, one can't say, following the French, "this did not lie." The construction "this was no lie" is thus the proper idiom any textbook would use. *Cela*, of course, is normally translated as "that" rather than "this" (perhaps Waldrop chose "this" for intimacy), but otherwise the line offers no other translation possibilities. Or again, Waldrop's translation of *"Il fallait faire connaissance avec la description"* as "I had to make friends with description" is not wholly literal (e.g., I had to get to know description), but "make friends" alludes slyly to Roubaud's own veiled reference to Gertrude Stein's important essay-poem "An Acquaintance with Description." In other words, there are alternate possibilities available to the translator even in the case of Roubaud, but only within rather narrow perimeters.

And there, of course, is the rub. Precisely because Roubaud's poetry is, at one level, so *translatable*, it doesn't give the translator very much scope. And this is the case even for the Oulipo lipogram, where the translator must be extremely gifted so as to match the original. To translate texts like *Quelque chose noir* or *La Disparition* is to subordinate oneself to the original, even as Wittgenstein's translators devote themselves to approximating the language of their master, so that there is surprisingly little talk, in Wittgenstein criticism, of the relative merits of translation *A* versus translation *B* or of the English translation of the *Tractatus* versus the French. The case of Rilke is the opposite. To speak of a translation of the *Duino Elegies* is to begin with the premise that *X*'s version cannot be commensurate with the poem itself.

Wittgenstein himself no doubt would have preferred Rilke's poetry to Roubaud's, even as he preferred Brahms to Bruckner. But ironically, his own understanding of poetry as *invention*, as conceptual art, became an important paradigm for those writers and artists who came of age in the immediate wake of the *Philosophical Investigations.* Consider Samuel Beckett, whose great *Trilogy* (*Molloy, Malone Dies, The Unnamable*) was published first in French, then in the author's own translation into English between 1951 and 1958. The relationship of the French to the English version of these short poetic novels raises interesting stylistic questions.[24] It is also the case that *Molloy*, say, in the German translation made by Erich Franzen, is quite true to the spirit of the original. Here is the opening page of what was originally a French novel—first in English, then in German:

> I am in my mother's room. It's I who live there now. I don't know how I got there. Perhaps in an ambulance, certainly a vehicle of some kind. I was helped. I'd never have got there alone. Perhaps I got here thanks to him. He says not. He gives me money and takes away pages. So many pages, so much money. Yes, I work now, a little like I used to, except that I don't know how to work any more. That doesn't matter apparently. What I'd like now is to speak of the things that are left, say my good-byes, finish dying. They don't want that. Yes, there is more than one, apparently. But it's always the same one that comes.

> *Ich bin im Zimmer meiner Mutter. Ich wohne jetzt selbst darin. Wie ich hierhergekommen bin, weiß ich nicht. In einer Ambulanz vielleicht, bestimmt mit irgendeinem Gefährt. Man hat mir geholfen. Allein hätte ich es nicht geschafft. Vielleicht habe ich es diesem Mann, der jede Woche erscheint, zu verdanken, daß ich hier bin. Er streitet es ab. Er gibt mir etwas Geld und nimmt das Geschriebene mit sich. So viele Seiten, so viel Geld. Ja, ich arbeite jetzt, ein wenig wie früher, nur verstehe ich mich nicht mehr aufs Arbeiten. Das macht nichts, wie es scheint. Ich möchte jetzt gern von dem sprechen, was mir noch übrig bleibt, Abschied nehmen, aufhören zu sterben. Das wollen sie nicht. Ja, es sind mehrere, wie es scheint. Aber der eine, der herkommt, ist immer derselbe.*[25]

Beckett's seemingly basic vocabulary, made up largely of personal and demonstrative pronouns, and ordinary verbs like "live," "know," "give," "take," and "work," applied to basic nouns like "mother," "money," "things," "pages," most of these organized into simple declarative sentences, translates neatly into German. And yet, like those propositions about "pain" or "colour" Wittgenstein lays out for us, Beckett's statements are highly elusive, indeterminate, and mysterious. The reference to the "ambulance" or "vehicle of some kind" in the fourth sentence suggests that it was at birth the narrator arrived in his mother's room, and so he has been there ever since, but the reference to "It is I who live there now" (*Ich wohne jetzt selbst darin*) suggests that this hasn't always been the case. In Wittgenstein's terms, the meaning can only be established by studying each word group or sentence in the larger context in which it occurs. What does "now" (*jetzt*) mean in "It is I who live there *now*"?

In *Philosophical Investigations* §383, Wittgenstein writes:

> We are not analyzing a phenomenon (e.g. thought) but a concept (e.g. that of thinking), and therefore the use of a word. So it may look as if what we were doing were Nominalism. Nominalists make the mistake of interpreting all words as *names,* and so of not really describing their use, but only, so to speak, giving a paper draft on such a description.

Most modernist poets, we might note, are in one form or another nominalists: Ezra Pound, as I suggest in a related essay here, builds his Cantos using collocations of proper names—a proliferation of restaurants, churches, frescoes, Provençal castles, Roman deities—so as to create a dense network of meanings. In more recent poetry, such nominalism has been practiced with beautiful irony by Frank O'Hara in poems like "Khrushchev is coming on the right day!"

But nominalism, as Wittgenstein understood so well, is a way of avoiding the concept "the use of a word." Unlike Pound, Beckett uses generic Irish names like Molloy, Malone, and Moran, and foregrounds everyday language—"Yes, I work now, a little like I used to"—puncturing this matter-of-fact statement with the qualification "except that I don't know how to work anymore." What could be easier to translate than the sentence "I don't know how to work anymore"? And yet what does such a sentence *mean*? Why doesn't Molloy know how to work anymore, and how does it relate to his past? Is he just making an excuse? Is his idleness the consequence of old age? Or has he lost one of his faculties or perhaps a limb?

It may well be that Beckett, like Wittgenstein, is so famous around the world because his enigmas are not so much textual as conceptual—and hence translatable. Such poetic language has great resonance at our moment of globalization—a moment when monolingualism is, unfortunately, increasingly common. In this context, as Roubaud also understands, poetry emphasizes not a specific language but simply *language* as an investigative tool. As Wittgenstein reminds us, "You learned the *concept* 'pain' when you learned language" (*Philosophical Investigations* §384).

In the fall of 1998, the Whitney Humanities Center at Yale University held a conference on the work of Eugene Jolas called "The Avant-Garde in transition." When I was invited, I must confess, I knew little of Jolas beyond his seminal editorship of the journal transition, *which serialized* Work in Progress, *the future* Finnegans Wake, *as well as a number of Gertrude Stein's experimental compositions. What I did not know until I began to read Jolas is that his multilingual poetry wrestles with issues so central to contemporary poetics. The essay was published in 1999 in the Australian journal* Kunapipi, Journal of Postcolonial Writing.

5

"Logocinéma of the Frontiersman"

Eugene Jolas's Multilingual Poetics and Its Legacies

Language became a neurosis. I used three of the basic world languages in conversation, in poetry and in my newspaper work. I was never able to decide which of them I preferred. An almost inextricable chaos ensued, and sometimes I sought a facile escape by intermingling all three. I dreamed a new language, a super-tongue for intercontinental expression, but it did not solve my problem. I felt that the great Atlantic community to which I belonged demanded an Atlantic language. Yet I was alone, quite alone, and I found no understanding comrades who might have helped me in my linguistic jungle.

Eugene Jolas, *Man from Babel*

Language as neurosis or language as "super-tongue for intercontinental expression"? For Eugene Jolas, a self-described "American in exile in the hybrid world of the Franco-German frontier, in a transitional region where people swayed to and fro in cultural and political oscillation, in the twilight zone of the German and French languages," language was clearly both.[1] For his was not just the usual bilingualism (or, more properly, the linguistic divisionism) of the Alsace-Lorraine citizen at the turn of the century; it was compounded by the acquisition of American English (already, so to speak, Jolas's birthright, born as he was in Union, New Jersey) in the years between 1909, when as a fifteen-year-old he emigrated to New York, and 1923, when he returned to Europe. What Jolas called "the long pilgrimage . . . through the empires of three languages" (65) was in many ways a great gift, the entrée to an international (or at least pan-European and North American) aesthetic. But it was also, as we shall see, a problem for a young man who aspired to be a great poet. When in the early twenties Jolas sent some of his poems to Frank Harris's magazine, *Pearson's,* Harris cautioned Jolas that he "came to English too late to become a real poet in [the English] language." "There is, in fact," Harris remarked, "no example in history of a poet who abandoned his native language in adolescence, and later succeeded in penetrating the mysteries of a new one. There are so many grammatical pitfalls that can never be overcome, unless the words have been felt in childhood" (49).

I shall come back to the poetry conundrum later, but for the moment let us consider what trilingualism did for Jolas the editor of *transition,* Jolas the impresario of the avant-garde and promoter of what he liked to call a "Eur-American philology" (65). From the first, Jolas's gift was an enormous sensitivity to different linguistic registers. Drafted in the U.S. Army in 1917, he concentrated neither on military strategy nor on political issues but on the "new words" that he heard from his fellow soldiers, most of whom, like himself, were recent immigrants: "profane words, crude words, voluptuous words, occult words, concrete words . . . a scintillating assemblage of phonetic novelties" (35). "I heard," he recalls, "the vocabulary of the bunkhouse, the steamer, the construction camp, the brothel, the machine shop, the steel mill. I heard that lexicon of the farmhouse and the mountain cabin. . . . Here was truly a melting-pot, Franco-Belgian-Serbian-German-Austrian-Bohemian-Americans in our outfit mingled with native-born Americans with Anglo-Saxon names, and our conversations were often filled with picturesquely distorted English and foreign words that quickened my Babel fantasies."

To put these remarks in context, consider the admonition made not so many years earlier by Henry James in a commencement speech at Bryn Mawr College. The new immigrants, James warned the graduates, were destroying the "ancestral circle" of the American language, turning it into "a mere helpless slobber of disconnected vowel noises," an "easy and ignoble minimum," barely distinguishable from "the grunting, the squealing, the barking, or the roaring of animals." "The forces of looseness," James warned, "are in possession of the field," and they "dump their mountain of promiscuous material into the foundations" of the language itself.[2]

From James's perspective, Jolas would be part of the "force of looseness . . . in possession of the field." But in the aftermath of the Great War, with the increasing traffic between Americans and Europeans (Marcel Duchamp, François Picabia, and Mina Loy in the United States; Gertrude Stein, Djuna

Barnes, and a host of American expatriates in Paris), the intactness of American English was threatened, and the stage was set for Jolas's own linguistic experiments and for his reception of Joyce's *Work in Progress*. When in late 1926 he heard Joyce read from the opening pages of his new manuscript, Jolas marveled at the "polysynthetic quality" of Joyce's language (*Man from Babel* 89), a language that was to become the touchstone for *transition*. The "repetitiveness of Gertrude Stein's writings" (89–90), on the other hand, was not really Jolas's cup of tea, even though, in deference to his coeditor, Elliot Paul, and to Stein's stature as the "*doyenne* among American writers in Paris" (116), he was to publish so many of her experimental pieces,[3] and even though he frequently came to her defense in the pages of *transition* as well as in the notes to his *Anthologie de la nouvelle poésie américaine* (1928).[4] In his autobiography, Jolas was more candid about what he called Stein's "esoteric stammering":

> Her mental attitude was remote from anything I felt and thought. For not only did she seem to be quite devoid of metaphysical awareness but I also found her aesthetic approach both gratuitous and lacking in substance. . . .
>
>   We published a number of her compositions in *transition,* although I am obliged to say that I saw, and see today, little inventiveness in her writing. The "little household words" so dear to Sherwood Anderson, never impressed me, for my tendency was always in the other direction. *I wanted an enrichment of language,* new words, millions of words. . . . (*Man from Babel* 116, my emphasis)

More vocabulary rather than less, Joycean "enrichment" rather than Steinian reduction: this "other direction" was of course Jolas's own. The famous manifesto "Revolution of the Word," which appeared in the summer double issue of 1929 (T 16–17), declared, "The literary creator has the right to disintegrate the primal matter of words imposed on him by text-books and dictionaries" (proposition #6), and "He has the right to use words of his own fashioning and to disregard existing grammatical and syntactical laws" (proposition #7).[5] In what Jolas understood to be the watershed year of the Great Crash, T. S. Eliot, as the February 1929 issue (T 14) had declared, was the enemy, his "reformatory forces" having been "constrain[ed]" "into the straightjacket of political and religious dogma" (T 14: 11). Fascism on the Right, Communism on the Left, a weak "desiccated humanitarianism" in the United States—all these, Jolas felt, conspired against the "new art" and made revolution "imperative." "The new vocabulary and the new syntax must help destroy the ideology of a rotting civilization" (T 16–17: 15).

But how exactly could the "disregard" of "existing grammatical and syn-tactical laws" contribute to the making of revolution? In Jolas's scheme of things, multilingualism was equivalent to racial and ethnic equality. In a piece called "Logos" (T 16–17), he addresses the issue of language borrowing and deformation: "In modern history we have the example of the deforma-tions which English, French and Spanish words underwent in America, as in the case of Creole French on Mauritius, Guyana, Martinique, Hayti [sic], Louisiana, and Colonial Spanish" (28). When he returned to New York in 1933, Jolas wandered the streets, recording the "inter-racial philology," the "fantasia of many-tongued words" (*Man from Babel* 147), accelerated by the presence of the new refugees from Hitler. He called the "embryonic lan-guage of the future" the "Atlantic, or Crucible, language, for it was the result of the interracial synthesis that was going on in the United States, Latin America and Canada. It was American English, with an Anglo-Saxon basis, plus many grammatical and lexical additions from more than a hundred tongues. All these, together with the Indian 'subsoil' languages, are now being spoken in America" (147). And after World War II, Jolas reconceived "Atlan-tica" as a universal language that "might bridge the continents and neutralize the curse of Babel" not by being an invention like Esperanto or Interglossa (272) but "by absorbing Anglo-Saxon, Greco-Latin, Celtic, Indian, Spanish, French Canadian French, German, Pennsylvania German, Dutch, Hebrew, the Slavic and Slavonic languages" (273).

Ironically enough, this Utopian dream of a common language had as its primary exhibit the most esoteric (and arguably private) of literary com-positions: Joyce's *Finnegans Wake,* each issue of *transition* presenting an-other installment of *Work in Progress,* as it was then called. Joyce's "excellent knowledge of French, German, Greek and Italian," wrote Jolas, "stood him in good stead, and he was constantly adding to his stock of linguistic infor-mation by studying Hebrew, Russian, Japanese, Chinese, Finnish, and other tongues. At the basis of his vocabulary was also an immense command of Anglo-Irish words that only seem like neologisms to us today, because they have for the most part become obsolete" (*Man from Babel* 167).

A comparable enthusiasm for Joyce's linguistic virtuosity was voiced by the young Samuel Beckett, whose essay "Dante . . . Bruno . Vico . . Joyce," appeared in the summer 1929 issue of *transition* along with "Revolution of the Word":

Here form *is* content, content *is* form. You complain that this stuff is not written in English. It is not written at all. It is not to be read—or rather it is not only to be read. It is to be looked at and listened to. His writing is not *about* something; *it is that something itself.* . . . When the sense is dancing, the words dance. The language is drunk. The very words are tilted and effervescent.

And again:

> Mr. Joyce has desophisticated language. . . . It is abstracted to death. Take the word "doubt": it gives us hardly any sensuous suggestion of hesitancy, of the necessity for choice, of static irresolution. Whereas the German "Zweifel" does, and, in lesser degree, the Italian "dubitare." Mr. Joyce recognizes how inadequate "doubt" is to express a state of extreme uncertainty, and replaces it by "intwosome twiminds."[6]

Beckett's own early poems and stories reflect this interest in polylingualism. In "Sedendo et Quiesciendo," which appeared in the March 1932 issue of *transition* (T 21), we read:

> Well really you know and in spite of the haricot skull and a tendency to use up any odds and ends of pigment that might possibly be left over she was the living spit he thought of Madonna Lucrezia del Fede. Ne suis-je point pâle? Suis-je belle? Certainly pale and belle my pale belle Braut with a winter skin like an old sail in the wind. . . . for many years he polished his glasses (ecstasy of attrition!) or suffered the shakes and gracenote strangulations and enthrottlements of the Winkelmusik of Szopen or Pichon or Chopinek or Chopinetto or whoever it was embraced her heartily as sure my name is Fred, dying all my life (thank you Mr Auber) on a sickroom talent (thank you Mr Field) and a Kleinmeister's Leidenschaftsucherei (thank you Mr Beckett). . . . (T 21: 16).

Here Belacqua's mix of fantasy and memory, prompted by the encounter with the astonishing Smeralda-Rima, gives rise to all sorts of foreign words and grammatical constructions: *haricot skull* (with its play on "bean"), *Lucrezia del Fede* (Italian for "Faith"), *Ne suis-je point pâle? Suis-je belle?* (French for "Am I not pale? Am I beautiful?"), *pale belle Braut* (English + French + German for "pale beautiful bride"), *Winkelmusik* (literally "cornermusic," here a spoof on "chamber music" and "chamberpot"), the phonetic plays and anagrams on Chopin's name and the parodic compounding of *Kleinmeister's Leidenschaftsucherei* ("Small master," on the analogy of *Bürgomeister, Haußmeister, die Meistersinger,* etc., combined with the grandiose neologism *Leidenschaftsucherei,* which translates as "lust-searching"). Such wordplay contradicts Beckett's complaint that English usually cannot capture the sensuous flavor of an image or action: *Winkelmusik,* for example, nicely captures the "tinkle" of the chamberpot, and the long open dipthong and voiceless stop in *Braut* has a very different phonetic aura from *bride* with its *ay* glide and soft-voiced stop. *Braut,* after all, rhymes with *Kraut* and *laut.*

Still, such contrived shifts from one language to another are ultimately distracting, taking us outside the text rather than further into it. Beckett seems to have sensed this. Writing in 1931 to Charles Prentice at Chatto & Windus, he remarked that "of course it ["Sedendo et Quiesciendo"] stinks of Joyce in spite of earnest endeavours to endow it with my own odours."[7] And surely the perceived "stink of Joyce" had something to do with Beckett's turn, in the fifties, to a "foreign" language—French—for the writing of *Waiting for Godot* and the *Trilogy.* It is interesting to note that in fictions like *Malone Dies,* he discarded the mannerisms of his early multilingual work in favor of a much sparer, starker, monolingual writing, no longer more than marginally Joycean.

But then Joyce's own multilingualism had its own very special parameters. Consider the following passage from "Anna Livia Plurabelle": as published in its first version in *transition* 8 (November 1927):

> Do you tell me that now? I do in troth. Orara por Orbe and poor Las Animas! Ussa, Ulla, we're umbas all! Mezha, didn't you hear it a deluge of times, ufer and ufer, respund to spond? You deed, you deed! I need, I need! It's that irrawaddying I've stoke in my aars. It all but husheth the lethest sound. Oronoko.[8]

Here the opening conversation of the washerwomen begins realistically enough but soon gives way to an allusion to the Spanish prayer *orar por Orbe y por Las Animas* ("pray for the Earth and the Souls of the Dead"), into which Joyce has embedded three river names: the Orara in New South Wales, the Orba in Italy, and the Orb in France. Further, *por* becomes "poor," so that, comically enough, the women seem to be talking about a friend or neighbor: "poor Las Animas." In the next sentence, *Ussa* and *Ulla* are both names of Russian rivers, and at the same time, as Walton Litz points out, the two words can be read as "us-ça," "you-là," referring to the near and far banks of the river. In the same sentences, *umbas* is a portmanteau word combining *umbra* ("shade, ghost") and the Umba River of East Africa. Then, in the next sentence, *Mezha* fuses the Italian stage direction *mezza voce* with the name of the Indian river Meza and the exclamation "ha," the latter leading to the shrill cries of the washerwomen: "You deed, you deed! I need, I need!" These repeated exclamations suggest that in the darkness (*umbra*), it has become more and more difficult for the women to hear one another. "A deluge of times" nicely underscores the river-flood motif, and the German "ufer and ufer" fuses riverbank (*Ufer*) and Russian river name ("Ufa") with the sound of "over and over." *Ufa* also means "medium-sized fir pole or spar," so we can read the end of the sentence as saying that spar after spar is spinning down the Liffey destined for the pond in "spond," with that word's further implication of "despond."

Without going any further and probing the complexities of the compound "irrawaddying" (the Irrawaddy River + "wadding" + "ear" + "irrational") or the final proper name "Oronoko" (the royal slave who is the hero of Aphra Behn's novel + the Orinoco River + a kind of Virginia tobacco), we can see that the linguistic paradigm of the passage in question is essentially absorptive. The language base, that is to say, is so firmly Anglo-Irish ("Do you tell me that now? I do in troth") that the foreign words and morphemes—in this case, Latin, Spanish, German, French, and Italian, not to mention the proper names of rivers in a variety of languages, all within the space of thirty-nine words—are absorbed into the fabric of English syntax and word formation, complicating and deepening meaning, without calling attention to themselves as foreign elements. Whereas a phrase like "my belle Braut" is additive (English + French + German), the question "Mezha, didn't you hear it a deluge of times, ufer and ufer, respund to spond," foregrounds the basic structure and rhythm of the English sentence and inserts coinages and portmanteau words that sound familiar enough, as in the case of "ufer and ufer" ("over and over"). The result is thus not so much a form of multilingualism as a reinvention of English as magnet language, pulling in those particles like *Ussa* and *Ulla* or deftly transposing a Spanish preposition (*por*) into an English adjective ("poor") so as to produce a dense mosaic of intertextual references.

Jean-Michel Rabaté has observed that the process of denaturalization I have just described, the undoing of the taxonomy of language, whether one's own or another's, was Joyce's way of declaring war against English, "against a mother tongue used to the limit, mimed, mimicked, exploded, ruined."[9] Jolas's multilingualism is of a different order. Neither in German nor in French, after all, did this writer have the command of English that Joyce possessed. The official language of his elementary school in Forbach had been German, a language inevitably associated in the boy's mind with the Prussian authoritarianism of his teachers. The French of his youth, on the other hand, was, properly speaking, a dialect "related to that of Luxembourg and the Flemish countries" (*Man from Babel* 9). And further, both French and German lost their hold over Jolas when as a teen-ager he gave up both for what he called the "linguistic jungle" of America. Thus, despite his expertise at translating one of his three languages into either of the others, an expertise that is everywhere manifest in *transition* as well as in such of his volumes as the superb *Anthologie de la nouvelle poésie américaine,* Jolas did not quite have the hard-core language base of a Joyce or a Beckett, the latter being able to write his novels in a "foreign" language (French), precisely because he was so sure of his native tongue.

For Jolas, in any case, the basic unit seems to have been not the sentence but the word, his compilation of "Slanguage: 1929"[10] and later "Transition's Revolution of the Word Dictionary"[11] testifying to his passion for what the Russian Futurists called *slovo kak takovoe*—"the word as such." In Jolas's dictionary, the list of neologisms begins with six items from Joyce: *constatation* ("statement of a concrete fact"), *couchmare* ("nightmare . . . cauchemar . . ."), *mielodorus* ("honeyed emphasis of odorous"), *Dance McCaper* ("An Irish *danse macabre*"), and *Besterfarther Zeuts* ("the Proustian divinity . . . Cronos . . . Saturn . . . who bests us all; in other words: Grandfather Time—here *Zeuts* suggests both Zeus and *Zeit,* German for 'time'"). Joyce is thus the presiding deity of the dictionary, but Jolas includes writers from Leo Frobenius to Bob Brown (*readie,* "machine for reading"), from Stuart Gilbert to Jolas's pseudonymous poet Theo Rutra, whose contribution is *flir* ("to glitter").

What, then, are the poems like? In *Man from Babel,* Jolas tells us that his "first poems in the New World were written in German" (180), for example this perfectly conventional Romantic quatrain in iambic pentameter:

Ich steh' auf himmelragendem Gemäuer,
Allein im Schmelz vom letzten Abendschein;
Die wilde Stadt umbraust mich ungeheur—
Mein Herz schlägt traumgebannt in Stahl und Stein.[12]

The transfer to English within the next few years made little difference: indeed, the themes of dream, loneliness, and adolescent lyricism remain constant, whether in metrical forms, as in:

I stand desolate before the funeral pyre of my youth.
Ours is the dance and the magic of blessed dreams;
And through the world goes a wind of despair. (25)

Or, in free verse:

> My nostalgias seek your moods
> In every meditative dusk,
> When I am tired with the tedium of machines,
> This age is distorted with madness . . .
> Fever stalks through the cities of stone . . . (51)

Now compare to these passages one of Jolas's early "Ur-Language" poems appearing in *transition* 8 (November 1927):

> Oor forest hear thine voice it winks
> Ravines fog gleamen and the eyes
> When night comes dooze and nabel sinks
> Trowm quills unheard and lize. (145)

Here is Jolas working toward the "revolution of the word," with the word itself as dominant: "Oor" for "Our" or *Ur*; "gleamen," a compound on the model of "snowmen"; "night comes dooze," that is, "down," fused with "doze" and "snooze"; "nabel" (the German *näbel* for "fog," and this "nabel" being one that "sinks / Trowm"—that is "down" in the form of *traum* (German for "dream") and perhaps over the "town." The stanza's final word, "lize," seems to be an intentional misspelling of *leise*, German for "softly," or "in a low voice."

The difficulty here is that the Anglo-German compounds and portmanteaus are more awkward than functional. Why is it more graphic, complex, or interesting to say "nabel sinks / Trowm" than to say "the fog sinks dreamily down"? Why transform the two-syllable *leise* (pronounced *layzé*) into what looks like a reference to lice or lizards, neither word applicable in the context? More successful than these multilingual poems of the late twenties are Jolas's experiments with sound play in the form of alliteration, assonance, onomatopoeia, metathesis, or echolalia. In *Man from Babel* he recalls:

> An expansion of language seemed necessary, also, in English and American poetry. Work on my translation of American poets had impressed me with the paucity of vocabulary and the poverty of the lyrical phrase, both of which seemed to me to be meager and often pedestrian. This, I felt, prevented the poet from expressing the deeper emotions which his unconscious might have evoked. I myself invented

a poet I called Theo Rutra, in order to project certain of my own neo-logistic work, and soon this fellow Rutra became my alter ego. I enjoyed playing him up to my friends, to which I described in detail the "Czech immigrant living in Brooklyn" (109).

Here is Theo Rutra's prose poem "Faula and Flona" (i.e., Flora and Fauna):

> The lilygushes ring and ting the bilbels in the ivilley. Lilools sart slinslongdang into the clish of sun. The pool dries must. The mor-rowlei loors in the meaves. The sardinewungs flir flar and meere. A flishflashfling hoohoos and haas. Long shill the mellohoolooloos. The rangomane clanks jungling flight. The elegoat mickmecks and crools. A rabotick ringrangs the stam. A plutocrass with throat of steel. Then woor of meadcalif's rout. The hedgeking gloos. And matemaids click for dartalays.
> (T 16–17 [June 1928], 34)[13]

Joyce is the obvious model for words like *ivilley* ("ivy" + "valley") and *plu-tocrass,* and Stein is also present, the sentence "The pool dries must" recalling "Render clean must" in her "Susie Asado." But however pleasurable the language games of "Faula and Flona," it is doubtful that, either here or in the multilingual poems, Jolas has found a way of "expressing the deeper emotions which his unconscious might have evoked," or that the ringing *lily-gushes* and *bilbels* "expand" the language as we know it. More important: the much touted "Revolution of the Word," a "revolution" that seemed so glamorous to Jolas and his friends in the late twenties, found itself increasingly under a cloud as it ran into the very real political revolution that brought the Nazis to power in 1932.

In his autobiography Jolas recalls a 1933 excursion he and his wife, Maria, made with the Joyces and the Siegfried Gideons to the Rhinefall of Schaff-hausen, on the Swiss-German border. Sitting on the terrace of a little inn, facing the beautiful iridescent waters of the swirling Rhine, "we suddenly noticed at nearby tables several grotesquely garbed Nazi youths who had crossed the border for a Sunday excursion. They wore their Hitlerite insignia with ostentation and seemed evidently proud of this affiliation. Soon we heard their raucous voices in a dull Germanic tavern song, and I could not help recalling the days in my childhood, when we used to hear the drunken voices of the Kaiser's soldiers in the little inn next to our house. Nothing had changed" (134).

Note that even here Jolas identifies people by their voices, by the way they *sound*. And note that the Nazis are aggressively monolingual—for Jolas, a sign of narrow nationalist identity. No wonder, then, that the worse the political situation in Europe became, the more insistently Jolas turned to multilingualism as defense. In the July 1935 issue of *transition* (now subtitled *An International Experiment for Orphic Creation*),[14] Jolas has a poem called "Mots-Frontiere: Polyvocables," which begins:

> malade de peacock-feathers
> le sein blue des montagnes and the house strangled by rooks the
> tender entêtement des trees
> the clouds sybilfly and the neumond brûleglisters ein wunder stuerzt
> ins tal with
> eruptions of the abendfoehren et le torrentbruit qui charrie les
> gestes des enfants. . . .[15]

Jolas's "Polyvocables" imply that if only poetry could contain French + German + English in equal additive measure, the treacherous frontiers increasingly separating the nations of Europe might be crossed. So the German *neumond* (new moon) *brûleglisters* ("burns and glistens") in both French and English, and the German *wunder stuerzt / ins tal* ("a wonder rushes into the valley") with English "eruptions." The "tender *entêtement*" ("stubbornness"), moreover, belongs not to *des arbres* but to "*des trees.*"

This last line reminds me of nothing so much as the refugee English spoken by some of my Austrian relatives and family friends in the United States of the early 1940s—for example, *Die bell hatt geringt* ("The bell rang"), with its normative German syntax and retention of the German prefix for the past participle. In his study of *transition*, Dougald McMillan judges such passages severely, arguing that "The circumstances of [Jolas's] trilingualism have left Americans, French, and Germans uncertain as to the national category he belongs in."[16] But this is to judge Jolas by the very norms he was attacking; the problem is not national indeterminacy but the somewhat clumsy additive technique Jolas, unlike Joyce, used in bringing his languages together. Indeed, another poem for the July 1935 issue, "Logocinéma of the Frontiersman," makes the A + B + C method quite overt: the elegiac meditation on the poet's words tracks Jolas's life from the German of his *Kindesworte* (*Immer leuchtete der Wunderkontinent*) to the French of his stormy *adolescence* (*mes mots chevauchaient une lavefrontière; mes mots sanglotaient dans une bacchanale de blessures*) and then the English of the poet's young manhood in the asphalt jungle of New York:

my words amerigrated
my words saw steelsparkle
my words nightstormed concrete. . . .
they asphaltwandered doom

manhattan words swarmed shiverdawn
                    (T 23 [July 1935]: 188)

Following this triad, the "Logocinéma" continues in the same vein for six
more sections of approximately sixteen lines each, now in English, but with
occasional German and French intrusions, as in "My homewords were *heim-
wehkrank* / my loamwords were full of *sehnsucht*" (part IV), and, as the
"motherwords" and "fatherwords" of the poet's Alsace-Lorraine childhood
come back, we find lines like "*mes mots pleuvaient doucement sur les boulevards*," with its echo of Blaise Cendrars.[17] As things become more complex
("my fatherwords luminousshone with sun" [part VII], and "my delugewords flowed through the heraclitean sluice" [part VIII]), Jolas tries to bring
his linguistic identities together ("patois words wedded artwords / sunverbs
flightrocketed against nightnouns" [part VIII]), and finally the cinematic
movement brings all three languages together in part IX, which begins "*Not
hatte die welt ergriffen* / the day was waiting for *erschuetterungen*" (i.e., "Suffering had taken hold of the world / the day was waiting for cataclysms," although the first word of the stanza can also be construed as the English
"Not") and culminates in a Last Judgment ("the *letzte Gericht*") of "*des dam-
nés de la terre*" (part IX). The last short stanza reads:

toutes les nuits étaient squelletiques
die hunde schrieen sich tot in den hecken
les forêts de la lune mystère brûlaient
the world was earthquakedarkling (191)

Here each of the four lines—French, German, French, English—is rhythmically independent, but each anticipates the next: the skeleton nights (line 1)
contain the dogs barking themselves to death in the hedges (line 2) and the
burning forests of the mysterious moon (line 3); thus (line 4) the world's en-
veloping darkness signals earthquake, cataclysm. The autobiographical frame,
with its emphasis on the coming into being of the "delugewords," provides
structure for the poet's kaleidoscopic "logocinéma of the frontiersman."
    But that "logocinéma," found again in such poems as "Intrialogue," "Ver-
bairrupta of the Mountainmen," and "Frontier-Poem," produced by Jolas

in the course of the following three years, did not survive World War II.[18] When, at war's end, Jolas was stationed in Germany by the U.S. Office of War Information (OWI) and assigned to various de-Nazification projects as well as to the task of setting up a new free German press, the dream of a common language was over. Postwar Germany, so Jolas tells us in *Man from Babel,* was characterized by a "vague-Neo-Romanticism"; "a good deal of poetry was being written and published, but the ferment and audacity of French, British, and American poetic creation was obviously lacking" (252). Indeed, the problems of the postwar years and the coming Cold War left little time for what now seemed like the luxury of polylingual poetry.

Yet this is not the end of the story; for Jolas's "polyvocables" of the 1930s, his *mots-frontiere,* look ahead to the intense poetic interest in marginal languages, dialects, creoles, pidgins, and alternate soundings that we have witnessed in recent decades, especially in the United States.[19] In the 1940s, the last decade of Jolas's own life (he died in 1952), the flow of American writers settling in Paris and other European capitals was reversed; New York becoming the home of Kandinsky and Mondrian, André Breton and Max Ernst, Willem de Kooning and Hans Hofmann, not to mention an entire colony of German exile writers (Thomas Mann, Bertold Brecht) and British expatriates (Aldous Huxley, Christopher Isherwood), who settled in Los Angeles. And in subsequent decades, as the United States has been transformed by the immigration of East Asians, Africans from the Caribbean, and especially Latinos from Mexico, Central America, and the South American countries, it was inevitable that the language of American poetry would begin to deviate not only from its nineteenth-century English model (Wordsworth to Hardy) but also from the Emerson-Whitman-Dickinson-Frost-Stevens paradigm that was its more immediate source.

"We tried," Jolas remarks sadly in the epilogue to *Man from Babel,* "to give voice to the sufferings of man by applying a liturgical exorcism in a mad verbalism." But "now that the greatest war in history is over, and the nations are trying to construct a troubled peace in an atomic era, we realize that the international migrations which the apocalyptic decade has unleashed bring in their wake a metamorphosis of communication" (272). The solution, he was quick to add, "will not be invented by philologists—we have seen their inventions: Idiom Neutral, Ido, Esperanto, Novial, Interglossa. These were pedantic, unimaginative creations without any life in them" (272–73). Rather, one must take one's own language—and English, Jolas felt, was now the most prominent, used as it was by seven hundred million people around the world—and "bring into this medium elements from all the other languages spoken today." The new language "should not number several hundred thousand words, but millions of words. It will not be an artificial language, but one that has its roots in organic life itself" (272).

The notion of interjecting "all the other languages spoken today" into the fabric of English is still a bit Utopian, but Jolas is on to something important—namely, that multilingualism functions not by mere addition but by the infusion *into one's own language* of the cultures that are changing its base. As a young reporter living in New Orleans, Jolas had been enchanted by the "Creole French spoken, by both whites and Negroes" as well as by the language of the descendants of transplanted French Canadians from Nova Scotia, which is Cajun. "Their children," he marveled, "were Ulysse, Télémaque, Olélia, Omen" (84), and he would no doubt have been intrigued by the following:

(1) From Kamau Brathwaite, *Trench Town Rock*[20]

L ass night about 2:45 well well well before
    the little black bell of the walk of my elec-
    tronic clock cd wake me—
      aweakened by gunshatt
—the eyes trying to function open too stunned to work
out there through the window & into the dark with its
various glints & glows: mosquito, very distant cock-
crow, sound system drum, the tumbrel of a passing en-
gine, somewhere some/where in that dark.   It must
have been an ear / ring's earlier sound that sprawled
me to the window.   But it was

TWO SHATTS

—silence—

not evening the dogs barking or the trees blazing
& then a cry we couldn't see of

do
do
do
do
nuh kill me

(2) From Alfred Arteaga, "Xronotop Xicano"[21]

Aguila negra, rojo chante.
Tinta y pluma.
Textos vivos,
written people: the vato
with la vida loca on his neck,
the vata with p.v., the ganga with
tears, the shining cross. Varrio
walls: Codices; storefront
placazos: varrio names,
desafíos, people names
Written cars, names etched
in glass, "Land of a Thousand
Dances." Placas
and love etched in schools.

(3) From Theresa Hak Kyung Cha, *Dictee*[22]

that. All aside. From then.
Point by point. Up to date. Updated.
The view.
Absent all the same. Hidden. Forbidden.
Either side of the view.
Side upon side. That which indicates the interior
and exterior.
Inside. Outside.
Glass. Drape. Lace. Curtain. Blinds. Gauze.
Veil. Voile. Voile de mariée. Voile de religieuse
Shade shelter shield shadow mist covert
screen screen door screen gate smoke screen
concealment eye shade eye shield opaque silk
gauze filter frost to void to drain to exhaust
to eviscerate to gut glazing stain glass glassy
vitrification
what has one seen, this view
this which is seen housed thus
behind the veil. Behind the veil of secrecy. Under
the rose ala derobee beyond the veil

voce velate veiled voice under breath murmuration
render mute strike dumb voiceless tongueless.

Brathwaite, Arteaga, Cha: all three write as outsider poets—poets for whom
English is in one way or another a foreign language. Kamau Brathwaite, to
take our first example, who was born Lawson Edward Brathwaite in Bar-
bados in 1930 and educated at Pembroke College, Cambridge, came, via a
decade spent in Ghana with the Ministry of Education, to a rediscovery of
his West Indian identity (the name Kamau was adopted in 1971) and to what
he called, in an important book by that title, *nation language*. He defined this
as "the submerged area of that dialect which is much more closely allied to
the African aspect of experience in the Caribbean,"[23] a language that combines standard English and Jamaican Creole, "to get at the pulse," as Joan
Dayan puts it, "of the street talk, gospel, or Rastafari he shared in and listened
to in Jamaica," the "riddim" (rhythm) of popular talk.[24] In the later work, of
which *Trench Town Rock* is an example, Brathwaite fused "nation language"
with what he called "video style":

> ... the video style comes out of the resources locked within the com-
> puter, esp. my Macs Sycorax & Stark (but not peculiar to them or me) in
> the same way a sculptor like Bob'ob or Kapo wd say that the images
> they make dream for them from the block of the wood in their chisel

> When I discover that the computer cd write in light, as X/Self tells his
> mother in that first letter he writes on a computer, I discovered a whole
> new way of SEEING things I was SAYING. . . . [25]

Defined this way, "video style" may be understood as another name for what
we usually call visual poetics: the use of typography (size, font, placement)
and page layout to create meaning.

Trench Town Rock, whose opening page is reproduced on p. 95, is an elaborate collage (or *métissage*, as Edouard Glissant called it[26]) based on the poet's traumatic experience of having had his house ransacked on 24 October 1990 by armed robbers while he, gagged and tied, helplessly waited for
the gun to go off. The book juxtaposes interviews, news reports, personal
diaries, and social commentary to create a powerful image of violence and
victimization within a culture that is itself a victim of more powerful cultures. In the passage in question, the mix of Standard English and Creole is
heightened by the urban rhythms of the Jamaican soundspace, beginning

with "Lass night about 2:45 well well well before / the little black bell of the walk of my elec- / tronic clock cd wake me"—a dazzling sound orchestration of /l/, /w/, and /k/ phonemes in rhyming words ("well well well"/"bell"), consonance ("walk"/"wake"; "electronic clock"), and alliteration ("little black bell," "clock cd"). Such double entendres as "aweakened by gunshatt" heighten the poem's meaning: the narrator is both awakened and weakened by the muggers; "gunshatt" recalls shit, "nuh" in "do / nuh kill me," has the force of an expletive as well as the injunction of "not." And Brathwaite's "video style," recalls Futurist typography in its heightening of the "**TWO SHATTS**," its emphasis on the italicized injunction "*do do do nuh kill me*," and its use of up-to-date business English shorthand, as in "cd," "wd," the ampersands, and the precision of "2:45." Further, the slashes within words ("some/where," "ear/ring's") create a series of emphatic breaking points, designed to represent the violence of the action. Everything is chaotic, dismembered, disabled.

Brathwaite's multilingualism is thus a compounding of English and Jamaican dialect, with visual language playing a central part. Alfred Arteaga's, by contrast, fuses two standard languages, English and Spanish, with a sprinkling of Aztec names and Chicano neologisms. Arteaga is a Mexican American poet, born in Los Angeles and educated at Columbia University and the University of California at Santa Cruz, where he received his doctorate in Renaissance literature. "These cantos chicanos," Arteaga says in his preface, "begin with X and end with X. They are examples of xicano verse, verse marked with a cross, the border cross of alambre y río, the cross of Jesus X in Native America, the nahuatl X in méxico, mexican, xicano" (*Cantos* 5). The cross (X) thus becomes the sign of two colliding cultures and languages. The title "Xronotop Xicano" presents one such crossing: a *chronotope* (Mikhail Bakhtin's term) literally means "time-space" and is defined as "a unit of analysis for studying texts according to the ratio and nature of the temporal and spatial categories represented."[27] In this case, the modern Western theoretical term *chronotope* is crossed with the adjective "Xicano," and refers, in the poem itself, to the language of Aztlan (the ancient Aztec empire that included Texas, New Mexico, Arizona, Colorado, and California). Within the poem itself, emblems of the Aztec Mexican past "cross" the present of Chicano ghetto children etching their names, their curses (*desafíos*), their *placas* ("graffiti"), and four-letter words on walls, storefronts, billboards, and car windows.

In defining the particular chronotope in question, Arteaga alternates Spanish and English phrases, the Spanish often made strange by "Chicano" spellings and adaptations. The opening line, *Aguila negra, rojo chante,* refers to the black eagle devouring the serpent on the red ground of the Mexican flag. But *chante* may be the imperative of *chantar* ("to plant") or a misspelled rendition of the English noun "chant" (or French *chanter*, "to sing"), so that the meaning of the line remains equivocal. And *vato* in line 4 (along with the feminine *vata* in line 5) is largely untranslatable—a term designating a victim or "lost boy" but etymologically related to the Latin *vates* ("prophet"), hence perhaps the boy as wise fool. The *vato*, in any case, has *la vida loca* ("the crazed life," "the life of the mad") hanging around his neck, even as the *vata's* fate is *p.v.* (*por vida*, "for life"). So the poet must take *tinta y pluma* ("ink and pen") and record the *textos vivos* of his people, caught up in their *ganga* ("bargain") "with tears," which is their own "shining cross" to bear, *ganga* also alluding to the gang life of the *varrio* (*barrio*), with its members' "names etched / in glass" on the schoolhouse walls.

Here language is the signifier of cultural hybridity, the "cross" between Spanish and English, which is the Chicano of the North American cities. To write only in English (or only in Spanish), Arteaga implies, would deny this experience its immediacy, its felt life. Whereas Brathwaite was raised as an English speaker, and hence resorts to dialect but not to other standard languages, Arteaga must include the "foreign" (Spanish) language base of his childhood.

A third alternative is that of Theresa Hak Kyung Cha, a Korean poet whose family immigrated first to Hawaii and then to California when she was eleven. At the Convent of the Sacred Heart all-girls school in San Francisco, she learned French, so by the time she attended Berkeley and studied film and performance art, her two written languages were a carefully acquired English and French. Accordingly, *Dictee*, the long poem Cha produced shortly before she was tragically murdered by a stranger in New York at the age of thirty-one, is an amalgam of English and French, the latter, so to speak, her memory language. The poem tells the story of several women who are united by their suffering: the Korean revolutionary Yu Guan Soon, Joan of Arc, Cha's mother, Demeter and Persephone, Hyung Soon Huo (a Korean born in Manchuria to first-generation Korean exiles), and Cha herself. The poet mixes writing styles (journal entries, allegorical stories, dreams), voices, and kinds of information, evidently as a metaphor of the dislocation of exile, the fragmentation of memory. Her text moves from verse to prose, from images to words, from history to fiction. Throughout her poem, Cha foregrounds the process of writing, its difficulties and revisions, its struggle to make sentences cohere, hence the broken sentences and Gertrude Steinian repetitions in the extract I have cited—"Point by point. Up to date. Updated"—the endless full stops, suggesting extreme cleavage, as in "Inside. Outside. / Glass. Drape. Lace. Curtain. Blinds. Gauze." The search for identity, for personhood, is continually subverted. Opaque glass, veil, screen, blind, curtain, shade—these are Cha's dominant images of oppression and occlusion.

In this context, French phrases, learned dutifully in school, are presented as welling up from the poet's subconscious. On the page prior to the extract above, a long passage begins with the lines *Qu'est ce qu'on a vu / Cette vue qu'est ce qu'on a vu / enfin. Vu E. Cette vue. Qu'est ce que c'est enfin* ("What have we seen? What is the seen that we have finally seen. Seen And. This thing seen. What is it finally?"). The "childish" French takes on a manic air as the sentence is broken apart and repeated for some ten lines. And as memories of school prayers and lessons intrude on the poet's fevered thoughts, the "veil" becomes *Voile. Voile de mariée. Voile de religieuse.* The wish to shed the veil is also put in French—*ala derobee* (correctly spelled *à la derobée*)—just as the need to suppress one's voice introduces the Italian stage direction *voce velata* ("veiled voice").

But where is Cha's native language, Korean? The cited passage does not contain a single transliterated Korean word, not a single ideogram or overtly Asian reference. The distant past of the poet's childhood, the difficult movements of her family from place to place during the Korean War—these are very much the referents of *Dictee*'s narrative and imagery, but the Korean language functions as absence in the life of a woman dutifully bound to English, with schoolgirl memories of textbook French. It is thus the English language that becomes the problem, the English language that must be fragmented, broken, deconstructed, reconstructed, and so on. The title *Dictee* (Dictation) refers to the indoctrination through language the immigrant must undergo. But *Dikte* is also the name of a Cretan goddess "whom Minos pursued for nine months until, about to be overtaken, she hurled herself from a cliff into the sea."[28] A victim, it seems, like the young girl who dutifully writes her *dictée*.

So much for Theresa Hak Kyung Cha's conscious devices. But surely there is another reason Cha avoids Korean. Polyglossia remains a noble ideal, but had Cha introduced sizable segments of Korean into her poem, she would be unlikely to command the readership she now has. French and Spanish: these still have a recognition quotient, and Brathwaite's Jamaican dialect can be sounded out and comprehended by any English speaker. But a multilingual poetry that would include Korean? Or for that matter, Chinese, Japanese, Vietnamese, Arabic? Or again, Portuguese? Hungarian?

The conundrum posed by *Dictee* is thus a conundrum Jolas could not quite anticipate. For the paradox of the contemporary situation is that the new version of multilingualism—and many poets are now following the example of Brathwaite[29]—far from supporting the internationalism that animated Jolas's poetry as well as the work collected in *transition,* has been prompted by precisely the opposite motive, a motive that is unabashedly nationalist, ethnicist, nativist. When the poet Brathwaite, who had been baptized Lawson Edward, became Kamau in middle life, he turned to the "nation language" of West Indian culture so as to provide a more accurate representation of a people largely erased by history. His interjections of dialect, street slang, folk rhythms, Rastafari, African myth, legend, and geographical markers are quite openly motivated by the desire to put the Caribbean experience on the map of modern poetry and fiction. In the same vein, Alfred Arteaga uses Spanish and its Chicano dialects to foreground a particular ethnic experience. And Theresa Hak Kyung Cha writes from the positionality of the displaced Korean American woman who cannot quite locate herself in the U.S. culture of her time. Indeed, Cha's shifts from English to French have nothing to do with any sort of tribute to the French language or French culture; on the contrary, the French phrases and idioms signal the deadness of a learned language that is not the poet's own. As for the language and culture she cares about—Korean—it can provide subject matter for narrative, myth, and pictorial image, but cannot function in its own right.

Jolas's polyglossia, designed to bring together diverse peoples, to erase borders between the European nations, to produce a large cosmopolitan and international consciousness—*E Pluribus Unum*—has thus been radically inverted. Not the melting pot, one of Jolas's favorite images, but the particular values of a particular underrepresented culture. Not the erasure *of* borders, but the focus *on* borders; not internationalism, but national and ethnic awareness: this is the realm of *mots-frontiere* that has replaced Jolas's dream of a "new language," his "super-tongue for intercontinental expression." Indeed, "intercontinental" is now a word used sparingly, and when it is, as in the case of those ICBMs with which we threaten weaker enemy nations, the vision is far from Utopian.

In 1998 the Beckett scholar Lois Oppenheim asked me to write an essay for her forthcoming collection Samuel Beckett and the Arts. *This was a tantalizing prospect: both the visual arts and music are central to Beckett's work. But I chose to explore another arena—the radio plays—to see how they differ from Beckettian theatre. My contribution was a study of* Embers. *Then in 2003 when Ruben Gallo at Princeton invited me to a conference specifically on radio, I wrote a paper on the more problematic radio piece* Words and Music, *for which Morton Feldman wrote the score. The essay below brings the two radio studies together.*

6

"The Silence that is not Silence"

Acoustic Art in Samuel Beckett's Radio Plays

> The primary purpose of radio is to convey information from one place to another through the intervening media (i.e., air space, nonconducting materials) without wires.
>
> *New Columbia Encyclopedia*

> Thesis: The phonograph emphasizes the self in the lack of subject. This machine bears a paradox: it identifies a voice, fixes the deceased (or mortal) person, registers the dead and thus perpetuates his living testimony, but also achieves his automatic reproduction *in absentia:* my self would live *without me*—horror of horrors!
>
> Charles Grivel, "The Phonograph's Horned Mouth"

The Samuel Beckett who began to write radio plays in the mid-fifties was no stranger to the medium: in Roussillon, where he lived in hiding from 1942 to 1945, the radio transmitter was *the* crucial information conduit for Resistance groups, and the BBC, which was to commission the radio plays, was its main source.[1] Half a century later, as the *New Columbia Encyclopedia* reminds us, radio is still primarily an information medium, a conductor of *messages,* whether news flashes, announcements of events, weather reports, and today the ubiquitous "sigalerts" that advise the driver about freeway conditions and traffic accidents even as they are taking place.

All the more reason, then, for the radio artist—and Beckett is surely one of the finest—to turn this information function, this relaying of messages from A to B, inside out. "Communication," writes Michel Serres, "is only possible between two persons used to the same forms, trained to code and decode a meaning by using the same key."[2] But communication is never without disruption: "in spoken languages: stammerings, mispronunciations, regional accents, dysphonias, and cacophonies. . . . In the technical means of communication: background noise, jamming, static, cut-offs, heteresis, various interruptions. If static is accidental, background noise is *essential* to communication" ("Platonic Dialogue" 66). "To communicate orally" is thus "to lose meaning in noise." Only at the level of mathematical abstraction, when form (e.g., the symbol x or the addition sign +) is distinguished from its empirical realizations, is dialogue entirely "successful." But "to exclude the empirical is to exclude differentiation, the plurality of others that mask the same" (9), and it is those "others"—the interference and noise that everywhere blocks the straightforward A > B model of transmission—that really matter in the communication paradigms that we actually use. "The transmission of communication," writes Serres, "is chronic transformation. . . . the empirical is strictly essential and accidental *noise*" (70).

The notion of "noise" as "the empirical portion of the message" is by no means confined to radio, but we see it heightened in this medium where everything depends upon sound, primarily the sound of the human voice as communicator. Martin Esslin, who worked closely with Beckett on his BBC productions and has written extensively on the radio plays, argues that "radio is an intensely visual medium. . . . Information that reaches [the listener] through other senses is instantly converted into visual terms. And aural experiences, which include the immense richness of language as well as musical and natural sound, are the most effective means of triggering visual images."[3] This may be true of the more mimetic variants of radio drama—Beckett's first radio play, *All That Fall*, is a case in point—but what happens when, as Klaus Schöning points out in a discussion of the new acoustic art, words are combined with "nontextual language, nonverbal articulations, quotation, original sound [i.e., ambient sound], environmental noises, acoustic *objets trouvés*, musical tones, [and] electronic technology"?[4] What do we visualize then?

Beckett's radio experiments did not, of course, go as far as, say, John Cage's *Roaratorio* (one of Schöning's key exhibits) in undermining the conventional linguistic base, but the dramatist was surely aware that if the transmission of information is one pole of the radio experience, soundscape is the other. Indeed, as Don Druker puts it in a discussion of radio, "it is necessary to consider *sound itself* as the raw material for analysis."[5] One must, for that matter, listen to radio more intensively than one does in the theater, where there is always something to *look at* as well. On the other hand, radio text also differs appreciably from the print media. When reading, one has the luxury of stopping to reconsider this or that point on a previous page, or one skims a given passage and moves ahead. Radio is much more coercively temporal; the sounds succeed one another, and the listener is challenged to take them in, one by one, and construct their relationships. Even when, as is usually the case, the radio piece is heard on tape or compact disc, so that one is free to fast forward and reverse, the listener remains deprived of the visual stimulus taken for granted by the theater or visual audience.

Even more important: because radio is essentially an information medium with what appears to be a linear structure, the listener feels compelled to pay close attention with the expectation of "finding out" something. But what does Beckett's radio audience find out? Here the theme of disembodiment put forward in my second epigraph becomes important. If radio (or the phonograph) has the capacity to bring *voice* into someone else's public or private space, the disembodiment of that voice, Beckett was quite aware, is a signifier of *absence,* of not being there, indeed of "death." Then, too, voice alone—or at least voice between puberty and extreme old age or serious illness—cannot define its owner's stage of life or status as can the visual image of a human body.

As a dramatic medium, radio is at its best when it takes this indeterminacy and absence into account. After *All That Fall,* whose characters are still represented as "real" people in a "real" Irish country setting, Beckett's radio art becomes more abstract and mediumistic, engaging in a dialectic of disclosure and obstacle, information and noise, in which the soundscape—which includes silence—provides conflicting, and hence tantalizing, testimony. In what follows I want to consider how this dialectic works in two Beckett radio plays—plays thematically related but raising different formal and technical issues. The first is *Embers,* written for the BBC and first broadcast in June 1959; the second, *Words and Music,* broadcast in November 1962.[6]

"No Sound"

Beckett commentators generally speak of *Embers* as a "skullscape" or "soulscape."[7] "The universe which the radio audience is confronted with," declared Clas Zilliacus in the first extended discussion of the piece, "is a totally subjective one: it is one man's world. The interplay between Henry and other characters takes place in Henry's mind" (*Beckett and Broadcasting* 82). The same point is made by Martin Esslin:

> The background—a background of sound, the sea, Henry's boots on the shingle—is still real, but the voices are all internal: Henry's internal monologue as he tries unsuccessfully to conjure up his dead father's presence, and later the voices of his wife and daughter and her instructors, which materialize in his memory. (Gontarski, *On Beckett* 368)

And in a survey of Beckett's radio and television plays for the recent *Cambridge Companion to Beckett*, Jonathan Kalb remarks that "*Embers* has no surface narrative other than that of a haunted man talking about talking to himself, telling stories that he never finishes, and sometimes experiencing (along with us) the ghostly people and things in his story." Kalb gives the following précis:

> Henry, who may or may not be walking by the sea with his daughter Addie nearby, addresses his dead father, who may or may not have committed suicide in the sea. The father fails to respond . . . and Henry tells a story about a man named Bolton (perhaps a father-surrogate) who has called for his doctor Holloway one winter night, for obscure reasons that may have to do with wanting to die. Henry then speaks to a woman, also apparently dead, named Ada, his former companion and mother of Addie, who speaks sympathetically but distractedly back to him. For most of the remainder of the action Ada and Henry reminisce about old times, some of which are dramatized as auditory flashbacks involving other characters. Henry complains several times of not being able to rid himself of the sound of the sea, and Ada suggests that he consult Holloway about both that and his incessant talking to himself. When Ada no longer answers him, Henry tries unsuccessfully to command the sound effects again, returns briefly to the Bolton story and then ends by seeming to make a note in his diary: "Nothing all day nothing." ("Mediated Quixote" 129–30)

This account of *Embers* as memory play taking place inside Henry's mind is accurate enough in its broad outlines,[8] but it seems to ignore the use of radio as medium, even though Beckett himself, in a much cited statement about his first radio play, *All That Fall*, insisted that the distinction between media had to be honored:

All That Fall is a specifically radio play, or rather radio text, for voices, not bodies. I have already refused to have it "staged" and I cannot think of it in such terms. A perfectly straight reading before an audience seems to me just barely legitimate, though even on this score I have my doubts. But I am absolutely opposed to any form of adaptation with a view to its conversion into "theatre." It is no more theatre than *End-Game* is radio and to "act" it is to kill it. Even the reduced visual dimension it will receive from the simplest and most static of readings . . . will be destructive of whatever quality it may have and which depends on the whole thing's *coming out of the dark.*[9]

"To 'act' it is to kill it": "radio text," Beckett here reminds us, is par excellence an art that depends on sound alone and hence cannot be converted to the stage. Furthermore, the sound in question is not just that of the human voice but also includes a complex network of nonverbal elements, musical or otherwise. It makes little sense, then, to complain, as does John Pilling, that Beckett should have included the voice of Henry's father, along with Ada's and Addie's voices, in the play:

> The puzzling thing is that Henry's control over voices does not extend to the most crucial figure of all, his father. . . . The failure to incorporate into the physical existence of the play its most important figure is not so much a failure of conception—though it might have served to link Henry's life to his story of Bolton—as of tact. There seems to be no good reason for the omission.[10]

But there is a very good reason for the omission, which is that, unlike the theater, radio makes it possible to represent characters by means of metonymic sound images: The ghost of Henry's father is indeed "heard" throughout the play—not only when his son acts the role of medium, imitating such parental exhortations as "Are you coming for a dip?" but also in the recurrent "Please! PLEASE!" that Bolton addresses to Holloway, and, most important, in the voice of the sea itself.[11] Indeed, Henry's is not quite an interior monologue like Malone's or the Unnamable's, for it moves easily in and out of the narrator's specific consciousness and depends heavily on the elaborate patterning of phrasal, verbal, and phonemic repetition.

Henry's first halting words in *Embers* are "On," "Stop," and "Down," each one spoken twice, the second time more emphatically, as the exclamation points indicate.[12] The predominant vowel sound is a long open "o" competing with the sound of the sea: "[*Sea, still faint, audible throughout what follows whenever pause indicated.*]" The "o" sound now modulates into the longer unit "Who is beside me now?" and after the response "[*Pause.*] An old man, blind and foolish. [*Pause.*] My father, back from the dead, to be with me. [*Pause.*] As if he hadn't died. [*Pause.*]," we hear the words, "No, he doesn't answer me." "No," which will soon become one of the key words in the Bolton narrative "no, hangings," "no light," "no, standing," "no sound"; and then the variant "not a sound" (which will be Henry's final words in the play), is of course a reversal of the opening "On." From "On" to "No": this is the trajectory of Henry's speech, his Omega (note that both "Bolton" and "Holloway" contain long "o's" as well) in conflict with the Alpha of his wife's name, "Ada," and the diminutive of Ada in the child's name "Addie." The narrator, Henry, for that matter, whose family name we never know, is caught phonemically between Alpha and Omega, so to speak. When one hears Ada speak lines like "Laugh, Henry do that for me" (97), the /e/ and /I/ phonemes stand out as distinct from the other names.

But it is not quite accurate to say, as Pilling does, that Henry has "control" over the voices in the play. For the dominant voice is not Henry's but the voice of the sea. It is that voice that punctuates each of Henry's questions about his father—"Can he hear me? [*Pause.*] Yes, he must hear me. [*Pause.*] To answer me [*Pause.*] No, he doesn't answer me [*Pause.*] Just be with me"—and that is presented as a character in its own right in the following strange speech:

> That sound you hear is the sea. [*Pause. Louder.*] I say that sound you hear is the sea, we are sitting on the strand. [*Pause.*] I mention it because the sound is so strange, so unlike the sound of the sea, that if you didn't see what it was you wouldn't know what it was. [*Pause.*] (93)

The "you" here can be taken to be the dead father, with whom Henry is sitting on the strand. But if so, it makes little sense, since, as we soon learn, the father lived at the sea's edge all his life and presumably would know how the sea sounds. Henry's information thus functions ironically, or even metalinguistically: on the one hand, it shows the narrator having a brief moment of power over the father, whose death haunts him; on the other, we can read the speech as an aside to the audience, especially in connection with the next sentence: "if you didn't see what it was you wouldn't know what it was"—an absurd statement given that of course the radio audience cannot "see" the "sea" (note the pun); nor can it, as Henry puts it a few lines further, "Listen to the light."

Such self-consciousness about the use of the medium and the constructed-

ness of the narrative is the "noise" Beckett introduces into the channel. We
are warned that the sea sound effects are not accurate and are exhorted to
"listen to the light." The "story" is thus immediately established as unreal in
the sense of unverifiable. If *Embers* were staged or televised, the seashore
setting would be so designated, whether more or less abstractly. But when
sound is our only guide and the narrator tells us that the sound we hear is
"unlike the sound of the sea," we cannot be sure where we are. It follows that
we cannot be wholly involved in Henry's private mental drama. The sea,
we are told a little bit further along, is the scene of his father's probable suicide, "the evening bathe you took once too often." But the next sentence
tells us that "We never found your body, you know, that held up probate an
unconscionable time, they said there was nothing to prove you hadn't run
away from us all and alive and well under a false name in the Argentine for
example, that grieved mother greatly. [*Pause.*]" (94). Indeed, Henry's obses-
sion is not with the sea as such but only with its *sound,* which he cannot
escape, even when he tries to "drown it out" by telling himself endless stories.
"I often went to Switzerland to get away from the cursed thing," he recalls,
"and never stopped all the time I was there" (94).

Ada cannot understand why Henry finds the sea's sound so oppressive.
"It's only on the surface, you know," she tells Henry, as if this would comfort
him. "Underneath all is as quiet as a grave. Not a sound. All day, all night,
not a sound. [*Pause.*]" And when Henry explains that he now walks around
with a gramophone so as to drown out the sea, Ada responds common-
sensically, "There is no sense in that. [*Pause.*] There is no sense in trying to
drown it" (101). Again, the ironies here are multiple. The silence of the sea
below the surface, "quiet as a grave," cannot comfort Henry, who knows that
the sea *is* a grave—his father's. And the use of gramophone or voice or rival
sounds to "drown it" has no chance against the sea's own drowning power—
power brought home to the listener by every sea-sound-filled pause. Yet, as
Henry says, "It's not so bad when you get out on it" (101). Again, an ambiguous wish: it might not be so bad to "get out on it," because one would no
longer be alive to feel the pain it evokes.

No sooner have the acoustics of water been established than Beckett introduces its opposite, fire, and the outdoors gives way to the indoors, as
Henry tells the story—a story "never finished . . . I never finished anything,
everything always went on for ever"—of "an old fellow called Bolton." It begins as follows:

Bolton [*Pause. Louder.*] Bolton! [*Pause.*] There before the fire. [*Pause.*]
Before the fire with all the shutters . . . no, hangings, hangings, all the
hangings drawn and the light, no light, only the light of the fire, sitting

there in the . . . no, standing, standing, there on the hearth-rug in the dark before the fire in his old red dressing-gown and no sound in the house of any kind, only the sound of the fire. [*Pause.*] Standing there in his old red dressing-gown might go on fire any minute like when he was a child, no, that was his pyjamas, standing there waiting in the dark, no light, only the light of the fire, and no sound of any kind, only the fire, an old man in great trouble. [*Pause.*] (95, ellipses are Beckett's)

The dominant feature here is the degree of verbal and phrasal repetition: the word "fire" appears eight times in combination with "light" and "sound," "only" and "no," as in "no light, only the light of the fire," "no sound of any kind, only the fire," and punctuated by the use of "no" as correction: "all the shutters . . . no, hangings," "sitting there in the . . . no, standing," "old red dressing-gown . . . no, that was his pyjamas." And "pause" also acts as a kind of "correction," for each pause is filled with the sea voice so that "no sound," and "not a sound" are not accurate descriptors.

Beckett's dense network of repetition places a curious burden on the sparsely used visual images in the passage. So abstract is the vocabulary that when we are suddenly introduced to the figure "on the hearth-rug in the dark before the fire in his old red dressing-gown," we hang on to the bright color image as a kind of signpost in the midst of shadow. Red is also the color of the fire, and then the embers—and phonemically both "red" and "embers" chime with "Henry," who is not overtly present at the scene in question.

But the power of visualization, activated momentarily in Henry's mono-logue, is repeatedly countered by rhythm, in this case the broken phrasal rhythm of "white world, great trouble, not a sound, only the embers, sound of dying, dying glow, Holloway, Bolton, Bolton, Holloway, old men, great trouble, white world, not a sound" (95). The sound structure here, as in many of Beckett's later works, is phrasal and linear, with two primary stresses per line:[13]

whíte wórld
greát troúble
nót a soúnd
ónly the émbers
soúnd of dýing
dýing glów

followed by the chiastic line, "Hóllowày, Bólton | | Bólton, Hóllowày," and then the same refrain with the lines in slightly different order:

óld mén
gréat troúble
whíte wórld
nót a soúnd

The effect of these elaborately stylized schema is again to occlude the information channel with noise. The message from sender to receiver, which radio, practically speaking, is designed to foreground, becomes progressively less well understood.

For what is the Bolton story about, and how does it relate to the death by suicide of Henry's father? John Pilling has complained that *Embers* "has a structural slackness deriving from the two main topics [the father-son plot and the Bolton-Holloway plot] failing to blend" (*Samuel Beckett* 98); Bolton, Pilling posits, is "simply an image in the imagination" (100), a reading that accords with Zilliacus's supposition that Bolton is somehow Henry's alter ego,[14] or with Donald Wicher's that he is "the fictive projection of the self."[15] But such thematic readings slight the piece's use of sound and silence, speech and pause. Just as outside there is no way of "drowning" the sound of the sea, inside the only sound is the sound of the fire and then its embers. However often Henry tells himself that there is "not a sound," whether on the shingle along the beach or in Bolton's sitting room, in both cases sound is steady and unstoppable.

The only way of interrupting the continuity of water and fire sounds, it seems, is to introduce another sound, one that is finite (and hence controllable) rather than continuous. Thus Henry summons "Hooves!" in the opening sequence, and although the hooves "*die rapidly away,*" he longs for a regular metrical rhythm, a beat that could "mark time. . . . a ten-ton mammoth back from the dead, shoe it with steel and have it tramp the world down! Listen to it!" (*Embers* 93). The parallel in the Bolton story is the drip:

> Holloway, Bolton, Bolton, Holloway, old men, great trouble, white world, not a sound. [*Pause.*] Listen to it! [*Pause.*] Close your eyes and listen to it, what would you think it was? [*Pause. Vehement.*] A drip! A drip! [*Sound of drip, rapidly amplified, suddenly cut off.*] Again! [*Drip again. Amplification begins.*] No! [*Drip cut off.*] Father! [*Pause. Agitated.*] Stories, stories, years and years of stories. . . . (95)

Again we have the exhortation "Listen to it!" and the auditory image of a sound that, unlike the sound of the ocean, which is present here again in the repeated pauses, can be identified, timed for frequency, and stopped. It is when the drip is finally "cut off" that Henry, supposedly telling a story unconnected to his family drama, cries out "Father!" So much for the unrelatedness of the two narratives.

Indeed, the verbal, imagistic, and acoustic symbiosis of the two "plots" is worked out with musical precision: they cross in the central sequence of the play, which is Henry's dialogue with Ada, and by extension, with Addie. Jonathan Kalb, in the comment cited above, says Henry and Ada "reminisce about old times," but this hardly gives the reader a sense of the hopelessness and futility that characterizes their exchanges or the epiphany toward which their desultory conversation moves.

Ada's vocal entrance follows the snatch of dialogue with Addie, whose presence, as Henry recalls it, evidently interfered with his need to "talk," to tell himself stories. Walking in the fields and holding his child's hand in what sounds like a parodic version of such Wordsworth poems as "We Are Seven," Henry says, "Run along now, Addie, and look at the lambs." But when she says "No papa," he turns "*Violent*": "Go on with you when you're told and look at the lambs!" which triggers Addie's "*loud wail*" (96). Addie's world, a pastoral world of fields, lambs, and the child Jesus, is one the sea-dweller Henry cannot abide. And it is in this context that Ada is remembered:

Ada, too, conversation with her, that was something, that's what hell will be like, small chat to the babbling of Lethe about the good old days when we wished we were dead. [*Pause.*] Price of margarine fifty years ago. [*Pause.*] And now. [*Pause. With solemn indignation.*] Price of blueband now! [*Pause.*] Father! [*Pause.*]

Another water sound—the "small chat to the babbling of Lethe"—that despite its promise to help the narrator forget, cannot counter the ongoing sound of the sea. Ada and Addie live in the mundane, everyday world where the price of margarine, or blueband, is the topic of discussion—a world that was, for a short time, Henry's own, as his rhyme "Daddy! Addie" (100) suggests. All the odder, then, that when Ada makes her entrance, there is for once no sound, and further "[*No sound as she sits.*]" For the radio listener, she is simply there; she may indeed have been there all along.

The Henry-Ada sequence is not simply flashback, for there are many time periods covered: their first lovemaking in the "hole," "Where we did it at last for the first time" (101); a moment long ago (is that the same moment?) when, as Ada recalls, "It was rough, the spray came flying over us. [*Pause.*] Strange it should have been rough then. [*Pause.*] And calm now" (98); Henry and Ada's parental dealings with their young daughter, who takes music and riding lessons; a somewhat older Ada given to nagging—"Did you put on your jaegers, Henry?" (97); "Don't wet your good boots" (99)—and then to warning Henry that "You will be quite alone with your voice, there will be no other voice in the world but yours" (102). And finally what is evidently the present moment in which Henry tells Ada, "I was trying to be with my father," and she says sardonically, "No difficulty about that." To which Henry responds, "I mean I was trying to get him to be with me. [*Pause.*] You seem a little cruder than usual today, Ada" (102).

But so fluid are the shifts from one time frame to another that there is no use in trying to establish a meaningful temporal sequence. When Henry says, in what seems to be the present, "let us get up and go," Ada responds, "Go? Where? And Addie? She would be very distressed if she came and found you had gone without her" (98). But when, a few minutes later, Henry asks Ada, "What age is [Addie] now?" it is Ada who demurs, "I have lost count of time" (101). When Henry counters, "Twelve? Thirteen? [*Pause.*] Fourteen?" the audience is even more confused, for Henry and Ada seem to be talking of a time in the distant past. Moreover, the one specific time signal given throws us off even further:

ADA: [*Twenty years earlier, imploring.*] Don't! Don't!
HENRY: [*Ditto, urgent.*] Darling!
ADA: [*Ditto, more feebly.*] Don't!
HENRY: [*Ditto, exultantly*]. Darling! (100)

If this prototypical "young love" scene took place twenty years before the present of the play, how could Addie now be twelve or thirteen? Beckett everywhere underscores the foolishness of such questions. And the radio medium makes it possible to shift ground at a moment's notice and to collapse time. Past and present are often indistinguishable, even as sound distinctions are rigidly maintained: sea-sound versus "hooves" in the first sequence, "drip" in the second, and finally the dashing together of stones in the third. When Ada insists that "there's nothing wrong with it [the sound of the sea], it's a lovely peaceful gentle soothing sound," Henry goes wild:

Thuds, I want thuds! Like this! [*He fumbles in the shingle, catches up two big stones and starts dashing them together.*] Stone! [*Clash.*] Stone! [*Clash. 'Stone!' and clash amplified, cut off. Pause. He throws one stone away. Sound of its fall.*] That's life. [*He throws the other stone away. Sound of its fall.*] Not this . . . [*Pause.*] . . . sucking!" (100, ellipses Beckett's)

The sound of stone falling *stops*, whereas the sea's "sucking" continues. "Sucking," with its harsh spirant and voiceless stop, now extracts Ada's monologue, which is, from the point of view of plot, the key to the play, providing as it does the crucial information Henry has sought all along.

The climactic scene in question begins with Henry's challenge: "I can't remember if he [Father] met you," and Ada's immediate reply, "You know he met me" (102). Henry demurs: "No, Ada, I don't know, I'm sorry. I have forgotten almost everything connected with you." Now comes the following dialogue:

ADA: You weren't there. Just your mother and sister. I had called to fetch you, as arranged. We were to go bathing together. [*Pause.*]
HENRY: [*Irritably.*] Drive on, drive on! Why do people always stop in the middle of what they are saying?
ADA: None of them knew where you were. Your bed had not been slept in. They were all shouting at one another. Your sister said she would throw herself off the cliff. Your father got up and went out, slamming the door. I left soon afterwards and passed him on the road. He did not see me. He was sitting on a rock looking out to sea. I never forgot his posture. And yet it was a common one. You used to have it sometimes. Perhaps just the stillness, as if he had been turned to stone. I could never make it out. [*Pause.*]
HENRY: Keep on! keep on! [*Imploringly.*] Keep it going, Ada, every syllable is a second gained. (102)

Ada cannot remember anything else, but she insists that "there are attitudes remain in one's mind for reasons that are clear" (103) and that she cannot forget "the great stillness of the whole body, as if all the breath had left it" (103). It remains for Henry to finish Ada's story for her: she sees, or so Henry imagines it, the old man sitting on the rock but keeps on toward the tram stop, gets on the next tram into town, but feels "uneasy" and gets off again. She retraces her steps: "Very unhappy and uneasy, hangs round a bit, not a soul about, cold wind coming in off sea, goes back down path and takes tram home" (103).

The critics have made very little of this whole sequence. "When Ada leaves Henry's mind," writes Cohn, "he tries to weave a story about her encounter with his father, but Ada 'takes tram home,' and Henry drops her" (*Just Play* 84). But then why is this the only moment in the play when Henry urges Ada to "drive on!" and "keep on!"? That "Every syllable is a second gained"? Note that for the first time it is revealed that Ada was the last person to have seen Henry's father alive. It is she who witnessed the scene at Henry's house when "they were all shouting at one another. Your sister said she would throw herself off the cliff." She who knows that Henry's "bed had not been slept in." And it is after the scene she witnesses—"your father got up and went out, slamming the door"—that she sees his figure "turned to stone" on the rock overlooking the sea. There is something so wrong with this picture that, having boarded her tram home, she gets off again and returns to the scene of the crime. But now there is "not a soul about."

This is the "message" Ada relays to Henry, but what does it mean? Evidently father and son have had a quarrel—"Your bed had not been slept in"—evidently something terrible has happened, but what? What would make the sister threaten to throw herself off a cliff? Why is everyone shouting? Why does the father go out, slamming the door? What drives him to drown himself? Why is the body, in a detail perfectly suited to radio, "never found"? Henry evidently knows some or all of these things, which is why he cannot drown out the voice of the sea. When Ada retells her tale, a tale she herself doesn't understand, his sense of guilt reaches fever pitch. If Ada could only remember more! "Every syllable is a second gained."

The Bolton story, far from being unrelated, provides the clue. Bolton has summoned Dr. Holloway, an old family friend, to help him in some desperate venture. Holloway finally offers to give his old friend a shot, but Bolton wants something else that Holloway won't give him: "We've had this before, Bolton, don't ask me to go through it again" (104). Does Bolton want Holloway to perform euthanasia? Or perhaps, given Ada's reference to Henry's sister's threat, an abortion? Or some other act of mercy? There is no way of knowing what Bolton's "Please! PLEASE!" refers to except that it is evidently something Holloway might dispense from his little black bag. The turning point, in any case, comes after the third "Please, Holloway!":

> Candle shaking and guttering all over the place, lower now, old arm tired, takes it in the other hand and holds it high again, that's it, that was always it, night, and the embers cold, and the glim shaking in your old fist, saying, "Please! Please! [*Pause.*] Begging. [*Pause.*] Of the poor. [*Pause.*] Ada! [*Pause.*] Father! [*Pause.*] Christ! [*Pause.*] (*Embers* 104)

"*Your* old fist": with the sudden and startling shift from third to second person, the text suddenly opens up. For who is Bolton but the father now immediately invoked in the sequence "Ada!" "Father!" "Christ!" each appellation punctuated by a pause bearing the sound of the sea? Far from being a projection of Henry's imagination, or Henry's alter ego, Bolton stands in for the father, who, having failed in his unspecified and final plea to Holloway ("Please! PLEASE!"), takes his own life. And it is Henry who, for reasons never made wholly clear, cannot stop feeling he is to blame. No removal to Switzerland, no memories of "normal" family life, no retelling of Ada's uncomprehending story of what happened the fatal day of his father's death, no invocation of horses hooves' marking time, of water dripping, of stones struck together with a loud grinding sound, can drown out the sea's endless sounding.

What is perhaps the key word linking the two narratives in *Embers* is the word "washout," which appears in Henry's opening monologue. He has just gone over the Bolton-Holloway story for the first time and has recounted Holloway's refusal to do what Bolton wants: "ghastly scene, wishes to God he hadn't come, no good, fire out, bitter cold, great trouble, white world, not a sound, no good. [*Pause.*]" At this point, "No good" is repeated, now referring back to Henry himself:

> No good. [*Pause.*] Can't do it. [*Pause.*] Listen to it! [*Pause.*] Father! [*Pause.*] You wouldn't know me now, you'd be sorry you ever had me, but you were that already a washout that's the last I heard from you, a washout. [*Pause. Imitating father's voice.*] "Are you coming for a dip?" "No." "Come on, come on." "No." Glare, stump to door, turn, glare. "A washout that's all you are, a washout!" [*Violent slam of door. Pause.*] Again! [*Slam. Pause.*] Slam life shut like that! [*Pause.*] Washout. [*Pause.*] Wish to Christ she had. (96)

The terrible irony here is that if Henry is figuratively a "washout," his father is literally one. But "washout" also refers to Henry's own death wish, his wish never to have been born coupled with his wish that he himself had never become Addie's father: "horrid little creature, wish to God we'd never had her" (96). An important intertext here is Beckett's late prose composition *Company,* specifically the following childhood memory:

> You stand at the tip of the high board. High above the sea. In it your father's upturned face. Upturned to you. You look down to the loved trusted face. He calls you to jump. He calls, be a brave boy. The red round face. The thick moustache. The greying hair. The swell sways it under and sways it up again. The far call again. Be a brave boy. Many eyes upon you. From the water and from the bathing place.[16]

The reference here, as James Knowlson notes in his biography, is to the "famous deep 'Gentlemen Only' Forty-Foot" into which Bill Beckett, a superb swimmer, enjoyed diving from the high rocks at Sandycove when his son Sam was small (*Damned to Fame* 32). In *Beckett Writing Beckett*, H. Porter Abbott rightly points out that the scene in question is of "an action that does not take place—no jump occurs":

> Nor, and this is equally important, is it the record of a refusal to jump (nothing in the scene indicates such a construction either). It is the not-taking-place of a following a father's command. It is the not-taking-on of an identity ("*Be* a brave boy"). It is the nonoccurrence of a baptism of total immersion with a father before the witness of many ("Many eyes upon you").[17]

For Abbott it is thus an example of Beckett's characteristic "Unwriting [of] The Father" (11), his intentional "sealing" of central autobiographical moments—his own Wordsworthian "spots of time"—"from meaningful, sequential narrative connection with any of the other spots in *Company*" (17).

Abbott convincingly separates Beckett's "autography" from full-fledged autobiography on the one hand, fiction on the other. *Company,* one might add, works more like a lyric poem than any kind of narrative, and the diving incident cited above is best understood in relation to another scene just a few pages earlier in the text, in which the author's father sets off on a mountain hike so as to avoid "the pains and general unpleasantness of [his wife's] labour and delivery," the delivery being Beckett's own. The father's urge is to get away: "Hence the sandwiches which he relished at noon looking out to sea from the lee of a great rock on the first summit scaled" (*Company* 13). The father who absents himself for the moment of his son's birth is not unlike the father of *Embers,* whose posture on a similar rock above the sea provides the death motif. And the son who cannot respond properly to the loved father's request to "Be a brave boy" and to "jump" is forever a "washout."

Knowlson records how devastated the twenty-seven-year-old Beckett was when his father died in 1933. It happened during the worst period of Beckett's life—the inability to leave home or to find a viable form of writing, the heavy drinking, the terrible fights with his mother. But his father, who made few demands on his son, was "a great source of strength to him" (*Damned to Fame* 164). As Beckett wrote to his friend Tom MacGreevy:

> Lovely walk this morning with Father, who grows old with a very graceful philosophy. Comparing bees and butterflies to elephants and parrots and speaking of indentures with the Leveller! Barging through hedges and over the walls with the help of my shoulder, blaspheming

and stopping to rest under colour of admiring the view. I'll never have anyone like him. (cited in *Damned to Fame* 165)

It was just a few months later that Bill Beckett collapsed with a heart attack: within a week he was dead. "I can't write about him," Beckett wrote MacGreevy, "I can only walk the fields and climb the ditches after him" (166), and more than fifty years later he told his biographer: "After my father's death I had trouble psychologically. The bad years were between when I had to crawl home in 1932 and after my father's death in 1933. I'll tell you how it was. I was walking down Dawson Street. And I felt I couldn't go on. It was a strange experience I can't really describe. I found I couldn't go on moving" (167).

The acute sense of guilt that produced this paralysis is not surprising when we consider that at the time of his death Beckett *père* could not know that his son would ever emerge from the bad phase he was in, a phase that gave his mother so much pain. And it is the son's guilt about this situation that is the subject of *Embers*. The sea-sound is forever linked to the dying embers, white world, and "no sound" that greets Bolton's "Please! PLEASE!" Beckett has written a searing play about what Dante called the "great refusal."

Information, Please

The question remains: what did Beckett gain by presenting this autobiographical drama of filial guilt as a *radio* play? If, as we have seen, *Embers* is closely allied to such of Beckett's later fictions as *Company,* which shares many of its actual images and incidents (and a similar case could be made for *Krapp's Last Tape* and *The Unnamable,* both of them written just a few years before *Embers*), why was Beckett so adamant in refusing to let his plays "for voices, not bodies," be staged or so much as read in front of a live audience? Why his insistence that "to 'act' it is to kill it"?

The answer cannot be that radio gave Beckett the best possible vehicle for "skullscape" or "soulscape," for certainly *Company* and *Krapp's Last Tape* are soulscapes too. Nor is it enough to say, as Beckett does of his radio plays, that the "whole thing com[es] out of the dark." Rather, I would like to suggest that the "radio-activity" of *Embers,* as of *Words and Music, Cascando,* and *Rough for Radio I* and *II* that followed in its wake, is that its sounding of disembodied voices makes it the perfect vehicle for the dance of death that is its subject. The dialectic of sea-sound/no sound, within which the sound of hooves, of a water drip, of stones grinding against one another cannot "drown" the continuity of the sea without and the fire within, is the vocal equivalent of a world in which all the characters—Ada, Addie, Henry's father, Bolton, Holloway, and Henry himself—are revenants, ghostly presences. When Ada tells Henry he "ought to see Holloway," she adds, "he's alive still, isn't he?" (*Embers* 100). But alive at which of the many discrepant times presented in this play? The Holloway we meet in Henry's monologue is an old man who says to the equally old Bolton, "for the love of God, Bolton, do you want to finish me?" (104). As for Henry himself, his living testimony exists, as it were, in absentia: his self, as Charles Grivel puts it in the passage that gives me my epigraph, lives *without him*.[18]

At the same time—and this is the paradox—*Embers* is an exciting whodunit. Inevitably, the audience tries to construct the plot, doled out in dribs and drabs of information. Why is Henry so obsessed with his father? How did the father feel about Ada? What, if any, role did she play in his death? What does Bolton want from Holloway, and why won't Holloway give it to him? And so on. Normally and conventionally, radio is the purveyor of messages: who killed whom and why? when and where did it happen? what are the latest police findings? what does the coroner's report say? But in *Embers* there are no findings, no announcement, no "late bulletin." Indeed, it is these features of radio discourse that Beckett parodies: the radio audience's demand for fact is consistently undercut by verbal and phrasal repetition, by unanchored visual image (e.g., red dressing gown, blue eye), and by rhetorical and sonic excess.

So stylized is the play's language, with its invocation of seemingly unrelated sounds and sights, that we all but miss the moment when disclosure actually occurs, when the noise dies down for an instant, allowing a bit of the "message" to come through. That moment occurs when Ada recounts her visit to the house, where "None of them knew where you were. Your bed had not been slept in." Her speech is significantly framed by Henry's "Drive on, drive on! Why do people always stop in the middle of what they are saying?" and "Keep on, keep on! [*Imploringly.*]" (102). When Ada stops, unable to remember anything else, Henry has to finish the story for her, a story that imperceptibly and inevitably modulates back into the Bolton narrative. And the narrator repeats the words "Not a word, just the look, the old blue eye" (104).

But if there is "Not a word, just a look," the radio narrative is over. "Every syllable" is indeed "a second gained," for if there is really no sound, the listener must assume that the receiver isn't working, that there is either failure in the particular channel of transmission or a mechanical failure that has somehow turned off the set. On radio, in other words, the only way to simulate silence is via sound. And it is this characteristic of the medium Beckett must have had in mind when he refused to allow his radio plays to be *visualized* in any form.

In a 1997 debate of the John Cage Internet discussion group, participants were discussing how to perform Cage's famous "silent" piece of 1952 called *"4.33"* The title refers to the four minutes and thirty-three-second length of the performance, designed for any instrument or combination of instruments, which are in fact not played during the "silent" performance. One member, Daniel Farris, suggests:

> When one records silence, one must make a number of decisions. As when recording sound, one must decide whether or not to mic it up close or at a distance. The purpose of close mic placement is to reduce the amount of intrusion caused by nearby instruments and ambient sound and not necessarily to capture the most accurate representation of the performance. The purpose of distance mic placement is to capture the complete sonic environment both completely and accurately. Both techniques are useful and the decision about which to use is a subjective but important one. . . . Given the average Western audience's predisposition toward movement and respiration (and occasionally more at a hot gig), if an audience were present, one would need to actually deploy microphones and roll tape. We could call this "the live version."[19]

Here Farris reminds us that silence is never in fact silent: to record it for radio or audiotape therefore presents special problems. On stage or in film, "silence" is represented by having some sort of visual movement (as in Beckett's own *Film*) during which nothing is "said." But on radio there is no such option, and so "silence" must be sounded as it is in *Embers*. The final sentence in the play, "Not a sound," thus denies its own assertion in ways that underscore the piece's overarching sense of emptiness. For Henry can't even have the silence he longs for and anticipates; there will always be another "syllable," but not the one he is looking for. Radio would seem to be a unique medium to achieve this particular pathos.

Toward *Hörspiel*

Words and Music, written three years later, is a somewhat different experiment, for here Beckett produced a radio play, a good portion of which is given over to music—a music to be written by a collaborator. For its first BBC production in 1962, the musical score was written by Beckett's cousin,

John Beckett. This score, evidently considered less than satisfactory by all concerned, was withdrawn shortly after the premiere. In the early seventies, Beckett scholar Katharine Worth produced a new version of *Words and Music* for the University of London Audio-Visual Centre, with music by Humphrey Searle. But this production, described at some length by Worth in an essay called "Words and Music Perhaps,"[20] was recorded for archival purposes only, and it was not until 1985, when Everett Frost undertook the production of *The Beckett Festival of Radio Plays* (see note 7), that the Beckett collaboration with Morton Feldman took place.

Feldman and Beckett had first met in 1976 in Berlin, where the latter was directing a stage version of *The Lost Ones*. They discovered that they shared a mutual hatred of opera. Beckett further told Feldman, "I don't like my words being set to music," to which Feldman replied, "I'm in complete agreement. In fact it's very seldom that I've used words. I've written a lot of pieces with voice, and they're wordless." Encouraged by these remarks, a few weeks later Beckett sent Feldman a card bearing a handwritten text (not quite a poem) called "Neither," which began with the words "to and fro in shadow / from inner to outer shadow / from impenetrable self to impenetrable unself / by way of neither." These short phrases became the germ of Feldman's 1977 "anti-opera" *Neither*, the composer's first work to consist entirely of the repetition and mutation of tonal forms. The composer thus became the logical choice to be Beckett's collaborator on *Words and Music*; indeed it was Beckett who recommended him to Frost. The radio piece was followed by a long composition called *For Samuel Beckett* (1986), which was Feldman's last work; he died a year later, before he had the opportunity to take on Beckett's other "musical" radio play, *Cascando*, as the two had planned.[21]

The relation of spoken word to music in *Words and Music* and *Cascando* has received curiously little critical discussion. Jonathan Kalb observes:

> *Words and Music* . . . presents a special problem. . . . Its action consists of a relatively conventional dialogic exchange, but the dialogue is missing half its lines—lines that the play implies should match, sentence for sentence, in musical terms, the specificity and subtlety of Beckett's language.
>
> It is hardly surprising that neither his cousin nor subsequent composers have been up to the task. In one case (John Beckett's score) the music proved unable to communicate ideas specific enough to qualify as rational lines, much less repartee, and in another (Morton Feldman's score for Frost's 1988 production) the composer came to feel constrained by the text's requirements. . . . Unless Music convinces us that

it has at least held its own in the strange mimetic competition with Words, the action of the play lacks dramatic tension. Beckett once reportedly said to Theodor Adorno that *Words and Music* "ends unequivocally with the victory of the music." Yet far from proving the superiority of music as pure sound, liberated from rational ideas and references, the play confines it to a function very similar to that of a filmic signature score. ("Mediated Quixote" 132)

Here Kalb is making some curious assumptions. First, the reference to the various composers not being "up to the task" implies that the work is really Beckett's and that the composer, whoever he or she may be, is merely an accompanist.[22] Thus Kalb does not discriminate between John Beckett, a relative who had done a little composing; Humphrey Searle, a fairly obscure Romantic serialist who had once studied with Anton Webern; and Morton Feldman, one of the great avant-garde composers of the century.

For Kalb, *Words and Music* is, in any case, a "play," whose "dialogue is missing half its lines—lines that, the play implies, should match, sentence for sentence, in musical terms, the specificity and subtlety of Beckett's language." But Beckett said nothing at all about such a "match" or about the "mimetic competition with Words" that music ostensibly "loses." In taking Feldman's composition to resemble filmic background music, Kalb, like Worth and other commentators, is assuming that the radio play is a vehicle for a particular theme—the familiar Beckett theme of the missed opportunity to have loved and been loved (see, for example, *Krapp's Last Tape*). But the fact is that in *Words and Music* frustrated love becomes, in its turn, the occasion for an analysis of the relative power of words and music to produce an emotional charge. And here radio has its field of action. In Gregory Whitehead's words:

> If the dreamland/ghostland is the natural habitat for the wireless imagination, then the material of radio art is not just sound. Radio *happens* in sound, but sound is not really what matters about radio. What does matter is the bisected heart of the infinite dreamland/ghostland. . . . the radio signal as intimate but untouchable, sensually charged but technically remote, reaching deep inside but from way out there.[23]

Radio sounds are intimate, but from where do they emanate, and to whom do they belong? When the sound source is thus uncertain, spoken word and musical sound can achieve a heightened interaction.

Consider, for starters, the role of "character" in the phantasmagoria of *Words and Music*. The "play" has three characters: Words, also called Joe; Music, also called Bob; and a mysterious third person named Croak, who issues commands to both. In the Beckett literature, Croak is usually considered a variant on the Master with Two Servants motif, as a Medieval Lord directing two minstrels, or as a Prospero figure with Words as his Caliban and Music as his Ariel. Or again, he is considered to be the Director who has commissioned Words and Music to "speak" their parts.[24] All of these readings assume that there are in fact three separate "characters" with separate identities. True, *Words and Music* still uses such naturalistic radio sounds as the shuffling of Croak's carpet slippers, the thump of his club on the ground, the rap of the baton prompting Music to play, and a series of groans on Croak's part, throat clearings and sighs on Joe's. But unlike the "real" characters in *All That Fall*, or even Henry and Ada in *Embers*, Croak, Joe, and Bob are not "individuals" at all but three dimensions of the same "voice," sometimes speaking, sometimes responding via musical sound. Indeed, when the play is heard rather than read, the voices of Joe and Croak are often indistinguishable, as in the "Joe"/"My Lord" interchanges near the beginning. Croak, for that matter, is regularly referred to as an old man, a designation that amused Morton Feldman when he first read *Words and Music*, because the Beckett who wrote the play was only in his mid-fifties. Yet both Croak and Words are given "old" voices, rather like the voice of Krapp in *Krapp's Last Tape*, not so as to present the dialogue of two old men (with musical interruption) but to heighten the difference between present and past and to stress, as radio perhaps best can, the gap between the discourse of memory and the actual past.

Clas Zilliacus has rightly observed that Croak "instigates two of his faculties at odds with each other, to provide him with solace and entertainment," and that the process described is that of "artistic creation" (*Beckett and Broadcasting* 95). But even here the notion of "solace and entertainment" is not quite accurate, for there is nobody to comfort or to entertain. It is best, then, to think of Croak as no more than the stimulus that prompts the complementary responses of Words and Music; indeed, we can't differentiate the three. In concert, they constitute the quintessential Beckett voice—a voice we know from *Embers* or *Malone Dies*, or, most immediately, from *Krapp's Last Tape*. But in *Words and Music* the setting is not an empty room as in *Malone* or *Krapp* but an abstract space. "The scene," writes Zilliacus, referring to Words's reference in the memory passage to "the rye, swayed by a light wind [that] casts and withdraws its shadow,"[25] is "a field of rye, the action of the scene is postcoital recuperation as reflected in the face of the woman" (109).

Again, this is to mimeticize what is largely abstract: when we hear the words in question, we focus, I think, on the astonishing shift in Words's discourse, willing, as he suddenly is, much to Croak's anguish, to tell his story. It is the *telling*, not the details of landscape or face, that is foregrounded. Indeed, we never know what the lost girl looked like: except for her "black disordered hair," her features are merely listed as brows, nostrils, lips, breasts, and eyes, without any specification.

Feldman's score, made up of thirty-three fragments, calls for two flutes, a vibraphone, piano, violin, and violincello. These fragments must be understood not as isolated units but as relational properties that play with and against the words they modify. Croak dominates only as long as Words and Music work against one another; as soon as they follow his order "Together!" Croak begins to lose control. In the final moments of the play we hear his club fall, his slippers shuffling away, and a "shocked" Words says "My Lord!" for the final time. But the shuffling suggests that Croak has not died; rather, his commands are no longer necessary, for Words and Music now sing together, their song invoking the depths of memory and desire.

In the case of opera—and, technically speaking, *Words and Music* is an opera—the question as to which takes precedence, the words or the music, has been hotly debated for centuries. Herbert Lindenberger cites composers from Monteverdi to Wagner and Berg as claiming that music must always serve the verbal text, whereas Berlioz declared that Wagner's crime was to make music "the abject slave of the word" rather than letting the music be "free, imperious, all-conquering."[26] *Words and Music* playfully alludes to these debates, rather in the spirit of John Cage's *Europeras*, first performed in Frankfurt in the very same year, 1987.

Thus the radio play opens with a compact fragment of orchestrated dissonance that subtly "improves" on the actual sounds of an orchestra tuning up. "Words" interrupts this bit of music with the single angry and anguished word "*Please!*"—Bolton's leitmotif in *Embers*—repeated so as to force the orchestra to stop. And the words that follow are, "How much longer cooped up here in the dark? [*With loathing.*] With you!" (Beckett, *Collected Shorter Plays* 127). The two personae could thus not be further apart, and to make that point Words now embarks on his first set text on a required theme, an absurd scholastic exercise, the set topic *Love* being lampooned, in the absence of Croak, by the substitution of the word "sloth": "Sloth is of all passions the most powerful and indeed no passion is more powerful than the passion of sloth. . . . " where *passion* is repeated three times in the first sentence alone, Words's voice being hoarse and "tuneless" as he pronounces *passion* in a dull monotone. The love theme thus hangs fire until Croak makes his entrance, shuffling into the blank space of Words and Music and calling on both as "My comforts." The address to Bob ("Music"), whose response is defined by Beckett as "*Humble, muted adsum,*" produces the repetition of a single atonal chord, led by woodwinds, and then a slight variation on the same, this time with strings. Music's role is surprising because Croak now asks both parties to "Forgive" (three times), and yet Music responds with the same soft and lovely chords as if to say that there is nothing to forgive. It is now Words's turn to speak his piece, given Croak's prompting: "The face" and "In the tower"—both references to the lost beloved who will haunt the rest of the piece, very much as she does in *Krapp's Last Tape*, where we hear "The face she had! The eyes! Like . . . (*hesitates*) . . . chrysolite!" (60).

The "theme tonight," Croak informs Joe, is "Love," and so Words repeats his first speech, now substituting "love" for "sloth" but slipping at one point and declaiming that "sloth is the LOVE is the most urgent . . . " (128). Joe becomes so heated that when Croak thumps his club and calls on Music (Bob), Words (Joe) keeps on talking. Croak has to reprimand him and call on Bob again. And now Music gets his chance: in a pattern of irregularly spaced intervals, woodwinds and strings combine to produce resonant chords worthy of love. These are interrupted, as at the play's opening, by protestations of "Please!" and "No!" from Joe, but now these agitated negatives sound more orgiastic than dismissive, and he himself waxes poetic with the line "Arise then and go now the manifest unanswerable," a play on the opening line, "I shall arise and go now," of Yeats's "Lake Isle of Innisfree." The presence of Yeats, the quintessential poet who writes of age and unfulfilled desire, has already been conjured up by the reference to "In the tower."

Croak repeatedly groans as Words dredges up the memory of the "love of woman" that his "master" is experiencing. In an absurdist passage, Words asks bombastically, "Is love the word? [*Pause. Do.*] Do we mean love, when we say love? [*Pause. Pause. Do.*] Soul, when we say soul?" (129). The referent of these basic words—*face, love, soul, age*—cannot be found. Croak realizes this and calls on Music, who responds with a strain played by the violin accompanied by the pedaled piano and then a more dissonant passage, its minimalist hypnotic repetitions mirroring Joe's halting words on age: "Age is . . . age is when . . . old age I mean . . . if that is what my Lord means . . . is when. . . . " Interestingly, here, for the first time Music echoes Words, prompting Croak to issue a new directive—"Together"—(three times), the third time adding the word "dogs." In response, Words tries, for the first time, to sing or at least intone the poem we will soon hear—a trimeter sonnet that begins with the line "Age is when to a man." Music now gives the cue with the note *La,* and Words responds with jagged *Sprechstimme,* in its turn "improved," as he puts it, with an ascending scale provided by Music, that Joe's words now mimic. Music now follows Words's lead, taking up Joe's suggestion as he tries to intone the whole song. But halfway through this sequence it is Music who makes the "suggestions" that Words now follows. And so Words is soon letting Music take the lead.

In its written form the words and rhythms of Beckett's song recall both the Yeats of *Words for Music Perhaps* and the young Stephen Dedalus, who mourns for his dead mother in *Ulysses:*

> Age is when to a man
> Huddled o'er the ingle
> Shivering for the hag
> To put the pan in the bed
> And bring the toddy
> She comes in the ashes
> Who loved could not be won
> Or won not loved
> Or some other trouble
> Comes in the ashes
> Like in that old light
> The face in the ashes
> That old starlight
> On the earth again.
> *(Collected Shorter Plays* 131)

The ungainly syntax ("Age is when to a man") and archaicizing language ("huddled o'er the ingle") give Beckett's poem a parodic edge: old men shiver, their "hag" brings them the bedpan and toddy, the beautiful girl emerges from the ashes, her face recalling "that old starlight / On the earth again." As such, the poem forces the listener to take each word like "toddy" separately, refusing the "flow" of the incorporating stanza. And meanwhile Music provides no more than an ascending line of plucked piano notes, repeated with the accompaniment of the vibraphone and then flute, as minimal and separate as the poet's words. Each monosyllable—"Who loved could not be won" or "Like in that old light"—has its own life. Like the incisions made by a sharp instrument, words and musical notes are etched into the mind.

This, at least, is the response of Croak to what are, after all, his own words and music. Having heard the familiar song, he can no longer give orders, no longer address Words and Music as his "Dogs" or "Comforts" or "Balms." Indeed, Croak no longer seems to be aware of Joe and Bob's presence, which has now been thoroughly internalized. He now enunciates only two words, repeated four times and punctuated by pauses: "The face [*Pause.*] The face [*Pause.*] The face [*Pause.*] The face" (131). For words and music have succeeded in bringing the woman in question back to life. And so music now plays for an entire minute, a series of repetitive chords, shifting pitches just slightly, after which Croak again says, now quietly, "The face."

It is as if these two little words give Joe (Words) license to speak. We now hear one of those agitated but perfectly "reasonable" and scientific formal set pieces, a description of the long lost night of lovemaking—first the face, framed by "black disordered hair as though spread wide on water," then "the brows knitted in a groove suggesting pain but simply concentration more likely all things considered on some consummate inner process, the eyes of course closed in keeping with this, the lashes.... [*Pause.*] ... the nose ... [*Pause.*] ... nothing, a little pinched perhaps, the lips...." (132). The mention of the word "lips" is too much for Croak, whose groans have been getting more and more pronounced. He cries in anguish the single word "*Lily!*"—evidently the girl's name. Now the rest of the narrative spills out, with the memory of "the great white rise and fall of the breasts, spreading as they mount and then subsiding to their natural ... aperture." The listener is expecting something like "natural condition" or "natural size," but the mention of the "aperture," which is, of course, not between the breasts but between the legs, arouses the hitherto soft-spoken Music, who now reappears in an agitated flute solo that is overwhelmed by percussion, even as Words interjects "Peace?" "No" and "Please!" yet again.

Words is now confident, his speech having such a marked effect on both Croak and Music. Accordingly, he places his love scene against the backdrop of the entire earth, illuminated on this particular autumn night by the variable star Mira, located in the constellation Cetus (the Whale), and known for being invisible half the time. Here Mira shines "coldly down—as we say, looking up" (132). Croak, recognizing that in Words's narrative the sexual union is about to be consummated, speaks his last word in the play, the loud and anguished "No!"—the open "o" reverberating in the listener's ear (133). But Words, now in league with Music, pays no attention to the "master."

WORDS:—the brows uncloud, the lips part and the eyes ... [*Pause.*] the brows uncloud, the nostrils dilate, the lips part and the eyes ... [*Pause.*] ...

a little colour comes back into the cheeks and the eyes . . . [*Reverently.*] . . . open. [*Pause.*] Then down a little way. . . . (133)

It is generally held (see Esslin above) that the radio listener automatically tries to visualize a scene like this one, to picture the lovers in the field of rye, coming together. But I think the speech just quoted, far from evoking a scene, is like a sound poem: the repetition of the assonantal "the br*ow*s un-cl*ou*d" and the intricate sound structuring of *li* in "the nost*ril*s d*ilate*, the *lip*s p*ar*t," leading up to the repetition of "the eyes," which, the third time round, "open." Words now has all the music he needs to complete the story. And with Croak gone, Words can indulge himself and let the Proustian involuntary memory take over. One cannot, the sound piece suggests, invoke *The Face* or *Love* intentionally, for such invocation leads to nothing but *talking about*. But to let go, to let, as it were, nonsemantic sound take the lead, produces the epiphany of the second song, which begins:

Then down a little way
Through the trash
Towards where . . . towards where. . . . (133)

Compared to the previous ballad, this poem, written in even more minimal lines, bearing two to four stresses, takes us, in language much more chaste than "Age is when to a man," to the bedrock of feeling. The poet, transfigured by love, can now accept the descent "down a little way / Through the trash." The soul empties out: "All dark, no begging, no giving, no words, / No sense, no need." Music, playing soft chromatic scales, leads the way while the poet sings, "Through the scum / Down a little way / To whence one glimpse / Of that wellhead." The sentence is left in suspension: the "wellhead" as goal remains a mystery. When these words are repeated, it is music that announces the melody and then becomes a discreet accompanist to Words. It is the final consummation: both parties now note that Croak is gone. "My Lord," Joe repeats twice, anxiously looking after Croak, and, turning for the first time to "Bob," begging him to respond.

It is a remarkable moment: Joe reaches out to his former antagonist, Bob, with a certain deference. Bob makes a brief "rude" musical flourish and suddenly becomes silent, so that it is now Words who summons Music with a sense of urgency. The situation of the radio play's opening has been completely reversed. When Music plays a short teasing chord, Words begs "Again! [*Pause. Imploring.*] Again!" Music obliges but only for a moment, the soft piano notes trailing off and Words concluding with a short satisfied sigh. The rest is silence—a silence that makes the very idea of competition between Words and Music seem foolish. And this, I think, is the thrust of the Beckett-Feldman collaboration.

It may be argued, of course—and here Kalb has a point—that the dependence on collaboration makes *Words and Music* a less important work than, say, *Embers,* that Beckett is at his best when he lets his own words do all the work, creating the semantic resonances and ambiguities we have in the complex monologue of a Henry or a Krapp. But if we think of *Words and Music* as an experiment, a move, contrary to Beckett's own purist instincts with regard to media, to create a new kind of *Hörspiel*—a *Hörspiel* that anticipates such later works as the John Cage *Roaratorio*—then we need not choose between *Words and Music* and *Embers*—both of them such superb examples of what Beckett's first master, James Joyce, called "soundsense."

Graçia Capinha, a professor at the University of Coimbra, invited me to give a keynote address on "the new poetries" in the summer of 1998. I thought this might be a good occasion to take up the issue of the subject in the Language poetries that had supposedly rejected all notions of individual "voice" in poetry. I revised the paper later that year and it appeared in 1999 in Critical Inquiry. Rereading the essay in 2003, I have a strong sense of the difference four years has already made in the poetic formations in question.

7

Language Poetry and the Lyric Subject

Ron Silliman's Albany, Susan Howe's Buffalo

> The "personal" is already a plural condition. Perhaps one feels that it is located somewhere within, somewhere inside the body—in the stomach? the chest? the genitals? the throat? the head? One can look for it and already one is not oneself, one is several, a set of incipiencies, incomplete, coming into view here and there, and subject to dispersal.
>
> Lyn Hejinian, "The Person and Description"

One of the cardinal principles—perhaps *the* cardinal principle—of American Language poetics (as of the related current in England, usually labeled "linguistically innovative poetries")[1] has been the dismissal of "voice" as the foundational principle of lyric poetry. In the preface to his anthology *In the American Tree* (1986), Ron Silliman famously declared that Robert Grenier's "I HATE SPEECH" manifesto, published in the first issue of the San Francisco journal *This* (1971), "announced a breach—and a new moment in American writing"—a rejection of "simple ego psychology in which the poetic text represents not a person, but a persona, the human as unified object. And the reader likewise."[2] From the other coast, Charles Bernstein similarly denounced "voice" as the "privileged structure in the organization and interpretation of poems."[3] And in his early essay "Stray Straws and Straw Men" (1976), Silliman is Bernstein's Exhibit A for a constructivist poetry, a poetry that undermines the "natural look," with its "personal subject matter & a flowing syntax."[4] "Ron Silliman," Bernstein writes, "has consistently written a poetry of visible borders: a poetry of shape"—one that "may discomfort those who want a poetry primarily of personal communication, flowing freely from the inside with the words of a natural rhythm of life, lived daily" ("Stray Straws" 40–41). And the essay goes on to unmask Official Verse Culture, with its "sanctification" of "authenticity," "artlessness," "spontaneity," and claim for *self-presence,* the notion, widely accepted in the poetry of the 1960s, that "The experience is present to me" (41, 42).[5]

Although Bernstein doesn't explicitly say so, the critique of voice, self-presence, and authenticity put forward in *Content's Dream,* as well as in such related texts as Ron Silliman's own *The New Sentence* (1987) or Steve McCaffery's *North of Intention* (1986),[6] must be understood as part of the larger post-structuralist critique of authorship and the humanist subject, a critique that became prominent in the late sixties and reached its height in the United States a decade or so later when the Language movement was coming into its own. It was Roland Barthes, after all, who insisted, in "The Death of the Author" (1968), that writing, far from being the simple and direct expression of interiority, is "the destruction of every voice, every point of origin. Writing is that neutral, composite, oblique space where our subject slips away, the negative where all identity is lost, starting with the very identity of the body writing." "Linguistically," Barthes declared, "the author is never more than the instance writing, just as *I* is nothing other than the instance saying *I:* language knows a 'subject,' not a 'person.'" And he famously concludes:

> We know now that a text is not a line of words releasing a single "theological" meaning (the message of the Author-God). . . . The text is a tissue of quotations drawn from the innumerable centres of culture. The writer can only imitate a gesture that is *always anterior, never original.* His only power is to mix writings, to counter the ones with the others. . . . Succeeding the Author, the scriptor no longer bears within him passions, humours, feelings, impressions, but rather this immense dictionary from which he draws a writing that can know no halt: life never does more than imitate the book, and the book itself is only a tissue of signs, an imitation that is lost, infinitely deferred.[7]

Here Barthes anticipates Foucault's equally famous pronouncement, in "What Is an Author?" (1969), that "The writing of our day has freed itself from the necessity of 'expression.'" In Foucault's words:

> Writing unfolds like a game that inevitably moves beyond its own rules and finally leaves them behind. Thus, the essential basis of this

writing is not exalted emotions related to the act of composition or the insertion of a subject into language. Rather, it is primarily concerned with creating an opening where the writing subject endlessly disappears.

The author is now replaced by the "author function"—the function of a particular discourse—and the pressing questions about a given text become not "what has [the author] revealed of his most profound self in his language?" but "where does [this discourse] come from; how is it circulated; who controls it?"[8]

What matter who's speaking? (Foucault 138). Beckett's question, as recharged and transmitted by Foucault, was to be historicized, along Marxist and specifically Althusserian lines, by Fredric Jameson in *Postmodernism; or, The Cultural Logic of Late Capitalism* (1991). Whereas Barthes, Foucault, and the Derrida of *Writing and Difference* were essentially talking about how to read—how, that is, to construct an existing text without taking its author's intentions as normative—Jameson takes the death of the author, or rather, the death of the subject, quite literally, that death being no more than one of the symptoms of the social transformations produced by late global capitalism. "The very concept of expression," Jameson posits, "presupposes indeed some separation within the subject, and along with that a whole metaphysics of the inside and outside" that characterizes great modernist artworks like van Gogh's *A Pair of Boots* or Edvard Munch's *The Scream*.[9] Postmodernism, in this view, no longer recognizes such "depth models" as inside/outside, essence/appearance, latent/manifest, authenticity/inauthenticity, signifier/signified, or depth/surface.

The "alienation of the subject is displaced by the latter's fragmentation," and indeed by "the 'death' of the subject itself—the end of the autonomous bourgeois monad or ego or individual" (*Postmodernism* 14–15). Coupled with that end is the end of a "unique style, along with the accompanying collective ideals of an artistic or political vanguard or avant-garde." The result is the now axiomatic "waning of affect" that manifests itself in an ability to produce satire or even parody, the latter giving way to "blank parody" or pastiche. "As for expression," writes Jameson, " . . . the liberation, in contemporary society, from the older *anomie* of the centered subject may also mean not merely a liberation from anxiety but a liberation from every other kind of feeling as well, since there is no longer a self present to do the feeling" (15).

In his first formulation of this "new depthlessness" or "waning of affect" (1984),[10] Jameson voiced some regret over the passing of modernism. But by 1990 (the date of the "Conclusion" to *Postmodernism*), he seems to find the passing of the modernist giants—Picasso, Kafka, Proust, Frank Lloyd Wright—the occasion of at least some satisfaction:

> [I]f the poststructuralist motif of the "death of the subject" means anything socially, it signals the end of the entrepreneurial and inner-directed individualism, with its "charisma" and its accompanying categorical panoply of quaint romantic values such as that of the "genius" in the first place. Seen thus, the extinction of the "great moderns" is not necessarily an occasion for pathos. Our social order is richer in information and more literate, and socially, at least, more "democratic" in the sense of the universalization of wage labor. . . . this new order no longer needs prophets and seers of the high modernist and charismatic type. . . . Such figures no longer hold any charm or magic for the subjects of a corporate, collectivized, post-individualistic age; in that case, goodbye to them without regrets, as Brecht might have put it: *woe to the country that needs geniuses, prophets, Great Writers, or demiurges.* (306)

I cite this passage at some length because its argument was so thoroughly internalized in the "advanced" discourses of the nineties about the place of the aesthetic in our culture. The demise of the transcendental ego, of the authentic self, of the poet as lonely genius, of a unique artistic style: these were taken as something of a given. In their group manifesto "Aesthetic Tendency and the Politics of Poetry" (1988), for example, Silliman, Carla Harryman, Lyn Hejinian, Steve Benson, Bob Perelman, and Barrett Watten concurred that "our work denies the centrality of the individual artist. . . . The self as the central and final term of creative practice is being challenged and exploded in our writing."[11] And, given the tedious and unreflective claim for the unique insight and individual vision that has characterized so large a portion of mainstream poetry, the case for an "alternative" poetics remains compelling.

At the same time, now that the exploratory poetries associated with the Language movement are more than twenty years old, Jameson's formulations (and related theories of the postmodern) have lost much of their edge. For even if we set aside the work of mainstream poets like the American laureates Robert Pinsky and Robert Hass, Mark Strand and Rita Dove, even if we restrict ourselves to the poets of the counterculture represented in, say, Jerome Rothenberg and Pierre Joris's *New Poems for the Millennium*,[12] differences among the various poets now strike us as more significant than similarities or group labels. Such counters as asyntacticality or the disappearance of the referent or even the materiality of the sign cannot alter the simple fact that we can easily tell a Charles Bernstein poem from one by Steve McCaffery, a Tom Raworth sequence from one by Allen Fisher, a Maggie O'Sullivan "verbovisivocal" text from one by Susan Howe. More important: the breakdown of the high/low distinction, accepted as a cornerstone of postmodernism by the theorists of the seventies and eighties, is coming under increasing suspicion as common sense tells us that all artworks are not, after all, equally valuable (whatever "valuable" means), and that when, for example, Frank Sinatra is called, as he has been in the wake of his death, one of the great artists of the century, this statement is not really equivalent to the proposition that John Cage is one of the great artists of the century. For one thing, the two assertions call for different speakers. For another, they posit different contexts. The word *great* in any case, means something different in the two cases, as does the word *artist*. Even *One of* is unstable: Sinatra fans were comparing their idol not only to other "great" singers and movie stars but to tycoons of the American record industry, those savvy entrepreneurs who know how to market a given label. In the case of Cage, on the other hand, *one of* would refer to the international avant-garde market—the *Hörspiele* heard on German radio as well as the Zen art of Japan.

Then, too, contemporary poetics has not satisfactorily resolved the relation of what Jameson calls the "new depthlessness" to the "genius" position now occupied by those evidently deep (read *complex, difficult*) theorists, whose word is all but law. Indeed, even as Jameson rejects the image of the "great demiurges and prophets" like "Proust in his cork-lined room" or the "'tragic,' uniquely doomed Kafka" (*Postmodernism* 305), on page after page he cites names like Theodor Adorno and Louis Althusser, Gilles Deleuze and Jean Baudrillard, Jean-Francois Lyotard and Ernesto Laclau. If genius theory is passé, if there is no such thing as unique or individual authority, why are these names so sacred? If Foucault has pronounced so definitively on the death of the author, why are we always invoking the name of the author Foucault?

In a recent essay for Bernstein's collection (1998), Silliman speculates on this phenomenon. Silliman begins by restating his opposition to "the poem as confession of lived personal experience, the (mostly) free verse presentation of sincerity and authenticity that for several decades has been a staple of most of the creative writings in the United States."[13] But in reevaluating what he calls Barthes's "ritual slaying of the author" ("Who Speaks" 364), Silliman wonders whether Barthes's theory of text construction hasn't gone too far. The insistence in "The Death of the Author" that "the reader is without history, biography, psychology; he is simply that *someone* who holds together in a single field all the traces by which the written text is constituted," is finally unsatisfactory: "The idealized, absent author of the New Critical canon has here been replaced by an equally idealized, absent reader. All that remains are the reports of other readers—call them critics—whose texts endlessly read textuality itself, whose claim to authority lies precisely in the self-knowledge of their texts as infinitely deferred, deferring, acts" ("Who Speaks" 365).

And where do these acts take place? Where else but in the university? As Silliman speculates:

> Perhaps it should not be a surprise, that while postmodernism in the arts has been conducted largely, although not exclusively, outside of the academy, the postmodern debate has been largely conducted between different schools of professors who agree only that they too dislike it. Thus the characteristic strategy of the ambitious critic and anxious graduate student alike is not the opening of the canons, but rather the demonstration of a critical move upon some text(s) within the already established ensemble of official canons. . . . Once incorporated into an institutional canon, the text becomes little more than a ventriloquist's dummy through which a babel of critical voices contend. ("Who Speaks" 365, 368)

Barthes could not, of course, have foreseen that the privilege he accorded the reader ("We know now that a text is not a line of words releasing a single 'theological' meaning") would so easily turn into the form of ventriloquism Silliman describes. But as those of us in the academy know only too well, this is precisely what has happened. "We know now" ("*On sait maintenant*"): we who are critics can practice our virtuosity on this or that poem, which is consequently accorded secondary status—hence the elevated status of Derrida or Deleuze vis-à-vis Beckett or Kafka.

What matter who's speaking? Perhaps it is time to reconsider the role of the subject in Language poetry. "The relation between agency and identity," writes Silliman, "must be understood as interactive, fluid, negotiable" ("Who Speaks" 371). It is a "relation between the poet, a real person with 'history, biography, psychology,' and the reader, no less real, no less encumbered by all this baggage. In poetry, the self is a relation between writer and reader that is triggered by what [Roman] Jakobson called contact, the power of presence" (373).

I find it interesting that Silliman, once an outspoken critic of the formalist lyric poem, here invokes the name of the great Russian Formalist critic. A similar shift may be noted in the work of Bernstein. In the mordantly funny essay "The Revenge of the Poet-Critic" (1998), Bernstein examines the issues posed by the poetics of cultural construction. "In the 1990s," he remarks,

> The problems of group affiliation (the neolyric "we") pose as much a problem for poetry as do assertions of the Individual Voice. If poems can't speak directly for an author, neither can they speak directly for a group. . . . Each poem speaks not only many voices but also many groups and poetry can investigate the construction of these *provisional* entities in and through and by language.
>
> If individual identity is a false front, group identity is a false fort.[14]

And in the related essay "What's Art Got to Do with It? The Status of the Subject of the Humanities in an Age of Cultural Studies," Bernstein gives a devastating critique of the current critical orthodoxy that treats literature as no more than "symptom" or "example," even as the theorist is taken to be above and beyond the fray. Isn't it possible, asks Bernstein, that Bourdieu's *Distinction: A Social Critique of the Judgment of Taste* is itself a "commodity whose status is determined by its role in the professional habitat to which he belongs?" Or, again, "Is Fredric Jameson's writing on postmodernism a symptom of postindustrial capitalism?" (62–63). "Behind every successful artist," Bernstein declares, "is a new historian who says it's all just a symptom. Behind every successful new historian is an artist who says you forgot to mention my work—and, boy, is it symptomatic!"[15]

Of course, as Bernstein would be the first to insist, there's no going back to earlier models. The workshop term *voice,* for example, a term that implies, quite inaccurately, that *speech* is primary and prior to writing and that hence a poem is simply the outward sign of a spoken self-presence (as in the ubiquitous cliché "She's really found her voice") is not adequate. Neither is the fuzzy term *style,* a term now thoroughly co-opted by the media and commodified in such titles as "Life and Style" (a daily section of the *Los Angeles Times*).

Perhaps a more accurate term to refer to the mark of difference that separates one identity from another, no matter how fully the two share a particular group aesthetic, is the word *signature.* According to the *Oxford English Dictionary* from 1580, from the Latin *signare,* "to sign or mark," a *signature* is "the name (or special mark) of a person written with his or her own hand as an authentication of some document or writing." "The fatal signature," we read in Robert Southey's *All For Love* (1829), "appear'd / To all the multitude, / Distinct as when the accursed pen / Had traced it with fresh blood." A subsidiary meaning (1613) of *signature,* now obsolete, was "A distinctive mark, a peculiarity in form or colouring, etc. on a plant or other natural object, formerly supposed to be an indication of its qualities, especially for medicinal purposes." A signature thus came to mean "a distinguishing mark of any kind": in 1626 Lancelot Andrewes wrote in one of his sermons, "The saviour . . . taking on Him 'Abraham's seed' must withal take on Him the signature of Abraham's seed, and be . . . circumcised." And in his translation of the *Odyssey* (1725) Alexander Pope writes, "Vulgar parents cannot stamp their race / With signatures of such majestic grace." In the seventeenth century *signature* was used to designate "a *naevus* or birth-mark."[16]

A second category of definitions comes from the discourse of printing: a *signature,* let's recall, is "a letter or figure, a set of combination of letters or figures, etc., placed by the printer at the foot of the first page (and frequently on one or more of the succeeding pages) of every sheet in a book, for the purpose of showing the order in which these are to be placed or bound." And, thirdly, there is the musical designation of *signature;* from 1806 on it has meant "a sign, or set of signs, placed at the beginning of a piece of music, immediately after the clef, to indicate its key or time."

The common thread of all three of the above categories is that of the *signature* as identifying mark. As such, it is not surprising that, like its cognate term, *author,* the word *signature* became suspect in post-structuralist theory. In *Les Mots et les choses* (1966), Foucault writes movingly of *signatures* as the key element in the system of similitudes that dominated the premodern world. As "the visible mark of invisible analogies," the signature was, for centuries, the external sign of a hidden but present interiority, and the world was "read" as a large open book, whose signs, characters, numbers, symbols, and hieroglyphs demand interpretation. "To find the law of signs," as Foucault notably puts it, "is to discover things."[17]

Foucault's *Les Mots et les choses* traces the historical dissolution of this Renaissance "episteme," a dissolution considered from a hermeneutic perspective by Derrida in "Signature Event Context" (1972). "A written sign," writes Derrida, " . . . is a mark that subsists, one which does not exhaust itself in the moment of its inscription and which can give rise to an iteration in the absence and beyond the presence of the empirically determined subject who, in a given context, has emitted or produced it."[18] But since the written sign inevitably breaks with its context, "with the collectivity of presences organizing the moment of inscription," "the absolute singularity of signature as event" can never fully occur ("Signature Event Context" 9, 20). Thus writing "is not the site, 'in the last instance,' of a hermeneutic deciphering, the decoding of a meaning or truth" (21).

From a hermeneutic perspective, this is no doubt the case. But even Derrida, posing the question "Are there signatures?" responds, "Yes, of course, every day. Effects of signature are the most common thing in the world" (20). And he ends his essay with the "counterfeit" signature "J. Derrida" (21). The implication is that however conscious we must be of the basic instability of a given signature, *in practice* we do take signatures seriously as markers of a particular individual, a cultural practice, an historical period, a national formation, a convention, and so on. Indeed, if our purpose is to understand specific writing practices, individual as well as generic, we can hardly avoid noting their individual stamp or mark of authorship. The Bilbao-Guggenheim Museum, for example, may bear witness to any number of postmodern architectural traits (and some modernist ones as well: witness the building's Frank Lloyd Wright allusions), but its indelible signature is that of its highly individual architect, Frank Gehry.

This brings me back to the question of the subject in the ostensibly "deauthorized" poetry of the Language school. In what follows, I want to look at signatures in two poetic texts, both of them written by what are nominally Language poets and both charting, in very specific ways, the geography of childhood. The first is Ron Silliman's own "Albany," the second, Susan Howe's *Frame Structures*.[19]

"Signatures of All Things I Am Here to Read"

"Albany" is a long prose paragraph made up of one hundred "New Sentences," to use Ron Silliman's own term, defined in a now well-known (and hotly debated) essay by that name. The "new sentence" is conceived as an independent unit, neither causally nor temporally related to the sentences that precede and follow it. Like a line in poetry, its length is operative and its meaning depends on the larger paragraph as organizing system.[20] Here, for example, are the first twenty sentences of "Albany":

> If the function of writing is to "express the world." My father withheld child support, forcing my mother to live with her parents, my brother and I to be raised together in a small room. Grandfather called them niggers. I can't afford an automobile. Far across the calm bay stood a complex of long yellow buildings, a prison. A line is the distance between. They circled the seafood restaurant, singing "We shall not be moved." My turn to cook. It was hard to adjust my sleeping to those hours when the sun was up. The event was nothing like their report of it. How concerned was I over her failure to have orgasms? Mondale's

speech was drowned by jeers. Ye wretched. She introduces herself as a
rape survivor. Yet his best friend was Hispanic. I decided not to escape
to Canada. Revenue enhancement. Competition and spectacle, kinds
of drugs. If it demonstrates form some people won't read it. Television
unifies conversation.

And here are the last twenty:

Client populations (cross the tundra). Off the books. The whole neighborhood is empty in the daytime. Children form lines at the end of
each recess. Eminent domain. Rotating chair. The history of Poland is
90 seconds. Flaming pintos. There is no such place as the economy, the
self. That bird demonstrates the sky. Our home, we were told, had been
broken, but who were these people we lived with? Clubbed in the stom-
ach, she miscarried. There were bayonets on campus, cows in India,
people shoplifting books. I just want to make it to lunch time. Uncriti-
cal of nationalist movements in the Third World. Letting the dishes sit
for a week. Macho culture of convicts. With a shotgun and "in defense"
the officer shot him in the face. Here, for a moment, we are joined. The
want-ads lie strewn on the table.

As in his long poems *Ketjak* and *Tjanting,* both written a few years earlier,
"Albany" relies on parataxis, dislocation, and ellipsis (the very first sentence,
for example, is a conditional clause, whose result clause is missing), as well
as pun, paragram, and sound play to construct its larger paragraph unit. But
it is not just a matter of missing pieces. The poet also avoids conventional
"expressivity" by refusing to present us with a consistent "I," not specifying,
for that matter, who the subject of a given sentence might be. Who, for example, says, "I just want to make it to lunch time"? Or, "Talking so much is
oppressive"? Who believes that "music is essential," and, by the way, essential
to what? Whose "best friend was Hispanic"? And so on.

At the same time—and this has always been a Silliman trademark—
indeterminacy of agent and referent does not preclude an obsessive attention
to particular "realistic" detail. Despite repeated time and space shifts, the
world of Albany, California, is wholly recognizable. To begin with, it is not
the Bay Area of the affluent—the Marin County suburbanites, Russian Hill
aesthetes, or Berkeley middle-class go-getters. The working-class motif is
immediately established with the reference to "my father withheld child
support, forcing my mother to live with her parents, my brother and I to
be raised together in a small room." And this is the white working class:

"Grandfather called them niggers." Later, when the narrator is living in a part of San Francisco where, on the contrary, many ethnicities are represented, we read "they speak in Farsi at the corner store." The poet is a political activist: he participates in demonstrations and teach-ins, is briefly jailed, avoids the draft, and so on. There are many explanations of everyday things the activist must deal with: "The cops wear shields that serve as masks." But the paragraph is also filled with references to sexual love: couplings and uncouplings, rape, miscarriage, and abortion. And, finally, there is the motif of poetry: "If it demonstrates form they can't read it." And readings: "It's not easy if your audience doesn't identify as readers." Writing poetry is always a subtext, but one makes one's living elsewhere: "The want-ads," as the last sentence reminds us, "lie strewn on the table."

"Silliman's work," observes Jed Rasula, "may be read as a grand refusal of the chronic strategies of authorial domination."[21] Here Rasula echoes Silliman's own early Language manifestos, with their emphasis on the avoidance of what Charles Olson called the "lyrical interference of the individual as ego," the refusal to create a consistent or controlling self, whose construction of events as of verbal forms controls the material in question.[22] The "realism" of "Albany," Rasula would no doubt argue, is properly understood not as a personal expression but as an elaborate network of signifiers in which conflicting vocalizations and linguistic registers come into play.

But must it be either/or? And is it really the case that Silliman eschews "authorial domination"? I find myself increasingly uncomfortable with such formulations. For who, after all, controls the specific language operations in the text before us? There is, to begin with, not the slightest doubt that "Albany" is a man's poem—a man who is aware of the sexual needs and difficulties of the women in his life but centrally caught up in the political: the need for demonstrations, the abuses of the cops, the "bayonets on campus," the question of "nationalist movements in the Third World." "How concerned was I," we read in sentence 11, "over her failure to have orgasms?" However much—and the question may have been posed to the narrator by a friend, a relative, a physician, or by himself—the very next sentence, "Mondale's speech was drowned by jeers," places the question about orgasms in ironic perspective. Even such seemingly neutral statements as "my turn to cook" identify "Albany" as the narrative of a young man who has consciously rejected the traditional male role: in his mother's household, after all, such a statement would have been absurd, given the traditional division of labor.

The signature of "Albany" is a "normal" declarative sentence ("I can't afford an automobile") or part of a sentence ("To own a basement," "Died in action"), sometimes commonsensical, sometimes aphoristic, sometimes an item in a newspaper or on television. In their curious collisions these "casual" sentences point to an author who is matter-of-fact, streetwise, and largely self-educated; his is the discourse of a working-class man (as even the first name Ron rather than Ronald suggests) who has slowly and painfully learned the craft of poetry, a man who's been around and has had to put up with quite a bit, beginning with his father's withholding of child support. Pain, violence, and injustice are the facts of his life; sentence after sentence refers to murders, shoot-outs, abortions, riots, asbestos poisoning and the like. And even at the trivial level difficulty dominates: "It was hard to adjust my sleeping to those hours when the sun was up." "Becoming to live with less space." "I used my grant to fix my teeth." And so on. Yet Silliman's characteristic formulations are by no means gloomy; on the contrary, his "voice" emerges as sprightly, engaged, curious, fun-loving, energetic, a voice that loves the wordplay of "they call their clubs batons. They call their committees clubs." Or, "Eminent domain. Rotating chair." Or, "There were bayonets on campus, cows in India, people shoplifting books. I just wanted to make it to lunch time."

No individual signature? Suppose we compare the prose of "Albany" to the following two extracts:

(1)   *A and Not-A* are the same.

My dog does not know me.

Violins, like dreams, are suspect.

I come from Kolophon, or perhaps some small island.

The strait has frozen, and people are walking—a few skating—across it.

On the crescent beach, a drowned deer.

A woman with one hand, her thighs around your neck.

The world is all that is displaced.

Apples in a stall at the street corner by the Bahnhof, pale yellow to blackish red.

Memory does not speak.

Shortness of breath, accompanied by tinnitus.

(2)   A man is standing in front of a window. In possession of
what he sees. A person becomes a lens on a room inside.
Then to walk into the room on sequent occasions. The
lights go down on the buildings outside. The window is
off of the kitchen, the room is filled with people. Smoke
coming out of the cracks. What can he have. All words
resolve this matter like a huge weight balancing on a single
point. That point is in motion, verging from one word to
the next. A cyclone covers the surface of the ceiling with
wavering lines. The room fills in with fragments of their
talk. But a window is an opening to the outside He is
contradicted in his rooms, imagining a better place to live.

Both of these passages were written by poets of Silliman's generation, then
living in San Francisco and associated with the Language community: the
first, Michael Palmer's "Autobiography" from *At Passages,* the second, Barrett
Watten's "City Fields" from *Frame (1971–1990).*[23] Both poets would insist, I
think, that theirs is not an "expressivist" poetry, that, in Palmer's words, "He
regards the self as just another sign." And it is true that read against, say, a
lyric by Mark Strand or Louise Gluck there is no doubt that, like Silliman,
both Palmer and Watten are trying, in the words of Jasper Johns, to "do
something else,"[24] that they have no interest in the closural first-person meta-
phoric model of mainstream poetry.

But to group these texts as Language poems tells us very little. Michael
Palmer's lineated poem is called "Autobiography," but the poet's tone is more
impersonal than Silliman's. His short sentences, separated by large areas of
white space, are enigmatic and parabolic, his images equivocal. Some of his
aphorisms—"*A and not-A*—are the same"; "The world is all that is displaced"
—allude to Wittgenstein, the latter a nice twist on "the world is all that is the
case."[25] Some sentences contain literary allusions: "My dog does not know
me," for example, inverts Gertrude Stein's, "I am I because my little dog
knows me."[26] In this context, "My dog does not know me" is equivalent to
saying "I am nothing." "All clocks are clouds" brings to mind a Magritte
painting; and such lines as "winter roses are invisible" and "Late ice sometimes sings" are written under the sign of French Surrealist dream poetry.

Unlike either Silliman or Watten, both of them insistently urban poets, Palmer is given to nature references like "roses" and "ice," like "the crescent beach, a drowned deer." And these nature images are underscored by references to foreign (usually European) locales, as in "apples in a stall at the street corner by the Bahnhof, pale yellow to blackish red." One thinks here of Apollinaire's "Zone" or Cendrars's "Panama, or My Seven Uncles." Or perhaps André Breton's *Nadja*.

Altogether, Palmer's imagination is more visual and literary than Silliman's, his memories more hallucinatory and dreamlike. His is the anxiety not of daily misfortunes but of the empty room: "Violins, like dreams, are suspect." "There is," David Levi Strauss has remarked, "a quite identifiable first person running through [Palmer's] books. It is usually male, neurasthenic, doubtful, by turns cheerful and morose: a reluctant survivor. If it had a visible companion, the other might be called Didi or Clov or Camier. This first person is trepidatious and apologetic, constantly undercutting its own authority."[27] In "Autobiography," not surprisingly, Silliman's sturdy resilience gives way to "shortness of breath, accompanied by tinnitus." And although, like Silliman, Palmer writes a poetry of parataxis, his is a juxtapositioning of poetic and philosophical fragments rather than the phenomenology of everyday life characteristic of Silliman.

Yet another kind of psychic drive can be found in Barrett Watten's prose poem, again part of a longer sequence. Unlike Silliman or Palmer, Watten uses the third person, but his narrator, who becomes "a lens on a room inside," functions as a kind of Jamesian register, through whom all "events" and items perceived are filtered. It is he who is "in possession of what he sees," first from outside the room and then from inside, he who feels cut off from the "fragments of their talk." Yet he is more confident than Palmer's self-critical "I," more assertive about "imagining a better place to live." Anxiety, for Watten, is socially constructed and hence to be overcome by social change: "All words resolve this matter like a huge weight balancing on a single point." For the moment, however, there is no escape: "A cyclone covers the surface of the ceiling with wavering lines."

In Watten's account of displacement and possible reconnection, each sentence leads to the next. If Silliman were writing these lines, "The window is off the kitchen" would be followed by a sentence like "net income is down 13%" or "they photograph Habermas to hide the harelip." Watten's prose is more chaste, consecutive, linear; his vocabulary less exuberant and varied. And even though his narrator never speaks in his own person, a voice—measured yet urgent, direct yet highly "educated"—comes through. Again, no one would mistake this passage for a work by Silliman.

The poet's *naevus* or birthmark, it would seem, is not so easily eradicated. It is interesting that when in 1997 Gale Research invited Silliman to contribute an autobiographical essay to its *Contemporary Authors* series, he used the sentences of "Albany" "to tell me what to write, where to focus, that moment in the essay. The whole premise of 'Albany' (or at least *a* premise) was to focus on things that were both personal and political, so when Gale called, it seemed like the right place to begin. *That poem always has been my autobiography, so to speak.*"[28] The resultant text, in which each of the one hundred sentences is printed in boldface, followed by a paragraph of varying length, is called "Under *Albany*"—"under," no doubt, because the poet now tries to get inside, behind, and *under* his earlier statements so as to make some sense of their psychological and social trajectory.[29]

Not infrequently, the "under" entry contradicts or qualifies the original sentence. For example (sentence 3):

Grandfather called them niggers.
So that I was surprised at how many elderly African American men, all, like my grandfather, members of the Veterans of Foreign Wars (VFW) came to his funeral. (31)

In the context of "Albany," the first sentence is taken at face value. Followed as it is in the original poem by "I can't afford an automobile," it gives us a sense of the bleak deprivation and petty racism of white working-class Albany. But in "Under *Albany*," the meaning of what is now a title shifts; perhaps, the reader here surmises, "calling them niggers" wasn't equivalent to simple racism, for as veterans of World War I black and white men may well have interacted more fully than have their grandsons.

I have discussed elsewhere the complex relationship of title to paragraph in "Under *Albany*,"[30] a text that is deeply moving in its account of the poet's empty childhood—a childhood that paradoxically paves the way for the remarkable resilience and optimism of Silliman's maturity:

I look forward to old age with some excitement.
Sixteen years later, I'm writing from my room 218 in the Motel Six of Porterville, in the Sierra foothills north of Bakersfield. My nephew, Stephen Matthew Silliman, is just four days old. Allen Ginsberg has been dead for 13 days. Their worlds never crossed, just as mine never crossed Gertrude Stein's. But I know people who have slept with people who have slept with people who slept with Walt Whitman. At 94, Carl Rakosi's mind clear as a bell. Others at 24, hopelessly muddied and

muddled. Once, walking on the beach at Stinson with Rae Armantrout during our student days at Berkeley, I knelt to pick up a beautifully pocked smooth gray stone (I still have it). She asked me what I was doing. "Looking for the good ones," I replied. (340–41)

In the context of Silliman's account of his day-to-day difficulties and trauma, the upbeat ending of this paragraph comes as a real surprise. His is a complex and engaging autobiography, but then "Albany," the prior text that supposedly exhibits what Jameson calls the "waning of affect," was always already autobiographical.

Hinge Pictures/Dividing Lines

Like "Under *Albany*," Susan Howe's *Frame Structures* (1996) refigures the poet's earlier work. It collects four of her earliest long poems (*Hinge Picture*, 1974; *Chanting at the Crystal Sea*, 1975; *Cabbage Gardens*, 1979; *Secret History of the Dividing Line*, 1978) in slightly revised versions and adds a long "preface" that gives the book its title. The poems are characterized by their distinctive visual layout: in *Secret History of the Dividing Line*, for example, the title (derived, minus the word "Secret," from William Byrd's eighteenth-century journal of explorations in the Virginia wilderness) appears in the center of a blank page with its mirror image, even as the opening horizontal rectangles (the four-line units have justified left and right margins and double spacing) play on the word "MARK" (89):

mark mar   ha   forest 1 a   boundary   manic   a   land a
tract indicate   position   2   record   bunting   interval
free also   event   starting   the   slightly   position   of
O   about both of   don't   something   INDICATION   Americ

made or   also   symbol sachem   maimed   as on her for
ar in   teacher   duct   excellent   figure   MARK   lead be
knife knows   his   hogs   dogs   a   boundary   model   nucle
hearted land   land   land   district   boundary   times un

Here *mark* refers first of all to the surveyor's (William Byrd's) mark made in delineating a boundary between "tract[s]" of forestland. But the mark is also a trace, a sign that points us to specific things that have happened: one thinks of Blake's "London," with its lines, "And mark in every face I meet / Marks of weakness, marks of woe."[31] The poem's opening "mark mar ha forest 1 a

boundary manic" gives the word *mark* a number of paragrammatic possibilities. "mark mar ha": stutter is followed by exclamation, an inability, perhaps, to "mark" the boundary in question. Or again, "mar ha" may be parts
of the name Martha, the *t* missing in the imagined source manuscript here
and throughout the text, "boundary manic" is central to the poet's thought;
she is mesmerized by questions of "secret" divisions, borders, boundaries,
fault lines. Then, too, *Mark* refers both to Howe's father (Mark DeWolfe
Howe) and to her son, Mark Von Schlegell, as the italicized line on the third
page of the poem, "*for Mark my father; and Mark my son*" tells us (91). Indeed, the frontispiece informs us that Mark DeWolfe Howe's *Touched with
Fire: The Civil War Letters and Diary of Oliver Wendell Holmes* is one of the
poem's sources.[32]

On the second page of *Secret History of the Dividing Line*, we find the following passage:

> Close at hand the ocean
> until before
> hidden from our vision
> MARK
> border
> bulwark, an object set up to indicate a boundary or position
> hence a sign or token
> impression or trace
>
> The Horizon

I am of another generation
> *when next I looked he was gone.*

The final line is repeated three times on this page and relates the colonial
expedition of William Byrd to the "MARK" who is the poet's father.

How does this allusive visual poem relate to Howe's so-called preface,
which interweaves autobiography, visual poetry, and the founding and early
history of Buffalo? For example:

> I was never sure what my father was doing in the army. Then I
> was never sure of anything what with his rushing away or changing
> cities and World War banging at windows the boundless phenomena
> of madness. I remember him coming back to Buffalo from basic train-
> ing by snapshot once or twice in a uniform. Absence is always present

in a picture in its right relations. There is a split then how to act. Laws
are relations among individuals.

When Theophile Cazenove reached America in 1789, he realized that
Philadelphia was the best scene for his operations because the future
of American funds, federal and state, depended on the actions of the
federal government. Pavements were in wider space and getting social
satisfaction he carried along a letter of introduction from his back-
ers in Amsterdam to Andrew Craigie in New York. The Van Staphorts
told Craigie their envoy came to America "to gratify his thirst after
knowledge in order to become better acquainted with the Genius of
their Government and the objects of their growing commerce." (*Frame
Structures* 6)

The common wisdom would be that these two paragraphs are "straight"—
although rather odd—prose; in the first sentence above, for example, the
noun phrase "the boundless phenomena of madness" is syntactically but not
semantically in apposition to the noun "windows." And the relation of syntax to semantics gets stranger as the paragraph continues: how, for example,
can the poet's father be "coming back from basic training by snapshot"?
Similar non sequiturs characterize the passage about Cazenove, as when
"pavements . . . in wider space" are linked to "social satisfaction."

How to construe this curious way of writing an autobiographical memoir, a memoir designed to serve as "frame structure" for the disjointed and
fragmentary lyric poems that follow? In one sense *Frame Structures* recalls
Robert Lowell's "91 Revere Street," that bemused account of the Beacon Hill
childhood and "Mayflower screwball" ancestry that makes "young Bob" the
neurotic and specially gifted child he is.[33] But whereas "91 Revere Street"
provides us with a series of snapshots, in which the Winslow-Lowell relatives come before us in all their foibles and futility, *Frame Structures* juxtaposes biographical sketches (for example, the poet's American grandfather,
Mark Antony DeWolfe Howe [1864–1960]) with the documentary history of
the founding of Buffalo, with allusions to Henry Wadsworth Longfellow's
Evangeline and James Joyce's *Eveline* as analogues to the family and social
drama of the Howes and Quincys, and with scraps ("flinders") of largely
illegible text, evidently drawn from Edward Gibbon. Again, whereas "91 Revere Street" is a kind of mirror image (in prose) of the autobiographical poems like "Commander Lowell" and "Beverly Farms" that comprise *Life Studies*, poems that culminate in Lowell's own very private "Skunk Hour," in
Frame Structures the connection between Howe's memoir and, say, the epi-
graphs from Boswell's *Life of Johnson* and Beatrix Potter's *Peter Rabbit* that

open *Cabbage Gardens,* remains elusive. Indeed, the oblique narrative that
follows, which begins with the lines

> The enemy coming on roads
> and clouds
> aeons.
> cashel has fallen
> trees are turf
> horizon thanks to myself, yes
> pacing the study.[34]

seems to have no identifiable lyric subject. Here, Howe's detractors would say,
is a cryptic Language poem that denies the very possibilities of the expressivity one wants from lyric.

Or does it? Consider the leitmotif of framing and being framed that runs
through both prose preface and visual poems, crisscrossing, in myriad ways,
the related motifs of war and colonization. The frontispiece (figure 4) is an
engraving from Frank Severance's *Picture Book of Earlier Buffalo,* based on
"an original sketch by Lt. Jesse D. Elliott, accompanying his report to the Secretary of the Navy on the Capture of the Detroit and Caledonia, dated Black
Rock Oct. 9, 1812." "The Second Oldest View of Buffalo," as this depiction
of schooners going up in smoke is captioned in Howe's book, thus immediately introduces the motif of war, in this case the War of 1812 (*Frame Structures* 1).

But if this is the "Second Oldest View of Buffalo," what would the first
look like? For Howe, origins cannot be known. "Lines represent the limits of
bodies encompassed by the eye" (5). The section "*Floating loans*" contains a
historical sketch of Joseph Ellicott's acquisition and settling of the land in
upstate New York that was to be called Buffalo. We can take in the facts, but
we cannot quite visualize the resulting city. "Space is a frame we map ourselves in" (9). When we finally do "see" the Buffalo harbor in the engraving,
we are witnessing a war scene: war, for that matter, is very much this poem's
condition. At the same time, "a picture," as Wittgenstein puts it, "held us
captive";[35] neither poet nor reader can get beyond the engraving, the stylized
image, to experience the "reality" of Buffalo. This is why names become so
tantalizing—Nicholas Van Staphorst, Christiaan Van Eeghen, Paul Busti—we
yearn for, but cannot get at, what's behind them. And consider the absurdity
of calling a city Buffalo. "Clans and individuals adopt the name of animals,"
Howe remarks, "cities seldom do." And she adds, "Prefaces are usually after-
images" (13).[36]

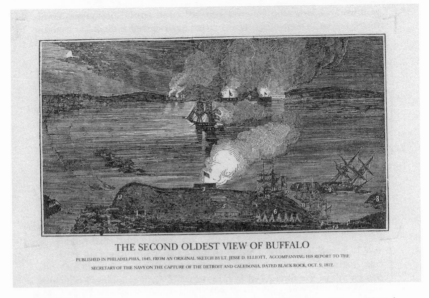

THE SECOND OLDEST VIEW OF BUFFALO

PUBLISHED IN PHILADELPHIA, 1845, FROM AN ORIGINAL SKETCH BY LT. JESSE D. ELLIOTT, ACCOMPANYING HIS REPORT TO THE
SECRETARY OF THE NAVY ON THE CAPTURE OF THE DETROIT AND CALEDONIA, DATED BLACK ROCK, OCT. 9, 1812.

Fig. 4. Frontispiece from Susan Howe's *Frame Structures* (Courtesy of Susan Howe)

The first sentence of Howe's "afterimage," under the heading *Flanders*, with its allusion to World War I, is: "On Sunday, December 7, 1941, I went with my father to the zoo in Delaware Park even now so many years after there is always for me the fact of this treasured memory of togetherness before he enlisted in the army and went away to Europe" (3). December 7, 1941 is, of course, Pearl Harbor Day, but this fact is not mentioned, the focus being on the "usually docile polar bears rov[ing] restlessly back and forth around the simulated rocks caves and waterfall designed to keep brute force fenced off even by menace of embrace so many zoo animals are accounted fierce" (3). The final clause here trails off, "so many" not anticipated by what comes before. The three polar bears are framed both literally and figuratively— literally behind the "iron railing" of their cage, figuratively by "the north wind of the fairy story" ["Goldilocks"] "ringing in my ears as well as direct perception" (3). From the opening image of (unstated) war malaise, through the accounts of King Philip's War, the Revolutionary War, World War I, and World War II, the text's war space is crisscrossed by "life-lines," lines of descent, connection, and association that, as the poet puts it, "I transmit to you from the point of impact throughout every snowing difficulty," lines "certified by surveyors chain-bearers artists and authors walking the world keeping Field Notes:" from "Flanders" to "*Flinders*";[37] from Nigeria, to Niger, to

Niagara; from the "iron railings" of the bear compound in the zoo to the "iron railings" of the Charles Street Jail; from Fanny Appleton Longfellow to the poet's younger sister, Fanny (28).

But the lines are also borders, boundaries, marks of enclosure—the line between the Boston Brahmin Howes and Quincys on the one hand and the Irish Mannings on the other. "Preface" thus paves the way for the poems that follow: "*Hinge* Picture," "Western *Borders*," "Secret History of the *Dividing Line*" (my italics). And even in *Cabbage Gardens*, the shifts in line justification and word placement, suggest that language is always in danger of becoming an enclosed space but that the poet refuses to let forms play their accepted role. Each segment is, so to speak, a "cabbage garden" that is planted differently.[38]

The extensive historical documentation in Howe's "Preface" thus serves to construct the past that has shaped what Howe takes to be her very palpable present. Weetamoo, "squaw-sachem of the Wampanoags, Queen of Pocasset (now Tiverton), wife of Wamsutta the son of Massasoit and sister-in-law of the Narrangansett sachem, Metacomet (King Philip to the colonial militia)," a figure Howe knows only from her reading of Mary Rowlandson, is just as "real" as "John d'Wolf, 'Norwest John,' another early venture capitalist [who] sailed to Russia by way of Alaska" (*Frame Structures* 21). The poet herself appears only in the interstices of the text: "Now draw a trajectory in imagination where logic and mathematics meet the materials of art. Canvas, paper, pencil, color, frame, title . . . " (27). Right after this catalogue of artist's tools (where "title" is the odd item), the cited overprint text becomes illegible (figure 5), forcing the reader to become a kind of viewer/voyeur.

"Preface" never spells out its "life-lines" to the lyrics that follow. In the words of the epigraph from Duchamp's *Green Box* that opens *Hinge Picture* (*Frame Structures* 32)—"Perhaps make a HINGE PICTURE. (folding yardstick, book. . . .) / develops in space the PRINCIPLE OF THE HINGE in the displacements 1st in the plane 2d in space"—"Preface" is a kind of "Hinge Picture" that contains connections to the historical and literary fragments that follow. Indeed, Howe's book is an elaborate trace structure: *Secret History of the Dividing Line* ends with a verbal rectangle on an otherwise empty white field:

sh	dispel	iris	sh	snow	sward	wide	ha
forest	1 a	boundary	manic	a	land	sh	
whit	thing	: target	cadence	marked	on		
O	about	both or don't	INDICATION	Americ			
sh	woof	subdued toward	foliage	free	sh		

(Frame Structures 122)

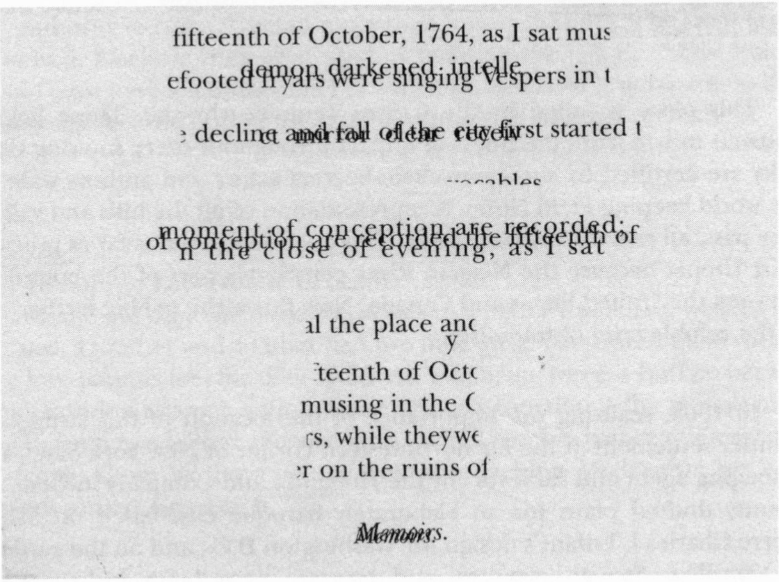

fifteenth of October, 1764, as I sat mus

efooted friars were singing vespers in t
demon darkened; intelle

: decline and fall of the city first started t

--ocables

moment of conception are recorded;
of conception are recorded the fifteenth of
n the close of evening, as I sat

al the place anc
y
teenth of Octc
musing in the (
rs, while they we
:r on the ruins of

Memoirs.

Fig. 5. Excerpt from page 27 of Susan Howe's *Frame Structures* (Courtesy of Susan Howe)

From "sh" to "sh," from "snow sward" to "foliage free," via a "boundary manic," a target cadence marked." "Sh." The rest is white space.

Compared to the "Robert Lowell" of *Life Studies*, Howe's "I"—female, maverick, only half New England blueblood—is much less of an insider, much more self-conscious about her particular origins. Her Boston is always shadowed by her Buffalo. Accordingly, she rarely speaks in her own person (e.g., "I was a deep and nervous child" [3]), preferring the voice of the chronicler ("Joseph Ellicott, sometimes called 'the father of Buffalo,' was born in Bucks County, Pennsylvania, in 1760 to Quaker parents from England" [5]), and the voices of others:

What are you crying for, Great-Grandmother?

For all the ruin so intolerably sad.

But we have plenty to eat.   We are lucky to be living in the United States, so very new and very old, lucky to be in the new part. Everything is clearer now we have electric light.

You must go on as if I was an open door. Go right on
through me I can't answer all your questions. (25)

Add to such voices the visual devices—line placement, typography, page
design—that characterize all four of the early books reprinted in *Frame
Structures,* as well as the new "Preface," and you have a signature (quite literally a series of marks made on paper) as unique and "personal" as any we
have in poetry today. Susan Howe and Ron Silliman, appearing side by side
as they do in the various Language anthologies, could hardly be more different in their modes of self-writing.

What then of the purported death of the subject? "The revolution of the
word," Silliman remarks in a recent interview, "is not an anarchist event."
On the contrary, "as the author, *I* get to determine *unilaterally* which words
in what order will set forth the terms through which the experience shall
occur."[39] A remarkable statement, this, for a Language poet, and yet at one
level it is simple common sense: every poet, after all, gets to determine the
words in his or her poem. The question remains, of course, what larger cultural and ideological constraints determine that determination. If Silliman's
and Howe's poetries are, as I have argued, characterized by their *difference,*
by a writing that is everywhere resisting its "Language" or "Experimental"
paradigm, how does that paradigm itself resist its contemporary others?

Suppose we read the poems of Silliman and Howe (or Palmer or Watten) not against one another but against those of a very different poetic
community—for example, the work of Charles Wright. Here is one of the
thirteen-line lyrics (there are twenty-four, divided into three sections) in
Wright's recent sequence "Disjecta Membra," included in James Tate's *Best
American Poetry 1997:*

O well the snow falls and small birds drop out of the sky,
The backyard's a winding sheet—
                                    winter in Charlottesville,
Epiphany two days gone,
Nothing at large but Broncos, pick-ups and 4 × 4s.
Even the almost full moon
                              Is under a monochrome counterpane
Of dry grey.
                      Eve of St. Agnes and then some, I'd say,
Twenty-three inches and coming down.
The Rev. Doctor Syntax puts finger to forehead on the opposite wall,

Mancini and I still blurred beside him, Mykonos, 1961,
The past a snowstorm the present too.[40]

The obvious thing would be to say that Wright's lyric sequence, which traces
the poet's emptying out, his night and death thoughts, and the gradual renewal of being, as defined by the seasonal cycle from the end of summer
to the end of winter in Virginia, is more "personal" or "expressive" than
the "Language poems" of Silliman or Howe. But strictly speaking, we learn
less about the particulars of Wright's personal life than we do about theirs;
people and places from the poet's past and present remain elusive as do the
causes that trigger the feeling of absence and emptiness described so lovingly
in this particular snow poem, where even "the almost full moon / is under a
monochrome counterpane / of dry grey."

What *is* different is not expressivity or subjectivity as such but the *authority* ascribed to the speaking voice—and here it is a particular voice that
is represented. Wright's speaker confidently uses metaphor to characterize
what he perceives ("The backyard's a winding sheet") and feels ("Epiphany
two days gone"); he compares the dismal sleety night to that of Keats's *Eve
of St. Agnes* and knows that what he sees when he looks out the window are
"nothing . . . but Broncos, pick-ups and 4 × 4s." In "Albany," on the other
hand, such connections and continuities (Wright's winter portrait is wholly
consistent and of a piece) are implictly judged to be impossible. Phrases like
"the bird demonstrates the sky" or "eminent domain" cannot be taken as
self-revelatory. For these utterances, in Silliman's scheme of things, are not
those of an observer located in a particular place; indeed, the distinction between inside and outside has been eroded. For Silliman, as for Howe, there
are no ideas or facts outside the language that names them—no "Broncos,
pick-ups and 4 × 4s," no "twenty-three inches" of snow, outside the poet's
verbal as well as literal window. Rather—and here the difference in epistemology is profound—language constructs the "reality" perceived. And this
means that perspective, as in the polar bear scene in Howe's "Frame Structures," is always shifting and that the subject, far from being at the center of
the discourse, as is the case in Wright's poem, is located only at its interstices.

It is not coincidental that "Disjecta Membra" has echoes of Keats (and,
later, Stevens), for its mode is Emersonian: "We live in the wind-chill, / The
what-if- and what-was-not, / The blown and sour dust of just after or just
before, / The metaquotidian landscape / of soft edge and abyss" (194). Nature always wears the colors of the spirit. There is no way Silliman or Howe
could write such a poem, because theirs is not a Romantic *Einfühlung* into
the external—is there an external?—world. And in this respect we can differ-

entiate quite readily between their ethos and that of such mainstream post-Romantic poets as Charles Wright or Mark Strand or Louise Gluck.

It was, of course, the declared opposition to this romantic paradigm that prompted the theoretical discourse of Language manifestos in the first place. And that oppositionality remains significant even though the "Us-versus-Them" rhetoric of *The L=A=N=G=U=A=G=E Book,* now twenty years old, has become complicated by the appearance of new poetic paradigms that don't quite fit the original theoretical frame.[41] The dialectic, in other words, has shifted ground, and it now seems more useful to look at special cases *within* the Language movement and related alternate poetries rather than at the group phenomenon.

Indeed, the paradox is that, like the earlier avant-garde movements of the century, Language poetics may well become most widely known when it starts to manifest notable exceptions. Imagism, after all, became interesting only when Ezra Pound declared that it had been diluted as "Amygism" and called himself a Vorticist instead. Dada, as I have suggested elsewhere,[42] derives much of its cultural capital from Duchamp, who had made his most "Dada" *readymades* before he had ever heard of the Cabaret Voltaire and who refused all his life to participate in Dada exhibitions. A renewal of interest in Concrete poetry was sparked by the decision of one Concrete poet, Ian Hamilton Finlay, to cultivate (quite literally) his own "concrete" Scottish garden. And the New York School, felt by many to have lost its center when Frank O'Hara died in 1966, is now getting renewed mileage from the increasing renown of one of its charter members, John Ashbery, even though Ashbery's poetry may well have more in common with T. S. Eliot's than with Kenneth Koch's.[43]

I do not mean to downplay the role of community, movement, cultural formation, or discourse in the making of avant-garde aesthetic. Community, after all, is crucial to the poets and artists who belong to it, especially in their formative stages. Indeed, the prominence of the lonely, isolated genius, which Jameson takes to be the hallmark of modernism (as opposed to postmodernism), was always something of a myth; even those "isolated geniuses" Joyce and Beckett needed a community of fellow writers and a set of publishing venues—for example, Eugene Jolas's *transition*—within which to circulate.

The poet has no obligation to be a responsible historian; indeed, the anxiety of influence precludes the possibility of reliable accounts of one's own genealogy. Here is where the poet's readers come in. In writing as critics or literary historians, even those who are themselves poets must maintain some critical distance, discriminating, for example, between the "Language" poetics of Michael Palmer, with its Celanian and French Surrealist cast, the New

York School–based poetics of Ron Silliman and Bob Perelman, and the fusion of "nation language" and "video style" in the work of a proto–Language poet like Kamau Brathwaite.[44]

Movement ethos, itself the stepchild of the post-structuralist critique of authorship, has for too long now occluded the critical need to discriminate *difference*, to define the signature of the individual lyric subject in its complex negotiations with its larger cultural and historical field of operation. In the words of Charles Bernstein's satiric little poem (*My Way* 3–4) on the limits of structuralism, "Don't Be So Sure (Don't Be Saussure)":

My cup is my cap
& my cap is my cup
When the coffee is hot
It ruins my hat
We clap and we slap
Have sup with our pap
But won't someone please
Get me a drink

In the spring of 1999 I was invited to give a paper at a conference called "Page Mothers" (the title refers to women editors of little magazines and experimental poetry journals), held at the University of California, San Diego. In my essay I discussed the origins of Language poetry—a movement whose original theorizers were a group of male poet-intellectuals. When I expanded the essay for presentation at the Barnard College conference on "Innovation in Contemporary Poetry by Women" (1999), I went on to trace the gradual transformation of early Language theory into a more inclusive "experimental" poetics that opened up the field to women and minority poets. But I concluded with a caveat—a caveat that aroused some resentment in my audience—as to the current demand on these "experimental" poets to write theoretical essays as had the founders of the Language movement. Edward Foster and Joseph Donahue requested the essay for their 2002 collection, The World in Time and Space: Toward a History of Innovative American Poetry in our Time.

8
After Language Poetry
Innovation and Its Theoretical Discontents

Are you sure, she asked, you're talking of ideas? Dark, emptied of touch would be entire, null and void. Even on an island.
Rosmarie Waldrop, *Split Infinites*

Innovate: from the Latin *in* + *novare*, "to make new, to renew, alter." In our century, from Rimbaud's "*Il faut être absolument moderne!*" and Ezra Pound's "Make It New!" to Donald Allen's *New American Poetry* (Grove Press, 1960) and Douglas Messerli's *From the Other Side of the Century: A New American Poetry, 1960–1990* (Sun & Moon, 1994), novelty has been the order of the day. Think of the (now old) New Criticism, the New Formalism, the New Historicism, *le nouveau roman*, and *la nouvelle cuisine*. As I was writing this essay, a message came over the Internet announcing the British poet-critic Robert Sheppard's *Poetics and Linguistically Innovative Poetry, 1978–1997*.[1] And in recent years, two important anthologies of women's poetry—*Out of Everywhere: Linguistically Innovative Poetry by Women in*

North America and the UK, edited by Maggie O'Sullivan for Reality Street Editions (London, 1996), and Mary Margaret Sloan's *Moving Borders: Three Decades of Innovative Writing by Women* (Jersey City, NJ: Talisman Publishers, 1998)—have made the case that, in O'Sullivan's words, "much of the most challenging, formally progressive and significant work over recent years, particularly, in the U.S. . . . . is being made by women" (*Out of Everywhere* 9), thus leading directly to the title of the Barnard conference: "Innovation in Contemporary Poetry by Women."

It was not always thus. The *Oxford English Dictionary* reminds us that *innovation* was once synonymous with sedition and even treason. In 1561 Thomas Norton wrote in *Calvin's Institute,* "It is the duty of private men to obey, and not to make innovation of states after their own will." Richard Hooker in 1597 refers to a political pamphleteer as "an authour of suspicious innovation." The great Jacobean dramatist John Webster speaks of "the hydra-headed multitude / That only gape for innovation" (1639), and in 1796 Edmund Burke refers to the French Revolution as "a revolt of innovation; and thereby, the very elements of society have been confounded and dissipated."

Indeed, it was not until the late nineteenth century that *innovation* became perceived as something both good and necessary, the equivalent, in fact, of *avant-garde,* specifically of the great avant-gardes of the early century from Russian and Italian Futurism to Dada, Surrealism, and beyond. I cannot here trace the vagaries of the term, but it is important to see that so far as our own poetry is concerned, the call for Making It New was the watchword of the Beats as of Black Mountain, of Concrete poetry and Fluxus as of the New York School. At times in recent years, one wonders how long the drive to innovate can continue, especially when, as in the case of Sloan's *Moving Borders,* fifty contemporary American women poets are placed under the "innovative" umbrella. Given these numbers, one wonders, who *isn't* innovative? And how much longer can poets keep innovating without finding themselves inadvertently Making It Old?

The problem is compounded when we turn to the relationship of innovation to theory. When the various French post-structuralisms of the postwar first became prominent, they were known as *la nouvelle critique.* But as time went on, *la nouvelle critique* became known as post-structuralism, just as the "new American poetry" was called, in Donald Allen's revised version of 1982, *The Postmoderns* (New York: Grove Press). What, then, is the relation of "new" to "post"? The issue is complicated, but it's fair to say that in the case of theory, "new" was an epithet applied from outside, for the theorists themselves were less concerned to Make It New than to establish certain truths—

for example, to study the relation of literary to so-called ordinary language, to determine the respective role of author and reader in the interpretation of a given text, and to establish the ways in which individual texts speak for their culture. For Barthes and Derrida, as earlier for Benjamin and Adorno, Bataille and Blanchot, *innovation* as such was of little interest. Benjamin, for that matter, had no use for the Dadaists who were his contemporaries, dismissing them as instigators of little more than "a rather vehement distraction," designed "to outrage the public."[2] And Adorno regarded most of what passed for "new" fiction or poetry as little more than kitsch.

Accordingly—and this is an important aspect of the Language movement, which stands squarely behind so much of contemporary "innovative" poetry—the "new" rapprochement between poetry and theory that we find in the first issues of $L=A=N=G=U=A=G=E$ (1978), and in such equally important journals as the San Francisco-based *This* and *Hills*, and the Canadian *Open Letter*—all these now a quarter-century old[3]—had less to do with innovation per se than with the conviction on the part of a group of poets, themselves keenly interested in philosophy and post-structuralist theory, that poetics was an intellectual enterprise, deserving a larger place than it had in the Creative Writing classroom of the seventies.

Consider the symposium edited by Steve McCaffery, published in the Canadian journal *Open Letter* in 1977 and reprinted by Andrews and Bernstein as $L=A=N=G=U=A=G=E$, Supplement Number One, in June 1980. The symposium was called "The Politics of the Referent"; it includes McCaffery's "The Death of the Subject: The Implications of Counter-Communication in Recent Language-Centered Writing," Bruce Andrews's "Text and Context," Ray DiPalma's "Crystals," Ron Silliman's "For Open Letter," and Charles Bernstein's "Stray Straws and Straw Men." Although three of the above were to be reprinted in their authors' own books on poetics, these early versions are revealing.[4] For so quickly did their authors soften their stance that the 1980 Supplement begins with the editorial disclaimer: "It seems worth remembering, in looking back on these essays, that the tendencies in writing McCaffery is talking about under such headings as 'language-centered' are as open to the entrapments of stylistic fixation as any other tendency in recent poetry."[5] And when McCaffery came to revise "The Death of the Subject" for his collection *North of Intention* (1986), he declared, "I was never happy with the title and both it and much of the content have been revised. The essay, whose original thoughts and materials were gathered through the mid-seventies, concentrates on a partial aspect of Language Writing: a concern primarily with the morphological and sub-lexemic relations present and obtainable in language. A decade later I can safely speak of this concern as an historic phase with attention having shifted . . . to a larger aspect—especially to the critical status of the sentence as the minimal unit of social utterance and hence, the foundation of discourse" (13).

McCaffery's original version begins dramatically with this declaration: "There is a group of writers today united in the feeling that literature has entered *a crisis of the sign* . . . and that the foremost task at hand—a more linguistic and philosophic then 'poetic' task—is to demystify the referential fallacy of language." "Reference," he adds, "is that kind of blindness a window makes of the pane it is, that motoric thrust of the word which takes you out of language into a tenuous world of the other and so prevents you seeing what it is you see" (Supplement 1). Such a thrust—the removal of what McCaffery calls later in the essay "the arrow of reference"—is essential because "language is above all else a system of signs and . . . writing must stress its semiotic nature through modes of investigation and probe, rather than mimetic, instrumental indications."

Here, in a nutshell, is the animating principle of the movement: poetic language is not a window, to be seen through, a transparent glass pointing to something outside it, but a system of signs with its own semiological "interconnectedness." To put it another way, "Language is material and primary and what's experienced is the tension and relationship of letters and lettristic clusters, simultaneously struggling towards, yet refusing to become, significations" (Supplement 2). McCaffery himself points to the Russian Formalists, to Wittgenstein, Barthes, Lacan, and Derrida as the sources for his theory, and indeed Language poetics, in this first stage, owes its greatest debt to French post-structuralism, although Charles Bernstein, for one, was much closer to Wittgenstein, whose work he had studied with Stanley Cavell at Harvard, than to Derrida, whose analysis of signification he distrusted, even as Silliman and Andrews were drawn to a more politicized Frankfurt School poetics. But McCaffery himself sounds a Derridean note when he declares that "the empirical experience of a grapheme replaces what the signifier in a word will always try to discharge: its signified and referent." Indeed, in poetry the signifier is always "superfluous," overloaded with potential meanings and hence more properly a *cipher* (Supplement 4).

There are two corollaries—one Barthean, one Marxist-Althusserian. "Language-centered writing," McCaffery tells us, "involves a major alteration in textual roles: of the socially defined functions of writer and reader as the productive and consumptive poles respectively of a commodital axis" (3). And again, "The text becomes the communal space of a labour, initiated by the writer and extended by the second writer (the reader). . . . The old duality of reader-writer collapses into the one compound function, and the two actions are permitted to become a simultaneous experience within the activity of the engager" (8). "Reading" is thus "an alternative or additional writing of the text." Indeed—and here the Marxist motif kicks in—"Linguistic reference is a displacement of human relationships and as such is fetishistic in the Marxian sense. Reference, like commodity, has no connection with the physical property and material relations of the word as a grapheme" (3). Direct communication, on this count, is the hallmark of the commodity fetish. Thus, "to remove the arrow of reference," to "short-circuit the semiotic loop" (9) becomes a political rather than a merely aesthetic act. In his "Text and Context," Bruce Andrews reinforces this notion, dismissing referentiality as the misguided "search for the pot at the end of the rainbow, the commodity or ideology that brings fulfillment" (Supplement 20).

As the Utopian manifesto of a twenty-eight-year-old poet, "The Death of the Subject" inevitably overstated its case. The call for "unreadability" and "non-communication," for example, was largely exemplified by sequences of disconnected word fragments and isolated morphemes, as in the citations from Andrews, Clark Coolidge, and Barbara Baracks, the latter giving us a two-column poem like

stint	grits
darts	file
gratis	ways to fit tins
dapper	angle
ill	apple

McCaffery calls on us to "produce [our] own reading among the polysemous routes that the text offers" (Supplement 4), a challenging invitation, even though, as soon became apparent, less stringent readers than McCaffery himself took him to mean that one reading would be just as good as another. Moreover, the rejection of all "instrumental" language as commodity fetish in favor of a poetic paradigm that, if we are to trust McCaffery's examples, includes only the most extreme form of wordplay, fragmentation, decomposition of words, and absence of all connectives, as in Andrews's "mob cuspid / welch / eyelet / go lavender / futurible" (5), could be seen as excessively dismissive of alternate ways of composing poetry.

But despite McCaffery's Ubulike iconoclasm, his basic premises—and this is the irony—were by no means as extreme or as new as both the proponents and opponents of Language poetics would have had us think. What McCaffery and Andrews (19) call the "referential fallacy" takes us right back to Roman Jakobson's central thesis that in poetry the sign is never equivalent to its referent and the corollary notion that poetry is language that is somehow extraordinary.[6] The case against transparency, against instrumental value and straightforward readability was the cornerstone of Russian Formalist theory as well as of Bakhtin's theory of dialogism and heteroglossia. In *The Noise of Culture,* William Paulson has shown that the concept of poetry as "noise," as blockage of the normal (transparent) channels of communication, is a notion that was already central, if intuitively so, for Romantic theorists.[7] As for Wittgenstein, who refused to distinguish between ordinary and extraordinary language, finding "ordinary" language quite "strange" enough, the basic tenet that there are no meanings outside of language gave McCaffery and his fellow symposiasts license to denounce what Bernstein called, in "Stray Straws and Straw Men," the "natural look" as itself a construction with particular implications. Poetry, Bernstein argued, is never really "natural" (e.g., "I look straight into my heart & write the exact words that come from within"); rather, "it emphasizes its medium as being constructed, rule governed, everywhere circumscribed by grammar & syntax, chosen vocabulary: designed, manipulated, picked, programmed, organized, & so an artifice."[8]

Twenty years after its appearance, we can read "The Politics of the Referent" symposium as an important statement, reminding readers on the one hand that poetry has always been "an artifice" and on the other that poetry cannot be too far out of step with the other discourses—philosophical, political, cultural—of its own time. By the mid-seventies, let's recall, these discourses, as studied on every campus across the United States, had produced a highly sophisticated and challenging body of texts about the nature and function of *écriture* or *writing,* whether "writing the body" (Cixous and Iragaray), the position of subjects in particular discourses (Kristeva), the relationship of truth to fiction (Todorov, Bakhtin), and so on. I remember clearly, in those years, walking into St. Mark's Bookshop in the Bowery and seeing on the central table the stacks of Barthes's *The Empire of Signs,* Derrida's *Of Grammatology* in the Gayatri Spivak translation, and Michel Foucault's *The Order of Things* (1970), which was published not by a university press but by Random House. These books were selling as if they were popular novels. At the same time, poetry, insofar as it had become the domain of the Creative Writing workshop, was no longer the contested site it had been in the days of Pound, Eliot, and Williams, or even of the "raw versus cooked" debates of the early sixties. In the seventies, for reasons too complex to go into here,[9] the production of poetry had become a kind of bland cottage industry, designed for those whose intellect was not up to reading Barthes or Foucault or Kristeva. The feeling/intellect split had probably never been wider. For even as students were absorbing Foucault's "What Is an Author?" and Barthes's "The Death of the Author," Official Verse Culture, as Bernstein called it, was spawning poems like the following, which I take from *The Morrow Anthology of Younger Poets*:

Hollandaise

The sauce thickens. I add more butter,
slowly. Sometimes we drank the best wine
while we cooked for friends,
knowing nothing could go wrong,
the soufflé would rise, the custard set,
the cheese be ripe. we imagined
we were reckless but we were just happy,
and good at our work. the cookbook is firm:
it is safer not to go over two ounces
of butter for each egg yolk. I try to describe
to myself how we could have been safer,
what we exceeded. If the sauce "turns"
there are things to be done, steps
to be taken that are not miraculous,
that assume the failed ingredients,
that assume a willing suspension of despair.[10]

Here McCaffery's arrow of reference is flying straight into the saucepan, ready to curdle that hollandaise. The lasting contribution of Language poetics, I would posit, is that at a moment when workshop poetry all across the United States was wedded to a kind of neo-confessionalist, neo-realist poetic discourse, a discourse committed to drawing pretentious metaphors about failed relationships from hollandaise recipes, Language theory reminded us that poetry is a *making* [*poien*], a construction using language, rhythm, sound, and visual image; that the subject, far from being simply the poet speaking in his or her natural "voice," was itself a complex construction; and that—most important—there was actually something at stake in producing a body of poems; and that poetic discourse belonged to the same universe as philosophical and political discourse.

None of this, of course, was all that new, but it was new within the particular context of "Naked Poetry," as an important anthology edited by Robert Mezey and Stephen Berg was called,[11] or vis-à-vis Allen Ginsberg's insistence on "First thought, best thought"—a precept Ginsberg fortunately didn't put into practice, at least not in his best poetry.[12] By the 1990s, in any case, all three of the Language principles that McCaffery put forward had been subtly transformed even as their force remains implicitly operative today. The referential fallacy, to begin with, has given way to a more nuanced emphasis on the *how* of poetic language rather than the *what*. The dismissal of instrumental language as the commodity fetish has come under criticism from both Left and Right, as readers have realized that so-called innovative writing—writing that is fragmented, asyntactic, non-sensical, etc.—can be just as fetishized as anything else. And the emphasis on readerly construction, an article of faith in the semiotic theories of Barthes, Foucault, and Eco, and, in the United States, of reader-response theory, has given way to a renewed perception that the alleged authority of the reader is, as Ron Silliman has remarked in a recent essay, merely a transfer of power whereby, in ways Barthes could not have foreseen, "the idealized, absent author of the New Critical canon has [merely] been replaced by an equally idealized, absent reader."[13]

Language poetics, let's remember, had a strong political thrust: it was essentially a Marxist poetics that focused, in important ways, on issues of ideology and class.[14] But it was less attuned to questions of gender and race: indeed, in the case of $L=A=N=G=U=A=G=E$, although one senses that every effort was made to include "innovative" women poets—for example, Rae Armantrout, Barbara Baracks, Abigail Child, Lynne Dreyer, Johanna Drucker, Barbara Einzig, Carla Harryman, Lyn Hejinian, Susan Howe, Bernadette Mayer, Leslie Scalapino, Rosmarie Waldrop, Diane Ward, and Hannah Weiner—the more overt theorizing itself was left, with rare exceptions, to the men in the movement.[15] Thus, students in the eighties were usually introduced to Language poetry by such "reference books" as Barrett Watten's *Total Syntax*, Charles Bernstein's *Content's Dream*, Steve McCaffery's *North of Intention*, and Ron Silliman's *The New Sentence*, all published between 1985 and 1987. The dominance of these founding fathers can be seen in the British reception of Language poetics, a reception coming largely from the Left, which was keenly interested in but also highly critical of the doctrines put forward in "The New Sentence," "Artifice of Absorption," or "The Death of the Subject," but had little to say about specific poems.[16]

What, then, of the women poets in the original movement?[17] Interestingly, their background was more literary and artistic than that of, say, Andrews and Bernstein, who had studied political science and philosophy, respectively. Susan Howe began her career as a visual artist and was very much influenced by Concrete poetry, especially the work of Ian Hamilton Finlay and

Tom Phillips. Johanna Drucker was trained as a printmaker and visual poet and wrote her PhD thesis at Berkeley on the Russian avant-gardist Iliazd. Rosmarie Waldrop was a student of modernism and of Concrete poetry, and a translator of Edmund Jabès, Maurice Blanchot, and many Austrian and German avant-gardists. Kathleen Fraser had studied with the New York poets, especially Kenneth Koch. And so on.

The increasing recognition of the women poets associated with L=A=N=G=U=A=G=E was made evident in Lee Hickman's superb journal *Temblor,* which began publication in 1985 and ceased, with issue 10, in 1989 because its editor was dying of AIDS and could no longer sustain the operation. Hickman is to my mind one of the great unsung heroes of the so-called innovative poetry scene. Unaffiliated with a university or even a specific movement, he published *Temblor* from his home on Cahuenga Boulevard in the much despised San Fernando Valley above Hollywood. *Temblor* had no editorial board, no mission statement and, until the last few issues, no grant money; Hickman simply published the poetry that interested him—a good chunk of it "Language poetry," but also the related poetries coming out of the Olson-Duncan school, the Objectivists, and the "ethno-poeticists" associated with Jerome Rothenberg: for example, Clayton Eshleman, Armand Schwerner, Rochelle Owens, Kenneth Irby, Robert Kelly, Jed Rasula, Gustaf Sobin, and John Taggart. *Temblor* was a portfolio with a 9 × 12–inch page that allowed for visual design, as for example in Leslie Scalapino's "Delay Series" (#4) and a long (28-page) section from Susan Howe's *Eikon Basilike* (#9).[18] The journal published Rosmarie Waldrop's *A Form of Taking It All* in its entirety (#6); Kathleen Fraser's sequence "In Commemoration of the Visit of Foreign Commercial Representatives to Japan, 1947" (#9); nine poems from Hejinian's "The Person" (#4); Susan Howe's "Heliopathy" (#4); sections of Rachel Blau DuPlessis's long sequence *Drafts;* and work by Barbara Guest, Rae Armantrout, Carla Harriman, Mei Mei Bersenbrugge, Johanna Drucker, Norma Cole, and Martha (Ronk) Lifson. The magazine introduced the work of poets from other countries and cultures: Anthony Barnett, Paul Buck, and Peter Middleton from Britain; Anne-Marie Albiac, Michel Deguy, Edmond Jabès, Jacqueline Risset from France; Saúl Yurkievich and Tomás Guido Lavalle from Argentina; Minoru Yashioka from Japan; and so on. And finally, unlike the various "Language" journals, *Temblor* focused on poetry rather than on theory, although it did include critical prose, especially on or by its own poets.

Here, then, was an opening of the field that nevertheless avoided the merely eclectic. Like any editor, Hickman had his idiosyncrasies (a number of poets, no doubt, were published simply because they were Los Angeles friends), but with rare exceptions no effort was made to recruit the mainstream. Hickman never published Derek Walcott or Galway Kinnell, Adrienne Rich or Rita Dove. Why not? We cannot, alas, ask Hickman himself, and there is no mission statement to guide us. But I suspect there were three reasons. First, I imagine the editor felt these other poets got enough of a hearing in the mainstream press, and if he was to edit and produce a journal, he might as well introduce lesser-known poets. Secondly, publication of the established poets would have been too expensive. And thirdly, although there is no *Temblor* manifesto, the journal's unstated aesthetic remained true to what had been the cornerstone of Language aesthetic—namely, that poetry is more than the direct voicing of personal feeling and/or didactic statement, that poetry, far from being transparent, demands indirection and verbal/syntactic deformations.

Consider, in this connection, Lyn Hejinian's "Two Stein Talks" in *Temblor* #3 (1986).[19] Hejinian makes a strong case for Stein's brand of "realism" as "the discovery that language is an order of reality itself and not a mediating medium—that it is possible and even likely that one can have a confrontation with a phrase that is as significant as a confrontation with a tree, chair, cone, dog, bishop, piano, vineyard, door, or penny" (129). In the course of her talks, Hejinian shows us how one can analyze such poetic language, how, for example, in the first of the *Tender Buttons*, "A Carafe, That Is a Blind Glass," the first phrase "A kind in glass and a cousin" "binds carafe with blind phonically." As for "blind," "A carafe is a container, a glass one, which, if filled with a thick liquid, that is a colored one, might be, so to speak, blind, opaque." "A blind glass," she adds, "might also be a blank mirror, or a draped window—as my aunt would say, 'Draw the blinds, it's dinner time'" (132).

The poet's offhand phrase "as my aunt would say" shows that reading semiotically rather than referentially, "in" rather than "for," need not be as impersonal an activity as it may have looked in its first incarnation. On the contrary, after citing Stein's sentence, "A gap what is a gap when there is not any meaning in a slice with a hole in it," Hejinian decides "to quote myself," in a stanza that begins "going / by the usual criteria for knowledge / I vowed not to laugh / but to scatter things" (133). Elsewhere in this issue we have Susan Howe's "12 Poems from a Work in Progress," which begins with a play on "sitt" / "site"/ "cite," in keeping with McCaffery's account of the *cipheral* text, and ends with an oblique prayer to "Keep and comfort come / unhook my father / his nest is in thick of my / work" (27). How does one "unhook" a father, and why? We never know for sure any more than we can paraphrase

Fanny Howe's observation, in her "Scattered Light," that "Some patios won't allow the shadow of a maid / It's where I want to go with my tray / See heat unbearably white / Each book must fall, a scholar's mind" (51).

Here, pun ("Sea heat unbearably white") and burlesque, as in the last line's play on "Into each life, a little rain must fall," complicate the story of this "shadow of a maid" carrying her tray on the forbidden patio. Throughout *Temblor* 4 (which contains the complete *Conduit* by Barrett Watten and *Demo* by Ron Silliman), the Language program is operative even if—and here we come to Hickman's own predilection—emotion, if by no means personal confession, is brought back into the equation. Further along in Fanny Howe's "Scattered Light" (#4) we read the following ten-line poem:

> It was a night to be left alone
> To dig out fifteen pounds of pumpkin guts
> Stick in a candle and water the curtains
> I phoned a friend with What do you want
> Money and luck they said
> When I asked the angel in the bottle
> She fluttered and cried
> I want to die!
> Sex, too, squeezes out a lot of pleasure
> Till nothing is left but the neck (52)

Failed domesticity probably looms as large here as it did in "Hollandaise," but the relationship between the pumpkin carving of the opening, the allusion to the Cumean Sybil trapped eternally in her bottle, and the image of the sex act hollowing out the body like an empty pumpkin cannot be transformed into any sort of coherent narrative. "Till nothing is left but the neck" is especially graphic. The neck of the bottle? The neck of the woman as external to the emptied-out body? The neck as all one has without money or luck? Oddly, my own image—if I am to follow McCaffery and become a co-constructor of the poem's meaning—is that of a chicken neck, the hard ugly piece of flesh (rather like a distorted penis or "stick in a candle") that remains when one has hollowed out the chicken, as opposed to the pumpkin, guts—the liver, heart, and other giblets, the fat along the inside chicken wall. Phonemically, in any case, the monosyllabic "neck" in final position connotes an unpleasant cut of some sort.

Fanny Howe's "Scattered Light" happens to be followed, a few pages later, by Nathaniel Mackey's "Uninhabited Angel," which begins

Sat up sleepless   in the Long Night Long, love
        Stood me up. Stayed away though its
Doing so stirred me. Wine on my shirtsleeve,
        Wind on my neck. (36)

Again, love standing the poet up, again that ugly word "neck" in final position. But here in Mackey's jazz-inspired lyric, rhythm is quite other—an allusion to the Dogon myth of the Andoumboulou fusing with the "attempt to sing the blues," as in the drumbeat of:

Tilted sky, turned earth.   Bent wheel, burnt
                                                    we.
        Bound I.   Insubordinate
                          us

where "we" is what's left when the wheel is bent and "I," bound to the wheel, becomes part of that "we" or "Insubordinate / us."

Nathaniel Mackey's poem serves as a reminder that even as women poets associated with post-structuralist experimentation were gaining recognition, persons of color had rarely been included. And here we come to a major shift in the nineties, when what could loosely be called a Language poetics has come into contact with one of color. A signal example is the poetry of Harryette Mullen, to which I now turn.

Musing & Drudging

In a 1997 interview for *Combo* #1, Harryette Mullen recalls her own initiation into poetry:

> I had come from Texas to Northern California. I was in graduate school at Santa Cruz. I was reading all of this theory as a student in Literature at UC–Santa Cruz. So, at that point when I would . . . be taken to these talks and readings . . . I had a context for it. . . . although of course no one at the university was dealing with the work of the [Language] poets. But [they] read the same theory that my professors did—in fact they probably read twice as much, and had read the same theory earlier than a lot of my professors had, and they were highly intellectual poets. . . . and they were saying interesting things. . . . for instance the idea of problematizing the subject.[20]

And Mullen jokes about her fellow minority graduate students at Santa Cruz, who used the argument that it was all very well for white male poets to renounce "voice" but that "We *need* our subjectivity." Either extreme, she decided, seemed unsatisfactory. In her drive to problematize her own subjectivity, she began to incorporate into the Language poetics that animated *Trimmings,* her book of prose poems based on Stein's *Tender Buttons,* the actual verbal games of her own culture—the childhood jump-rope rhymes and "pseudo-courtship, formulaic exchanges" of preadolescence, like the male "What's cookin' good lookin'?" with its female response, "Ain't nothin' cookin' but the beans in the pot, and they wouldn't be if the water wasn't hot."

Trimmings is a wonderful example of the new fusion of Language poetics and a renewed "Personism," to use Frank O'Hara's phrase. In an interview with Barbara Henning, Mullen remarks that "*Tender Buttons* appeals to me because it so thoroughly defamiliarizes the domestic, making familiar 'objects, rooms, food' seem strange and new, as does the simple, everyday language used to describe common things."[21] But Mullen's own version of *Tender Buttons* also becomes, as she puts it, "a reflection on the feminization and marginalization of poetry: a whole poem composed of a list of women's garments, undergarments, & accessories certainly seems marginal & minor, perhaps even frivolous & trivial" (Henning, Interview). Consider the following:

> Tender white kid, off-white tan. Snug black leather, second skin. Fits like a love, an utter other uttered. Bag of tricks, slight hand preserved, a dainty. A solid color covers while rubber is protection. Tight is tender, softness cured. Alive and warm, some animal hides. Ghosts wear fingers, delicate wrists.[22]

This glove poem takes its inspiration from Stein but is really quite different. Mullen keeps her eye more firmly on the object than does Stein, whose cushions, umbrellas, and hats quickly give way to other related items, often quite abstract. Mullen's poem immediately raises the issue of color with the punning of "Tender white kid," and "off-white tan." For the poet, the "Snug black leather" is in fact "second skin," and so it "Fits like a love" even as it is "utter other," with its play on "udder"—the female body—and the need to speak, to give poetic voice to what has been voiceless. Further, the emphasis on "utter other" leads to classification: rubber gloves, leather gloves, gloves that are too tight, gloves that fit. But also an unease as to the source of leather gloves that is quite un-Steinian: "Alive and warm, some animal hides," where the pun on "hides" (as of "softness cured") leads directly to the image of ghosts known by their large white fingers in the dark. Do those ghost fingers belong to the predominantly white glove wearers? Mullen doesn't press the point: gloves are "tender" and "dainty"; they make the wrists look "delicate."

The *Trimmings* poems thus have a complicated derivation. On the one hand, one could read this particular playful prose poem in conjunction with the short paragrammatic pieces cited by McCaffery in his essay for "The Politics of the Referent"—poems by Bruce Andrews, bpNichol, and McCaffery himself. On the other hand, Mullen's piece is more overtly political and engaged in the contemporary discourse about gender and race. Indeed, Mullen internalizes the theoretical paradigm of Language poetics so as to refigure the relationship between the various ethnicities and communities to which she belongs.

In a 1993 lecture called "Visionary Literacy: Art, Literature and Indigenous African Writing Systems," for example, Mullen uses the deconstructionist analysis of *écriture* to call into question the standard explanatory models of African American vernacular orality:

> That black literary traditions privilege orality . . . has become something of a commonplace, in part because it's based upon what seems to be a reasonable and accurate observation . . . Presumably, for the African-American writer there is no alternative to production of this authentic black voice but silence. This speech-based and racially inflected aesthetic that produces a black poetic diction requires that the writer acknowledge and reproduce in the text a significant difference between the spoken and written language of African Americans and that of other Americans.[23]

As pointed out by Aldon Nielsen, who discusses this lecture in his *Black Chant*, Mullen's proposed study of African *signage*, as the background for understanding the relationship of oral to written, "has much to tell us about the falsity of the assumed opposition between singing and signing in both Africa and America" (36). And he cites Mullen's statement:

> The larger question I am asking is this: How has the Western view of writing as a rational technology historically been received and transformed by African Americans whose primary means of cultural transmission are oral and visual, rather than written, and for whom graphic systems are associated not with instrumental human communication but with techniques of spiritual power and spirit possession . . . In or-

der to construct a cultural and material history of African-America's embrace and transformation of writing technologies one might ask how writing and text functioned in a folk milieu that valued a script for its cryptographic incomprehensibility and uniqueness rather than its legibility or reproducibility.(36)

Here is a theoretical project that has very real poetic implications, involving, as it does, the struggle against the received idea that one is either "black *or* innovative." "*Muse & Drudge*," Mullen explains, "really was my attempt to show that I can do both at the same time."

Muse & Drudge was written, seemingly against the "Language" grain, in irregularly rhyming and heavily syncopated ballad quatrains. Its eighty pages have four quatrains per page, with no stops or indeed any punctuation except for the capitalization of proper nouns and apostrophes marking the posses-sive, as in "galleys upstart crow's nest." Each page, as Kate Pearcy points out in an excellent essay on the book, seems to be a discrete unit, unbroken dur-ing oral performance.[24] Accordingly, the lines of contiguity—that is, the net-work of metonymic associations—are offset by an oral paradigm that insures temporal reception of a given four-quatrain unit. Consider the following:

Sapphire's lyre styles
plucked eyebrows
bow lips and legs
whose lives are lonely too

my last nerve's lucid music
sure chewed up the juicy fruit
you must don't like my peaches
there's some left on the tree

you've had my thrills
a reefer a tub of gin
don't mess with me I'm evil
I'm in your sin

clipped bird eclipsed moon
soon no memory of you
no drive or desire survives
you flutter invisible still[25]

Of this pseudo-ballad, we might say, in Steve McCaffery's words, "a reading activates certain relational pathways, a flow of parts, and . . . a structural 'infolding' of the textual elements" (Supplement 11). In the first stanza, each of the fourteen words functions paragrammatically. "Sapphire's lyre" (the play on Sappho places Mullen's own blues singer in a rich poetic tradition),[26] "styles" (or is "styles" a noun, designating Sapphire's lyric styles?), "plucked eyebrows," where "plucked" can also be a verb as can the "bow" in "bow lips." "Bow lips and legs" is a witty false parallel: it refers to being "bow-legged," but "bow lips" are the Cupid's mouth, a lovely rounded form. Or do the "lips and legs" bow down? Most important, "lyre styles" sounds like "life styles," and, lo and behold, the last line reads, "whose lives are lonely too."

Now consider the role sound plays—the rhyming of "Sapphire's"/"lyre"/ "styles"; the consonance of "lyre," "lives"; the alliteration of "l"s in seven of the fourteen words; the eye rhyme of "brows"/"bow." We can hear "Sapphire" playing the blues in this poignant and droll love song. What's more, in the second stanza, the "lucid music" comes to incorporate the Southern Black idiolect of "you must don't like my peaches / there's some left on the tree."[27] Individual morphemes create tension: "chewed up the juicy fruit" refers to a common brand of chewing gum, but "chewed up" relates that "juicy fruit" to those rejected peaches. Again, "you've had my thrills" is a brilliant send-up of the expected "I've had my thrills / a reefer a tub of gin / don't mess with me I'm evil." And "I'm in your sin," with its allusion to the Bessie Smith song "A Pig Foot and a Bottle of Gin," undercuts self-recrimination (e.g., "I'm full of sin") by putting the blame squarely on the lover. Then again, "you've had my thrills" can be read as, "you've had my best moments; I've given it all to you!" Finally, the semantic and phonemic conjunction of "clipped bird" and "eclipsed moon" plays on the standard romantic clichés about love. Is the poet herself the "clipped bird"? Or is she getting rid of the lover? The poem's last line, "you flutter invisible still" makes for a comic rhyme with the "thrills" of line 9; it also echoes the image of the swans who glide through the water "Unwearied still" in Yeats's "Wild Swans at Coole." The substitution of "invisible" could hardly be more deflating: if "you" (the lover) has been reduced to no more than an invisible flutter, it is surely time to move on. And in the penultimate line, "drive" rhymes with the second syllable of "survives," the chiming of "drive"—"desire"—"survives" underscoring the poet's case for survival.

"Despite random, arbitrary, even nonsensical elements," Mullen has remarked of *Muse & Drudge*, "the poem . . . is saturated with the intentionality of the writer." "I intend the poem to be meaningful," she insists, "to allow, or suggest, to open up, or insinuate possible meanings, even in those places where the poem drifts between intentional utterance and improvisational wordplay." And she talks of the poem's amalgam of "topical references to subculture and mass culture, its shredded, embedded, and buried allusions, its drift between meaning and sound, as well as its abrupt shifts in tone or emotional affect" (Henning, Interview). Metonymy and pun, already much in evidence in the earlier *Trimmings,* are the key tropes, but they function in a traditional lyric form that ironizes their mode of operation, and is itself ironized by these figures. In the words of a later stanza:

> down there shuffling coal
> humble materials hold
> vestiges of toil
> the original cutting tool
> > (*Muse & Drudge* 11)

where the consonance of "coal"—"hold"—"toil"—"tool" contradicts the ballad account of the miner's dreary work routine. Lyric and linguistic play combine to create a vision at once detached and oddly "personal."

Caveat Lector

I come back now to the question of "innovation." To call *Muse & Drudge* "innovative" is not especially helpful, because it would be just as accurate to say that as the very title, with its nominal/verbal collocation of inspiration and hard work, suggests, the book is quite traditional in its respect for the lyric contract, the emphasis on sound structure, the personal signature, and the mimetic grounding of experience. What matters more than "innovation," I think, is that *Muse & Drudge* is a book that speaks very much to its own time, that taps into various writings and speech formations in ways that are compelling. If Mullen's is a "theoretical" poetry, it is one that has deftly internalized the theories in question.

But—and this is where the situation has become problematic—such internalization is hard earned. Like any mode, the production of "text without walls," as McCaffery called it, can become a mere tick. And so can the theory that ostensibly animates it. One of the most problematic manifestations of what we might call post–Language poetics is that in the wake of the foundational theory that filled the pages of avant-garde little magazines of the eighties, poets have engaged in a good bit of "soft" theorizing. This has been especially true of women poets, perhaps because they have felt, quite understandably, excluded from the earlier formulations of poetics (a situation that can be traced back to the homage paid to Charles Olson's "Projective Verse"). Indeed, exploring such venues as the "Women/Writing/Theory" symposium for *Raddle Moon* (#11 and #13), the "Poetics and Exposition" section of *Moving Borders* (1998), or the final issue of *Poetics Journal* (#10, June 1998), I find myself wishing that the poets in question would engage in more stringent critique of one another's poems rather than producing so much "theoretical" prose.

In an essay for the "Poetics" section of *Moving Borders*, for example, I came across the following sentence: "Mimesis can partner metonymy, another obstruction to either/or."[28] What can this mean? Metonymy is the trope that relates one image or phrase to another along the axis of contiguity, as in "hut," "hovel," "poor little house," "shack" (Jakobson's example). The discussion of mimesis or representation is perhaps the cornerstone of literary theory from Plato on down, but however we construe mimesis, the word refers to the mode of the verbal construct itself and its relation (or nonrelation) to an external reality. Metonymy, on the other hand, is a trope and hence exists, if it exists at all, *within* the mimesis, not side by side with it. Tolstoy's *Anna Karenina,* for example, is considered a highly mimetic novel, and one of its main verbal devices is metonymy, as when Anna sees her husband at the train station after she has already fallen in love with Vronsky and notes that Karenin's ears stick out underneath his hat in a peculiar (and unpleasant) fashion, the protruding ears becoming a synecdoche (the most common form of metonymy) by which Karenin is known throughout the novel. Not only can't mimesis "partner" metonymy, there being no equivalence between the two ("another obstruction to either/or"), but metonymy is in fact one of the key features *of* the mimetic contract.

Farther down on the same page we read, "Can the rational accommodate the irrational? Can forms exist which truly allow for the accidental, absurd, grotesque, horrific, incommensurate—is this what Adorno meant?" The answer is quite simply *no,* for Adorno never equated "form" with the "rational"; he knew it was quite possible to have complex and subtle forms that are by no means "rational"; moreover, he did not conceive of form as the container of the thing contained. Again, in an essay called "In Re 'Person,'" there is a statement that reads, "The *value* of perspective to nascent capitalism was that it eventually aided in the creation of a new reality, a rationalized objectified space which could then be opened to exploitation."[29] What artist can this author have in mind? Perugino? Raphael? Leonardo? Giorgione? All those wonderful Italian painters who used perspective to create the most amazing sense of palpability of nearness and distance, of mysterious background events that complicate what is seen in the foreground? Was theirs a "rationalized objective space"—a space of nascent capitalism?

Such theory buzz, like the current spate of what I call Big-Name Collage—the large theoretical essay or even poem that is no more than a collage of nuggets by Big Names—Heidegger and Giorgio Agamben, Cixous and Kristeva, Deleuze and Baudrillard—without any real analysis of what the philosophers in question are actually arguing—is problematic, because this particular form of "innovative" writing may well alienate the very readership it hopes to capture. That readership is, I think, more attuned to specific issues, as when Mullen tries to walk the minefield between the particular idiolects or, as Jeff Derksen has called them, "communolects" of our increasingly multilingual society;[30] for those "communolects" now have everything to do with the one revolution that really has occurred in our own time—namely, the habitation of cyberspace. This is not the place to discuss the poetic experiments—and many of these really are experiments in that they fail as often as they succeed and are replaced by more adequate models—on Web sites like Kenneth Goldsmith's *UbuWeb: Visual/Concrete/Sound Poetry*, but clearly, two important things are happening.[31] The first is the increasing visualization of poetic text—a visualization that is by no means new but has been reconfigured in important new ways in works like Johanna Drucker's *The Word Made Flesh* or Susan Howe's *Eikon Basilike*. The second is a form that I call, for want of a better name, "differential poetry," that is, poetry that does not exist in a single material state but can vary according to the medium of presentation: printed book, cyberspace, installation, or oral rendition.

In the performative work of Laurie Anderson and Suzan-Lori Parks, Joan Retallack and Caroline Bergvall, for example, the issue is less the referential fallacy, as it was for McCaffery in the mid-seventies, than it is the semiosis of the verbal/visual field itself, where words and phrases can be moved around, reconfigured, and assigned to different slots so that the "poem" has a variety of different forms. In a piece called "RUSH (a long way from H)," for example, Caroline Bergvall has designed a text you can access and activate on the Electronic Poetry Center Web site or read in book form, but it can also be seen and heard as performed and videotaped for the Internet, in which case temporality becomes an important determinant of meaning.[32] As a barstool monologue cum brawl, interrupted and qualified by visual diagrams, media argot, and verbal breakdown, "RUSH" puts an ingenious spin on such pub monologues as that of Lil's "friend" in *The Waste Land*.

Is it "innovative"? Is it, in Bergvall's words, "kindajazz or excitingly passée"? Well, there are surely Dada precedents for this performance model, and

"RUSH (a long way from H)" recalls the work of John Cage and various Fluxus artists. So, to rephrase the question, is Bergvall's an *interesting* rendition of a lonely, anxious, and hilarious conversation, presumably between two women, in the neighborhood pub? A close look at the work's linguistic deformations and repetitions lays bare the complex layering that defines "this gigantic submarined trancehall" as it takes shape on the cyberpage. And the next step, one we find taken in Kenneth Goldsmith's Java Applet called "Fidget," is to have the words themselves put in motion, touch and intersect with one another, and vary according to what time of day one accesses the site.

How does such work relate to the original $L=A=N=G=U=A=G=E$ manifestos? How is the "death of the author" playing itself out in such works as "RUSH (a long way from H)" or "Fidget"? These are questions I try to answer elsewhere, with respect to particular works.[33] But whatever the answer, there is no doubt that the poetic action is already moving elsewhere and that we will have to come to terms with a given work's specific materiality as well as its *difference*. As Gertrude Stein put it so nicely in "An Acquaintance with Description":

> What is the difference between three and two in furniture. Three is the third of three and two is the second of two. This makes it as true as a description. And not satisfied. And what is the difference between being on the road and waiting very likely being very likely waiting, a road is connecting and as it is connecting it is intended to be keeping going and waiting everybody can understand puzzling.[34]

In 1999 David Jackson of Yale's Department of Spanish and Portuguese orga-
nized a symposium in honor of the seventieth birthday of the Brazilian poet
Haroldo de Campos. Known chiefly as one of the founders of the Concrete
movement, Haroldo went on to produce important theoretical works as well
as what I call here "Concrete prose." I wrote a paper for the occasion and
then enlarged it to include contemporary U.S. poets whose work moves in
similar directions. The essay was published in the special issue on the nine-
ties, edited by Thomas Gardner for Contemporary Literature *(2001).*

9
The Invention of "Concrete Prose"

Haroldo de Campos's *Galáxias* and After

> [Gertrude Stein's] prose is a kind of concrete poetry with justified margins.
> David Antin, "Some Questions about Modernism"

> The language act is also an act of survival. Word order = world order.
> Steve McCaffery and bpNichol, "The Search for Non-Narrative Prose"

On the face of it, Concrete poetry and prose poetry (or poetic prose) would
seem to represent two extremes, with the lyric (lineated text framed by white
space) as middle term. The Concrete poem is, by common definition, a visual
constellation in which, as the "Pilot Plan for Concrete Poetry" published
by the *Noigandres* poets of Brazil put it, "graphic space acts as structural
agent."[1] Indeed, in the words of Dick Higgins, the Concrete poem charac-
teristically "defines its own form and is visually, and if possible, structurally
original or even unique." And further, unlike the Renaissance pattern poem
or the Apollinairean *calligramme*—forms that are in many ways its precursor—
the Concrete poem's "visual shape is, wherever possible, abstract, the words
or letters within it behaving as ideograms."[2] But unlike, say, Ezra Pound's
ideograms in *The Cantos,* the text from which the *Noigandres* poets of Brazil took their name,[3] the Concrete poem is usually short: "its most obvious
feature," as Rosmarie Waldrop puts it, "is reduction. . . . both conventions
and sentence are replaced by spatial arrangement."[4] "We do not usually *see*
words," Waldrop remarks, "we *read* them, which is to say we look through

them at their significance, their contents. Concrete Poetry is first of all a revolt against this transparency of the word."[5]

Take, for example, Haroldo de Campos's well-known Concrete poem "fala / prata / cala / ouro" ("speech / silver / silence / gold"),[6] which plays with the hackneyed proverb "Silence is golden" as well as the classical epithet "silver-tongued":

fala

prata

    cala

    ouro

        cara

        prata

            coroa

            ouro

                fala

                cala

            para

        prata   ouro

        cala   fala

                    clara

Of the constellation's sixteen words, four—*fala, prata, cala,* and *ouro* ("speech," "silver," "silence," "gold") appear three times each: *fala* ("speech") is first *prata* ("silver"), and its rhyming partner *cala* ("silence") is *ouro* ("gold"). But the application of epithets seems to be no more than a matter of chance—"heads" (*cara*) or "tails" (*coroa*)—and so the fifth pair—*fala / cala*—joins the two contraries ("speech / "silence") and is followed by a stop (*para*) that disrupts the poem's staircase structure. Accordingly (below stairs, so to speak), a double reversal sets in: "silver" (*prata*), in a reversal of noun and adjective, is now "silent" (*cala*) and it is gold (*ouro*) that speaks (*fala*). Indeed, what is *clara* (the poem's final word, used for the first time here, combines *cala* and *cara* both visually and phonically) is that *ouro* is the dominant, the one word that doesn't match any of the others, containing as it does the only *u* in the poem and being the only word that doesn't end in *a* and has no rhyming partner. Silence, Haroldo implies, may be golden, but, at least in our culture, it is gold that speaks![7]

The poem is a good example of the reduction Waldrop speaks of: it has only eight different words (the count is $[4 \times 3] + 4 = 16$), and its syntax is minimal, there being no connectives relating paired nouns and adjectives.

Visual placement is central to meaning: the possible pairs—almost nudes descending a staircase—are blocked in line 11 by the isolated word *para,* followed by the reversed matching pairs of the penultimate lines, which yield to the final *clara.* The modulation from the initial *fala / prata* to the final *clara* is certainly temporal, but the text is also self-reflexive, each item pointing back to its previous partner as well as forward, the constellation as a whole resembling, as Haroldo himself notes, serial structure in music—for example Anton Webern's "Klangfarbenmelodie" (see *Concrete Poetry* 12).

Whereas a Concrete poem like this one is to be understood as what the *Noigandres* poets, following Joyce, called *verbivocovisual* (see *Concrete Poetry* 72), the prose poem, read as it must be from beginning to end, is primarily temporal. No matter how disjunctive or semantically open it may be, no matter how fully it is constituted by what Ron Silliman has called "the new sentence,"[8] the prose poem is usually a block of print whose words, syllables, and letters have no optical significance. In the case of Western prose, as R. P. Draper notes, "it is an automatic assumption that letters forming words are separated by space from other letters forming words, that these letters march across the page from left to right, and that the lines so formed are strictly parallel and progress downwards at equal intervals."[9]

In their *Rational Geomancy,* Steve McCaffery and bpNichol remind us that the conventional book "organizes content along three modules: the lateral flow of the line, the vertical or columnar build-up of the lines on the page and thirdly a linear movement organized through depth (the sequential arrangement of pages upon pages)."[10] Practically speaking, this means that "the book assumes its particular physical format through its design to accommodate printed linguistic information in a linear form" (60). And further, "Prose as print encourages an inattention to the right-hand margin as a terminal point. The tendency is encouraged to read continually as though the book were one extended line" (60). The page, far from being a visual unit, thus becomes "an obstacle to be overcome" (61). Even when the prose poem avoids narrative, it generally exhibits the very continuity Concretism rejects in favor of spatial form.

Here, for example, is James Tate's prose poem "Casting a Long Shadow," which appears in the 1998 issue of the journal *The Prose Poem:*

> This is where the child saw the vision of the Virgin Mother. She was standing right here and the Blessed Mother was up there on that rock (smoking a cheroot—but we don't believe that part). The child wept for joy and ran to get her mother. The mother was watching her favorite soap opera and accused the child of playing pranks. When the soap

opera ended the mother agreed to go outside. Several ravens were talking to one another. Storm clouds were moving in. The mother suddenly
slapped the child across her cheek.[11]

The subgenre of prose poetry represented by Tate's piece is that of the sar-
donic fable, the seemingly casual little tale that leads up to an ironic epiphany
—in this case the reality of motherhood that deflates the child's dream. Max
Jacob was an early master of this form. In this parabolic variant of the prose
poem, the semantic dominates, the visual playing no appreciable part: the
reader's eye moves from start to finish without paying attention to the right
margin. Indeed, the narrative ("This is what happened") demands continuity and hence there is little internal sound play or eye rhyme. The page, as
McCaffery and Nichol put it, is little more than an obstacle to be overcome.

But as the authors of *Rational Geomancy* argue, there can be prose that
doesn't satisfy these conventions. To begin with, the prose poem is itself a
calling into question of lineation. *Verse,* even free verse (the word *verse* [Old
English *fers*] comes from the Latin *vertere,* "to turn," which is to say, to move
from *a* to *b* and, in turn, from *b* to *c*) is by definition a kind of container, and
hence poets from Baudelaire to the present have tried, at particular junctures,
to circumvent it. "Linear progression," McCaffery notes, "we have come to
understand not merely as a spatial arrangement but as a way of thinking."[12]
A way of thinking, one might add, called into question as long ago as the
1860s, when Baudelaire, in the dedication to Arsène Houssaye (1862) that
prefaces *Le Spleen de Paris* (*Les petits poèmes en prose*), declares, "Which of
us in his moments of ambition, has not dreamed of the miracle of a poetic
prose, musical, without rhythm and without rhyme, supple enough and rug-
ged enough to adapt itself to the lyrical impulses of the soul, the undulations
of reveries, the jibes of conscience?"[13]

Baudelaire's own prose poems are set as normal printed pages: visual design
plays an appreciable role. Paragraphs are often quite short, and the longer
ones are often interrupted by snatches of dialogue. Indeed, since the narrative element is so marked here, the *Spleen de Paris* poems might more properly be designated short fictions. Neither Baudelaire's nor Rimbaud's (nor
even Mallarmé's) prose poems, for that matter, set the stage for Concretist
experimentation with prose. Rather, the *Noigandres* poets looked to two
prose writers: Gertrude Stein and especially James Joyce. The de Campos
brothers had been translating *Finnegans Wake* since the late fifties, and in
1962 they brought out a book called *Panorama do Finnegans Wake,* which
contains, among other things, what Haroldo calls "the creative transposition
('transcréation') of eleven fragments (bilingual presentation), accompanied

by interpretative comments."[14] Indeed, Haroldo reminds us, "the 'verbivocovisual' elements of Joyce's prose, the 'montage word,' regarded as a composite
mosaic unit or a basic textural node ('silvamoonlake,' for instance), were
emphasized from the very beginning of the Concrete Poetry movement"
("Sanscreed" 55). And he cites an earlier formulation by Augusto de Campos: "The Joycean 'micro-macrocosm,' which reached its pinnacle in *Finnegans Wake*, is another excellent example [of proto-Concrete poetry]. . . .
Here counterpoint is *moto perpetuo*. The ideogram is obtained by super-
imposing words, true lexical montages. Its general infrastructure is a circular
design of which every part is a beginning, middle, and end."[15]

It may seem strange that Concrete poetry, with its emphasis on graphic
space as structural agent and its conviction that in the verbivocovisual constellation, form and content are isochronous, would take as its exemplar a
628-page work of continuous prose—a "novel" that, except for Book II, chapter 2 ("UNDE ET UBI"),[16] with its marginal glosses, pictograms, musical scores,
and geometric forms, does not seem to exploit the visual dimension of the
text at all. But perhaps it is the word *visual* that needs reconfiguration here.
A hint is supplied by Haroldo in his essay "The Open Work of Art" (which,
incidentally, preceded Umberto Eco's well-known *Opera Aperta* by a number
of years).[17] In discussing the "circular organization of poetic material" in *Un
coup de dés*, Haroldo adds:

> The Joycean universe also evolved from a linear development of
> time toward space-time or the infusion of the whole in the part ("all-
> space in a notshall"—nutshell), adopting as the organogram of *Finne-
> gans Wake* the Vico-vicious circle. . . . each "verbi-voco-visual" unit
> is at the same time the continent-content of the whole work and in-
> stantly myriadminded. . . . a whole metaphoric cosmos is contained in
> a single word. This is why it can be said of Finnegans [*sic*] that it retains
> the properties of a circle, of the equidistance of all points on it from
> the center. The work is porous to the reader, accessible from any of the
> places one chooses to approach it. (*Dispositio* 6)

The implication of such "allspace in a notshall" is that, for Haroldo, Concrete
poetics is not a matter of word placement or innovative typography (as it is
for some of his colleagues), but rather the phonemic, ideogrammic, paragrammatic character of the morphemes and words themselves. Accordingly,
the distinction between "visual poem" and "prose" breaks down. Consider
the following passage from the *Anna Livia Plurabelle* section of *Finnegans
Wake*. Haroldo's translation, which becomes Fragment 8, covers the better

part of page 202 (seven lines from the top of the page and three from the bottom). Here is the original:

Tell me, tell me, how cam she camlin through all her fellows, the neckar she was, the diveline? Casting her perils before our swains from Fonte-in-Monte to Tidingtown and from Tidingtown tilhavet. Linking one and knocking the next, tapting a flank and tipting a jutty and palling in and pietaring out and clyding by on her eastway. Waiwhou was the first thurever burst? Someone he was, whuebra they were, in a tactic attack or in single combat. Tinker, tilar, souldrer, salor, Pieman Peace or Polistaman. That's the thing I'm elwys on edge to esk. Push up and push vardar and come to uphill headquarters! Was it waterlows year, after Grattan or Flood, or when maids were in Arc or when three stood hosting? Fidaris will find where the Doubt arises like Nieman from Nirgends found the Nihil. Worry you sighin foh, Albern, O Anser? Until the gemman's fistiknots, Qvic and Nuancee! She can't put her hand on him for the moment. Tez thelon langlo, walking weary! Such a loon waybashwards to row! She sid herself she hardly knows whuon the annals her graveller was, a dynast of Leinster, a wolf of the sea, or what he did or how blyth she played or how, when, why, where, and who offon he jumpnad her and how it was gave her away. She was just a young thin pale soft shy slim slip of a thing then, sauntering, by silvamoonlake and he was a heavy trudging lurching lieabroad of a Curraghman, making his hay for whose sun to shine on, as tough as the oaktrees (peats be with them!) used to rustle that time down by the dykes of killing Kildare for forstfellfoss with a plash across her. She thought she's sanhk neathe the ground with nymphant shame when he gave her the tigris eye!

Reading this "chattering dialogue across the river by two washer-women," as Joyce himself described it,[18] one cannot proceed from left to right and from top to bottom as one does in the case of standard "see-through" prose. Since the page is not broken up by dialogue, paragraphing, or indented quotation, the reader intuitively searches for configurations that might "organize" the verbal flow that is equivalent to the river Anna Liffey, which is its nominal subject. Punctuation marks—exclamation points, question marks, capital letters—become important as do proper names, both real and those created by punning, especially when they alliterate. Consider the following sentence, which comes roughly in the middle of the sequence:

Fidaris will find where the Doubt arises like Nieman from Nirgends found the Nihil.

The eye moves up the page past "Flood" to "Fonte-in Monte" (Fountain in the Mountain) in line 3; the coinage *Fidaris* contains the morpheme "Fid" that gives us *Fides* (faith) and *Fideles* (faithful). Faith is thus pitted against "the Doubt that arises," but the capitalization of Doubt suggests that this is also one of the myriad river names in the sequence, as in "the Doubt river rises." The first half of the sentence is, in any case, put into question by the second in which *Nieman* (*Niemand* = no one) from *Nirgends* (nowhere) finds *Nihil*. But—and here the "vocovisual" comes in—there can be no "Doubt" about the intricate relationship between words:

> *Fidaris* (with "Flood" in the sentence right above it)→*find*→*from*→*found* (alliteration of *f, d, n*)
> Fidar*is*— aris*es* (rhyme)
> *Ni*eman—*Ni*rgends—*Ni*hil (anaphora)

Further, there is assonance of *i*—the letter appearing ten times in the space of fourteen words. The "Fidaris" cluster thus stands out as do "Albern, O Answer" and "Qvic and Nuancee" in the next lines. "Nuancee" is a particularly complex compound, containing "nuance," so that we read the words as the command "Quick (with a German accent) and with nuance!" even as "Nuancee" contains "Nancy," "antsy," and "see."

The opposite of such a cluster effect is to have a clause comprising the most ordinary of monosyllables, as in:

She was just a young thin pale soft shy slim slip of a thing then

Cliché piled on cliché with all the connectives in place! But the sentence now shifts from these clipped words to further compounding, neologism, and play on proverbial wisdom, in the phrase "sauntering, by silvamoonlake and he was a heavy trudging lurching lieabroad of a Curraghman, making his hay for whose sun to shine on, as tough as the oaktrees (peats be with them!) used to rustle that time down by the dykes of killing Kildare for forstfellfoss with a plash across her." The punning here must be *seen*, especially "peats [peace] be with them!"—a perfectly reasonable reference to the care of oaktrees, "killing Kildare," where the first morpheme in the proper name of the county is taken literally, and "for forstfellfoss," perhaps just a tongue twister when heard, but visually a pun on such phrases as "first fell frost" or "forced [and she] fell [in the] foss." The *ru* of "tru*dging*" reappears chiastically in "l*ur*ching" and "C*urr*aghman," and "*us*" in "*us*ed" reappears in "r*us*tle."

In his study *Ideograma: Lógica/Poesia/Linguagem* (only a section of which has been translated into English),[19] Haroldo discusses Ernest Fenollosa's study of the Chinese written character. Unlike Pound, who took Fenollosa at face value, Haroldo recognizes that the sinologist's notion that in Chinese words are much closer to things than in English, that there is a natural connection between the ideogram and what it represents, is incorrect. Rather, using Roman Jakobson and Charles Peirce's theories of semantic and syntactic motivation, Haroldo argues that Fenollosa's argument must be understood somewhat differently:

> Since . . . at a second level, poetry "naturalizes" (reifies) the sign by virtue of its "self-reflecting" function and the emphasis on the materiality of the message. . . . Fenollosa's genetic *parti pris,* highlighted by his "magic realism," loses in importance to the formal (intrinsic) pertinence of the description. At this point the Peircean notion of diagram makes it possible to transfer ("translate") the Fenollosian (and Poundian) conception of the ideogram and the ideogrammic method of composing (relational, parallelistic, paratactic syntax) to the sphere (where the palpable side of the sign comes to the fore), wherein Saussure (the Saussure of anagrams as "asyndetic successions" of paradigms) and Jakobson (above all the Jakobson of the poetry of grammar) are privileged mediators. (*Dispositio* 14)

For Haroldo, in other words, the interest of the ideogram is not in its status as a visual sign that stands for a particular meaning; rather, the ideogram brings to our attention the "palpable side of the sign" in its "relational, parallelistic, paratactic syntax." *Relationality* becomes the key term, and the units to be related are phonemes and morphemes as well as words and phrases.

From this perspective, Concrete poetry is less a matter of spatial form and typographic device than of "ideogrammatizing" the verbal units themselves. The *ru/ur* constellation in "and he was a heavy tru*dging* l*ur*ching lie*abroad* of a C*urr*aghman," with its punning on "lie" and "broad"—these are items that must be seen. But—and this has been the role the *Wake* obviously played for Haroldo and the other Concretists—the ideogrammic method, reconceived as it is in Haroldo's study, can be used in "prose" quite as easily as in verse or in the spatial constellation characteristic of the Concrete poem.

Now we are in a better position to understand the following statement in Haroldo's 1977 essay "Sanscreed Latinized":

> In 1963 I began to write my BOOK OF 'ESSAYS/GALAXIES. . . . The book was conceived as an experiment in *doing away with limits between poetry and prose*, projecting the larger and more suitable concept of *text* (as a *corpus* of words with their textual *potentials. . . .* The *text* is defined as a "flux of signs," without punctuation marks or capital letters, flowing uninterruptedly across the page, as a *galactic* expansion. Each page, by itself, makes a "concretion," or autonomously coalescing body, interchangeable with any other page for reading purposes. There are "semantic vertebrae" which unify the whole. . . . [The book] constitutes a search for "language in its materiality," without "beginning-middleend." "Exterior monologue" was the phrase I used to express this "materiality" "without psychology," that is, *language that auto-enunciates itself.* (58, my emphasis)

The notion of the "galaxy" as *limit text* is reiterated in Haroldo's afterword to the *Galáxias,* where he refers to his text as operating "at the extreme limits of poetry and prose."[20] And in an interview with Roland Greene, Augusto similarly endorses a writing "where the criteria of poetry and prose co-exist in a boundary-situation, where the words of prose are as though ionized by their poetic function." "Such," adds Augusto, "is the case in *Finnegans Wake,* in many texts of Gertrude Stein, and in the *Diaries* of John Cage, which are analogous to those lyric works that incorporate the language of prose, such as certain passages in the *Galáxias* of Haroldo de Campos."[21]

The case of Gertrude Stein is especially interesting because, unlike the Concretists or Joyce before them, Stein does not use innovative typography and rarely includes foreign words, proper names, or allusions—in other words, the exotic items whose coordination makes for visual interest in *Finnegans Wake.* Yet consider the following paragraph from "Regular Regularly in Narrative," from Stein's 1931 text *How to Write:*

> They be little be left be killed be left be little be killed be killed be little be little be left be killed be his father be his mother be his father be little be left be killed be his mother be his father be left be killed be little be his father be his mother. Be little be his mother be left be his father be little be his father be left be killed be his father be left be killed be his father be his mother be killed be his mother be left be his mother be little be killed be left be his mother be his father be his father be his mother be his father be left be his mother be killed be left be his father.

This is what did not happen to happen to be this brother
to his brother to his father to his father to be left to his mother
to his father.[22]

"Successions of words," remarks Stein at the opening of "Arthur a Grammar," "are so agreeable" ("How to Write" 35). And so they are in the faux-narrative above, which alludes mysteriously to a "they" who are "little" and have been "left" to "be killed," possibly by their father and/or mother, but then again mother and father are themselves evidently there to be killed. We "see" these verbal configurations before we take in their meaning—no doubt because, for Stein, narrative is not nearly as interesting as description, and here the wholly reductive vocabulary—there are only eight different words in this 131-word paragraph—forces the reader's eye to dwell on the visual design produced by the ceaseless conjunction of *little* and *killed*, *little* and *left*, with *father*, *mother*, and especially the word *be* placed at key junctures of the word square.[23] The only punctuation Stein uses here is a period, and in the paragraph before us, there are only two sentences and hence two periods. Accordingly, when the second paragraph introduces a succession of new words—"*This is what did not happen to happen*"—followed by reference to another new word, *brother*, the "plot" thickens, almost as if Stein were about to recount the tale of Cain and Abel, only to "sacrifice" these characters to her abstract and minimalist grid.

Haroldo de Campos has clearly learned from both Joyce and Stein. Here is the opening text of the *Galáxias*, "e começo aqui," as translated into French by Inés Oseki-Depré and into English by Suzanne Jill Levine.[24]

e começo aqui e meço aqui este começo e recomeço e remeço e
arremesso e aqui me meço quando se vive sob a espécie da
viagem o que importa não é a viagem mas o começo da por isso
meço por isso começo escrever mil páginas escrever
milumapáginas para acabar com a escritura para começar com a
escritura para acabarcomeçar com a escritura por isso recomeço
por isso arremeço por isso teço escrever sobre escrever é o futuro
do escrever sobrescrevo sobrescravo em miluminoites
milumapáginas ou uma página em uma noite que é o mesmo
noites e páginas mesmam ensimesmam onde o fim é o começo

et ici je commence et ici je me lance et ici j'avance ce commencement
et je relance et j'y pense quand on vit sous l'espèce du voyage ce

n'est pas le voyage qui compte mais le commencement du et pour
ca je mesure et l'epure sépure et je m'élance écrire millepages
mille-et-une pages pour en finir avec en commencer avec l'écriture
en fincommencer avec l'écriture et donc je recommence j'y
reprends ma chance et j'avance écrire sur écriture est le futur de
l'ëcriture je surécris suresclave dans les mille-et-une-nuits les
mille-et-une pages ou une page dans une nuit ce qui se ressemble
s'assemble pages et nuits se miment sensoimênt où le bout c'est le
début

and here I begin I spin here the beguine I respin and begin to
release and realize life begins not arrives at the end of a trip which
is why I begin to respin to write-in thousand pages write
thousandone pages to end write begin write beginend with writing
and so I begin to respin to retrace to rewrite write on writing the
future of writing's the tracing the slaving a thousandone nights in a
thousandone pages or a page in one night the same night the same
pages same semblance resemblance reassemblance where the end is
begin

Galáxias is, loosely speaking, written in prose, although its jagged right margin reinforces the notion of the page as "constellation," its look perhaps more Steinian than Joycean, created as it is primarily by rhyme (both auditory and visual) and what we might call hyper-repetition. Haroldo's text permutates the words *começo* (*commence, begin*) and its variants like *meço, recomeço, remeço, acabarcomeçar, arremeço,* as well as two other galaxies, the first referring to writing—*escrever, escritura, sobrescrevo, sobrescravo* (this last item punning on the notion of writing as slaving)—and the second to the page in its isolated or multiple incarnations: *uma página em uma noite,* or *miluminoites milumapáginas,* the page and the night becoming interchangeable. The image of the circle, *onde o fim é o começo* (*où le bout c'est le début, where the end is begin*), is enacted phonemically and visually by the elaborate turn and return of words and morphemes. In the words of Eliot's *East Coker,* "In my beginning is my ending": *acabarcomeçar, fincommencer, beginend.*

The long word *acabarcomeçar,* with its internal rhyme stands out visually on the page, leading the eye in various directions that follow the paths of *começo* and related words containing *e*'s and *o*'s. As the eye moves down the page, the notion of writing as circularity—the tracing and retracing of words on a hitherto blank page—is conveyed not only by the meanings of the words but by their visual configurations. In the Levine translation, the emphasis is on the second syllable of *begin*, which leads to *in* and *spin*, and farther down the page to *finish, fine, line*, and so on. The latter are eye rhymes only, suggesting what care is taken to ensure *seeing* rather than *seeing through* on the reader's part.

Galáxias can thus be regarded as a visual poem—visual, not in the sense of calligrammatic, as in the case of Apollinaire's "Il pleut" or Eugen Gomringer's "Wind," but in its attention to letters and morphemes as well as paronomasia and paragram. A series of "exterior monologues" in prose, *Galáxias* thus points the way from the "prose" of modernists like Joyce and Stein to the new prose poetry of the late twentieth century. I am thinking less of the current predilection for fusing prose with pictogram, the alternation of prose and verse, or the use of typography (different font size, boldface, italics, lines reversed or upside-down) for "special effects" in the great tradition of Futurist page design. Such design, as I suggest in *Radical Artifice*,[25] all too easily shades into the now familiar formats of advertising, billboard, magazine, and Web page layout. Rather, I want to look at some "limit-texts," at "prose poems" that, like the *Galáxias*, challenge the distinction between poetry and prose and emphasize the materiality of the text.

Consider, for example, the seemingly normal "prose" of Rosmarie Waldrop's sequence *Lawn of Excluded Middle*, published in 1993. Waldrop, herself one of the early theorists of Concrete poetry, has experimented with various verse and prose forms; in *Lawn* the norm is the short verse paragraph, one per page. Here is section 3:

> **I** put a ruler in my handbag, having heard men talk about their sex. Now we have correct measurements and a stickiness between collar and neck. It is one thing to insert yourself into a mirror, but quite another to get your image out again and have your errors pass for objectivity. Vitreous. As in humor. A change in perspective is caused by the ciliary muscle, but need not be conciliatory. Still, the eye is a camera, room for everything that is to enter, like the cylinder called the satisfaction of hollow space. Only language grows such grass-green grass.[26]

When we look at this block of print, with its justified left and right margins, at first nothing especially stands out except perhaps the first letter, a boldface capital *I*, and even this is a well-known print convention. And, as in the case of normal prose format, we read the text from left to right and from sentence to sentence to its conclusion. Waldrop's is not primarily a paragrammatic text where morphemes or phonemes within a given word split off and form new constellations, although of course the book's title is a play on the law of the excluded middle, the law of formal logic that everything must be either true or false, which Waldrop herself rejects as a falsification of experience.

Language is just as important to Waldrop as it is to Haroldo de Campos, only for her, as for the Wittgenstein she cites in her "Endpaper," "Poetry [is] an alternate, less linear logic." "Wittgenstein," she writes, "makes language with its ambiguities the ground of philosophy. His games are played on the Lawn of the Excluded Middle," which "plays with the idea of woman as the excluded middle. . . . more particularly, the womb, the empty center of the woman's body, the locus of fertility." Accordingly, the "logic" that governs Waldrop's prose poem is absurd in its hyperliteralism. The poet puts a ruler in her handbag, "having heard men talk about their sex." "Now," the poet notes proudly, "we have correct measurements," but the "stickiness" that results seems to be in the wrong place: "between collar and neck." The next sentence derives, I would guess, from Wittgenstein's proposition that "A picture held us captive. And we could not get outside it, for it lay in our language." [27] "It is one thing," we read, "to insert yourself into a mirror, but quite another to get your image out again." One can generate one's own image merely by placing oneself in front of a mirror, but of course one can't "get" that image "out again" and still have it, for a mirror image obviously has no life of its own. Then, too, from the woman's perspective, "to insert yourself" is a male prerogative, one that calls into question the woman's efforts to "get your image out again" and to "have your errors pass for objectivity." The situation, as the next word tells us, is "Vitreous," as glassy and slippery as the "grass-green grass"—a phrase defying the rule of logic that an attribute of a thing can't be identical to that thing.

"Vitreous. As in humor." What does that "As" mean? Is humor glassy? Transparent? Brittle? In Waldrop's poem, a given phrase or sentence only seems to "follow" its predecessor, either logically or temporally. Indeed, the familiarity of the print block on the white page turns out to be as open to question as is the law of the excluded middle. For one thing, the very fixity of Waldrop's grid is contradicted by her phrasing, the words, not cut into syllables at the margin, fitting into the confined area only by allowing for uneven spacing that leaves prominent white gaps. In the prologue to *Reluctant Gravities*, Waldrop refers to this practice as "gap gardening which, moved inward from the right margin, suspends time. The suspension sets, is set, in type, in columns that precipitate false memories of garden, vineyard, trellis."[28]

Thus, in this particular passage, the characters per line vary between 45 (line 1) and 53 (line 4). The wider spacing given to certain words like *conciliatory* emphasizes their phonemic and visual relationship to other words, in this case *ciliary* (of an eyelash) in the sixth line and *cylinder* in the eighth. The spacing of line 8 (it has only 47 characters), moreover, creates the very "hollow space" that is its reference point, and the reader's eye is inevitably drawn to the words "Only language grows" that follow and that have no words beneath them on the page. There is only the "grass-green grass" on the left. And that *grass* points back to *grows* so as to create a "galaxy" on this lawn of excluded middle.

A second example of a prose block that is attentive to the right-hand margin is Steve McCaffery's "Aenigma":[29]

when i   am read   i   am sentenced   and detached from
equivalence when the shadow   lifts its box   i'm light when
my fingers turn to foreheads i'm an eagle's heart instructing
scorpions to dance when they are cities i'm the colour grey
when there's a   national blaze i am a bed of shared water
wherever i am tempted by precision i become a wrinkle elsewhere
if they modify my centre i repeat a word   before the next
word has a meaning should my voice be grafted to a question
then the   third persona will replace a cardboard cover if i tell
myself these possibilities i tell myself a canvas has subsided so
that when i am eaten in   the   answer i am still proposed.

The key phrase in this twelve-line composition is "I am" (used twice in the first line and twice in the last), the "Aenigma" (archaically spelled) of the title being "what am I?" The answer depends upon adverbs of time and place: direct at dead center, we see the phrase "wherever I am," and the reference to "elsewhere" right beneath it follows hard upon five instances of "when." "My centre," "my voice," "if I tell myself," "I tell myself": self-reference is foregrounded throughout the piece. And yet this is the least personal of poems, an "exterior monologue," as Haroldo would call it, in which "language autoenunciates itself." Indeed, the ubiquitous "I" is not a particular individual but a function of the larger language game.

The opening, "When I am read I am sentenced and detached from equivalence," sets the stage for the poem's paragrammatic activity. To be "read" is inevitably to be sentenced: readers of prose process consecutive sentences—but that demand (which this poet cannot fulfill) also becomes a kind of death sentence. Furthermore, the text is "detached from equivalence"—from equivalent line lengths, equivalent statements. And since there is no punctuation, the "when, then" constructions become equivocal, clauses often pointing both forward and back, as in "when there are cities I'm the colour grey when there's a national blaze." Indeed, throughout the text, *post hoc* is never quite *propter hoc*. Punning, moreover, regularly undermines the possibility of communication. "When the shadow lifts its box, I'm light," for example, plays on the gerund "shadowboxing" and perhaps, more specifically, on the well-known Duke Ellington song "I'm Beginning to See the Light," which contains the stanza, "Used to wander in the park / Shadowboxing in the dark, / Then you came and caused a spark, / That's a four-alarm fire now." That fire becomes, in line 5, a national blaze, and *when* that occurs, *then* "I'm a bed of shared water." Nice for putting out the flames, but how does one share water? McCaffery's mode, as line 8 puts it, is one of suspension: "I repeat a word before the next word has a meaning." Thus, "sentenced and detached from equivalence," the text must fend for itself. If the "aenigma" of the title is never resolved, textuality nevertheless forces itself on the reader: "when i am eaten in the answer I am still proposed."

Note that this last line is the only one that fails to meet the justified right margin, calling the reader's attention to the proposal. McCaffery's "Aenigma" thus enacts its meanings visually, concretely, even though it looks like an ordinary prose paragraph. Typography, we see, has come a long way in deconstructing the categories "prose"/"verse."

A somewhat different "Galaxial" prose is that of Joan Retallack in a piece from her book *How to Do Things with Words* called "Narrative as memento mori":[30]

At breakfast in the Ramada Inn Paul
needed to test the procedure for de
veloping a photogram. (He does not
wish to call it a Rayograph for pol
itical reasons.) Doug ordered 2 egg
s sunnyside up with ham. I ordered
Special K and a banana. Paul ordere
d French toast and began the photog
ram placing a blue rectangular piec
e of sensitive paper on his noteboo

k, sticking push pins in each of th
e four corners to hold it in place.
He placed a spoon, an ashtray, and
4 packets of sugar on the sensitive
paper and then took it outside to d
evelop, returning a few minutes lat
er without the photogram, but with
a rectangular aluminum pan filled w
ith water. He placed the pan on the
table next to his French toast. Dou
g said he was embarrassed by all th
e food on his plate. I was disappoi
nted because the waitress didn't br
ing me a whole banana. I told the s
tory of the flying banana sighted I
n the same village in Russia (Voron
ezh?) where aliens were recently re
ported strolling in the park with t
heir robot. Paul went out to check
the photogram. He said when the sen
sitive paper turns pale the images
are developed. He was worried there
might not be enough light. It was a
foggy morning. Doug said he had tal
ked with Marcia on the train coming
up about her daughter's post-punk r
ock band. He said they were into vi
olent lyrics. Somehow the subject o
f misogyny arose. Paul came back an
d said the photogram wasn't ready a
nd he was *really* worried there wasn
't enough sun. I thought the slices
of banana on my Special K were less
than 1/3 of a whole banana. Paul we
nt back out to check the progress o
f the photogram. Doug had finished a
ll the food on his plate. I realiz
ed I didn't want the orange juice I
had ordered, but I drank it anyway.

Retallack's "narrative"—an account of breakfast in the Ramada Inn with Paul and Doug—is a story that goes nowhere, except on the page, but on the page there is plenty of verbal "action." If Waldrop and McCaffery adjust spacing so as to meet the demands of the justified right margin, Retallack begins with a specific constraint, 35 characters per line, including spaces that function as rests. When a sentence reaches the margin formed by this firm rule, the word in question must be spliced, giving us such items as "ordere / d," "noteboo / k," "w / ith," "Dou / g," "br / ing," "t / heir," "a / ll," "wasn / 't." The left margin thus becomes a letter column, vertically producing words like "eke" and "pee." How strange, the poet suggests, word formation really is. Throughout, Paul's making of the photogram ("he said when the sen / sitive paper turns pale the images / are developed") is analogous to the poetic process itself, where words are endowed with a new life by their decomposition and placement on the "light sensitive" page. Decisions: what to order for breakfast, what to do to the paper—these come together in quirky ways as the woman who speaks expresses her disappointment that "the waitress didn't br / ing me a whole banana," an item that somehow becomes conflated with the potential misogyny of her two male companions. Like the photogram (which can't be called "a Rayograph for pol / itical reasons," evidently to avoid reference to the inventor of this art form, Man Ray, Retallack's "memento mori" memorializes not death but everyday trivia: "I realiz / ed I didn't want the orange juice I / had ordered, but I drank it anyway."

My fourth and last example is taken from Kenneth Goldsmith, *No. 111 2.7.93—10.20.96*, chapter II:

A door, à la, a pear, a peer, a rear, a ware, A woah!, Abba, abhorred, abra, abroad, accord, acère, acha, Ada, ada, add a, adda, adore, Aetna, afford, afire, afore, afyre, ah air, ah car, ah ere, Ah Ha, ah ha, ain't tha, air blur, air bra, airfare, alder, all ears, all yours, alla, Allah, aller, allya, alpha, alswa, ama, amber, ambler, AmFar, amir, amor, Ana, ana, and ka, and uh, and war, anear, Anka, Anna, anvers, apes ma, appeere, aqua, ara, arbour, archer, ardor, ardour, are our, are there, Are there?, Are uh?, arm bears, armoire, armor, armour, arrear, as far, ashore, asper, ass tear, asthore, atcher, atma, au pair, au poivre, auntre, aura, austere, Auxerre, aw arrgh, aw awe, aw war, award, aware, awed jaw, Ayler, bazaar, baba, babka, bacca, baga, bagba, bagger, baiter, bamba, bancha, baner, bang your, bania, banker, banter, bar burr, bar straw, barbed wire, barber, barbour, bare rear, bare tears, Barère, batter, baxa, be here, be square, Beans Dear?, beau-père,

beaver, BeavHer, bedder, bedsore, beeba, beemba, been there, beer blare,
beer blur, beer here, begba, beggar, beggere, Bel Air, Bela, bela, belcher,
ben wa, Ben-Hur, bencher, bender, Bernard, Bertha, bestir, beta,
betcha, betta, better, bettre, bever, beware, bezoar, bibber, bicker, bidder,
biddler, bider, bien sûr, bifore, Big Star, Big Sur, bigga, bigger, bim-ba,
bird's rear, bismer, BiStar, biter, bitter, bittre, blabber, black tears, blah
corps, Blair's, blare, blanca, blare blur, blaster, blather, blazer, bleahhh,
blear corps, bleeder, bleeper, blender, blinder, blisker, blisper, blister,
blixa, blobber, blonder, bloomer, blooper, blubber,[31]

Goldsmith's prose is the most rule-generated of the four, although, like John
Cage, in many ways his mentor, Goldsmith has obviously "collected" his
words and phrases "according to taste." The amazing 606–page "useless encyclopedic reference book" that results was composed by collecting all the
phrases the poet came across in the given time period of the title (whether
in books, on radio or TV or on the internet or in actual conversation), words
and phrases that end in the common sound of American English linguists
call *schwa* (ə, er). The phrases are organized alphabetically by syllable and
letter count, beginning with one-syllable entries for chapter 1 ("A, a, aar, aas,
aer, agh, ah, air . . . ") and ending with the 7,228-syllable "The Rocking Horse
Winner" by D. H. Lawrence, which is never identified. The page in question
is the opening of chapter 2, where the units are two-syllable. Recitation of
the passage is a great feat, but note that when the page is seen, the words and
phrases create all manner of rhymes and repetitions, as in "be / here, be
square, Beans Dear?, beau-père, beaver, BeavHer, bedder, bedsore, / beeba,
beemba, been there." The reader's eye can proceed vertically ("betcha, bicker,
bigga, bittre, blare") as well as horizontally and even diagonally as we move
from "A door" to "blooper." Capitalized words stand out ("Anka, Anna, anvers, apes ma" or "Big Star, Big Sur, / bigga") creating fascinating disjunctive
inventories of the language we actually use today in the United States.

    The absurdist cataloguing that is the basis of *No. 111*—for example, "Are
there?, Are uh?, arm bears, armoire, armor, armour, arrear, as far, ashore, asper, ass tear, asthore, atcher, atma, au pair, au poivre, auntre, aura, austere,
Auxerre"—and, as the syllables get longer, such units as "How do you spell
'onomatopoeia'? How long do you plan to be 'almost there?'" (from Chapter X, p. 137)—constitutes a sociopoetic document, a memento mori, as it
were, for the discourses that characterize the 1990s, from those of the *National Enquirer* and the TV talk shows to the argot of daily conversation and
the beautiful prose of D. H. Lawrence. Along the way, Goldsmith gives us
passages in which the faulty transmission of verbal information (usually the

transcription from oral to written that is such a common phenomenon today) produces language like the following:

CXCV

My son is under the doctor's care and should not take P.E. today. Please execute him. Please excuse Mary for being absent. She was sick and I had her shot. Please excuse Fred for being. It was his father's fault. Please ackuse Fred being absent on Jan. 28 29 30 31 32 and 33. Mary could not come to school today because she was bothered by very close veins. Mary was absent from school yesterday as she was having a gangover. Please excuse Mary from Jim yesterday. She was administrating. Please excuse Fred for being absent. He had a cold and could not breed well. Please excuse Mary. She has been sick and under the doctor. Please excuse Mary from being absent yesterday. She was in bed with grandpa;
    (*No. 111*, 490).

This parodic catalogue of standard medical excuses produced by the parent for the teacher—I especially like "She was sick and I had her shot," "she was having a gangover," and "she was bothered by very close veins"—is nothing if not a verbovisivocal construct. What Haroldo de Campos perceived in the early sixties, when he produced such concrete poems as "**fala / prata,**" is that the technological revolution of our time would produce a situation where "reading" increasingly means "seeing," where the dichotomy is less between "poetry" (verse) and "prose" than between *seeing* and *seeing through*. "Please excuse Fred for being absent. He had a cold and could not breed well."

In 2001 Joel Bettridge and Eric Selinger asked me to write an essay for their collection on Ronald Johnson in the National Poetry Foundation's "Life and Poetry" series. I decided to explore Johnson's early Concrete poetry, which has interesting analogues to the work of Haroldo de Campos discussed in chapter 9. But the difference is also telling: Johnson's Concrete has a stronger sound component, deriving from particular musical compositions rather than from the Pound-Fenollosa ideogram, as was the case with Brazilian Concrete.

10

Songs of the Earth

Ronald Johnson's Verbivocovisuals

> Words which sound alike belong together.
> Oyvind Fahlström

Songs of the Earth (1970) was Ronald Johnson's favorite among his own books of poetry. Johnson's editor, Peter O'Leary, tells us that "he thought of it as nearly perfect,"[1] and accordingly O'Leary reproduces all twelve of these minimalist Concrete poems in his *Selected Poems*. In his preface Johnson explains that these "squarings of the circle" or "strains" were based on the "musics of silence" as recorded by Thoreau on his night walks in the Concord woods as well as on "a progression of hearings of Mahler's *Song of the Earth* [*Das Lied von der Erde*] on records, in concert, and in my head."[2]

The reference to Thoreau, a key figure for many poets of the sixties and seventies, especially John Cage, is not surprising. But the homage to Mahler, who would seem to be too musically complex and melodic to suit Johnson's minimalist bent, seems anomalous until one recalls that Mahler's *Song of the Earth* (1908) had its own minimalist/imagist base in the Chinese poems translated (quite freely) in Hans Bethge's collection *Die Chinesische Flöte* (*The Chinese Flute*)—poems by Li Po, Ts'ien Ts'i, and Wang Wei. Indeed, notes Henry-Louis de La Grange, "the discovery of Chinese music stimulated Mahler to adopt certain features, such as the pentatonic scale, and to use instruments suggesting those of China, such as the mandolin harp, winds and tambourine." And La Grange cites two key innovations in the composition of the song cycle: (1) "the use of the same motifs in both the principal and secondary voices—prefiguring one of the basic principles of Schoenberg's serial composition, 'total thematicism'"; and (2) "heterophony (or 'imprecise union'), a principle in which a melody and an ornamented or varied version of it are heard simultaneously, or in which identical voices diverge slightly in rhythm or in interval structure."[3]

These principles, as we shall see, also operate in Johnson's *Songs of the Earth*, where the Mahlerian themes of love and death are treated to the concentration and simplification characteristic of the Chinese lyric. Mahler's six songs—"The Drinking Song of Earth's Sorrow," "The Lonely One in Autumn," "Youth," "Of Beauty," "The Drunkard in Spring," and "The Farewell" —become Johnson's twelve condensed "squarings": the composer's delicate sonorities and exquisite orchestral refinements, filtered through the minimalism of Li Po and Wang-Wei, provide the impetus for Johnson's particular brand of Concrete poetry.

The founders of the Concrete movement—Eugen Gomringer of Switzerland and the *Noigandres* group of Brazil—equated "concrete" largely with the visual aspect of the poem. "Concrete Poetry," wrote Gomringer in 1960, "is the general term which includes a large number of poetic-linguistic experiments, characterized—whether constellation, ideogram, stochastic poetry, etc.—by conscious study of the material and its structure." This new poetry, emphasizing as it does "formal pattern" in "reduced language," should be "as easily understood as signs in airports and traffic signs."[4] And *Noigandres* similarly focuses on "graphic space as structural agent" rather than "mere linear-temporistical development."[5] Central to their concept of the concrete poem was the Poundian ideogram, and although the ideogram was defined in Joycean terms as "verbivocovisual," *Noigandres* concerned itself with typography, word and letter placement, and spatial disposition rather than sound as such.[6] Concrete poetry, after all, was poetry *to be seen*.

The one early Concretist who qualifies this emphasis on visual art was the great Swedish poet-artist Oyvind Fahlström. In discussing various verbal systems in his "Manifesto for Concrete Poetry" (1953),[7] Fahlström remarks: "I can construct . . . for example, a series of 12 vowels in a certain succession and make tables accordingly, even though a twelve vowel series as such does not make the same sense as the series of the twelve-tone chromatic scale" (75). And again:

Above all I think that the rhythmic aspect contains unimagined possibilities. Not only in music is rhythm the most elementary, directly physically grasping means for effect; which is the joy of recognizing something known before, the importance of repeating; which has a connection with the pulsation of breathing, the blood, ejaculation. It is wrong that jazz bands have the monopoly of giving collective rhythmic ecstasy. The drama and poetry can also give it. (76)

And Falhström goes on to formulate the axiom that I cite as my epigraph above, "Words which sound alike belong together." In tracking etymological links—e.g., "*Laxar* [salmon] has to do with *laxering* [laxatives] and *taxar* [dachshund] has to do with *taxering* [tax assessment]" (76). Chinese, the poet argues, is especially suited to poetry because "its classless words and meaning derived from word order." Concrete, in this context, refers less to the visual poem as such than to the "squeez[ing]" of the "language material":

> Throw the letters around as in anagrams. Repeat the letters in words; lard with foreign words . . . with foreign letters. . . . Of course also "lettered," newly-discovered words. Abbreviations as new word building, exactly as in everyday language. . . . Always it is a question of making new form of the material. (78)

These statements look back to such Russian avant-gardists as Velimir Khlebnikov and Alexei Kruschenykh, whose etymological and phonemic wordplay is legendary,[8] as well as forward to sound poets, *lettristes,* verbo-phonetic poets, and so on. But Johnson avoided the complex iconoclastic exercises of the latter, preferring the defamiliarization described by Fahlström when he writes:

> You can also . . . put well-known words in such realized strange connections that you undermine the reader's security in the holy context between the word and its meaning and make him feel that conventional meanings are quite as much or quite as little arbitrary as the dictated new meanings. (77)

Consider the first of Johnson's "twelve squarings":

earthearthearth
earthearthearth
earthearthearth
earthearthearth
earthearthearth
earthearthearth

"Earthearthearth," Johnson remarks in the preface, "is a linkage of ear to hear and heart. Art and hearth are also hid in it." Certainly all these words become paragrammatically present. But what strikes me as especially odd is that the words "heart" and "hearth" only stand out (and then dominate) when the line is repeated. When we read

earthearthearth

by itself, the word "earth"—containing, as it does, "ear"—remains intact, but the longer the column above, the more dominant the *th* becomes in the constellation, with "heart" right at the center between them. And further, the column makes "the" prominent, even as *arth* suggests *arthrography,* the radiographic examination of a joint—what lies behind the surface.

Johnson's seemingly simple and innocuous little columnar poem thus has an interesting relation to Mahler's "Drinking Song of Earth's Sorrow." The *ear* and the *heart,* the fire in the *hearth*—these are basic components of human life on earth, the substratum of all else, the Stevensian "the the" of the "world on the dump" that must be treated to the *arthrography* or *art* that sees into the life of things.

From the *earth,* seen in this light, the cycle moves to what is above and beneath it:

s tone s
s tone s
s tone s
s tone s

C L O U D
A L O U D
A L O U D
A L O U D
A L O U D
A L O U D

dark behind and
dark beyond and

underneathunder

To begin, we might note that Johnson's typography is conservative: I can re-produce it with reasonable accuracy on the computer, using my default font (Verdana), boldface, and centering cues. Perhaps Johnson wanted to avoid expense: the original edition of *Songs of the Earth,* with its disappointingly routine cover design (small green, orange, and yellow squares and circles on a cream-colored background), is not an elegant artist's book. Or perhaps Johnson wanted to invent a form that could be reprinted as it is in the *Selected Poems.* Composition, in any case, becomes, as Steve McCaffery notes, "largely a syntactic and a spatial matter, of the re-arrangement of existing phrases into new combinations, implying a synchronic sense of 'literature' as an ac-cessible word-supply."[9] In this paragrammatic mode, the Mahlerian *tones* are also the *stones* beneath the *earth,* just as the clouds above ground demand an increase in loudness and font size. As above, so below: the chaos of darkness "underneath under."

Poem #3 is more of a constellation:

```
s    p    r    i    n    g
s    p    r    i    n    g
s    p    R    I    N    G
s    p    R    I    N    G
s    p    R    I    N    G
S    P    R    I    N    G
```

```
be 11 to
11 be 11
to 11 be
11 to 11
```

"Spring" is configured as a square: the six-letter word repeated six times and hence forming two diagonals as well as the horizontal. The gradual shift from lower-case to capital letters, first in line three to form "RING" and then in the final line, the whole word "SPRING" is evidently designed to present the arrival of spring by visual means. But the refrain brings in a tonal com-plication. The letters spell out "bell toll bell toll bell toll," thus fulfilling the promise of the "ring" above. But the spacing, separating the coupled "l" pho-nemes from the words that contained them, designates the number eleven, and, more indirectly, parallel lines, and indeed the opening "be ll to" gener-ates parallels both horizontally and diagonally, as in the diagonal "be be be" of lines 1–3. The spring "ring" or rondo thus becomes a square, whose tolling bell brings us full circle.

In Poem #4, the decisive bell gives way to the contrasting sound of the "wood / wind," and in #5, that motif is developed:

```
        c    h    o    r    d
             o    o    o
             W O O D
        o    o    o    o    o
             W I N D
             o    o    o


        c    l    o    u    d
```

dark-clouded
spring birds
lark-colored

spring clods

loud   strings

Here is an example of the heterophony La Grange describes in Mahler. The letters and phonemes repeat with delicate variations: we see and hear the opening "chord," played on the woodwinds and finally transformed (perhaps under the pressure of "wind"?) into a reprise of the "cloud" of poem #2. The little coda brings back the "dark" and "cloud" of that earlier lyric, transforms "dark" into the "lark" of spring, "cloud" into "clods" as well as its rhyming partner "loud," and signals the shift from wind instruments to strings. *Strings* further echoes "spring," substituting only one phoneme, even as "colored" is almost equivalent phonemically to "clouded." And of course "WOOD WIND" refers here not only to musical instruments but also to the "earth" of poem #1 and the "cloud" of #2. Squares within squares and echo structures throughout provide a delicate exercise in sameness and difference.

The two central poems, #6 and #7, present a slightly different development. One of the first and most famous exhibits of the Concrete movement was Eugen Gomringer's "Wind":[10]

```
          w    w
        d    i
        n    n    n
      i    d    i    d
      w              w
```

Mary Ellen Solt writes:

> Had [Gomringer] simply printed the word "wind" in the center of the
> page, it would simply have sat there. Arranging it spatially so that we
> can read the word in four directions, he is able to introduce an element
> of play into the "reading" of the poem that captures the nature of the
> wind far more truly than a longer poetic statement of many words. The
> letters actually seem to float as if the wind were acting upon them.
> (*Concrete Poetry,* 9)

Such iconicity, carrying on the tradition of such avant-garde poems as Apollinaire's *calligrammes* (e.g., "*Il pleut*") and characteristic of first-stage Concrete poetry, has since been called into question. Can letters and words actually represent the signified, in this case the wind itself? Johnson was surely
aware of this discussion when he produced his two constellations:

poem upon poem

form from form
from form from
form from form

open open open

```
      m        i       n       d

      i                        n

      n                        i

      d     n     I     w
      w                 d
               i     n
               i     n
      w                        g
```

Here "poem upon poem" alludes to the Gomringer derivation as well as to
the relation of #6 to the earlier and later lyrics in the sequence. Change a
single phoneme in "form" and you have "from"; "form," moreover, literally
comes "from" a prior form and is in turn "open" to a new one. Here, moreover, "wind" is not represented in its supposedly actual movement and effect,

as is the case in Gomringer's constellation, but transforms into "mind" by a simple reversal of *w* to *m*. What a difference a letter makes! In #7 a second transposition transforms "wind" into "wing," while the separation of "in" from the four-letter words suggests that the bird's wing flies *in* the wind, even as it is recalled "in" the "mind" of the previous lyric. In the ninth lyric, the two-word "world / wind," this motif is repeated, the expected whirlwind now seen as universal, as indigenous to the earth (poem #1) and hence the "world."

The magic of letter reversal has always fascinated Johnson. Asked to comment on the concrete poem "**MAZE, MANE, WANE,**" [see Solt, *Concrete Poetry* 251), the poet writes:

> It is a maze mostly because one tends to read left to right at first & it makes no sense.
>
> Then one sees the vertical words: MAZE, MANE, WANE & thinks, trapped as I planned, to it that way. But the way out of the maze is a visual one & one sees at last that it is simply three words MAZE (since the M's & W's are made exactly alike, as are the Z & N's, so that the W is simply an upside down M, etc.). So it is actually the word maze making itself into one. And as an added delight, there are the handsome words MAZE, MANE, WANE. (*Concrete Poetry* 52, 311)

A similar form of verbal play characterizes the eighth Song of the Earth:

W   A   N   E

W   ᵃA ⁿ ᵉN ʷ E
      a n e w
W   ᵃA ⁿ ᵉN ʷ E
      a n e w

W   A   N   E

A N E W

A N E W

A N E W

A N E W

Here the first letter *w* of "wane" becomes the last letter of its anagram "anew." And further, *w* is an upside-down *m*, the letter preceding *n*, and hence made new by it. Throughout the first part of the poem, the capitalized "WANE" trumps the small "anew," as if to question the very possibility of life "anew" —renewal. At the same time, a triangle is formed out of the words "AN / a new," thus preparing the ground for the antiphon in which the four-letter "ANEW" is repeated four times, thus making a new square that takes precedence over the prior waning.

After the "world / wind" of "anew," the bell sounds of "be ll to" of poem #3 come back in the seemingly conventional "fa la la la la" refrain of #10:

$$f \quad a \quad l \quad l \quad a \quad l \quad l \quad a \quad l \quad l \quad a$$
$$l \quad l \quad a \quad l \quad l \quad a \quad l \quad l \quad a \quad l \quad l$$
$$a \quad l \quad l \quad a \quad l \quad l \quad a \quad l \quad l \quad a \quad l$$
$$l \quad a \quad l \quad l \quad a \quad l \quad l \quad a \quad l \quad l \quad a$$
$$l \quad l \quad a \quad l \quad l \quad a \quad l \quad l \quad a \quad l \quad l$$

By careful spacing and italicizing, Johnson finds the "fall," "all" and parallel *l*'s that recapitulate earlier elements in the sequence. "Fall" follows "wane" in #8, "all" follows "world" in #9, and both "all" and the earlier "anew" are also sly allusions to Johnson's poet-mentor Louis Zukofsky's lyric sequence "Anew" and to his *All* (*Collected Shorter Poems*). Indeed, it was probably from Zukofsky that Johnson first got the idea that one could make poetry from the smallest and least conspicuous words in the vocabulary—words like "all" and "anew."

After the "fall," again an ascent:

and ascend
and ascend
and ascend

to the end

st air st air st air
st air st air st air
st air st air st air
st air st air st air
st air st air st air
st air st air st air

The staircase shape here is one of the most iconic elements in the sequence, but the splitting of the word "stair" into "st air" brings in the notion of the saint (he who ascends the stair to heaven), but a saint that has no proper name and is no more than "air"—a fitting designation vis-à-vis the "earth" of #1. Then, too, the dialectic between "wane" and "anew" is contained in the morpheme *end* in "ascend" and foregrounded in "to the end." No way to "ascend," it seems, without the terminus of the "end" in sight. And that paradox leads to the lovely final lyric that plays exquisite variations on two letters, *o* and *n:*

on on on on o
noon on on on
on on on on o
noon on   noon

on on on . . .

Johnson's little finale contains a Beckettian "on" (as in "I must go on I can't go on I'll go on . . . "), juxtaposed to the exclamatory particle *o* and the word "noon," with its paragram on "no one." Indeed "no" is the mirror image of "on," and the poem asks to be read from both left and right.

But the lyric "On" has a clinamen that is especially interesting. It is the only one of these lyrics that introduces excessive spacing (see line 4) so as to make the sides of the square equal. This lyric is also the only one that has a foreshortened final line, thus fulfilling the promise of the "open open open" of #6.

Commenting on the final bars of Mahler's last song, *Der Abschied* ("The Farewell"), Henry-Louis de La Grange remarks:

> The dimension of "openness" . . . is preserved until the very end, when the final C major chord upon which the flute and the clarinet obstinately maintain a dissonant A instead of letting it descend to G, as traditional harmony would require. It imparts a sense of timelessness to the final bars, in which the last two notes of the solo voice ("Ewig," E-D) are also not allowed to reach the tonic (C). Furthermore, three of the four notes in this final chord are those of the main leitmotif of the word—A-G-E. The movement ends in near-silence with the pianissimo tonic chord sustained by three trombones and woodwinds, and brief arpeggio fragments plucked at by the harp, mandolin, and celesta. (*Mahler* 468)

What interests me here is that although Johnson's words are by no means comparable to the formal diction of Mahler's *Lied* ("*Die liebe Erde allüberall/*

blüht auf im Lenz und grünt aufs neu."), his rendition of "On . . . " uncannily captures the spirit of *Das Lied von der Erde.* The main leitmotif of the sequence is recapitulated, and the dissonance of the final foreshortened line produces the "near-silence" of the tonic chord.

In his 1995 interview with Peter O'Leary, Johnson explains that his major long poem *ARK* owes its major debt to the Concrete poetry he was practicing in the sixties. "I learned all the visual things I did," he remarks, "from concrete poetry. I wanted to take it further, like Ian Finlay who now makes gardens." And he adds:

> I think the thing I'm proudest of in concrete poetry is a late work after the movement was nearly over. I'd looked at and admired Jonathan Williams's *Mahler* where for each movement of the symphonies he wrote a poem, and I thought, "Ah, but he didn't do *Das Lied!*" So I did *Songs of the Earth* and made them each a concrete poem. . . . It's a sequence of squares with different statements in a different orientation. It's a very romantic poem. And I think it can stand beside *Das Lied.*[11]

In the "Beams" of the *ARK,* of course, these Concretist experiments are carried much further. But *Songs of the Earth* marks a key transition between the more programmatic visual Concretism of the 1950s and 1960s and the visual/sound poetries of the last two decades, especially those of Susan Howe and Johanna Drucker, Christian Bök and Brian Kim Stefans. Indeed, Johnson's central insight that the semantic is only one element in poetry, that poetry is to be *seen* and *heard* rather than *seen through, heard through,* and primarily to be paraphrased and interpreted, is only now coming fully into its own.

In 2002 the Spenser Society, which regularly sponsors a session or two at the annual Modern Language Association convention, asked me to participate in a panel on the legacy of the Spenserian stanza. I am hardly a Spenser expert, but when I studied the stanza, with its ingenious interlocking rhyme scheme (ababcdcdd), in which eight iambic pentameter lines are followed, to great effect, by a final alexandrine, it struck me that although after the nineteenth-century poets no longer use the Spenserian stanza, its complexity and especially its deployment of the alexandrine have much to teach a poetry culture that is increasingly indifferent to the role of sound in poetry. Indeed, the free verse, now dominant not only in the United States but also around the world, has become, with notable exceptions, little more than linear prose, arbitrarily divided into line lengths. But there are two sites where sound is once again being foregrounded. The first, as we have already seen, is in Concrete and post-Concrete visual poetries. The second may be found in procedural (rule-governed) poetics, whose center today is probably the French movement called Oulipo. The following essay takes up the Oulipo alexandrine and some of its Anglophone derivates.

II
The Oulipo Factor

The Procedural Poetics of Christian Bök and Caroline Bergvall

Loyal practitioners of the alexandrine, our hexameter, unhinge from within the meter of this rigid and puerile mechanism. The ear, freed from a factitious counting, takes joy in discerning, on its own, all the possible combinations of twelve tones.

Stephane Mallarmé, "Crise de vers"

Our words must seem to be inevitable.

W. B. Yeats, *Letters on Poetry to Dorothy Wellesley*

In 1988 Jacques Roubaud, the remarkable poet-novelist-theorist-mathematician, published a book called *La vieillesse d'Alexandre* (*The Old Age of Alexander*), which makes the case that the death of the alexandrine—the twelve-syllable line that is the staple of French poetry from the Renaissance to the late nineteenth century—has been grossly exaggerated.

Roubaud's dramatic story begins in the twelfth century with a short fragment of a Provençal poem dedicated to the exploits of Alexander the Great, written by one Alberic de Pisançon.[1] This poem, written in octosyllabics, was soon followed by a decasyllabic (pentameter) *Alexandre,* and then in 1170 Lambert le Tort de Chateaudun introduced the decisive innovation destined to create an indissoluble link between the hero and the meter in which his exploits were to be celebrated in the many Alexander poems that followed—a line that had twelve syllables and a complex set of rules. In the Alexander poems that now proliferated, the hero was depicted as conqueror and lover; he tamed and mastered the wild horse Bucephalus, descended into the underworld in a glass barrel, and was always the perfect *chevalier courtois.* By the mid-fifteenth century, the twelve-syllable line was named the alexandrine, and it became the celebrated verse form that extended from Corneille and Racine, as in the latter's famous reference to Phèdre as

La fille de Minos et de Pasiphaé

down to Baudelaire, whose alexandrines often break up not into hemistichs, as in the above example, but into trimeters, as in:

A la très belle, à la très bonne, a la très chère

In its variable forms, the alexandrine remained intact until the fall of the Paris Commune in 1870. In that year it experienced a catastrophe—the word is well chosen because etymologically it means *kata* (down) plus *strophe* (turning) and hence has metrical overtones—at the hands of Rimbaud's "revolutionary" poem "Qu'est-ce pour nous, mon coeur" (see *La vieillesse d'Alexandre* 20–26). For here the rules, especially those relating to the necessary prominence of the sixth syllable and the place of the silent *e,* were consistently violated. And Roubaud relates this violation to the violation of the social order, which is the impetus of Rimbaud's oppositional poem. After Rimbaud, so the common wisdom would have it, the "broken" alexandrine was increasingly replaced by free verse: Apollinaire's and Cendrars's rhythms set the stage for what Roubaud calls *"le vers libre international"*—the free verse now dominant around the world, whose only distinguishing feature is lineation as such. Free verse, Roubaud notes, easily adapts linguistic units to linear ones and is characterized by its formal indifference (204). Its absence of rules makes it suitable for a global age, for free verse passes readily from language to language and is potentially translatable. Indeed, says Roubaud, the passage of free verse across frontiers is metrically duty-free (205).

The "death of Alexander," by this argument, is inevitable in the would-be egalitarian twentieth and twenty-first centuries. The common wisdom goes something like this: (1) Verse is not necessarily poetry, (2) conversely, then, poetry is not equivalent to verse, and hence, (3) verse is of no importance (*La vieillesse d'Alexandre* 10). Contemporary poetry criticism, Roubaud further suggests, has followed suit. Even when it is concerned with poems written in fixed verse forms, it pays no attention to prosody, discussing the texts in question as if they were in fact written in prose. All of us have experienced this situation. On an oral exam I once asked a student who was writing a dissertation on Shelley to name the verse form of "Adonais" and of "Ode to the West Wind." He was at a complete loss.

But the apparent hegemony of free verse, Roubaud suggests, was never all that complete. The key figure in this story is Mallarmé, whose *Crise de vers* (1896), cited in my epigraph above, performs the crucial analysis of the relation of verse to language itself. Let me again cite the passage, which refers to the modernist state of the art:

> Loyal practitioners of the alexandrine, our hexameter, unhinge from within the meter of this rigid and puerile mechanism. The ear, freed from a factitious counting, takes joy in discerning, on its own, all the possible combinations of twelve tones.[2]

Roubaud calls this "a marvelously Schoenbergian Utopian definition of a new alexandrine, where all the possibilities of twelve—not in the arithmetical sense, the current impoverished sense according to which mathematics is no more than a rigid, puerile, and facticious counting—but where a hieratic rhythmic entity with almost infinite variety, would be in play (for the new *jouissance* of the ear)" (53).

Roubaud is referring here to the "mathematical" poetry of Oulipo (the *Ouvroir de littérature potentielle*), a poetry that unlike the ubiquitous free verse paradigm on the one hand, and the traditional metrical forms of the New Formalists on the other, is produced by those "restrictions of a formal nature" known as constraints. As Roubaud puts it in his "Introduction" to *The Oulipo and Combinatorial Art* (1991):

> Obviously a complex relation exists between the requirements of an outwardly imposed rule and the artist's inner freedom. (This is why

the choice of mathematics, arguably in fundamental opposition to poetry, is anything but haphazard.)

And there follows the well-known Oulipo "law": "A text written according
to a constraint describes the constraint."[3]

According to Oulipo rules, there are as many possible constraints as there
are poems, and the constraint is not an external form that is readily recognized but may be a rule that remains largely hidden to the reader. Whereas
a Petrarchan sonnet may be understood as a kind of envelope (octave plus
sestet), whose parameters govern the poem's composition, the Oulipo constraint is a *generative* device: it creates a formal structure whose rules of composition are internalized so that the constraint in question is not only a rule
but a thematic property of the poem as well.

Consider Michel Bénabou's 1986 assemblage of *perverses,* lines obtained
by splitting two familiar lines of poetry and crossing them (see *Oulipo Compendium* 78). Titled "Alexandre au greffoir" ("Alexander Transplanted"), it
appeared as #29 in *La Bibliothèque Oulipienne* and is dedicated to "Jacques
Roubaud / qui ressemble à Baudelaire / et rime avec Rimbaud."[4] In his headnote Bénabou notes that however monotonous the alexandrine may have become in its recent incarnations, it remains the verse form that gave France
its golden age of poetry, the cornerstone of its metric, perhaps because its
rules are so very strict. Accordingly, with Roubaud's help, Bénabou sets out
to give the alexandrine new life. Their project has two stages: (1) to make
a list of all the alexandrines they know by heart, which are thus part of
their everyday lives, and (2) to liberate the hemistichs by separating and re-
combining them, thus producing a whole new set of alexandrines. The latter
process produces a sizable body of *perverses.* Bénabou's list has 260 alexandrines, each one divided into hemistichs and printed in two columns. The
source texts are then re-formed into single aphoristic lines, couplets, quatrains, and whole poems. Here for example is the first quatrain of a poem
called "Les Chats":

Les amoureux fervents des fleuves impassibles
Aiment également, à l'ombre des forêts,
Les chats puissants et doux comme des chairs d'enfants
Qui comme eux sont frileux dans les froides ténèbres.[5]

The source text is Baudelaire's "Les Chats":

Les amoureux fervents et les savants austères
Aiment également, dans leur mûre saison,

Les chats puissants et doux, orgueil de la maison,
Qui comme eux sont frileux et comme eux sedentaires.[6]

Bénabou joins the first hemistich of each line to the second of another: the first alexandrine thus selected (#8) is the opening line of Rimbaud's "Bateau ivre": "Comme je descendais des fleuves impassibles." The second (#107) is Phèdre's disclaimer in Racine's great tragedy: "Ah, que ne suis-je assise à l'ombre des forêts"; the third (#163) comes from Baudelaire's own "Correspondances": "Il est des parfums frais comme des chairs d'enfant"; and the fourth (#162) from Baudelaire's "Chanson d'Automne": "Bientôt nous plongerons dans les froides ténèbres."

Here, we might argue, is the Schoenbergian "12-tone" fantasy par excellence. For by fusing Baudelaire's lines with Racine's or Rimbaud's, something very interesting happens. The "new" poem is by no means absurd; it makes perfectly good sense, for example, to compare soft cat fur to the skin of small children. The cat lovers in this version are not those who are aging and hence sensitive to the cold, but those, like the Rimbaud of "Bateau ivre," who are lovers of those impassive rivers that will take them far away. But the shadows of the forests (here Phèdre's lament comes in) are also threatening—of a piece with the cold darkness of Baudelaire's "Autumn Song." Then, too, the Oulipo game is an eloquent homage to the French poetic tradition in general and to Baudelaire in particular, testifying to the continuity of a tradition that in French letters has never been surpassed. Bénabou and Roubaud allow us to see that poetry is always intertextual, that even the strongest urge to "Make It New!" involves familiarity with what came before. Indeed, to take the hemistichs apart, as we would a musical phrase, is to see how complex and intricate a form the alexandrine really is. There need be nothing passé or dated about its use, provided its mathematical variability is honored.

In *Oulipo Compendium* Harry Mathews gives us some English examples of Bénabou's *perverses,* this time in iambic pentameter, which is to English what the alexandrine is to French. For example, from Shakespeare's "They that have power to hurt and will do one," and Milton's "They also serve who only stand and wait," Mathews produces the couplet:

They also serve who hurt and will do none
They that have power to only stand and wait

Or he invents a sonnet like "the Maoist's Regrets," which begins

Shall I compare thee, China to Peru?
That is no country! Amid the alien corn,

The wood's decay, the yielding place to new,
The old order changeth! blow his wreathed horn!

The pentameter does not break into two equal parts, and so it doesn't lend itself as well as the alexandrine to Bénabou's particular constraint. But iambic pentameter has its own potential, which Matthews exploits in a brilliant piece for the poetry journal *Shiny* called "35 Variations on a Theme from Shakespeare."[7] The source text is "To be or not to be, that is the question." Here are some examples of Mathews's variations:

02. *Anagram*
    Note at his behest: bet on toot or quit

04. *Lipogram in* a
    To be or not to be, this is the question

05. *Lipogram in* i
    To be or not to be, that's the problem

06. *Lipogram in* e
    Almost nothing, or nothing: but which

09. *Missing letter*
    To be or not to be hat is the question

10. *One letter added*
    To bed or not to be, that is the question

13. *Emphasis*
    To be, if you so what I mean, to *be,* be alive, exist, not
just keep hanging around; *or* (and that means or or the other, not
getting away from it) *not* to be, *not* to be alive, *not* exist, to—putting
it bluntly—check out, cash in your chips, head west: *that* (do you read
me? Not "maybe this" or "maybe something else") *that* is, really is,
irrevocably is, *the* one and only inescapable, overwhelming, and totally
preoccupying ultimate question.

14. *Curtailing (different)*
    To be or not to be, that is

31. *Homophony*
      Two-beer naughty beat shatters equation

And so it goes, the famous line being put through such other hoops as *"Double Curtailing"* ("Not to be, that is"), *"Antonymy"* ("Nothing and something; this was an answer"), and *"Permutation"* ("That is the question: to be or not to be)."

What is the purpose of Mathews's little Hamlet game? First, it demonstrates the difference syntax and morphology can make, the changes that meaning undergoes by means of something as seemingly trivial as the addition of a single phoneme or a change in word order. "That is the question: to be or not to be" has an entirely different emotional aura from the original, and amplication (#13) turns Hamlet's meditation on suicide into a Woody Allen comedy passage. More important: as in the case of Roubaud and Bénamou's alexandrines, Mathews's "35 Variations" is an anatomy of the *untranslatability* that makes poetry what it is. For, as the variations show, there is no other way to say "To be or not to be, that is the question." Consider the rhythm:

To **be** or **not** to **be** // **that** is the **ques**tion

where the clash of stresses in the fifth and sixth syllables and the extra unstressed final syllable enact what the line is saying. The lipogram "to be or not to be, that's the problem" has the requisite ten syllables but loses the force of the terrifying eleven-syllable original. For one thing, "Problem" cannot compete with "Question" with its paragram on *quest.* For another, "that" must be isolated for emphasis. Sound and syntax, in this scheme of things, are all.

The Linear Fallacy

In the United States, Oulipo has long had its counterpart in the work of John Cage, Jackson Mac Low, and the Fluxus poets. Cagean constraints are not as literary as those of Oulipo—the rules are not likely to involve rhetorical figures like anagram or homophony—but the counting devices are often more elaborate than such Oulipo rules as N + 7.[8] The poetry of constraint, in any case, is now becoming an interesting alternative to the dominant poetic mode of the anthologies and journals—dominant, incidentally, not just in conservative but in so-called experimental circles as well. Consider the following examples, some of them lyric, others narrative, which I have selected at random, by opening the recently published *Norton Anthology of Modern and Contemporary Poetry* and copying out the beginnings of poems, written during the 1990s:

> On Fridays he'd open a can of Jax
> After coming home from the mill,
> & ask me to write a letter to my mother
> Who sent postcards of desert flowers
> Taller than men. He would beg,
> Promising to never beat her
> Again.

> When his Excellency Prince Norodom Chantaraingsey
> Invited me to lunch on the battlefield
> I was glad of my white suit for the first time that day.
> They lived well, the mad Norodoms, they had style.
> The brandy and the soda arrived in crates

> On my way to bringing you the leotard
> you forgot to include in your overnight bag,
> the snow started coming down harder.
> I watched each gathering of leafy flakes
> melt round my footfall.

> Menial twilight sweeps the storefronts along Lexington
> as the shadows arrive to take their places
> among the scourge of the earth.

> A young black girl stopped by the woods,
> so young she knew only one man: Jim Crow
> but she wasn't allowed to call him Mister.
> The woods were his and she respected his boundaries
> even in the absence of fence.

> "Look how they love themselves,"
> my mother would lecture as we drove through
> the ironwoods, the park on one side,
> the beach on the other, where sunworshippers,
> splayed upon towels, appeared sacrificial,
> bodies glazed and glistening like raw fish in the market.

For many years I wanted a child
though I knew it would only illuminate life
for a time, like a star on a tree; I believed
that happiness would at last assert itself,
like a bird in a dirty cage, calling me,
ambassador of flesh, out of the rough
locked ward of sex.

Seven poems, all of them by distinguished prize-winning poets: in order of their appearance, Yusef Komunyakaa, James Fenton, Jorie Graham, Rita Dove, Thylias Moss, Cathy Song, and Henri Cole.[9] Yet, different as these poets are from one another with respect to gender, ethnicity, and thematic concerns, all of them observe what is currently a poetic formula: their "free verse" is really—and perhaps intentionally—no more than lineated prose.[10] Here are my transpositions of the seven extracts above:

On Fridays he'd open a can of Jax after coming home from the mill, & ask me to write a letter to my mother who sent postcards of desert flowers taller than men. He would beg, promising to never beat her again.

When his Excellency Prince Norodom Chantaraingsey invited me to lunch on the battlefield, I was glad of my white suit for the first time that day. They lived well, the mad Norodoms, they had style. The brandy and the soda arrived in crates.

On my way to bringing you the leotard you forgot to include in your overnight bag, the snow started coming down harder. I watched each gathering of leafy flakes melt round my footfall.

Menial twilight sweeps the storefronts along Lexington as the shadows arrive to take their places among the scourge of the earth.

A young black girl stopped by the woods, so young she knew only one man: Jim Crow[,] but she wasn't allowed to call him Mister. The woods were his and she respected his boundaries even in the absence of fence.

"Look how they love themselves," my mother would lecture as we drove through the ironwoods, the park on one side, the beach on the

other, where sunworshippers, splayed upon towels, appeared sacrificial,
bodies glazed and glistening like raw fish in the market.

For many years I wanted a child though I knew it would only illuminate life for a time, like a star on a tree. I believed that happiness
would at last assert itself, like a bird in a dirty cage, calling me, ambassador of flesh, out of the rough locked ward of sex.

When we examine these models, we note that the line break, so central to
free verse in its early manifestations in the twentieth century, no longer has
the semantic function it exercised in poetry from Ezra Pound and William
Carlos Williams, to George Oppen and Lorine Niedecker, Robert Creeley and
Frank O'Hara, down to Clark Coolidge and Rae Armantrout. Indeed, in
these recent poems, all of them written in complete sentences, the attention
paid to sound structure or syntactic patterning is so minimal that one can
only conclude that the term "poetry" currently designates not the melopoeic
origins of lyric poetry or the page designs of visual prosody but rather an
ironized narrative or, more frequently, the personal expression of a particular
insight, presented in sometimes striking figurative language: "desert flowers
/ Taller than men," "leafy flakes melt round my footfall," "Menial twilight
sweeps the storefronts," bodies are "glazed and glistening like raw fish in the
market," "happiness" asserts itself "like a bird in a dirty cage."[11]

But since fiction can—and does—foreground these same devices, the same
"sensitive," closely observed perceptions or ironic, parabolic tales—one wonders if "poetry" at the turn of the twenty-first century isn't perhaps expendable. Do we really need it? Or is "real" poetry to be found, as some people
now argue, in hip-hop culture or at the poetry slam? Or perhaps in New Formalist attempts to restore the iambic pentameter or tetrameter to its former
position? Whatever our position on the New Formalism, close reading of its
exemplars suggests that, like the clothing or furniture of earlier centuries,
the verse forms of, say, the Romantic period cannot in fact be replicated except as museum curiosities. Consider the opening of Wordsworth's "Tintern
Abbey":

Five years have past: five summers, with the length
Of five long winters! And again I hear
These waters, rolling from their mountain-springs
With a soft inland murmur.—Once again
Do I behold these steep and lofty cliffs,

That on a wild secluded scene impress
Thoughts of more deep seclusion; and connect
The landscape with the quiet of the sky.

A whole essay could be written on the subtle ways these lines enact the "con-nect[ion]" of "the landscape with the quiet of the sky." The assonance of "quiet," "sky," the internal rhyme of "steep" and "deep," "soft" and "loft-y," the permutation of "secluded" into "seclusion," and the relation of enjamb-ment to the creation of that "soft inland murmur" of line 4: each rhythmic unit here is carefully calibrated. But the mere choice of meter is obviously not enough: here, in a poem called "Rough Country," is Dana Gioia's account of coming across a hidden waterfall:

not half a mile from the nearest road,
a spot so hard to reach that no one comes—
a hiding place, a shrine for dragonflies
and nesting jays, a sign that there is still
one piece of property that won't be owned.

Here the dutiful elaboration of the iambic pentameter does little to relate meaningful units: consider the monotony of "and NESTing JAYS, a SIGN that THERE is STILL." Again, word and rhythm seem to have no necessary connec-tion: if the first line read "not half a mile from the nearest highway" and the second, "a spot so tough to reach that no one comes," I doubt anyone would notice.

It is not just that Gioia is untalented; even poets of much greater tal-ent have found that, as Roubaud suggests in *La viellesse d'Alexandre,* the re-cycling of a verse form that had a raison d'être at a particular moment in history at a particular place cannot be accomplished. The alexandrine, in other words, can still live, but only when it is understood as what Roubaud calls a "hieratic rhythmic entity." Specific sound patterns change in response to their time and culture, but the principle that sound structure controls meaning remains the same.

The Jouissance of Sound

Consider, to begin with, the role of sound in the poetry of ancient cultures, not just in Greece and Rome but in Chinese and Hebrew, Arabic, or African texts as well. In the Lianja epic of the Congo, for example, the bards, so we learn from the *New Princeton Encyclopedia of Poetry and Poetics*, were interested "not merely in the rhythmic flow of the narration following distinctive patterns of line and syllable count"; they also looked for such sound effects as "alliteration, sound-imitating words, sonorous names . . . appositives . . . lyrical evocations and inversions of normal word order."[12] Or again, in Tang dynasty poetry (usually considered China's Golden Age), what was called "regulated verse" consisted of a prescribed eight-line stanza, distinguished by its level-tone rhyme, falling at the end of each couplet. Tang regulated verse also had specific rules governing the distribution of parallelism. "Each component in the first line [is] matched by a grammatically similar and semantically related, yet tonally antithetical, component in the corresponding position of the second line, thus forming a perfect mirror effect." "The coherence of the poem's phonic pattern," moreover, is "governed by the cumulative effect of contrast (*dui*) and connection (*nian*)" (*Encyclopedia of Poetry* 194). For Tang dynasty aesthetic, the successful poem was one whose elaborate mathematical form could accommodate personal lyric vision.

Procedural poetry, in this scheme of things, marks a return to tradition—but not quite the Englit tradition the New Formalists long to re-create. Consider again the adage that "A text written according to a constraint describes the constraint." A recent exemplar of this axiom is Christian Bök's *Eunoia*, published in Toronto by Coach House Press in 2001 and to everyone's amazement, since it is hardly a standard volume of poetry, the recipient of the Griffin Poetry Prize for 2002. In the postface to this one-hundred-page book, Bök explains the book's particular constraint as follows:

> "Eunoia" is the shortest word in English to contain all five vowels, and the word quite literally means "beautiful thinking." *Eunoia* is a univocal lipogram, in which each chapter restricts itself to the use of a single vowel. *Eunoia* is directly inspired by the exploits of Oulipo . . . the avant-garde coterie renowned for its literary experimentation with extreme formalistic constraints. The text makes a Sisyphean spectacle of its labour, willfully crippling its language in order to show that, even under such improbable conditions of duress, language can still express an uncanny, if not sublime, thought.[13]

Bök's chief model was probably Georges Perec's *La Disparition*, the tour-de-force novel written without the letter *e*—a feat almost impossible in French, depending, as it does, on approximately one-eighth of the total lexicon. Gilbert Adair's translation, *A Void*, does the same thing in English. *La Disparition* followed Roubaud's central rule in making the constraint the novel's theme as well: the book deals with disappearances and loss, with oblique reference to the disappearance of Perec's family as a result of the Holocaust.

Bök reverses Perec's process by using only one vowel rather than eliminating one. But there are further rules:

All chapters must allude to the art of writing. All chapters must describe a culinary banquet, a prurient debauch, a pastoral tableau, and a nautical voyage. All sentences must accent internal rhyme through the use of syntactical parallelism. The text must exhaust the lexicon for each vowel, citing at least 98% of the available repertoire (although a few words do go unused, despite efforts to include them: *parallax, belvedere, gingivitis, monochord,* and *tumulus*). The text must minimize repetition of substantive vocabulary (so that, ideally, no word appears more than once). The letter Y is suppressed. (103–04)

Finally, the poem's visual layout is rule-bound. The chapters vary in length, but each chapter is divided into units made up of the same number of lines: twelve in A, eleven in E and I, thirteen in O, twelve in U. The print blocks, with their justified margins, look like squares and are placed in the upper part of their respective pages.

The operations described obviously can't be carried out by a computer: no program could readily sort out the words needed to present a prurient debauch or culinary banquet. And that, of course, is Bök's point. To see how the process works, let me reproduce the five **A, E, I, O, U** sections that "allude to the art of writing." These occur, in all five cases, at the opening of their respective chapters, although questions of poetics come up again later in each text:

CHAPTER A (for Hans Arp)

Awkward grammar appals a craftsman. A Dada bard as daft as Tzara damns stagnant art and scrawls an alpha (a splapdash arc and a backward zag) that mars all stanzas and jams all ballads (what a scandal). A madcap vandal crafts a small black ankh—a hand-stamp that can stamp a wax pad and at last plant a mark that sparks an *ars magna* (an abstract art that charts a phrasal anagram). A pagan skald chants a dark saga (a Mahabharata), as a papal cabal blackballs all annals and tracts, all dramas and psalms: Kant and Kafka, Marx and Marat. A law as harsh as a *fatwa* bans all paragraphs that lack an A as a standard hallmark.

CHAPTER E (for René Crevel)

Enfettered, these sentences repress free speech. The text deletes selected letters. We see the revered exegete reject metred verse: the sestet, the tercet—even *les scènes élevées en grec*. He rebels. He sets new precedents. He lets cleverness exceed decent levels. He eschews the esteemed genres, the expected themes—even *les belles letters en vers*. He prefers the perverse French esthetes: Verne, Péret, Genet, Perec—hence, he pens fervent screeds, then enters the street, where he sells these letterpress newsletters, three cents per sheet. He engenders perfect newness wherever we need fresh terms.

CHAPTER I for Dick Higgins

Writing is inhibiting. Sighing, I sit, scribbling in ink this pidgin script. I sing with nihilistic witticism, disciplining signs with trifling gimmicks—impish hijinks which highlight stick sigils. Isn't it glib? Isn't it chic? I fit childish insights within rigid limits, writing shtick which might instill priggish misgivings in critics blind with hindsight. I dismiss nitpicking criticism which flirts with philistinism. I bitch; I kibitz—griping whilst criticizing dimwits, sniping whilst indicting nitwits, dismissing simplistic thinking, in which phillipic wit is still illicit.

CHAPTER O for Yoko Ono

Loops on bold fonts now form lots of words for books. Books form cocoons of comfort—tombs to hold bookworms. Profs from Oxford show frosh who do postdocs how to gloss works of Wordsworth. Dons who work for proctors or provosts do not fob off school to work in crosswords, nor do dons go off to dorm rooms to loll on cots. Dongs go crosstown to look for bookshops known to stock lots of topnotch goods: cookbooks, workbooks—room on room of how-to books for jocks (how to jog, how to box), books on pro sports, golf or polo. Old colophons on schoolbooks from schoolrooms sport two sorts of logo: oblong whorls, rococo scrolls—both in worn morocco.

CHAPTER U for Zhu Yu

Kultur spurns Ubu—thus Ubu pulls stunts. Ubu shuns *Skulp-
tur;* Uruk urns (plus busts), Zulu jugs (plus tusks). Ubu scripts
junk *für Kunst und Glück.* Ubu busks. Ubu drums drunks, plus
Ubu strums cruths (such hubbub, such ruckus): *thump, thump,
thrum, thrum.* Ubu puns puns. Ubu blurts untruth: much bunkum
(plus bull), much humbug (plus bunk)—but trustful schmucks
trust such untruthful stuff; thus Ubu (cult guru) must bluff
dumbstruck numbskulls (such chumps). Ubu mulcts surplus
funds (trust funds plus slush funds). Ubu usurps much usufruct.
Ubu sums up lump sums Ubu trumps dumb luck.

Bear in mind, as you read these curiously dissimilar "stanzas," Bök's rule
that "the text must exhaust the lexicon for each vowel." The poet has not, in
other words, chosen particularly silly-sounding **U** words or harsh **A** ones, for
he must, in the course of the poem, use all the **A**'s, **E**'s, etc. What the poem
thus teaches us is that, Saussure notwithstanding, vowels do have semantic
overtones. A poetics of **A,** to begin with, evokes an alien, often exotic East:
**Hassan, Agha Khan, Arab, Mahabharata, cabal, pagan, fatwa, bachannal,
altar, naphtha, maharajah, baklava, Tartar, drachmas, mandala, Cassandra,
karma, Allah, Sahara, Rwanda, Shah, Ghana, Katar, Japan, Samarkand,
Kandahar, Madagascar, lava sandflat.** In the Western world that exoticism
is transferred to **A Dada bard as daft as Tzara.** A poetics thus involves **awkward grammar** that **appalls a craftsman.** Dada, we know, always involved
the destruction of "normal" syntax and preferred a **slapdash arc and a backward zag** to the orderly **stanza** or **ballad.** Again, **A** art seems to be largely
abstract: **a pagan skald chants a dark saga.** The authors associated with **A**
lack the gentleness of **E** or lightness of **I**: they include such heavies as **Kant**
and **Kafka, Marx** and the revolutionary **Marat.** No doubt, this is because **A**
is not only the letter of the exotic East but also of the **law** and of **bans.**

E poetics could hardly be more different. **We prefer,** as Bök puts it in the
stanza following the one cited here, **genteel speech, where sense redeems
senselessness. E** is mostly genteel and soft-spoken—the language of the
French esthetes. The **E** poet is a **revered exegete** who is familiar with but
rejects metred verse: the sestet, the tercet. If **A** poetry is abstract, **E** is the
language of **cleverness**—perhaps a shade too clever, since that quality can
exceed decent levels. E poets may be primarily clever like Jules **Verne** or
masters of riddling like the surrealist Benjamin **Péret** or the Oulipo master
Georges **Perec.** The work of such writers can appear too tricky: **We sneer
when we detect the clever scheme.** But then of course, despite all its gentle-

ness and gentility, **E** is the language of **stress, of wretchedness, dejectedness,** and **the deepest regrets,** which are invariably **secret.**

I poetics initially presents itself as **light** and **tripping,** the language of **wit** and **impish hijinks. I** is the realm of **writing** and **singing** as well as of **criticism.** But **criticism** that resists **nitpicking** in favor of **philippic wit. Isn't it glib? Isn't it chic?** asks the poet. And why not: in later sections of **I,** we meet **singing birds, six kinds (finch, siskin, ibis, tit, pipit, swift), whistling shrill chirps, trilling chirr chirr in high pitch.** For Bök, this **I** world is the charmed world of **gliding flight, skimming limpid springs.** No **fatwa** here, no long and heavy **Mahabharata.** Yet lightness of being may contain the seeds of its own destruction: I note that **I** is also the lexicon of **crippling** and **wincing, cringing, spitting,** and **itching,** of the **riding whip** and the **Blitz.** Even as **A's abstraction** can veer toward exotic fantasy on one hand, serious philosophical thought (**Kant, Marx**), on the other, **I** is slippery: **Klimt** and **Liszt** are its emblematic artists.

I take Bök's **O** chapter to be the most solemn and scholarly. **O,** as Bök presents it, is the language of the **book,** of **school,** and of the **Word. God** is also an **O**-word. In Bök's sequence, much is made of **Oxford dons, provosts,** and **proctors,** of **schoolrooms** containing **books** and **rococo scrolls—both on worn morocco. Schoolbooks** bear **old colophons. Monks** belong here, as do the **dorms** where **Oxford dons hold forth.** But again the reverse side operates as well: **O** gives us the world of **tombs** and **donjons,** of **Sodom** and **Moloch,** of the **mondo doloroso** of **Job** and **Lot,** of **porn shops** and **blond trollops.** The **Word** has never been taken more to heart. And the emblematic poet of **O** poetics is none other than **Wordsworth.**

None of this can fully prepare us for Bök's **U** chapter. In English, **U** is the dirty vowel—the emblem of **slut, lust, fuck, cunt, dugs, humps, bum, stuffs, rumps, crud, bust**—one could go on and on. This is Bök's shortest chapter, because monovocalic words with **U** are much less common than those with the other vowels and also, as we see here, much less varied. Bök can write about **Ubu** here, but Alfred Jarry's hero is one of the only authors available in the **U** pantheon. True, there is the biblical **Ruth** and Krenek's **Lulu,** but we find neither philosophers nor poets in this chapter. The only art in the **U-world** is **sculpture,** but here perceived as primarily **junk sculpture;** the one musical instrument is the **drum,** the one gourmet dish is **duck,** served, possibly, with **rum punch.** Not much variation here, not much finesse, delicacy, lightness, or the exotic other. Yet, before we write off **U** words entirely, we should remember that this is the chapter of **truth** and of those who **blush** when they violate it.

Eunoia thus differentiates the vowels only to imply, in the end, that there are no hard and fast divisions between their values. Be vigilant, this poetic sequence tells us; don't fall into the sorcerer's trap. Don't let the intricate musical structure and elaborate internal rhyming of the stanza sequence lull you into apathy. In this sense *Eunoia* recalls such classic poems as Keats's "Eve of St. Agnes," a poem that, like *Eunoia*, dramatizes the inextricability of pain and pleasure—an inextricability carried through, of course, on the sound and visual level as well. *Eunoia* may seem, on a first reading, like mere language game, but it soon reveals itself to be a game where everything is at stake and where struggle is all. As the poet puts it in the **I** chapter, "Minds grim with nihilism still find first light inspiring."

If *Eunoia* is overtly an Oulipo work, following the chosen rule quite literally to the letter, other recent poetic texts have adapted the paradigm to their own purposes. I am thinking of the performance texts of such British poets as Chris Cheek, John Cayley, and especially Caroline Bergvall, who performs frequently in the United States. Bergvall's hybrid work—it is composed for live and digital performance, installation, video, as well as book form—derives from post-punk music and sound poetry as well as from literary movements like Oulipo. Her sonic, verbal, and rhetorical devices are extremely sophisticated, encompassing Duchampian pun, phonemic bilingual (French-English) transfer, paragram, ideogram, allusion, and found text. In their complex assemblages, these function to explore such areas as our conceptual approaches to female (and feminine) representation as well as the power structures within which these sexualities must function. The doll, the bride, the daughter, the mesh: these participate in any number of games at once sexual and verbal.

Bergvall's most orthodox Oulipo work is "Via: 48 Dante Variations," which recalls Harry Mathews's "35 Variations on a Theme from Shakespeare." Her base text is the opening tercet of Dante's *Inferno*:

Nel mezzo del cammin di nostra vita
mi ritrovai per una selva oscura
che la diritta via era smaritta

As she recalls her procedure in the headnote:

I had started to collect Dante translations like others collect stamps or good wines, at first simply following a lead to see what might come through, in the dark of dark, in the wood of wood, in the musicalised sense of panic. 1-2-3 lines, and three menace him, and the one at the crossroads and the one who speaks and the one who remains hid-

den. A perfect plot in the massing of time, lost already walking. Faced
with the seemingly inexhaustible pool of translations into English of
Dante's *Inferno,* I decided to collate all translations archived at the British Library up until May 2000—seven-hundred years after the date
fixed by Dante for the start of the Comedy's journey.

Forty-seven exemplars emerged from this process. The resulting piece was
first presented as a recorded text-sound piece with the Irish composer Ciíaran
Maher, who, Bergvall recalls, "worked on the vocal fractals from this recording to create a 48th variation running underneath the recording." The translations were then alphabetized, the list thus collapsing historical time and
emphasizing the relativist nature of translation. The resulting musical structure emphasizes similarity where we might expect difference, and yet the al-
phabetization ("Halfway . . . ," "In the middle of . . . ,") reminds the reader
or listener that no two of the translations are exactly the same. As Bergvall
explains it:

> Unlike the graphic causal horror of linear travel, these point by point
> interceptions spin a spiraling musicality, its horror is abstracted, a
> build-up of interrupted motion, pulling together into a narrative of
> structure, stop-start, each voice trying itself out, nothing looped, yet
> nothing moving beyond the first line, never beyond the first song, never
> beyond the first day, the forest walls, the city walls, my body walls. Hav-
> ing to look for points of exit, further in, further down, rather than
> out.[14]

The chain of variations thus produced is fascinating in the delicate shading
of its differences: the "dark wood," for example, appears again and again, and
yet the wood is also "sunless," "gloomy," "darkling," and "obscure." Some
translations use archaic language and rhyme:

> Midway the path of life that men pursue
> I found me in a darkling wood astray
> For the direct way had been lost to view (#31)

Some are slangy:

> Halfway through our trek in life
> I found myself in this dark wood,
> Miles away from the right road (#7)

Some emphasize the darkness of the wood, others the darkness of the speaker's consciousness, unable as she is to find the straight road, the right path, the narrow way, the rightful pathway, or the true road. In Oulipo terms, the sequence enacts its constraint because there is no progress, no "direct path" or "path that does not stray" to take us out of the maze of alternate tercets. *Via* is *Vita*, no more, no less.

Like Mathews's "35 Variations," Bergvall's poem thus demonstrates the power of the poetic word. Dante's tercet has three basic strands: the middle of one's life, the dark wood, and the crossroads where the true path is lost. These three topoi can be varied in countless ways to create a riveting narrative. Who is speaking? How did that speaker come to be in this obscure place? And how do we know the path he's on is not the right one? What is a "true" path, anyway? Since the reader does not know whose these translations are, s/he concentrates on the differentials, especially the issue of cause in the third line: is the path "lost to view" to mankind, or is it that "I had missed the path and gone astray" (#44)?

"Via" is a fascinating exercise, but even more interesting are such Bergvall sound performance works as her recent "About Face" (part 2 of her larger project, *Goan Atom*), notes and early drafts of which may be found in a recent issue of *How 2*.[15] "About Face" is not a rule-governed composition, although the title pun is exploited in just about every line of the poem, which is twelve manuscript pages long.[16] In a note on the poem, Bergvall explains:

> "About Face" started out in 1999 for a performance in which I was interested to explore the format of a reading-performance as an explicit balancing between audibility and inaudibility (the listener's/viewer's) . . . between what you see and cannot hear, what you hear and cannot see. . . . the piece was more structured and articulated by word and sound associations ("faceless" leads by contraction and code-shift to "fesse" [French for buttock] and openness to accidents, rather than as a procedural or constraint-led piece.[17]

Bergvall goes on to say that she used interrupted transcripts of recorded conversations so as to foreground "social opacity and historical erasures." Then too the form enabled her to reflect on "games of face in relation to intimacy, love, intimate pleasure" and to test such common oppositions as that between Hellenic/Christian concepts of the face as a marker of presence and Judaic/Moorish traditions in which "face" can only be "symbolic/inscriptive." "The acrobatics of trying to write face," writes Bergvall, "leads to reflecting on it as a speech act."

Here is the opening:

> Begin a f acing
> At a pt of motion
> How c lose is near to face a face
> What makes a face how close too near
> Tender nr pace m
> Just close enough makes faceless
> Too close makes underfaced

> Ceci n'est pas une fesse
> Past nest urn face
> Sees here your passing

> This is not a face
> Yes transcrpt
> S easier li this
> A face is like a rose
> The n fss
> correlated to ah yes tt t
> waltzing t change

The technique here is not procedural, but "About Face" shares with Oulipo poetics the desire to decompose words so that their phonemic, morphemic, and paragrammatic properties emerge. Take the first line, "Begin a f acing." Many poems begin with "begin"—for example, Wallace Stevens's *Notes Toward a Supreme Fiction* ("Begin, ephebe . . . ")—but here the space between "f" and "a" that produces "ace" (perhaps an allusion to Tom Raworth's long columnar poem by that title) suggests that facing someone or something is always an interrupted activity, a "point of motion," as we read in line 2. Lines 3 and 4 work similarly—the breakup of "close" gives us the very different word "lose," and central questions about the phrases "face to face" and "about face" are now posed. Bergvall mimics speech patterns—"Tender nr pace m"—a line that can be heard as opening with "tender near" or "tenderness" but remains visually opaque. This line modulates, in its turn, into the discriminations of "pace"/"faceless"/"underfaced" and the permutations on "how close," "just close," "too close."

Sound repetition and permutation, together with various graphic variants, thus govern meaning in Bergvall's poem. There are obvious relations to Language poetry, especially to the work of Charles Bernstein, Steve McCaffery, or Joan Retallack, as Bergvall would be the first to admit, but her particular focus here is on verbal/visual contradiction.[18] The Magritte allusion of line 8, for example, "*Ceci n'est pas une fesse*" ("This is not a buttock") is heard as "*Ceci n'est pas une face.*" And line 9, "Past nest urn face" is a homophonic translation-reversal of "n'est pas une," the transposition reminding us of the faces carved on Greek urns, those "nests" where the remains of the dead body are contained as so much dust. The "urn face" thus "sees here your passing": its stability is that of death, which will soon be the fate of the passing observer.

In the next stanza, what is *sounded* cannot be properly seen: "yes transcrpt / s easier li this" is heard without difficulty as "Yes, [the] transcript's easier like this," but on the page the words break down into presemantic morphemes. "A face is like a rose" in the stanza's fourth line alludes to Gertrude Stein, for whom the rose remains a noun to be "caressed" but finally rejected in favor of non-nouns. Bergvall refuses to leave it at that. Her "face" is just as easily a verb as a noun and hence calls up the lines "n fss / correlated to ah yes tt t / waltzing t change"—lines that take us back to those buttocks (*fesses*), whose "correlation" remains an unnamable ("ah yes tt t"). The off-color allusion remains masked; we know only that there is "waltzing t change," that somehow an about face has been accomplished.

This is only the beginning of a complex network in which found prose texts from artists like Christian Boltanski, whose astonishing photographs of students at the Lycée Chases in Vienna modulate into blow-ups that recall skulls—the skulls these faces would become in the course of the Holocaust—alternate with complex poetic passages that explore the meanings of *facing the other* (Levinas), *faceless, face up,* and so on. "About Face" is a bravura performance that must be both heard and seen, the aural and the visual undermining one another so as to produce a very dense investigation of our facings and facelessness. Toward the end, one of the stanzas reads:

Like a curtain pulled a face it violent
Fc t
fc
vile unforgiving like a spectacle

where "fact" transforms aurally (but not necessary visually) into a "fuck" that is somehow "vile" and "unforgiving"—no longer a face to be seen as the Other, but mere Spectacle.

Like Christian Bök, whose initials serendipitously match hers, Caroline Bergvall takes the semantic to be produced both aurally and visually. In one sense her strategy is perfectly traditional: poetry is, after all, the language art, the art that, in Hugh Kenner's words, "lifts the saying out of the zone of things said."[19] Kenner's reference here is to Williams, who was a master of that art, as were, in the next generation, Lorine Niedecker and George Oppen, and in ours such poets as Charles Bernstein and Susan Howe, Steve McCaffery, and Tom Raworth—poets not especially given to the use of procedural methods but always aware, even in their ways of organizing free-verse units, of the figure sound makes. There are, in other words, serious alternatives to the lineated prose of the Norton poets that do not necessarily move in the direction of the procedural poetics I have been discussing. It is patently not a case of either/or.

If the inventions of younger poets like Bök and Bergvall deserve our close attention, as I have suggested they do, it is because sequences like *Eunoia* point us back with special force to a poetic moment that has been largely displaced by the sonic indifference that characterizes contemporary anthologies, journals, and poetry readings—an indifference that is satisfied to produce poems or, from the reader's perspective, to call texts poems merely because they are lineated, never mind the absence of rhythmic figure, sound structure, and visual configuration. Faced with such prosaic flatness, it is, in Bergvall's words,

> Time to keep pple in the drk
> Face-wash
>   In need
> Face-grip

In 2002 Nate Dorward, the young editor of a little magazine in Toronto called The Gig *and an authority on contemporary British poetry, asked me to contribute to the special Tom Raworth issue he was assembling. I've always wanted to write more on Raworth, to my mind one of the most exciting but also most difficult of contemporary poets. I had a chance recently to review his* Collected Poems *(Carcanet, 2003) for the* Times Literary Supplement *and believed I was beginning to sort things out. For the Dorward collection, I chose a little-known Raworth text, "Letters from Yaddo," an epistolary memoir (or, more accurately, anti-memoir) that opens up new possibilities for poetic prose. Unlike the "Concrete prose" of Haroldo de Campos or Rosmarie Waldrop, Raworth's mode here is assemblage, his letters to Ed Dorn being constantly interrupted by "extraneous" material—some of it verse, some of it found text. Dorward turned out to be a most exacting editor. Draft 1 elicited thirty-five pages of e-mail commentary and correction, draft 2 another ten or so. Finally, Dorward felt I got it more or less right. Himself one of Raworth's best readers, he certainly taught me a great deal about Raworth's poetics.*

12
Filling the Space with Trace

Tom Raworth's "Letters from Yaddo"

The more formless I try to be, the more objects push themselves into a shape.

Yes, the wheel turns full circle: but the flaw in the rim touches the ground each time in a different place.

Tom Raworth, "Letters from Yaddo"

"Letters from Yaddo," the first text in *Visible Shivers*,[1] was written in April–May 1971 when Tom Raworth was on fellowship at the Yaddo writers' colony in Saratoga Springs, New York. The piece was originally to be published by Frontier Press in a book called *Cancer*, together with the two texts "Logbook" and "Notebook." But *Cancer* never materialized, and the appearance of "Letters from Yaddo" was delayed for some fifteen years. In *Visible Shivers* the unpaginated (34-page) text of "Letters" is followed by a twenty-five-page set of shorter poems and the sonnet sequence "Sentenced to Death," both from the mid-eighties. Meanwhile, the aphoristic "Notebook" had appeared in David Levi-Strauss's journal *Acts* (No. 5, 1985), and *Logbook,* one of Raworth's most intricate and carefully structured sequences—a poetics in the form of a parodic travel narrative—was published in 1976 by Poltroon Press in Berkeley.

Given this publication history, it is not surprising that "Letters from Yaddo" seems to have fallen through the cracks: it is little known, even among Raworth's admirers. Perhaps genre has been a stumbling block. The title and standard letter format place "Letters from Yaddo" in the tradition of such short volumes of correspondence as Charles Olson's *Letters for Origin.* But whereas Olson's letters, however wild their typography and syntax, are written to convey particular information, ideas, and desires to their recipient, Cid Corman, "Letters from Yaddo" subordinates conversation with Ed Dorn to the intricate collage structure of what is essentially a poetic text. "Letters" incorporates poems and found texts from various decades; it includes letters from Tom's father and son as well as documentary fragments like the legends on the photographs found in a nest of drawers in the main house at Yaddo (*Visible Shivers* 17–18). The narrative itself, moreover, moves imperceptibly from sober reportage to hyperreal list making, from expository comment to dream sequence and complex time shift, where visual memory and present sound are interlaced. The text has passages as oblique and "difficult" as those in the long poetic sequences *Writing* or *Ace,* but on the whole, "Letters from Yaddo" is surprisingly readable—even suspenseful. As such, it may be a good place to begin to understand Raworth's highly individual poetic ethos.

I want to begin with the final pages of "Letters from Yaddo," which describe, in the third person, Raworth's own experience of undergoing open-heart surgery, performed to repair the hole in his heart (actually atrial septal defect).[2] We know from an earlier incident that when, in 1955, at the age of seventeen the poet tried to enlist in the armed forces, he learned that he had been born with "a hole in [his] heart" (*Visible Shivers* 21). Indeed, there are oblique references throughout the text to that hole and to the accompanying leakage of the heart valve. In the original *Cancer* manuscript, "Letters from Yaddo" had as its epigraph a sentence taken from Edward Crankshaw's much-cited "Interview with Mao": "He was, he said, just a lone monk walking the world with a leaky umbrella."

Cardiac arrhythmia, moreover, plays a role not only thematically but formally as well. The dislocation of rhythm is hardly unique to Tom Raworth—indeed it is a staple of experimental poetries today—but in comparison to the rhythmic units of, say, Bruce Andrews or Steve McCaffery, Raworth's starts and stops connote a curious breathlessness, as in

blur blur   blur blur
what's what's that that!!   Oh oh
              crew crew (17)

And even Raworth's prose sentences are unusually short, as if they need to catch their breath. Here is the open-heart surgery passage:

> He is dressed in a white gown and lies on a trolley being wheeled along a corridor. He is drowsy. Outside the operating theatre the trolley stops, and a doctor in green overalls with a green face-mask leans over and looks at him. He feels hands on his right arm, the chill of alcohol, the prick of a needle. A voice tells him to count backwards from 10. At once he feels wide awake, though his eyes are shut, and thinks "this is taking a long time to work." As he thinks "work" he opens his eyes. There is an enormous weight on his chest; he is inside an oxygen tent. Eight hours have passed and the operation is over. He runs the thought through again: "this is taking a long time to work." He can see no break in it. He screams for them to take him out of the oxygen tent—the clear plastic only a few inches from his face seems to be suffocating him. Two days later, when the nurse is out of the room, he forces himself out of bed and over to the table where, in a drawer, is his file. He reads how his heart was stopped, his blood pumped through a machine: how his breastbone was sawn in half, his heart stitched, his chest sewn up. He reads of the pints of blood poured into him, and how, at the end of the operation, after his heart had been re-started, it had stopped again, and how he'd been given massive shots of adrenalin to bring him back to life. Nowhere can he find the key. (34)

These are the perceptions of a seventeen-year-old patient, as retold by the survivor of the operation, now twice that age. But the retrospective account, searing as it is, cannot really convey what it was that happened. Here is the text's concluding paragraph:

> I still run that thought through sometimes. Somewhere there must be a flaw in it. Somehow, I must find the weak point and snap it. It's too perfect to be human. It tastes of technology. When I wrote "I feel like an android" I knew what I was writing. (34)

The "thought" that Raworth still "runs through" (see line 9 in the long paragraph above) is that "this is taking a long time to work." In his memory, this thought has continuity: indeed, it is all he remembers, for the operation itself is a total blank: it is not a part of the poet's experience. "Somewhere," accordingly, "there must be a flaw in it." The "it" may be the step-by-step account of the operation recorded in his file, on which he bases his own narrative. Or again it may be his memory, which has transformed the whole affair into someone else's "story." Or "it" may be the process of trying to remember just what happened. In any case, that story "tastes of technology" and can thus only be relayed in the third person. In Rimbaldian terms: not *Je pense* but *On me pense*, or *Je est un autre.* "When I wrote 'I feel like an android' I knew what I was writing."

The inability to have access to one's own experience colors much of Raworth's poetry and gives it its peculiar poignancy. The opening pages of "Letters from Yaddo" explore this perception from a different angle. The sequence begins matter-of-factly, "Dear Ed: sorry to have missed you when I called, but I was happy to hear Jenny [Ed's wife] and to learn that you are all o.k. I got here yesterday on the bus from New York: now it's a bright spring morning" (1). But then the flat diaristic style gives way to a "joke poem," written back home in Colchester, with the punning title "Sonnet Daze":

> I watch myself grow larger in her eyes
> and clutch a yellow feather near its tip
> as if to mark with ink that never dries
> the yet uncharted voyage of my ship
>
> those two flat images project and form
> the looming solid that contains my mind
> whilst independently the quill writes "warm"
> dreaming its tip still in the bird's behind
>
> since those two stanzas many days have passed
> now percy thrower speaks of roses on t.v.
> morecambe and wise with full supporting cast
> will soon be on—I call for val to see
>
> the fire is red the cat licks down her tail
> i close my eyes and read the rest in braille

England—the England still feeding on its Elizabethan heritage: Sir Thomas Wyatt's "lover, [who] compareth his state to a ship in a perilous storm tossed on the sea," and Sidney's Astrophel, who woos his Stella, "biting my trewand pen"—is parodied in the poet's "uncharted voyage," in which the "quill" is "dreaming its tip still in the bird's behind." By the third stanza the Petrarchan tradition has given way to burlesque Romantic nostalgia—"since those two stanzas many days have passed"—leaving the poet somewhere in the drab seventies TV world of Percy Thrower's gardening show and the Morecambe & Wise comedy hour.[3] The final rhyme, "tail"/"braille," suggests that the only way to tolerate the Percy Throwers of the TV scene is to practice some form of sensory deprivation. So the poet closes his eyes and "read[s] the rest in braille," which is to say that he tries to see what happens when we don't look at the screen but merely hear what is being said. To do this is to defamiliarize the talk of roses by means of a new language game.

Such sensory experimentation is central to Raworth's aesthetic: on the next page he recalls an earlier moment when "talking to someone—or, rather, listening to someone talk" becomes a double exercise, first in "making mental notes of what was being said to write up later" and, conversely, in blocking out the talk so as "to catch the name of a record that was playing [on the radio] and the voice was drowning it out." In a neat reversal in which background noise trumps individual speech, "I scribbled it all down as it was because I realised that's what a writer is, and you can only use yourself in the most truthful way possible at the time." And he adds the proviso that "I'm not going to sublimate it by putting it into the mouths of 'characters' . . . or/and letting them take over. If you can't give it straight, there's no point in being a radio" (2). A few pages later the poet adds, "Fighting off 'characters' is taking time. The words form themselves into speeches and project faces to say them. . . . Treacherous bastards I'm going to cork you in until you understand you're PLOT not CHARACTER" (9).

This is an important statement of poetics. "Character," for this poet, is always a threat, because it posits a coherent, identifiable self, interacting with other such selves in a plausible fictional universe. For Raworth, it is fictionality that is the fiction—the notion that one can write a novel that places identifiable characters in particular "plots," that one can create "character" out of the bits and pieces of overheard conversation, whether in the "real" world or on the radio. Realism, after all, is just a convention: the realistic narrative depends on a high degree of selectivity. "To give it straight," on the other hand, is to refuse to discriminate between fore and background. Like John Cage's *Roaratorio*, Raworth's is a construct where noise is just as important as the "information" ostensibly conveyed. Fidelity to the actual texture of experience means sensitivity to the complex interplay of foreground and background, information and noise.

This is by no means to say, as many of Raworth's critics have complained, that the texts in question are merely non-sensical, that they have no "meaning." On the contrary, "you can only use yourself in the most truthful way possible at the time" (2). The word *truth* crops up again and again. "If it's done with truth and love," we read in a slightly later letter, "and no wish to profit, in any sense, then it will take shape. The final thing I find in any art that moves me is the clear message 'there is no competition because I am myself and through that the whole'" (18). Each artwork, once made, is uniquely itself. At the same time, the poet can never quite achieve what he wants to: "I look at the poems and they make a museum of fragments of truth. And they smell of vanity, like the hunter's trophies on the wall. . . . I have never reached the true centre, where art is pure politics" (22–23).

Art at its most uncompromising would be "pure politics," the will to change one's entire world. But this poet also knows that at the true center—his "true centre"—there is that hole in the heart we read about throughout. To "give it straight" like a turned on radio, "you can only use yourself in the most truthful way possible at the time." It is in this context that we must understand Raworth's emphasis on minute literal description of daily routine. Yaddo, the writers' colony, is a good site for the practice of self-discipline, for there are only so many options. Consider the following passage:

> I've trained myself (now that's a ridiculous phrase) during the past week to wake at five to seven. At seven o'clock I start running past the garage, down through the woods and around the lakes. I am back at the house at 7:15. I wash, make my bed, and walk to the garage building for breakfast. Each day I have a glass of orange juice, cornflakes with cold milk, two scrambled eggs and two cups of coffee. Then I leave any letters I've written in the basket by the door and collect any that have arrived. I walk back to the house, read the mail in my bedroom, go down to the kitchen to collect my lunchpail and thermos, then walk to my cabin. There I clean the ashes from the stove, light the first fire with the paper bags yesterday's food was wrapped in (plus any scraps from my wastepaper basket) and some kindling from a cardboard carton. I then read my mail again, by which time the kindling has caught and I can put a couple of logs into the stove from the rack in the corner. I usually look out of the window for a while, at the trees and birds and squirrels. I crumple up whatever cake or cookie is in the lunchpail, and throw it out the door. Then I listen to the traffic for a while. I can just see the highway through the trees. After that I sweep the floor and write letters. At four o'clock I take my lunch things back to the kitchen and read in my bedroom until five thirty, when I go down to the kitchen, make a drink, and take it into the library. Dinner is at six

thirty. Back to the house at eight. Make some phone calls. Drink some more. Go to bed. At least that's the theory. Well, we're all going to die, that's for sure. Like the mouse that hasn't moved. (20)

On the surface, such passages may look like exercises in self-revelation: here's what I've done and what it means to me. But Raworth's "self-centeredness" works the opposite way. "I'm going on the vague assumption," he remarks a few pages later, "that if I can completely and correctly describe my self, then that self will wither and blow away" (30). But of course that cannot happen: the "self," dispersed and dislocated as it may be at any one point, reappears at the interstices where actual letters received, overheard conversations, and remembered incidents, collaged together without comment, produce their own "noise." At the same time, as we saw in the story of the open-heart operation, the poet's own experience cannot be represented. His "character" too must be reconceived as "plot." Thus, at points of stress, time shifts and prose often gives way to fragmentary lyric, as when contemplation of the inscription on the poet's yellow pencil—"THINK AND SUGGEST—STATE OF N.J.500"— is juxtaposed to the notebook version of a poem written on April 1, before Tom came to Yaddo:

> very profound
> and almost round
>
> the story of the three verbs
> light   time   and space
>
> their coast
> isn't my coast
>
>   *
>
> good evening
> I am worn away by your kisses
> god i was good
>
>   *
>
> that song
> that you remember
>
>   *

After that last asterisk we move into the prose of "turning and turning and turning it is really scandalous how we jump up and down on the international date line. I follow the sun—and they call them the backward nations" (3).

John Barrell has talked of the "refusal of all affect," in Raworth's poetry (performed orally, as it is by Raworth, at high speed with little change in emphasis), "a refusal which seems to offer the words of the poem as an empty succession of empty signs."[4] But when we remember the narrator's fear that "Somewhere there must be a flaw in it," the fragmentary lines begin to fall into place. The shift from prose to verse, to begin with, represents a refusal not of affect but of continuity with the diaristic passage about "character" that precedes it. The minimalist couplets invert reader expectation: if something is "almost round," there might be a "very profound" meaning at stake, but as an afterthought the second line is absurd. Again, "the story of the three verbs / light time and space" has its own "flaw," since this could just as well be the story of the three nouns "light," "time," and "space," and in any case, the items are not parallel. "Their coast / isn't my coast" is an overheard snatch of a larger conversation in which the principals argue about geographic preferences. The following tercet contains a pastiche of popular song—"I am worn away by your kisses"—and plays on various meanings of "good" and the sonic linking of "good" and "god." "That song / that you remember" then modulates into "turning and turning and turning," which recalls both Yeats's "Turning and turning in the widening gyre" ("The Second Coming") and, closer to home, the song "Turn, Turn, Turn," recorded by the Byrds. Early British rock is a motif throughout: the notebook entry on the preceding page refers to "jimi hendrix castles made of sand" as pointing to "the separation of character and life." Raworth now shifts to the Beatles—"I follow the sun"—and modulates into a droll send-up of the narcissism of British pop, "another pretentious English group / thinking the audience is a mirror" (4). But "that song that you remember" is also Raworth's own "song," which begins so tunefully and then makes the linguistic turn by contemplating such ordinary words as "that."

By now we can understand how Raworth's poetic mode works. First, presentation must replace representation ("too perfect to be human"); the "truth" of experience is always elusive. Hence, continuity is always misleading: the present of Yaddo consistently gives way to incidents from the past, poems recorded in earlier notebooks, memories, allusions. Disconnected as these fragments, whether verse or prose, seem to be, they are by no means random or chaotic, for the same metonymic threads come up again and again, whether in the poet's past or his present, whether in pop song or Elizabethan sonnet. Thus, when we come to a passage like "it is really scandalous how we jump up and down on the international date line," we realize that the poet's own movements, memories, and tall tale, as recorded here, present precisely such a "jumping up and down," there being, in fact, no way to get off that line and stay fixed in one familiar place.

"Letters from Yaddo" proceeds not in any sort of linear fashion nor by the creation of "character" but by a "plot" consisting of telling juxtapositions and displacements. Consider the passage on pages 6–8 that begins with a Yaddo conversation, evidently over breakfast, with "a Korean novelist here named Kim whose eyes are good to look through":

> He was telling how he'd learned English from old movies. Like Shirley Temple's "You have to ess em eye el ee / to be aitch ay double-pee why." Then the first time he left Korea and landed in America he saw a newspaper with enormous headlines saying SHIRLEY TEMPLE DIVORCED and thought "Ohhhhh . . . these people BLIND!" The only problem with the movies was that kissing was never shown, so the plots suddenly jumped.

Here again, the technique is to "give it straight" by refusing to make Kim any sort of "character." In using himself "in the most truthful way possible," Raworth focuses not on the individual but on the delicious absurdity and irrelevancy of discourse. "The plot suddenly jumped," as someone else in the room starts to talk about "an SDS girl saying, 'Communism good/Capitalism is bad'. . . . and a novelist from the South said 'What tahm of deh was it?" Oh . . . mahnin'. . . . I thought it was the ahfternoon she math hev bin hah on some o that marijooahna" (6). One non sequitur leads to another, the vapid conversation sending Tom, who had smoked his last joint before breakfast, right back to his cabin, where he writes picture postcards to his children.

From "literary" conversation at Yaddo to the silence of Tom's cabin to another "literary" document: this time a long letter to "Tommy" from the poet's father. This letter within a letter is perhaps the centerpiece—or should I say "offcenterpiece"?—of the sequence. For in the context, the "real" letter, with its reference to "real" people and incidents, seems more fantastic than the mock-Petrarchan "Sonnet Daze" or the gnomic "very profound / and almost round." It begins as follows:

> Dear Tommy, Wherever you are when you read this, we hope all goes well. We were very pleased to get your letter, and it was kind to send the book so carefully packed (I almost threw away the letter written on the cardboard). We read it with interest (including the laudatory words on the back of the jacket) and hope it will add to your reputation. I

shall try to get the Penguin book in May. There seems to have been a
poetry explosion, and the resulting poeticised particles are too small
for me to handle mentally with any satisfaction. Sometimes I seem to
hover on the edge of a meaning to these minutiae of sensibility, but
finally it eludes me. Perhaps it is a private world that I am not supposed
to enter. A pity, because beauty does not lose by being shared.

And there follows the famous anecdote about Joyce's reprimand to his aunt
upon her failure to respond to the gift of *Ulysses*.

Raworth's father is thus nothing if not learned, and the letter contains an
almost unbearable mix of affection and alienation, of pride in Tommy's ac-
complishments offset by an inability to understand what those accomplish-
ments might be. Father and son obviously see each other infrequently; later
in the letter the father notes, "We scarcely recognised you from the photograph on the back of the book." Moreover, from the covering letter written
on the packing cardboard (which was almost thrown out) to the poems
themselves, perceived by the father as so many "poeticised particles" or "minutiae of sensibility," Tom's writing clearly eludes the older man's grasp.

But this is not the familiar cliché of bourgeois father unable to understand artist son. On the contrary, this father alludes not only to Joyce's *Ulysses*
but also to Plato and to Plotinus in the Stephen McKenna translation much
touted by Yeats, and he intriguingly tells Tom: "I must have been thinking
about your poems when I went to bed last night, because I dreamed that you
had exploded Bridges' 'London Snow' and I was trying to reconstruct it from
the particles." He seems to understand only too well that his son's poetry
represents some sort of "explosion" of the literary convention represented by
Bridges's poetry.

In his autobiographical essay for the Gale *Contemporary Authors* series,
Raworth has commented on the pathos of his father's life.[5] A very bookish
boy, the accidental death of his own father, a dockworker, forced him to leave
school at fourteen and go to work. After various clerkships, Thomas Alfred
Raworth became an editorial assistant on the Jesuit magazine *The Month*,
where, as Raworth put it in a letter to me, "his reading was catholic to start
and Catholic to finish":

After he died, I found things like the early Criterion appearances of
sections of Finnegans Wake bound up. . . . Stein, the Imagists, all were
there . . . then masses of theology, lives of the Saints. Inside a copy
of the Knox translation of the Bible I found a letter to him from Knox
thanking him for the list of typographical and other errors in his version he'd detected and listed. He could write equally well with either

hand and, to my knowledge, had perfect recall of anything he read. That's one of the reasons, I'm sure, I have no memory: just a mulch. I still (in storage) have a hand-written anthology of poetry he made for me when I was a child.[6]

The gap between the two literary worlds—between that of the Catholic *Month*, with its maudlin late-Victorian locutions ("Your mother loves to look after the flowers, and I begin to think they love to see her") and the postmodern world of Tom Raworth and Ed Dorn, is obliquely figured in the image, at the close of the letter, of "Carlyle [who] used to order a box of long clay pipes from Paisley and smoke a new one every day, putting the old one on the doorstep, before he went to bed, to be taken by who would." Carlyle's pipes, smoked and discarded on the doorstep, have given way to the joints smoked by young Tom, who also leaves things on the doorstep—stale cake crumbs for the birds and squirrels. Clearly, the literary son owes much to his literary father, but the gap between the two is too wide to bridge. "I shall type the address in caps," writes Tom's father, as I don't know if YADDO is the name of a person or a place or the initials of an organization." And he signs his letter "May God bless and direct you," where "direct" must be the ultimate verb from which the son is prone to recoil.

Between the receipt of this letter and the publication of "Letters from Yaddo," both Mary Raworth née Moore and Thomas Alfred Raworth died— she in 1983, he in 1986, when *Visible Shivers* was already in press. The book is dedicated to their memory. But the text itself makes no commentary on family relationships; rather, the next letter to Ed is conceived by the poet as "a cassette of winter 1947 (visual) with a sound track from 1971" (10). Actually, the "cassette" may be said to have three tracks: the first is a visual image of a sick child in a freezing room, whose mother and father are trying to comfort him with hot water bottles during a terrible cold spell. Returning to this passage once we have read the concluding account of Raworth's diagnosis and operation, we can see that even then he was suffering from his congenital defect, although no one seemed to know it. This visual track, in any case, intersects with a second visual one, recording terrifying dreams, whose time and location is not specified, particularly one in which the dreamer has lost all the money in his tin box (but is also the policeman who stole it) and has "dropped the key down a drain outside King's Cross Station." And the third, or sound, track takes place in the present of Yaddo, Tom receiving a letter from his twelve-year-old son that reads in part:

I hope it's o.k. in America for you. If you see a Hell's Angel take a photo for me.

I have been out with Gaynor and the family to a café and the waitress was hopeless; forgot everything. Saw a super funny cowboy film, began like this. Out in the west there are many cowboys. Some are good, some are bad. Some are bad with a bit of good in them, some are good with a bit of bad in them. This story is about some pretty good bad cowboys. See postcard. (11)

Ironically, the distance between Tom and this young enthusiast for Hell's Angels and cowboy flicks may be greater that that between Tom and his father. Accordingly, the world of dream and of memory take over: in the poem's present Tom finds himself irrelevantly searching the Yaddo library for a "collected Bridges," where he might "check on that 'London Snow' poem" (12). And increasingly, as the "plot" of *Letters* develops and Tom finds himself, especially after Mr. Kim's departure from Yaddo, "Adrift and alone . . . inside my head" (17), the poet increasingly fixates on the world of his adolescence and youth.

This lower-middle-class world of the 1950s and early 1960s, with its hectic rhythms, its jazz, drugs, and fashion-consciousness, contrasts sharply with the isolation and singularity of the present, in which the poet sometimes feels so anxious that he goes down to the main house and rummages through the drawers, finding old sepia pictures of "Snow-Crowned Popocatapetl and Ixtaccahuatl Guarding Cathedral, Puebla, Mexico" or "The Flower of Venezuela's Regular Army" (17). Appropriately enough, there is even a picture depicting the slaughtering of the "fatted calf" in the parable of the Prodigal Son. But if Tom is himself a Prodigal Son, the narrative of the fifties is made poignant by its very chronology. It is in 1954, a year before the discovery of the hole in his heart, that Tom and his friends sport narrow trousers and "slim-jim ties," play hookey, and go into Central London, where they eat huge meals at Lyon's Corner House and sip Manhattans, Side-Cars, and the other exotic cocktails of the 1950s. There is, as yet, no inkling of the future. The narrative now elides the hospital years and gives a hilarious account of Tom's job with the Continental and International Telephone exchange in 1964:

... I liked the job. Apart from the usual Civil Service shit, and the 200 different varieties of ticket to fill out for calls, you were left pretty much to yourself. I would "accidentally" disconnect people whose tone I didn't like or who were rude to me. I'd let girls phoning their soldier boyfriends in Germany for three minutes from a call box (over 10/-) talk for perhaps ten, instead of cutting them off. One Christmas I linked the East Berlin operator to the West Berlin operator (there was no direct link then) and left them connected all evening. (23)

Here Tom is already practicing what will be his poetic mode, the accidental "connect" and "disconnect" between overheard utterances that comes together to "fill the space with trace" (6). It is a poetic challenge that takes years of discipline. As a five-year-old, writing his first poem in 1943, Tom produced the "following little lyric":

o what fun
to be a boy
and have a toy

i teach my soldiers to fight
and my lions to bite

o what fun
to be a boy
and have a toy (25)

This "cry from the heart," to use Yeats's phrase, is immediately deflated by Uncle Arthur's charge that young Tom must have copied his poem from somewhere:

"Copied," he said, continuing downstairs, "you must have copied it from somewhere—you couldn't have written it." The valves that blew out in my head then are still dead. I shine the torch around over them but they can't be repaired. I feel the wall under my hands, the roughness of the stippled distemper. I taste the powder in my mouth as I bite my nails and try to tell him "I DID write it!" And so I lose my faith in truth. (25)

But the irony is that in a larger sense, Tom's "o what fun / to be a boy" is in fact "copied"—not from a particular poet but from the conventions of lyric mastered by the young at the time and taken as the law. When, on the contrary, the poet defies convention so as to "tell it straight," as Tom does in the letter to Ed in which "o what fun" is embedded, he notes flatly, "It's so grey here. Five days of rain, mist in the mornings. . . . Trucks pass on the highway I can barely make out through the trees, but my chair vibrates." And after

recounting the quarrel as to the authenticity of his first poem, the poet sets
down these lines (25):

timber   truck   vibrates
     my   s   pine
                           is how I'd write it
now, I suppose.

Here is the aesthetic of reduction and paragrammaticality that animates Raworth's mature poetry. Indeed, the insistence that "I DID write it!" is precisely
one that Raworth knows the poet must avoid in the move beyond individual
ego. In Raworth's two-line passage, "timber" and "truck," separate in the
prose section that precedes it, come together phonemically, whereas "vibrates" is now transferred from chair to truck. The detachment of "s" from
"spine" gives us a tree to go with timber—"pine"—but the layout also makes
it possible to read the passage as "my trucks pine." Poetry is not the linear "I
teach my soldiers to fight / and my lions to bite" but language construed as
reflexive, multiple.

How this process works is shown in the short poems reproduced on the
next four pages. Here Raworth gives us a string of playful punning poems,
culminating in

blur   blur   coming up fast
it overtakes him as they blend into the window
play with marked watches the set
is switched off the images deviate   life
goes on in the album   for the record
our noises are off (29)

If "the set / is switched off," how can the images that we first see as "blur
blur" and "blend into the window," "deviate"? Deviate from what? Well, in
the punning "for the record," "life / goes on in the album," even though the
"noises" of the sound track are "off." But the passage also refers to sporting
events, probably horse races ("blur blur coming up fast,"), in which those
with "marked watches" time the players. And there are a number of other
ways of construing this dense lyric passage.

Lyric, I remarked earlier, oscillates throughout "Letters from Yaddo" with
the sort of sober flat description of his room that Tom produces for Ed in his
next letter.

I never did describe this room, though I gave you the measurements. The floor is wooden, painted grey, as is the skirting board. The walls and ceilings (high, pointed) are white. The door is in the centre of the wall to my right. It is wooden, stained, as are all the window frames. There is a window either side of the door, two windows in the wall opposite me, two in the wall to my left (between which is the stove), and four behind me. I sit at my desk, facing the centre of the room, on a wooden chair. Slightly behind me, to my left, is a tall metal lamp. Beside it are the log-rack and cardboard boxes of kindling. Between the kindling and the stove are a white metal and plastic chair and a bucket filled with ashes. The stove stands in a wooden tray full of sand, and there is a bent brown metal reflecting screen behind it. (31–32)

What is the point of this obsessive description—description that occurs again, now distanced in the next paragraph by the third-person pronoun, which details the poet's cardiac catheterization, probably performed in 1956 in preparation for the open-heart surgery? The first step in the search for "truth," Raworth suggests, is the close, patient observation found in the two passages in question. But as we know from the final page, with its account of the operation itself, "Somewhere there must be a flaw in it. Somehow I must find the weak point and snap it" (34). There is always a point when literal description breaks down, and ghosts people the scene "As if all those who have been here have filled the space with trace" (6).

One such ghost, as we have seen, is the poet's father, whose letter raises interesting questions about the status of realism. The text reproduces the *real* letter and yet, in the context of the poet's ruminations throughout, its "reality" often shades into the absurd, as when Tom's father remarks, "Valarie [Tom's wife, Val], I expect, will be back in Colchester in time to cope with the census form," or, "Your mother is at present absorbed in Treasure island. She is truly omnivorous" (7). Again, the father, mostly very down-to-earth, is given to pompous flowery locutions like "I am in no hurry to exchange my lease of life for a freehold in eternity." Even he, then, does not become a "character," a consistent, coherent self. And in keeping with the shifting linguistic registers we find in this letter, the lyric poems refuse to "cohere" in normal imagistic or syntactic ways.

The most surprising thing about "Letters from Yaddo" is that they really are letters to be mailed and that they were really sent to Ed Dorn. Because "we are the product of people's battles inside our heads" (4), the letters do not serve as conduit from *A* to *B*; on the contrary, Ed's chief role in this strange correspondence seems to be as stimulus to the poet's imagination. However complex the time shifts and the "cassettes" where the visual track from one time period is spliced with the verbal track of another, Tom's assumption is that Ed will understand what he is saying. And so the letter, one of the most traditional literary forms, curiously enough becomes a perfect vehicle for dense and oblique multivocal speculation. Even the final tale of the long-ago open-heart operation, never directly witnessed but always on the edge of Tom's consciousness, can be told. And the addressee—whether Ed or his double, the reader—is drawn into the poet's circle by the consistent discrimination of alterity, of difference between one moment or one reaction and another. The epistolary anti-memoir thus manifests itself as a genre with great possibilities. Yes, "the wheel turns full circle: but the flaw in the rim touches the ground each time in a different place" (22).

In the summer of 1999 Joan Retallack organized a conference at Bard College on the topic "Poetry and Pedagogy: The Challenge of the Contemporary." I was unable to attend the conference but promised I would contribute an essay to the volume based on it, to be edited by Retallack and Juliana Spahr. The prospective contributors were sent a list of questions revolving around the central issue: how does teaching the new experimental poetries differ from teaching the poetry of "the familiar canon"? Since the conference included workshops for high school teachers, this question was evidently designed to elicit specific strategies that might be replicated. But to my mind, the more important questions were ones that hadn't been posed: how does one tell a good "experimental" poem from a bad one? And what is an experimental poem anyway? In the essay that follows, first published in the Buffalo journal Kiosk in 2002, I take a stab at these questions.

13
Teaching the "New" Poetries
The Case of Rae Armantrout

How does the avant-garde poetry being written today play out in the contemporary college classroom? Having taught courses in "Modern Poetry" since 1965, when I began my teaching career at the Catholic University of America, let me begin by saying that, paradoxically, the poems of, say, Bruce Andrews or Harryette Mullen are at one level more accessible to students than are those of W. B. Yeats or Ezra Pound. For however scrambled a new "experimental" poem may be—however nonsyntactic, nonlinear, or linguistically complex—it is, after all, written in the language of the present, which is to say the language of the students who are reading it. On the other hand— and here's the rub—since the contemporary undergraduate is likely to have almost no familiarity with poetry, beyond the obligatory Robert Frost poem that may or may not have been taught in high school, the class will have a lot of catching up to do. Indeed, the notion of teaching "beyond the familiar canon" that I have been asked to discuss here is something of a mystery to me, because there is no longer a canon beyond which to go! At Stanford University, where I now teach, we have English PhD candidates who have never read Keats's "Ode on a Grecian Urn," much less Milton's "Lycidas." And when

I recently gave an invited lecture to the Engineering Honors Club at the University of Southern California on the topic "What Is Poetry?" I learned that most of these juniors and seniors—high I.Q. students, all of them—had never read *any* poetry and couldn't cite the name of a single poet. The only work they had all read—and I doubt it will help them with the analysis of radical poetries today—is Charlotte Perkins Gilman's *The Yellow Wallpaper*.

So much for the "familiar canon," the irony being that the lack of consensus is not necessarily a blessing for the avant-garde. For the absence of any serious discourse about poetry, of a real debate as to the merits of *X* or *Y*, coupled with a commercial poetry scene controlled by only a few publishing houses whose chosen poets win the big prizes and find their way into *The New Yorker*, makes it difficult to teach students how poetry actually works and when a given poem has value. Accordingly, those of us who want to broaden the readership for the new poetries must take nothing for granted, must take up the work of the contemporaries we care about and read their work closely and critically, bearing in mind that Official Verse Culture, as Charles Bernstein has dubbed it, tends to valorize very different models.

Let me illustrate how this might work, using as an example a subtle and intriguing book published by Green Integer Press: Rae Armantrout's *The Pretext*.[1] Armantrout is a leading and, we might say, established Language poet—the author of seven previous collections, including one in French, and a prose memoir—but she is hardly canonical on the New York publishing scene represented by Norton or Viking, Knopf or Farrar, Straus & Giroux, by the *New York Review of Books* or *New York Times Book Review*.[2] I shall speculate later in this essay why this might be the case, comparing Rae Armantrout's poems to some recent work by a woman poet of the very same generation whose poetry has won every prize and honor, including a MacArthur Fellowship, and who is currently the Boylston Professor of Rhetoric at Harvard. I am thinking, of course, of Jorie Graham.

For the moment, however, let's consider how one might teach *The Pretext*. Like Armantrout's earlier books, this one is slender and compact; its ninety-one pages include forty short poems, typically made up of two- and three-line free-verse stanzas. There are also some prose poems, like "Performers," and some mixed verse-prose ones, like the title poem. Although the lyrics are self-contained poems, this book does have a narrative thread of sorts: it concerns the poet's regular visits to a nursing home where her mother is evidently dying. Only a number of the poems are directly "about" the mother, but death is, however obliquely and sardonically, a presence throughout. Here is a representative poem:

Direction
Age as a centripetal force.

She can't hold the fictive
panoply of characters
apart.

Is *that* scary?

Origin's a sore point.

(When the old woman sheds tears,
I say, "What's wrong?"

as if surprised

the way Peter denied
he knew Jesus in the bible.

But Jesus too
refused to recognize his mom.)

We want a more distant relation

like that of Christmas tree ornament
to fruit. (60–61)

How would I go about discussing this poem in the classroom? Students who
have at least some familiarity with poetry are likely to have two contradictory reactions. On the one hand, "Direction" looks familiar on the page. Its
short free-verse lines and small stanzaic units, its largely casual, colloquial
diction and phrasing, its everyday references—these are fairly standard in poetry anthologies today. If the students have already been exposed (as I hope
they have) to the poetry of William Carlos Williams and Robert Creeley,
they will recognize these poets as obvious influences on Armantrout. A less
obvious, but perhaps more striking, presence here is that of Sylvia Plath; such
one-line observations as "Age as a centripetal force" and "Is *that* scary?" recall
poems like "Cut Thumb" and "Love Song."

On the other hand, in Armantrout's poem there is much less continuity than in either Creeley's or Plath's lyric. There is no positioned observer, whose insights are detailed one by one. The first line, "Age as a centripetal force," sets the stage: the reference is to the increasing inward turn, the withdrawal from contact with the outside world that characterizes old age, as memory comes to replace action as well as anticipation of a possible future.

The "Direction" of the title is thus inward. But who is "she" and why can't she hold even "the fictive / panoply of characters / apart"? Evidently "she" is the "old woman" who "sheds tears" in line 7; even the soap opera she watches on TV, perhaps, has become too complicated for her to follow. And "*that*" of course is "scary" to the "I" of line 8, who is evidently at her bedside. But "Is *that* scary?" may also be the old woman's question about the "fictive panoply" she is watching on TV or reading about. Indeed, everything is scary in this context, especially since "Origin's a sore point." The "Origin" of what? Of illness? Of the first signs of memory loss or Alzheimers? Of the lack of rapport between the two people in question, who may well be (but we can't say for certain) mother and daughter. Armantrout doesn't spell it out, so it seems all the more sinister and frustrating.

The narrator tries to keep things normal, unemotional: "When the old woman sheds tears / I say, 'What's wrong?' / as if surprised." Such pretense is perhaps necessary, but it can also be perceived as cruel—a denial that the poem likens to Peter's betrayal of Jesus and, in turn, Jesus' refusal to acknowledge Mary as his mother. The poet is uncomfortable with bedside scenes, and she may not be close to this "old woman" even though the situation is obviously painful for them both. The last lines, in any case, are equivocal: "We want a more distant relation," she says, "like that of Christmas tree ornament / to fruit." Who, to begin with, is "we"? Human beings in general in their dealings with relatives or perhaps even friends? Young people? Children of the elderly and sick? Or specifically daughters? Or certain kinds of daughters? The simile, far from being graphic, is purposely open to interpretation. If the Christmas tree ornament is an angel, its relation to fruit is indeed "distant." If it is a blue metal ball that looks rather like a plum, the distance decreases. Then again, the piece of fruit may *be* the Christmas tree ornament itself. In that case, how distant is a "more distant relation"? And how easily can the "I" actually detach herself from the old woman's plight?

Let us now step back and see what assumptions have been made thus far: First, that any serious poem, however disjointed and "nonsensical," is meaningful. Second, that the poem's meanings are never quite paraphraseable, never univocal—numbers of alternate readings are possible. And third, that the only way to *get at* the poem is in fact to read it, word for word, line by line. Much of what passes for poetry criticism today refuses to do this: it picks up on one item that arrests the reader's attention and often ignores the rest. But a close reading—and there is no other way to understand poetry, which is, as Ezra Pound so succinctly put it, "news that stays news"—has to account for all the elements in a given text, not just the ones that support a particular interpretation.

From this perspective, we read Armantrout's poem as we would any other, whether "experimental" or conventional, contemporary or Renaissance. But such a preliminary reading is not worth much unless we now start to ask larger questions. What matters, after all, is not what this little poem "says" about old age or mother-daughter relationships but *how* it says it and why. The next step, then, is to place the poem in a number of larger frames: first the book in which it appears and Armantrout's oeuvre as a whole, then its genre and stylistic conventions, and then its cultural and historical markers vis-à-vis other comparable poems of the period.

First, then, context. The opening poem of Armantrout's book is called "Birthmark: The Pretext" and begins as follows:

You want something, that's the pretext. I recently abandoned a
dream narrative called "Mark." You can see it, since you asked.

MARK

I'm with three friends.
We've parked in a lot downtown,
lucky to get a slot.

My son's friend
asks him if he's divided
his homework in three parts;
luckily he has.

Suddenly, I'm the teacher.
I see a line of Milton's
I'm glad I haven't marked it wrong;
at first I thought it didn't fit.[3]

Here is the same mix of the colloquial and the oblique, the literal and the punning, that we witnessed in "Direction." A "pretext" is both an excuse for doing something and a pre-text or preface that anticipates what is to come. In the poet's case, the "pretext" has to do with a series of recent events. But this is never said directly. Instead, she gives us a "dream narrative" called "Mark" that at first seems absolutely naturalistic and flat except that the three stanzas don't cohere. What do the three friends of the first have to do with dividing homework into three parts and the issue of "marking" (with its pun on "Mark") a line of Milton's (the poet or a student in the poet's writing class) that didn't "fit"? In the prose that follows, we read:

> That's not very interesting or it's only interesting because it's real. It's a real dream composed of three banal vignettes in which the same elements appear, luck, parts, and fit. It's interesting to the extent that the divisions and the fitting together arise spontaneously, without pretext. In other words, to the extent that there is a stranger in my head arranging things for me. Of course, I divided the poem in three parts. I chose the word *lucky*. (*Veil* 91)

Luck, parts, and *fit:* Armantrout's "three banal vignettes" indeed fuse these three elements: the luck of finding the parking space, the tripartite division, both of the son's homework and of her own poem, and the issue of parts—in this case, lines—that fit. In real dreams, Armantrout posits, images obviously don't cohere. The poet must capture that "reality" even as she is the one *choosing* the words and dividing her poem into particular parts.

Here, then, is a statement of poetic that is itself poetically rendered. The rest of the piece turns to Armantrout's own "reality": the strawberry-colored birthmark on her outer left thigh, her small breasts, her rebellion against gender identification related in her reaction to the image of Marilyn Monroe. Here again the threefold topos of the poem—luck, parts, and fit—becomes the object of self-scrutiny. Was Monroe lucky to have her particular parts? Is the poet comfortable with her own? "Funny," she remarks, "how you can be excited without fitting in anywhere." This seemingly casual observation provides the "pretext" for the rest of the book, with its peculiar tension between not "fitting in" and "excitement," of separation and absorption into what is an alien but enticing culture—the culture in which the great star, blessed with those amazing breasts, nevertheless has "a squeaky little girl voice." "The Birthmark" ends with the sentence "But I've gone off on a tangent when what I wanted to do was swallow my own pretext." The metaphor is apt: what may look "tangential" is really a "pretext" the poet has carefully "swallowed" or made her own as the motive that looks ahead to, and is the raison d'être for, what follows.

What sort of poetry is this, and where is it positioned in the culture? Why, for example, is this "poem" written primarily in prose? Readers new to such work sometimes object that poems like "The Birthmark" and "Direction" are not sufficiently concrete or graphic, that this poet's ruminations on "luck, parts, and fit" are not properly "emotive" and hence "moving." Isn't poetry, at least in the extracts from the *Norton Anthology* the student may have seen, the expression of powerful feelings? Why, then, Armantrout's largely abstract diction? And why speak of the female gender as an oppressive "birthmark" rather than dramatizing the specific sexual feelings this particular woman might have?

To answer such potential objections, the instructor must confront issues of genre and convention. It is not enough to say that Armantrout's predilection for abstract nouns and adjectives and "prosaic" rhythms has to do with her status as a "Language poet," or again, that the "fragmentation" and dislocation of her phrasing is a feminist response to patriarchy. Armantrout herself has remarked, in an interview with Lyn Hejinian, "I don't think we can say that fragmentation and polyvalence are feminine styles sometimes appropriated by men. . . . Aren't these the techniques of all the great modernists (Joyce, Pound, Eliot, and the later Williams as well as Stein and H. D.)?"[4] At the same time—and I shall come back to this point—gender obviously does make a difference in *The Pretext* as does Armantrout's long involvement with the Language community. But for the moment it should be noted that Armantrout's poetry is really very *unlike* that of Ron Silliman or Bob Perelman or even that of Lyn Hejinian. What, then, is it like? What assumptions govern its verbal and rhythmical choices?

The first thing to say—though it may seem obvious—is that Armantrout's is a decidedly *American* poetic. There are in her lyrics no appreciable echoes of canonical English poetry, no allusions to Wordsworth or Keats or, for that matter, to such early modernists as Yeats and Hardy. This exclusion immediately differentiates Armantrout's lyric not only from a poet like Allen Ginsberg, for whom Blake was central, but also from John Ashbery's, where, despite an overlay of French Dada and Surrealism, allusions to and borrowings from the Romantic and Victorian poets are decisive. Then, too, Armantrout's syntactic structures are largely those of American working-class speech, minimally grammatical and often slangy, as in "She said, 'If you're gonna hire / the dummies, I quit!'" ("The Past," *Pretext* 21). And the minimalism of her free-verse stanzas, with their curious line breaks and incorporated silences, suggest that traditional verse forms have long since lost any attraction as have such classical genres as ode or pastoral elegy. Armantrout's is poetry written in the Williams mode as that mode was developed by Creeley, George Oppen, and especially Lorine Niedecker. Like Niedecker, whose poems the students might be given as analogues, Armantrout writes as a self-acknowledged outsider, a loner. "I myself," as she puts it in "Writing" (*Pretext* 10), "was always a forwarding address." But, again like Niedecker, this poet is tough-minded and self-reliant: "People come first, but / categories outlast them," she tells herself (21). And like Niedecker, she has a crusty, quirky sense of humor that distinguishes her poetry from the surface sophistications of its New York counterpart. "Sound / as a drum / or tight as a drum?" she asks wryly in "The Past" (21), and then responds with the single word "Quick!" followed by the poignant question "Is recognition / sentimental?"

Neither Niedecker nor Plath, however, foregrounded pop culture as does Armantrout in *The Pretext*: the difference, no doubt, is generational. Armantrout's particular discourse radius is that of comic books and late-night TV, movie stars and department store clerks, the CBS evening news and the parking lot. Domesticity, in this world of "Flagpole[s] on a traffic island," is itself mediated by media images: to be a housewife, this poetry suggests, is not to be baking a cake or making new curtains but to be watching TV and daydreaming about Art Garfunkel and Joanne Woodward. In this sense Armantrout's is very much a poetry of our moment—a poetry of bedroom communities in Southern California, where neighbors don't really know one another and half of one's waking hours are spent driving around in one's car. Indeed, even without any biographical knowledge, the reader surmises that Armantrout's giant peonies and clunky telephone poles are located in communities that have little history, that her "yard strung with plastic Jack-O-Lanterns, / some filled with poinsettias" is remarkable precisely for its lack of distinction. Her landscape is a long way from Robert Lowell's Boston Common or Frank O'Hara's lunch-hour Manhattan.

This brings us to larger historical and cultural issues. What does it mean, for starters, to have a book of poems so dismissive of everything that traditionally goes with poetry: intricate sound repetition, stanzaic layout, and especially a coherent "I" whose reflections one can follow throughout the poem, a lyric self that stands behind the poem's metaphors and symbols? Then, too, what happens when "poetry" declares itself to be without generic markers, whether with respect to larger verse forms—sonnet, sestina, quatrain—or conventions, such as those of the dramatic monologue, the pastoral elegy, ode, or ballad? If the "new poetry" does without all these, what does it substitute?

Armantrout herself suggests that what she is writing is collage. "I do a kind of faux-collage where I'm mixing familiar tones and voices—say the *diction* of a TV anchor man with that of an Alzheimer's patient" (*Wild Salience* 12). But collage is actually not quite the right term for Armantrout's "tone-shifting" and "peculiar overlaps," as she calls them, for collage entails the juxtaposition, on the same verbal plane, of concrete images pasted together, whereas an Armantrout poem consists of a sequence of tenuously interconnected clauses and phrases, where the connections between abstract statements are regularly blurred. Brian Reed has referred to this mode as an "attenuated hypotaxis"[5]—a useful designation, reminding us that disjunction need not be, as is often thought, paratactic—phrases and clauses strung together by a series of "and's"—that a pseudo-hypotaxis in which B seems to follow A, only to turn out to be a disconnect, is another interesting mode of procedure. Indeed, it is a more radical mode than collage, which was, after all, the dominant poetic mode of modernism.

What is the meaning of such hypotaxis? For many poets of Armantrout's generation, all ordering principles are suspect as are the conventional genres. In the age of media, as I have argued in *Radical Artifice: Writing Poetry in the Age of Media* (1992), linear structures with beginning, middle, and end and forms of musical repetition have been viewed as failing to "measure" and critique the actual social and political structures within which we live in late-twentieth-century (now twenty-first-century) America. And from her position as a woman and hence, as we see throughout the pages of *The Pretext*, forced to assume the role of caretaker, whether of her son or her mother, the institutional structures seem especially oppressive:

> When her mother worsens,
> She imagines the funeral
> Of a living celebrity.
>
> Who would attend?
> Why or why not?
>
> Is this dream logic?
> ("Her References," *Pretext* 18)

In her willingness to do without so much of the usual accoutrements of poetry, Armantrout gives her full attention to its one indispensable element: language. "All our nouns / will be back momentarily" we read in a poem called "No," which ends with the couplet "As if it were needless / to say," with its play on that most common of qualifiers, "Needless to say . . . " (46–47). What a close reading of *The Pretext* will reveal is that this is a poetry obsessive about language itself, its "luck, parts, and [especially its] fit." Poetry, in other words, can do without symbol, metaphor, metrical elegance, and so on, but what it cannot do without is what Aristotle called *to prepon*—fitness or relatedness. In the line "Origin's a sore point," for example, "sore point" is obviously a dead metaphor, but in the poem "Direction," in which the old woman "sheds tears," the "sore point" is also a literal reference. In the metonymic network of the poem, cliché is regularly twisted (often into pun) so as to yield new meanings, as in "To postpone withdrawal / by spreading oneself thin."

In this scheme of things, poetry is, as David Antin has put it, the *language art,* and so the relative success of a given set of poems has to do with its recharging of the language, its ability to make words and lines resonate. Sound (repetition, internal rhyme, consonance) does play a part as does the poem's placement of text and white space. The question, one of Armantrout's favorite rhetorical devices, is regularly left hanging, and when, down the page, a putative answer comes, it seems to be to another question. And the sudden shifts from concrete image to abstract noun and verb, many of them placed within pseudo-propositions, suggest that one cannot make present the world outside oneself; there are only tentative moves in that direction. In "Greeting," for example, the image of the telephone pole, "shouldering a complement / of knobs" (68), suddenly yields to thoughts of *circumstance:* "the way a single word / could mean / necessary, relative, / provisional." The force of these meditative lines is to transform the image of the "wood pole's / rosy crossbar" into an anticipation of the death prefigured in the bird's "flick past" on the final lines. We can't read "Greeting," we can only reread it.

The complexities of this disjointed, minimalist poetry will make more sense to students if it is read against its alternatives on the current poetry scene. An interesting counterpart, as I mentioned above, is found in the poetry of Jorie Graham, one of the most admired poets writing in America today. Consider a recent poem called "Evolution," which appeared in Graham's *Never* (2002) less than a year after Armantrout's *The Pretext:*[6]

One's nakedness is very slow.
One calls to it, one wastes one's sympathy.
Comparison, too, is very slow.
Where is the past?
I sense that we should keep this coming.
Something like joy rivulets along the sand.
I insist that we "go in." We go in.
One cannot keep all of it. What is enough
of it. And *keep*?—I am being swept away—
what is *keep*?—A waking good.

Visibility blocking the view.
Although we associate the manifest with kindness,
we do. The way it goes, where it goes, slight downslope,
Like the word "suddenly," the incline it causes.
Also the eye's wild joy sucked down the slope the minutes wave
                                                    by wave

pack down and slick.
The journey—some journey—visits one.
The journey—some journey—visits me.
Then this downslope once again.
And how it makes what happens
            Always more heavily
laden, this self only able to sink (albeit also
                        lifting as in a
sudden draught) into the future. *Our* future. Where everyone
                                            is patient.
Where all the sentences come to complete themselves.
Where what wants to be human still won't show
                        its face.

Like Armantrout's poems, this twenty-seven-line lyric is written in free verse, although Graham's "free verse" is obviously quite unlike Armantrout's.[7] Graham's lines are mostly long and prosaically understressed, but they culminate in the iambic hexameter of the conclusion: "where áll the séntencés cóme to compléte themsélves. / Where whát wánts to be húman stíll won't shów its fáce." The move toward metrical stability is not surprising, for Graham's lyric exhibits an emotive and temporal coherence. However oblique some of its images and references, B follows from A here, and C from B in a sequence that has its own inner logic. One cannot, for example, reverse the order of these largely grammatical sentences and clauses.

Again, like Armantrout's, Graham's language is predominantly abstract: her poem contains primarily conceptual nouns like "sympathy," "Comparison," "past," "joy" "good," and "kindness," even as the predominant verb is the copula, as in "Where is the past?" or "what is *keep*? A waking good." But "Evolution" has none of the gaps we find in, say, "Direction," where the line "Age is a centripetal force" is followed by the words "She can't hold the fictive panoply," with no indication of who "she" is. Nor does "Evolution" use the casual diction, slang, or popular culture references we find in Armantrout's work. Graham's language is stately and remote—rather like the language of the later books of Wordsworth's *Prelude*. "Joy *rivulets* along the sand," "what happens" is "Always more heavily / laden," the self is "only able to sink (albeit also / lifting as in a / sudden draught)," and so on. True, these elaborate phrases are punctuated by staccato, more colloquial ones like "I insist that we 'go in.' We go in," but its general tenor is one of high seriousness. Then, too, the poet's voice is carefully distanced by the use of the pronoun "One" (five instances) and "we" or "our" (six instances), as compared to only three references to the first person, in each instance brought in only to qualify a generalization about "one" as in:

> The journey—some journey—visits one.
> The journey—some journey—visits me.

"Evolution" is an oblique and highly wrought poem, but its central meanings are not difficult to understand once we recognize that it uses the subject of Darwinian Evolution as a pretext (that word again!) or occasion for a meditation on what it means to be "human," to have "evolved" from the animals into a "higher" species. Where does such evolution leave our powerful sexual instincts? The poem's difficulties are generated not by semantic gaps and dislocations, as is the case in Armantrout's lyric, but by circumlocution and indirection. The first line, "One's nakedness is very slow," for example, seems puzzling since nakedness is a condition and hence cannot be either "fast" or "slow," but what the poet is really saying here is that one's acknowledgment of one's nakedness, or one's awareness of one's nakedness, is what comes only slowly. And as the prosopopoeia of the second line suggests, we are trained to regard the body as somehow outside the self so that "One calls to it, one wastes one's sympathy."

As such locutions testify, in Graham's poem the irony is multiplex. One wants to live instinctually, the poem suggests, but "One cannot keep all of it." Then again, "what is *keep*? A waking good." So, much as the "I" dutifully insists "that we 'go in,'" and "We go in," one resists such rational behavior and is "swept away" down "the incline." Graham's is in fact a latter-day "Dialogue of Self and Soul" (Yeats), a *débat* between the longing for "something like joy" that "rivulets along the sand" and the recognition that "the eye's wild joy sucked down the slope the minutes wave by wave / pack down and slick." The Shakespeare echo ("Like as the waves make toward the pebbled shore / So do our minutes hasten to their end") paves the way for a moment of self-recognition. Facing oneself and letting go is hard: it is not darkness but ironically "visibility" that is "blocking the view." The future of

Evolution—a future where perhaps we accept ourselves as we are—is never quite complete.

These speculations on the aporias of sexual love and responsibility evidently have urgency for the poet. But it is interesting to compare such generalizing statements as the concluding line's "Where what wants to be human still won't show its face," to the laconic reference to "Age as a centripetal force" in Armantrout's "Direction." In the latter case, as I remarked earlier, what is said about old age remains equivocal: is the increasing solipsism a good thing or not? In Graham's "Evolution," on the other hand, the assertion is presented as a hard-earned truth that the narrator has made her own. True, the conclusion is presented obliquely. "What wants to be human" is evidently the woman's inner "animal" nature, the "wild joy sucked down" that "still won't show its face." But if the line is designed to mystify the *reader,* the poet herself seems to know exactly how she feels about Darwinism, sexuality, and the need for restraint. It is not, in other words, that the speaker herself has doubts as to the "wisdom" put forward in her ruminations on the erotic life. Indeed—and here is an unanticipated irony—despite the talk of "wild joy" and the "sinking" that is also a "lifting," there is no abandon in the formal structure of the poem. On the contrary, its elements are everywhere controlled, its tone carefully modulated. *Tone,* more specifically voice and address, is one of the hardest things to talk about when analyzing poetry. But consider the following: Why is Graham's poem, with its evident desire for letting go, a series of complete sentences and clauses? To whom is she speaking when she asks questions like "Where is the past?" or "What is *keep*?" She is clearly not asking herself, because having raised these issues she goes on to spell out what the whole situation means. Nor is she addressing her lover, the person referred to in lines like "I insist that we 'go in.' We go in" or in the allusion to "*Our* future."

Who, then, is the addressee? By all accounts it is the reader, the reader who is to be made wiser by the poet's oblique and ominous account of what sexual passion does to human beings. But the profundity of the "message" is undermined by the reader's recognition that in fact the poem exhibits no appreciable conflict. No worry about "luck, parts, and fit" here. The lovers, as this poem makes clear, aren't about to give each other up; they aren't conflicted about what they should do, or at least the speaker is not, since, in all fairness, her lover is not given much a chance. Indeed, it is the narrator who calls the shots. "I insist we 'go in.' We go in."

But, then, what *is* the actual situation that haunts this poem? We never know. In *The Pretext* Armantrout presents us with her difficult, by no means "pretty" response to her dying mother's behavior in the nursing home; she is unsparing in showing her own failings as well as those of others. Every reader can identify with such a situation. But in "Evolution" the world-weary narrator, curiously *knowing* about the relation of past and present, the journey into the future, and the fate of the self, seems unable to see herself as others see her. Difficulty in such a poem is less the inherent difficulty of a complex response to a particular situation than it is a calculated "difficulty," designed to impress readers with the profundity and importance of the issues at stake.

Why, then, have "Evolution" and related Graham poems won such extravagant praise from reviewers and prize committees? The answer, I think, is that such poems are just familiar enough to hit a responsive chord without quite giving themselves away. "Evolution" is a neo-Romantic lyric meditation, the representation of a thought process that culminates in the recognition that "*Our* future" would ideally be one where we could be ourselves, in all our nakedness, even as, so we know, "all the sentences come to complete themselves." Shades of the prison house inevitably close in on us. Given these parameters, the poem's willed indeterminacies like "What is enough / of it? And *keep*?" are curiously contained within a formal fixity (the passage from "nakedness" to "show its face") that belies these ostensibly open meanings.

Yet—and this is what makes the comparison of Armantrout to Graham valuable—"Evolution" testifies at every turn to its author's awareness of the Language movement, even as it doesn't want to take dislocation and discontinuity to the extremes of Armantrout or Bruce Andrews, of Charles Bernstein or Clark Coolidge. Consider the lines "The way it goes where it goes, slight downslope, / like the word 'suddenly,' the incline it causes." The reference is to the fact that "súddenly" is a dactyl and hence "inclines" downward (/ x x), thus making "súddenly" itself a verbal "downslope." But unlike Armantrout's recognition, in the poem "No," that "The copula may take the form of a cable / or snake" (*Pretext* 46), the reference to "suddenly" seems more clever than integral to the poem.

Comparison and contrast, in any case, can make a poetry class learn to differentiate between enigmas that cannot be resolved because the poet has no answers and those that are, more properly, surface difficulties, easily penetrable on a second or third reading. Graham's is usually considered a "philosophical" poetry, what with its frequent allusions to Heidegger and Agamben, Levinas and Lacan, and it is true that hers is highly unlike the more transparent mode of such of her contemporaries as Sharon Olds or Rita Dove. If we wanted to place Graham's poetic, we might assign it to the "Romantic esoteric" slot—highly complicated and serious but with none of the intransigence, the edge, that we find in the best Language poetries. Its audience may well be wider, but its reach, probably narrower.

The challenge of Armantrout's quirky lyric may thus be more satisfying than the stylishness we have come to associate with Jorie Graham. Seemingly slight as Armantrout's poems sometimes seem to be, especially when one compares a book like *The Pretext* to a Graham volume like *The Swarm* (2000) or *Materialism* (1997), they exhibit everywhere a strenuous thinking that takes nothing for granted. I don't claim for a moment that they surpass, in any way, their great modernist forebears; to my mind—and this is too complicated a subject to develop here—the real "revolution of the word" came early in our century, even if its promise is only now being realized. And I also don't want to argue that Armantrout is always successful: in "Direction," for example, the reference to Mary as Jesus' "Mom" strikes me as excessively cute. But what reading her work against Graham's suggests is that even as we must take the Other of "experimental" poetry quite seriously, noting that there are many overlaps between Graham's "Evolution" and Armantrout's "Birthmark," we must also discriminate between their respective poetic stances and their place in literary as well as cultural history.

I am by no means making the case for a false and easy ecumenicalism that takes its poetry wherever it happens to find it and treats it as so many discrete items, all of them interesting and somehow of value. But I do feel that before we decide who is writing what claims to be the truly innovative poetry and how we should teach it, the more closely we weigh the various alternatives before us. How to teach the new "experimental" poetry? Take nothing for granted. In Armantrout's words:

> Just reproducing it
> requires
> all the concentration
> you are: this
> taut prong
> holding forth.
>
>   (*Pretext* 83)

In 1999 Jeffrey Di Leo, the editor of Symploke, *was putting together a volume of essays on the subject of* affiliations, *those complex relationships between individuals and the institutions for which they work or the disciplines in which they perform. In response I wrote the following essay, which first appeared in* Symploke *and then in Di Leo's expanded book version, published by the University of Nebraska Press in 2003. The following essay is more personal than the others here. Oddly, it thus set the stage for the writing of my memoir,* The Vienna Paradox *(New Directions, 2004), a reconsideration, now that I think of it, of yet another of my affiliations—that of Austrian Jewish refugee in the United States.*

14

Writing Poetry/Writing about Poetry

Some Problems of Affiliation

> I am not a painter, I am a poet.
> Why? I think I would rather be
> A painter, but I am not. Well. . . .
> Frank O'Hara, "Why I Am Not a Painter"

Academics like myself, who write about contemporary poetry and poetics, often have an affiliation problem. On the one hand, our subjects are alive, kicking, and ready to praise but also challenge our interpretations of their work. On the other, our more traditional colleagues regard our area of expertise as "soft" and trivial. When the time comes to hire for the Creative Writing program, moreover, they are convinced they can "judge" the poetry to be evaluated at least as well as we do. Creative Writing is only a fun "extra" activity anyway, isn't it? A few years ago, when my brilliant colleague Gilbert Sorrentino ventured an opinion as to a "regular" job applicant's understanding of James Joyce (whose work Gil taught almost every year), I heard a second colleague say, "What does Gil know? He's only a *writer!*"

I am not myself a "writer"; I have, as one of my favorite Oberlin professors, F. X. Roellinger, told me tactfully many years ago, more talent for the "critical" than the "creative" essay (much less, for the poem), but I do have a special affinity for *work in progress,* the writing that is not yet canonical or fixed, the attributes of which I like to try to define and put in some perspective. And in a curious way, I am—I might as well confess it—in love with the twentieth century (this despite all its elitism and imperialism, its Eurocentrism and even, in its Continental variant, its phase of totalitarianism)— the twentieth century whose first half gave us so many extraordinary poets and artists and composers and architects and dancers that it blows the mind, and whose second half, if less dazzling, is fascinating for its working out of the problems the early century produced. Then too it is *our* century and, again in the words of Frank O'Hara, "I am ashamed of my century / for being so entertaining / but I have to smile."[1]

But throughout graduate school and for the first ten years of my academic career (1965–1975), my affiliation was with the world of academic scholarship. I had been taught in graduate school to "back up" every statement with a footnote, to provide the necessary evidence to buttress an argument, and especially to observe academic decorum. This meant that as critics we never declared *X*'s argument "wrong" and certainly not "preposterous" or "silly"; rather, we would say, "I wonder if Harold Bloom's reading of Wallace Stevens's *Auroras of Autumn* takes into account that . . . ," or "Thus far, no critic has noticed that A. R. Ammons's poetry is informed by . . . ," and so on. As academics, we were taught to write straightforward, coherent prose in which "*B*" follows logically from "*A*." Clarity, the telling example, and thorough documentation using the *PMLA* style sheet—these were, and largely continue to be, the order of the day.

My first two books, and certainly my articles for scholarly journals, followed these prescriptions to the letter. When I was writing my dissertation, *Rhyme and Meaning in the Poetry of Yeats,* I used to go to the Library of Congress and ferret out obscure scholarly articles in German that might have something to do with the theory of rhyme. Or if I wrote on the elegies of Robert Lowell, I began with Theocritus, looked up the etymology of the word *elegy* as well as its history, and then read whatever my fellow scholars might have said on the subject, no matter how obscure the monograph or journal in which they had published their findings. Indeed, to find a topic for a paper meant, as we had been taught in graduate school, to find an original angle. Thus, when I wrote on the "consolation theme" in Yeats's great elegy "In Memory of Major Robert Gregory," I argued that the reason this particular poem didn't seem all that mournful—indeed, seemed rather bracing and self-confident—was that it presented the poet himself as wise witness and survivor, superior, in fact, to the young Robert Gregory who was ostensibly the poem's subject. The editor of *Modern Language Quarterly* was satisfied that mine was an original reading of the poem—not *too* original, of course, because there was already a body of received opinion on the Gregory elegy, beginning with Frank Kermode's remarks in *Romantic Image*. The goal was—and is—to participate in a discourse that, as Michel Foucault and, more recently, Pierre Bourdieu have taught us, is nothing if not rule-bound.

For a decade or so, then, my goal was to make it in the world of *Modern Language Quarterly* and *ELH*, *American Literature* and *PMLA*. When my essay "Spatial Form in Yeats's Poetry" appeared in the last of these (it was my first and last article in *PMLA*), I was overjoyed to receive a note of praise from the great Yeats and Joyce biographer-critic Richard Ellmann. "Thank you," he wrote me in a magisterial handwritten note, which I have preserved for posterity, "for writing your article." I felt that I had indeed found my professional niche!

But then in 1975 I was asked, on the basis of a review essay on Frank O'Hara's *Art Chronicles* that I had written for *The New Republic,* to write a book on O'Hara for George Braziller, a small but elite New York publishing house that specialized in art books. The book that resulted marked a shift in affiliation. Not that I ever quite pleased the publisher, who wanted more anecdotes and fewer footnotes, more biography and good gossip and less assessment of O'Hara's debt to French Surrealism. But in the course of writing *Frank O'Hara: Poet among Painters* (1977), I met the deceased poet's sister, Maureen O'Hara Smith, and his editor, Donald Allen, as well as many of O'Hara's poet and painter friends, including John Ashbery, David Shapiro, Grace Hartigan, Larry Rivers, and Norman Bluhm. Some of these became close friends, and through them I became affiliated with the poetry/art world of New York, although in a minor way. And I must confess that this world seemed (at least at first) much more enjoyable and stimulating than academe. Here people really *loved* poetry, although they couldn't always say why they loved a particular poem; more important: my new poet/artist friends really *cared*—they thought poetry and painting made a difference: it was their life, not just a way to get tenure. Best of all, they were not subject (or so I thought!) to the institutional constraints that made life in the English department seem so confining. No curriculum planning or PhD oral committees, no tenure meetings or job candidate lunches in the faculty club!

My affiliation with this world expanded when I wrote my next book, *The Poetics of Indeterminacy: Rimbaud to Cage* (1981). I couldn't, of course, have conversations with Rimbaud or Ezra Pound or Gertrude Stein, but I came to know Ashbery much better and met his younger friends, John Yau and David Shapiro, Ann Lauterbach and Marjorie Welish. And I developed a strong friendship with David Antin—the subject, along with John Cage, of the final chapter of my book. David, who teaches at the University of California–San

Diego, was close at hand (I was then teaching at the University of Southern California), and we must have had literally hundreds of phone conversations that I now wish I had recorded. David is a kind of quiz kid, a voluble genius who can talk impromptu about Diderot's *Rameau's Nephew* or Mark Rothko in such detail that every conversation was like a lesson. It was David who first introduced me to the work of Wittgenstein, the subject of my later book *Wittgenstein's Ladder* (1996), which, in turn, produced a long and fascinating review-essay on his part published in *Modernism/Modernity* (1998). Through David, moreover, I came to know Jerome Rothenberg (the two poets have been friends ever since their City College days), whose wide-ranging work in ethnopoetics and Dada helped me to see beyond the canonical poets I had studied thus far.

The Poetics of Indeterminacy also led to a friendship with John Cage, a friendship that I can safely say changed my life. Not that I saw John often, but he remains my role model for what an artist can be. For John and his partner, Merce Cunningham, there was no real separation between art and life, which meant, in practice, that art had to take on the arena of everyday life and respond to it. At the same time—and this is the paradox that still fascinates me—John was nothing if not an aesthete: he would work for hours to get a particular word or musical phrase just *right,* and art, for him, was always *work.* Then, too, I admired the way John went his own way; he never did anything in order to be "popular," which is not to say that he was not a shrewd career builder. He knew how to seize an opportunity—like composing music for a synchronized swimming event at UCLA—but he never betrayed his own aesthetic in order to go up the ladder. He did not read reviews of his work, holding that such reading would only distract him. I had occasion, several times when John stayed with us, to witness his typical day. In the morning he would fix himself his macrobiotic breakfast and act as if he had nothing whatever to do except chat with me and cook. But within five minutes after breakfast, he'd be seated at the dining table, wholly at work. He never wasted a minute—just pure concentration and *attention.*

From the early eighties on, in any case, I have had a dual allegiance and dual affiliation. My essays and books have remained "academic" in that they are written in straightforward expository prose (I don't know how to write what I would consider effective freeform "alternate" prose) and have lots of footnotes. But the subjects I write about have more and more been contemporary poets like Charles Bernstein and Susan Howe, Lyn Hejinian and Johanna Drucker, Steve McCaffery and Rosmarie Waldrop, as well as artists and photographers. And a number of these I have come to count among my closest friends. Without them, I don't know what I would have done in an academy that I often find stuffy and irrelevant. True, I have had some wonderful colleagues, but on the whole I find that I just don't speak the same language as most of the members of my department. Yes, we read the same theorists, but whereas most academics tend to adopt a particular paradigm (psychoanalytic criticism, Marxist criticism, Deconstruction, the Frankfurt School, Cultural Studies, Gender criticism, etc.), I've always felt skeptical toward such allegiances—largely, no doubt, because the adoption of a theoretical model always puts the literary work in a secondary position—a position where the poem tends to be no more than an example of X or a cultural symptom of Y.

Why should this be the case? Why does "theory" (whether feminist or postcolonial, psychoanalytic or the new globalization theory) now have so much more cultural or academic capital than even the most central of literary texts: *Hamlet* or the *Divine Comedy* or *Ulysses*? I would argue that the death of the canon—of a list of texts that one expects the student to know—makes it extremely difficult to maintain a sense of cohesiveness or community at the departmental, much less the institutional level. How can a medievalist specializing in, say, *Piers Plowman*, be expected to know about the Harlem Renaissance or *film noir*? And vice versa: can we expect a specialist in, say, Latino cultural studies to know Jacobean drama? Increasingly, the only way of engaging one's colleagues in other periods or literatures is to find an umbrella—whether Queer Theory or Lacanian criticism, or the Frankfurt School—that might embrace the now largely disparate areas of "literary" study.

But where does this leave the poet? Ironically, however new and up-to-date the theoretical paradigm in question, that paradigm is more user-friendly when it comes to the work of earlier periods than in relation to the cutting-edge poetry or artwork of our own moment. The paradigmatic, in other words, is inevitably at odds with the confusion and richness of work-in-process. Bakhtinian narrative theory, for example, has proven enormously useful vis-à-vis the novel from Diderot to Toni Morrison, but what about the video art of Bill Viola? Or a hybrid lyric narrative/documentary/historical text like Susan Howe's *Pierce Arrow*? Or the "Little Sparta" sculpture park of Ian Hamilton Finlay?

Given these aporias, for a critic of contemporary writing like myself, academic affiliation tends to take an institutional rather than intellectual form—namely, the bonding with one's colleagues, however disparate, over issues of academic politics—hiring, departmental governance, curriculum planning, all of the above easily turning into what we all enjoy, namely, academic gossip. On this level I can engage my colleagues in colonial American or Medieval studies. The latest tenure case or promotion scandal, the job market news, the new endowment gift or budget shortfall: these keep us in close contact. At the same time, academic "who's who" talk can also be the kiss of death, so far as imaginative work is concerned. For how can one concentrate on *poeticity* or related issues when one has to prepare for the upcoming tenure meeting or the Q & A session for a job candidate in a field quite remote from one's own?

On the other hand—and this is my subject here—affiliation with the "unaffiliated" poetry community for someone who is not one of "them" is not without its problems either. Since my own allegiance has been and continues to be to the poetic avant-garde, whether that of the early twentieth century or the present, I am in many ways a natural enemy for the Creative Writing cohort in the English department. By definition—although there are now notable exceptions like SUNY–Buffalo or Brown—the Creative Writing workshop is, by definition, conservative. For one thing, its appointments tend to be made through the English department, which means that its members, whether poets or fiction writers or even dramatists, must be acceptable to the entire department. I am continually astonished by the tastes of most of my colleagues when it comes to hiring faculty for Creative Writing. I have seen the most stringent critics of, say, Renaissance literature be satisfied to hire someone who writes *New Yorker*-style short stories that are "entertaining" and "well done" but that on a serious level don't have the slightest artistic merit. English professors who are rigorous about the canon when it comes to, say, eighteenth-century fiction will endorse work of the late twentieth century that they would never dream of including in a course reading list. And so those of us who are postmodernists are often caught between the scholars and the "creative writers," with uneasy affiliations with both.

But my dual—or perhaps, more accurately, divided—affiliation has a second aporia. In *Radical Artifice: Writing Poetry in the Age of Media* (1992) and related studies, I have enthusiastically advocated the breaking down of the traditional genres, the production of "theorypo" or "poessays"—which is to say the writing, much of it very exciting, that, strictly speaking, is neither lyric poetry nor literary theory or cultural criticism but an inspired blend of all three, as is the case with Susan Howe's *My Emily Dickinson* and *The Birthmark,* Charles Bernstein's *Content's Dream* and *My Way,* Steve McCaffery and bpNichol's *A Rational Geomancy,* or Johanna Drucker's *A History of The/My Wor(l)d.* Wonderful as these works are, they are now spawning a second generation of self-proclaimed hybrid texts that are less successful, at least from the point of view of someone like me who has had, like it or not, academic training. As more and more "experimental" poets have entered the academy—a recent phenomenon—they have wanted to out-theory the theory gurus whom they sense to be the premier members of a given English or Comparative Literature department—the members who possess cultural capital. And so we now have the bizarre phenomenon of the poets trying to emulate the very scholars who have tended to ignore their presence by jumping on the theory bandwagon operative across the hall.

Ironically, the production (or overproduction) of these new poets' "theory-essays" does nothing so much as remind me of my academic roots. When I read generalizations about the nature of narrative or rhythm in poetry, I want to cry out, "Wait a minute! That's not accurate! Where is your documentation? Hasn't X already done this? And why don't you just look it up?" And in raising such caveats, I become aware that I am making my poet friends angry. They want me to write blurbs for their books, produce flattering reviews, and invite them to give readings at Stanford or at conferences. But, understandably, they resent my inadvertent stance of "Criticism belongs to me, and poetry to you!" They are hurt that I, who have advocated the breakdown between primary and secondary discourse, poetry and its criticism, now sound like any other traditional academic. And when they really want to put me down, they say that I'm not so different from Helen Vendler!

This last comment raises a really interesting affiliation problem. Helen Vendler and I have extraordinarily different views on contemporary poetry and different critical methodologies, but it is assumed we are affiliated because we are both women critics of a certain age in what is still a male-dominated field. Recently Michael Scharf wrote a piece for *Poets and Writers* called "The Perloff/Vendler Standoff/Handoff,"[2] in which he characterized us as "late-career professionals" and said we had had similar career trajectories.

I wonder whether Harold Bloom has ever been characterized as a "late-career professional." Or John Hollander? Or Richard Howard?—all roughly my age. More important: I wonder if two men would be said to have had the same career trajectory if, as is the case with Helen Vendler and myself, one is a Boston Irish Catholic, the other a Jewish refugee from Vienna whose roots are deeply European and hence, in the case of poetry, often geared toward German and French materials. Helen Vendler received her PhD from Harvard but, due to the sexism of the sixties, could not get a teaching position there immediately and hence taught at Boston University. I, on the other hand, was a fifties housewife who decided to go back to school in the immediate neighborhood—which in my case meant the Catholic University. I had no valuable connections, no Ivy League prospects, but I also experienced little of the sexism that Vendler experienced, because I did not travel in her particular competitive circuit. Helen Vendler has written books on Shake-speare's sonnets and Keats's odes, whereas I myself have gravitated to the ar-tistic and philosophical affiliations of the twentieth-century poets we both study.

It is odd, then, that we are often endowed with an affiliation neither of us sees herself as having. Then again, as I realized recently when Helen and I were invited to be on a joint panel at the Poetry Society of America, in one sense we *are* affiliated—namely, so far as our attitudes toward work are con-cerned. We both came of age in an academy that, as I have mentioned, de-manded a criticism informed by *knowledge*. If we didn't know the Romantics, then we couldn't write intelligently on Yeats or Stevens or even on Ashbery. If we weren't able to recognize a particular reference, we went to the library and looked it up; we didn't just speculate or go online to ask our chat group friends what a certain word might mean. *Professionalism,* in other words, was and remains a deeply ingrained reflex.

But then what does *professional* mean vis-à-vis new poetries? I have learned, the hard way, that if one says something about a living poet at a conference or in a critical journal, and that poet happens to "disagree" with what one says, he or she won't hesitate to stand up in the audience and make an objection or to write vituperative letters to the author and her friends. The poet Tina Darragh, objecting to a statement I made about another poet, Leslie Scalapino, in an essay published in *Critical Inquiry* (summer 1999),[3] had no compunction about reading an "open letter of protest" about me at various poetry readings around the country. It does not seem to have oc-curred to this poet, whom I know very slightly, that this is not appropriate professional behavior. As I wrote to her, she might have written a letter to the editor of *Critical Inquiry,* or she might have challenged me to debate on an MLA panel or comparable event, but to read a statement of attack as part of a poetry reading, at which I was not present to defend myself, seemed quite appalling to me until I realized that it was a question of conflicting concepts of affiliation. In the circle of Language poets to which Darragh belongs, her behavior was evidently not considered inappropriate. No one, I gather, got up and walked out when she read her protest statement at the Small Press Traffic auditorium in San Francisco.

Ironically, although for over two decades Language poets have argued that the author does not "own" his or her poem, that the reader constructs the text, and that there is no one "right" (and hence "wrong") reading, it remains the case that when an outsider like me (professor rather than poet) says something the poet herself finds questionable, her fellow-poets rally to that poet's cause in an us-versus-them pattern at least as insidious as the Stanford academic's dismissal of Gilbert Sorrentino as being "just" a writer. Thus, Darragh's censuring letter was a salutary if painful reminder of my primary affiliation. It was very much like being a Jew who has never been subject to anti-Semitic slurs and who hence does not think of herself as different from anyone else, finding herself suddenly in a situation where that Jewishness becomes a relevant fact that must be acknowledged. The absence of any overt objection to the Darragh protest in a setting—Small Press Traffic—in which I had thought I felt at home, momentarily made me withdraw and recognize that, after all, I am not a poet and at a certain point my affiliations have to be elsewhere. And it made me recognize that I am more "academic" than I had probably thought, since I do firmly believe in reasoned discourse. In other words, I felt that argument is one thing—and I would have been happy to engage in public debate with Darragh on what I had said—but that name-calling is another and is something that the rules of our profession make more or less impossible. Think of the conferences you attend and the articles that you read, and consider how little straightforward accusation or even direct attack there is.

Perhaps, I thought, I had gone too far in the other direction, siding with the poets against the academy. Perhaps I had written one too many blurbs, praised one too many poets, and invited too many of them to give readings at my university. Oddly, I now found myself pulling back with a measure of enormous relief! I wanted to do nothing so much as to write on dead poets and artists, on historical movements and trends. When, by coincidence, I was asked a week later to do an omnibus review of Rilke translations, including William Gass's fascinating new book on what translating Rilke means, I was delighted!

This, then, was my lesson in the aporias of affiliation. The poetry community to which I felt I belonged turned its back on me and I responded in kind. But, as I have remarked, only for a moment. For whatever my own situation, I persist in believing that my poet friends are more interesting and often much better read (at least in modern literature) than most of my colleagues, and that poets, despite some of the misguided forays I have mentioned, have the potential to be the best critics. I know that by saying this I am putting myself and people like me out of business, but just as Sir Philip Sidney wrote one of the best poetic treatises of the sixteenth century, just as Samuel Johnson's *Prefaces to Shakespeare* are much greater Shakespeare criticism than that of the professional critics of his day, just as Baudelaire's *Salons* are much more profound works of art criticism than that of the Goncourt brothers, and just as Eliot and Pound put forward poetic principles that are still with us at the beginning of a new century, so I believe that the finest, the most perceptive, the most genuinely engaged criticism of our own time is that of poets. I am thinking of John Ashbery on Raymond Roussel, John Cage on Jasper Johns, Lyn Hejinian on Gertrude Stein, Susan Howe on Emily Dickinson, or Lydia Davis on Maurice Blanchot.

What does all this tell us about affiliation, about the relation of the creative to the critical, which is my subject? As I hope these speculations make clear, the complexity of affiliation today demands ceaseless and uneasy negotiation. And in the long run, that is all to the good. I don't want to be classified by gender, race, religion, or ethnicity, even though these play such a large and complex part in my makeup—or anyone's makeup. I don't want to have to write on women poets because I'm a woman or on Jewish poets because I am Jewish. I also don't want to be classified as an academic *tout court* and have it be assumed—as it is in, say, the MLA—that as academics in the humanities or, more narrowly, in English, we inevitably write for other academics. Nor do I want to be classified as an apologist for one community of poets (in this case, Language poets) at the expense of other writers.

Affiliation—like that in the Language community of the late seventies and eighties—is a two-edged sword. True, by their group manifestos and journals, their small presses, meetings, readings, symposia, and "talk" sessions, the Language poets brought many lesser figures into the fold and created a real sense of community and outreach. Their sheer number and marvelously energetic activity ensured that the rest of the poetry world had to take them into account. At the same time, as individuals within that community have come to the fore—an inevitable evolution in any avant-garde cénacle—back-biting, jealousy, and jockeying for power begin to splinter the field, and the next generation is already on the barricades objecting to the poetic principles of their elders. Without affiliation, it seems, it is impossible in a mass society to function at all, but affiliation, whether academic or literary, whether based on gender or race, ethnicity or class, Ivy League or large state university, can easily become a straitjacket. Once pegged as *X* or *Y*, you no longer need to expand your horizons, to *do better*, or, in Jasper Johns's words, to *do something else*.

Affiliation, I would conclude, involves a necessary dialectic: one moves toward it to move away from it and then back again. When I am with poets I suppose I wear my academic hat; when I'm with academics I find myself speaking for the poetry community with which I have such close ties. If divided loyalties often make me feel I am walking on eggshells, I nevertheless savor the possibility of participating in a discourse unlike the one in which I've been so thoroughly trained and disciplined. Indeed, as our academic routines—the job talk, the syllabus, the interview, the *PMLA* article—

become, as they have, increasingly formulaic, some form of counteraffiliation becomes increasingly appealing. Flexibility, as Frank O'Hara knew so well, is all:

> But me? One day I am thinking of
> A color: orange. Pretty soon it is a
> Whole page of words, not lines.
> Then another page. There should be
> so much more, not of orange, of
> words, of how terrible orange is
> and life. Days go by. It is even in
> prose. I am a real poet. My poem
> is finished and I haven't mentioned
> orange yet. It's twelve poems, I call
> it ORANGES. And one day in a gallery
> I see Mike's painting, called SARDINES.
>   ("Why I Am Not a Painter," *Collected Poems* 262)

Notes

Introduction

1. William Carlos Williams, "The Young Housewife," in *The Collected Poems of William Carlos Williams*, vol. 1, 1909–1939, ed. A. Walton Litz and Christopher MacGowan (New York: New Directions, 1986), 57. "The Young Housewife" was first published in the 1916 issue of *Others* and in book form in *Al Che Quiere* (1917).

2. See Reuben A. Brower, *The Fields of Light: An Experiment in Critical Reading* (New York: Oxford University Press, 1951). Brower's method was to take a poem like Donne's *Extasie* and show that the central metaphor of "interanimation" controls the structure of the whole poem: every word and image underscores the basic notion of interrelatedness. Or again, in *The Tempest* the key design is metamorphosis, the "sea change" that makes everything "rich and strange." And so on.

3. Hugh Kenner, *The Pound Era* (Berkeley: University of California Press, 1971), 404, and see 397–99.

4. My scansion is a simplified version of the standard Trager-Smith scansion using four stresses: primary (/), secondary (/\), tertiary (\) and weak ( ). A caesura is indicated by a double bar (||), a lesser pause by a single bar (|) For an extended analysis of Williams's prosody, see my "'To Give a Design': Williams and the Visualization of Poetry," in *William Carlos Williams: Man and Poet*, ed. Carroll F. Terrell (Orono: National Poetry Foundation, University of Maine at Orono, 1983), 159–86.

5. James E. B. Breslin, *William Carlos Williams, An American Artist* (1970; rpt. Chicago: University of Chicago Press, 1985), 51–52.

6. Hugh Kenner, *A Homemade World: The American Modernist Writers* (New York: Alfred A. Knopf, 1974), 58.

7. Gertrude Stein, "Miss Furr and Miss Skeene," in *Writings, 1903–1932* (New York: Library of America, 1998), 308–09.

8. Cleanth Brooks, *The Well Wrought Urn: Studies in the Structure of Poetry* (New York: Harcourt, Brace, 1947), 163.

9. See John Barrell, "Subject and Sentence; The Poetry of Tom Raworth," *Critical Inquiry* 17 (winter 1991): 386–409; Colin MacCabe, "Dissolving the Voice," Review of Raworth, *Writing, Times Literary Supplement*, 30 December 1983: 1455.

10. Nate Dorward, "On Raworth's Sonnets," *Chicago Review* 47, no. 1 (spring 2001): 17–35, see 18, 21.

11. Tom Raworth, *Collected Poems* (Manchester, Eng.: Carcanet Press, 2003), 37.

12. Philip Larkin, "Home Is So Sad" (1958), *Collected Poems,* ed. Anthony Thwaite (New York: Farrar Straus, 1989), 119.

13. *Microsoft Word Dictionary,* Software for Microsoft Word. MAC OS9.2.

14. *Ace* was originally published by Trigram Press, London, in 1973, with illustrations by Barry Hall. It is now available from Edge Books, Washington, D.C. (2001). *Ace* is reproduced in Tom Raworth, *Collected Poems,* 201–22.

15. See Marcel Duchamp, *Notes,* bilingual edition, presented and trans. Paul Matisse (Paris: Musée National d'Art Moderne, Centre Georges Pompidou, 1980); rpt. Boston: G. K. Hall, 1983, unpaginated, but each example is numbered.

16. See Marjorie Perloff, *Twenty-first-Century Modernism: The New Poetics* (Oxford, UK: Blackwell, 2002), 114–16.

17. Gilles Deleuze, *Difference and Repetition,* trans. Paul Patton (1968; New York: Columbia University Press, 1994), xx–xxi. My emphasis.

18. Ludwig Wittgenstein, *Philosophical Investigations,* 3rd edition, trans. G. E. M. Anscombe (New York: Macmillan, 1958). Where applicable, numbers are those of propositions, not pages.

19. Jennifer Ashton, "Modernism's 'New' Literalism" (review essay), *Modernism/Modernity* 10, no. 2 (April 2003): 387–88, 384. Along with the Language poets, my book *Twenty-first-Century Modernism* is one of Ashton's targets, indeed the occasion for her polemic.

20. Donald Allen and George F. Butterick, eds., *The Postmoderns: The New American Poetry Revised* (New York: Grove Press, 1982). By 1982 Language poetry was already on the scene, but *The Postmoderns* does not yet recognize their presence, focusing on the poets of Allen's famous *New American Poetry, 1945–1960* (1960), with the addition of such of their heirs as Anne Waldman, Joanne Kyger, and Ed Sanders.

21. Jacques Roubaud, "Poésie et pensée: quelques remarques," *Poésie* 92 (April 2002): 49.

22. Oulipo is the acronym for the Ouvroir de littérature potentielle, the Workshop for Potential Literature, founded in Paris in 1960.

23. Susan Howe, *The Midnight* (New York: New Directions, 2003), 49.

Chapter 1

1. Robert Weisbuch, "Six Proposals to Revive the Humanities," *Chronicle of Higher Education,* 26 March 1999, B4–5.

2. In a follow-up article in the *Chronicle of Higher Education,* Weisbuch outlines more fully his plan for "aggressively promulgating the value of what we do in [the humanities]." The Woodrow Wilson National Fellowship Foundation's new project, "Unleashing the Humanities: The Doctorate Beyond the Academy," with a budget of about one hundred thousand dollars, will award grants to academic departments that "encourage students to interact with the world as part of their graduate training." A

second program will award up to thirty grants of fifteen hundred dollars each to support doctoral students who are using their training in a nonacademic setting. The third program seeks "to match top doctoral students with companies, schools, and other employers that can offer them 'meaningful' positions outside academe." See Denise K. Magner, "Finding New Paths for Ph.D.s in the Humanities," *Chronicle of Higher Education*, 16 April 1999, A 16–17.

3. See, for example, Brigitte Hamann, *Hitler's Vienna; A Dictator's Apprenticeship*, trans. Thomas Thornton (New York: Oxford University Press, 1999), 62.

4. See Randal Johnson, "Introduction," Pierre Bourdieu, *The Field of Cultural Production: Essays on Art and Literature*, ed. Randal Johnson (New York: Columbia University Press, 1993), 7.

5. Cited by Patrick Healy, "Today's News," *Chronicle of Higher Education*, 20 September 1999, Internet version at http://chronicle.com.

6. According to the *OED*, *literature* (from the Latin *littera* or letter of the alphabet) as "Literary work or production; the activity or profession of a man of letters; the realm of letters" was first used by Samuel Johnson in the *Life of Cowley* (1779): "An Author whose pregnancy of imagination and elegance of language have deservedly set high in the ranks of literature." The more restricted sense of literature, as a "writing that has claim to consideration on the ground of beauty of form or emotional effect," does not appear until 1812. *Literature* in the sense of "the body of books and writings that treat a particular subject" is first found in 1860.

7. Aristotle, *On Rhetoric: A Theory of Civic Discourse*, trans. George A. Kennedy (New York: Oxford University Press, 1991); Cicero, *Brutus*, trans. G. L. Hendrickson (Cambridge, MA: Loeb Classical Library, 1952); Quintilian, *Institutio Oratoria*, 4 vols., trans. H. E. Butler (Cambridge, MA: Loeb Classical Library, 1921–1922).

8. Groupe Mu, *Rhetorique générale* (Paris, 1970).

9. Michel Meyer, *Questions de rhétorique: langage, raison et séduction* (Paris, 1993); Nancy S. Struever, "Rhetoric: Historical and Conceptual Overview," *Encyclopedia of Aesthetics*, 4 vols., ed. Michael Kelly, vol. 4 (New York: Oxford University Press, 1998), 151–55, esp. 155.

10. Stephen Halliwell, *Aristotle's Poetics*, 2nd edition (Chicago: University of Chicago Press, 1998), 44.

11. Roman Jakobson, "Marginal Notes on the Prose of the Poet Pasternak" (1935), in *Language in Literature*, ed. Krystyna Pomorska and Stephen Rudy (Cambridge, MA: Belknap Press, 1987), 301–17.

12. Stanley Fish, "How Ordinary Is Ordinary Language?" *New Literary History* 5 (1973), Special issue, "What Is Literature?": 41–54; rpt. in Fish, *Is There a Text in This Class? The Authority of Interpretive Communities* (Cambridge, MA: Harvard University Press, 1980), 97–111. I discuss the problems of this essay in *Wittgenstein's Ladder: Poetic Language and the Strangeness of the Ordinary* (Chicago: University of Chicago Press, 1996), 54–57, 88–89.

13. Ludwig Wittgenstein, *Zettel*, ed. G. E. M. Anscombe and G. H. von Wright, trans. G. E. M. Anscombe (Berkeley: University of California Press, 1967), #160, 28.

14. Aristotle, *Poetics*, trans. W. Hamilton Fyfe (Cambridge, MA: Harvard Univer-

sity Press, 1960), 36–37. I have translated the word *philosophoteron* as "philosophical" rather than "scientific," which is misleading. Otherwise, I stick to the Fyfe translation, designating the traditional numbers for paragraphs.

15. Plato, *Republic*, in *The Collected Dialogues of Plato*, ed. Edith Hamilton and Huntington Cairns, trans. Lane Cooper, et al., Corrected edition (Princeton, NJ: Princeton University Press, 1963), #387b, my emphasis. I give the standard paragraph number rather than page since there are so many translations and editions of *Republic*.

16. Hayden White, *Metahistory: The Historical Imagination in Nineteenth-Century Europe* (Baltimore: Johns Hopkins University Press, 1973).

17. Rossetti's work, both verbal and visual, is the subject of Jerome J. McGann's astonishingly comprehensive, beautifully produced, and learned *Rossetti Archive* at http://www.iath.virginia.edu/rossetti.

18. The URLs are, respectively, http://www.samuel-beckett.net; http://www.beckett.english.ucsb.edu; and http://www.literaryhistory.com/20thC/Beckett.htm.

19. See http://www.futurism.org.uk; http://www.toutfait.com; and http://www.ubu.com.

20. See Peter Bürger, *Theory of the Avant-Garde*, foreword by Jochen Schulte-Sasse, trans. Michael Shaw (Minneapolis: University of Minnesota Press, 1984), esp. chapter 3.

21. See Theodor W. Adorno, "On Lyric Poetry and Society," *Notes to Literature*, vol. 1, ed. Rolf Tiedemann, trans. Shierry Weber Nicholsen (New York: Columbia University Press, 1991), 37–54, esp. 45.

22. Theodor W. Adorno, "Heine the Wound," *Notes to Literature*, 80–85; esp. 82.

23. George Steiner, "The Humanities—At Twilight?" *PN Review* 25, no. 4 (March–April 1999): 23. The essay (18–24) was originally presented as a lecture at Boston University on 2 April 1998.

24. Frank O'Hara, "Poem (Lana Turner has collapsed!)," *The Collected Poems of Frank O'Hara*, ed. Donald Allen (Berkeley: University of California Press, 1995), 449.

Chapter 2

1. See T. S. Eliot, letter to Ezra Pound, 24 January 1922, in *The Letters of T. S. Eliot*, vol. 1: 1898–1922, ed. Valerie Eliot (San Diego: Harcourt Brace Jovanovich, 1988), 504. On 27 January, Pound replied to Eliot's query, "I do *not* advise printing G. as preface. One don't miss it AT all as the thing now stands" (*Letters*, 505).

2. The same collection, with minor changes, was published a month later in New York by Alfred A. Knopf under the title *Poems* and has come to be known as *Poems 1920*. The variant texts of the poems in these two volumes is reprinted as Appendix C in T. S. Eliot, *Inventions of the March Hare, Poems 1909–1917*, ed. Christopher Ricks (New York: Harvest Books, 1998), 347–84.

3. See Unsigned Review, "A New Byronism," *Times Literary Supplement*, 18 March 1920; rpt. in *T. S. Eliot: The Critical Heritage*, vol. 1, ed. Michael Grant (London: Routledge & Kegan Paul, 1982), 108; Desmond MacCarthy, "New Poets: T. S.

Eliot," *New Statesman* 8 (January 1921); rpt. in *T. S. Eliot: The Critical Heritage*, 111–17, 115.

4. The text used for "Gerontion" is Eliot's *Collected Poems, 1909–1962* (New York: Harcourt Brace, 1970), 29–31.

5. Bernard Bergonzi, *T. S. Eliot* (New York: Collier, 1972), 55.

6. Stephen Spender, *Eliot* (London: Fontana, 1975), 66–67.

7. In all editions prior to the 1962 *Collected Poems*, the word "Jew" was not capitalized.

8. See Rachel Blau DuPlessis, *Genders, Races, and Religious Cultures in Modern American Poetry, 1908–1934* (New York: Cambridge University Press, 2001), 144.

9. Ludwig Wittgenstein, *Wittgenstein's Lectures, Cambridge, 1930–1932; From the Notes of John King and Desmond Lee*, ed. Desmond Lee (Chicago: University of Chicago Press, 1980), 112.

10. Ludwig Wittgenstein, *Philosophical Investigations*, 3rd edition, trans. G. E. M. Anscombe (New York: Macmillan, 1968), #19.

11. For Eliot's sources and allusions in "Gerontion," see B. C. Southam, *A Guide to the Selected Poems of T. S. Eliot* (New York: Harcourt Brace & World, 1968), 43–47. Most Eliot commentaries like Grover Smith's *T. S. Eliot's Poetry and Plays: A Study in Sources and Meaning*, rev. ed. (Chicago: University of Chicago Press, 1960), explain these references. The most recent step-by-step explication of the poem is Denis Donoghue's in *Words Alone: The Poet T. S. Eliot* (New Haven, CT: Yale University Press, 2000), 77–95.

12. Hugh Kenner, *The Invisible Poet: T. S. Eliot* (New York: Harcourt Brace, 1959), 125.

13. Scansion is as follows: primary stress (/), secondary stress (/\), plus juncture or short grammatical pause (|), caesura (||), enjambment (>). Alliterative and assonantal letters are italicized.

14. Julius relates Gerontion's "Here I am" to Abraham's "Behold, here I am," spoken in response to God's call in Genesis. But whereas Abraham's words fix his identity, Gerontion's never do (63).

15. See, for example, Southam, *Guide to the Selected Poems*, 45–47.

16. See Lyndall Gordon, *T. S. Eliot: An Imperfect Life* (New York: Norton, 1999), 137.

17. Leyris's translation may be found, next to some passages translated by Jean Wahl, in a very useful essay by Joan Fillmore Hooker called "Visions and Revisions: 'Gerontion' in French," in Laura Cowan, ed., *T. S. Eliot: Man and Poet*, vol. 1 (Orono: National Poetry Foundation, University of Maine, 1990), 125–48; see Appendix, 146–48.

18. Jewel Spears Brooker, "Eliot in the Dock: A Review Essay," *South Atlantic Review* 62, no. 4 (fall 1996): 107–14, 112.

19. Christopher Ricks, *T. S. Eliot and Prejudice* (Berkeley: University of California Press, 1988), 29. Hugh Kenner (129) similarly notes that "the Jew who was spawned in some estaminet of Antwerp cannot but prolong into the present the reputation of another who was born in a different inn," and Brooker notes that the etymology of *estaminet* (little café) is *barn* or *cowhouse* (310), so that the reference is indeed to Christ in the Bethlehem manger.

20. *Letters,* 310–11, emphasis mine. Cf. Eliot's letter of 17 June 1919 to his niece Eleanor Hinkley. Here he describes at length the petty jealousies and endless gossip of Bloomsbury, where "A. gets in a funk lest I hear of this and trace it to her, and anxiously confides in Vivien. A. you see hates B. and also is jealous of her. She therefore repeats my remarks to D" (*Letters,* 304–05). And so on. Such a dinner party, Eliot tells Eleanor, is harder to manage than "the best fencing match or duel" (305).

21. For the sordid story of Vivien Haigh-Wood's affair with Russell, which went on intermittently from 1915 to 1918, see Ray Monk, *Bertrand Russell: The Spirit of Solitude, 1872–1921* (New York: Free Press, 1996), 432–50, 487–91; Carole Seymour-Jones, *Painted Shadow: The Life of Vivienne Eliot, First Wife of T. S. Eliot, and the Long-Suppressed Truth about Her Influence on His Genius* (New York: Nan A. Talese, Doubleday, 2001), 93–106 and *passim.* Seymour-Jones, whose sympathies are always with Vivien, may be exaggerating Russell's treachery, but her basic story accords entirely with Monk's.

22. See *Collected Poems,* 57–59, and cf. Seymour-Jones, *Painted Shadow,* 308–10.

23. According to the *OED:* "*Scapegoat* (1530). 'Goat sent into the wilderness on the Day of Atonement, symbolic bearer of the sins of the people,' coined by Tyndale from scape (M.E. aphetic form of escape) + goat, to translate L. caper emissarius, mistranslation in Vulgate of Heb. 'azazel (Lev. xvi.8, 10, 26), which was read as 'ez ozel 'goat that departs,' but is actually the proper name of a devil or demon in Jewish mythology (sometimes identified with Canaanite deity Aziz). Meaning 'one who is blamed or punished for the mistakes or sins of others,' first recorded 1824."

24. In *Eliot in Perspective, A Symposium,* ed. Graham Martin (New York: Humanities Press, 1972), 83–101, Gabriel Pearson points out that the plural ending of *rocks* "is disturbed by being echoed by the singular 'moss' to be pluralled in its own turn by the initial *s* of 'stonecrop.' . . . Though one gets images, a landscape of sorts, one hardly reads past and through the words to a world without" (85).

25. In the typescript and in *Ara vos prec,* these two lines were set off from the rest; see Ricks, *March Hare,* 349.

26. John Crowe Ransom, "Gerontion," in Allen Tate, ed., *T. S. Eliot: The Man and His Work; A Critical Evaluation by Twenty-six Distinguished Writers* (New York: Delacorte, 1966), 151.

Chapter 3

1. Sanehide Kodama, "Cathay and Fenollosa's Notebooks," *Paideuma* 11 (fall 1982): 207–40. The Fenollosa manuscript in question is File #20 in the Yale Collection of American Literature, Beinecke Library, Yale University. The poem itself may be found in Ezra Pound, *Personae: The Shorter Poems of Ezra Pound,* a revised edition prepared by Lea Baechler and A. Walton Litz (New York: New Directions, 1990), 134.

2. See Ronald Bush, "Pound and Li Po: What Becomes a Man," in *Ezra Pound among the Poets,* ed. George Bornstein (Chicago: University of Chicago Press, 1985), 35–62; Wai-Lim Yip, *Ezra Pound's Cathay* (Princeton, NJ: Princeton University Press,

1969), 88–92; Robert Kern, *Orientalism, Modernism, and the American Poem* (Cambridge, Eng.: Cambridge University Press, 1996), 197–201.

3. See K. K. Ruthven, *A Guide to Ezra Pound's Personae, 1926* (Berkeley: University of California Press, 1969), 206: "Japanese *Cho-fu-sa* from Chinese *Ch'ang-feng-sha* . . . the long Wind Beach . . . in An-hwei, several hundred miles up the river from Nanking."

4. Hugh Kenner, who cites this example in *The Pound Era* (Berkeley: University of California Press, 1971), 204, also notes that in "Song of the Bowmen of Shu," the reference to the "flying general" "Ri" (he was the famous Ri Shogun during the Kan dynasty) becomes "Rishogu" (see 221).

5. Yunte Huang, e-mail letter to the author, 17 April 2002. I am indebted to Huang's suggestions about Chinese names, idioms, and references throughout this essay; see his *Transpacific Displacement: Ethnography, Translation, and Intertextual Travel in Twentieth-Century American Literature* (Berkeley: University of California Press, 2002), 60–92.

6. See "A Retrospect" (1918), *The Literary Essays of Ezra Pound*, ed. T. S. Eliot (London: Faber and Faber, 1954), 3; Ezra Pound, "I Gather the Limbs of Osiris" (1911–1912), *Selected Prose, 1909–1965*, ed. William Cookson (New York: New Directions, 1973), 21–25; Ezra Pound, *ABC of Reading* (New York: New Directions, 1960), 36.

7. Ezra Pound, *Gaudier-Brzeska; A Memoir by Ezra Pound* (1916; New York: New Directions, 1970), 81–92.

8. *ABC of Reading*, 21.

9. Ezra Pound, "The Approach to Paris," *New Age* 13 (1913): 662; *Selected Prose*, 23.

10. Hugh Kenner, "The Possum in the Cave," in *Allegory and Representation*, ed. Stephen J. Greenblatt (Baltimore: Johns Hopkins University Press, 1981), 140, and see Kenner, "The Invention of China," *Pound Era*, 192–222. The poem, says Kenner, "may build its effects out of things it sets before the mind's eye by naming them" (199). Cf. Richard Sieburth, ed., *A Walking Tour in Southern France: Ezra Pound among the Troubadours* (New York: New Directions, 1992), "Introduction," vii–xxi.

11. Ezra Pound, "Digest of the Analects," *Guide to Kulchur* (New York: New Directions, 1952), 16. The reference is to *Analects* 13, 3.

12. Fung Yu-Lan, *A Short History of Chinese Philosophy*, ed. Derk Bodde (1948; New York: Free Press, 1976), 41–42.

13. Ezra Pound, *The Cantos* (New York: New Directions, 1993), 298. Subsequently cited as C. Numbers after slash mark refer to line number in a given Canto.

14. Michael André Bernstein, *The Tale of the Tribe: Ezra Pound and the Modern Verse Epic* (Princeton, NJ: Princeton University Press, 1980), 45–46.

15. See *Oxford Paperback Encyclopedia* (Oxford: Oxford University Press, 1998).

16. Jean-Michel Rabaté, *Language, Sexuality, and Ideology in Ezra Pound's Cantos* (Albany: SUNY Press, 1986), 175. Daniel Tiffany, in *Radio Corpse: Imagism and the Cryptaesthetic of Ezra Pound* (Cambridge, MA: Harvard University Press, 1995), 20–36 and passim, carries this even further, arguing that for Pound, "Image is equivocally, but intentionally, *nonvisual*, insofar as it resists, contests, and mediates the ex-

perience of visuality, but also in its preoccupation with the invisible" (21); as such, the Image is part of a larger "submerged economy of loss and mourning" (27).

17. Pound's dates are 1885–1973; Duchamp's are 1887–1968.

18. Marcel Duchamp, *A L'Infinitif,* in *The Essential Writings of Marcel Duchamp: Salt Seller = Marchand du Sel,* ed. Michel Sanouillet and Elmer Peterson (London: Thames and Hudson, 1975), 74. See "The Conceptual Poetics of Marcel Duchamp," Perloff, *Twenty-first-Century Modernism* (Oxford, UK: Blackwell, 2001), 77–120.

19. See Marcel Duchamp, *Notes,* presentation and translation by Paul Matisse (Paris: Musée National d'Art Moderne, Centre Georges Pompidou, 1980; rpt. Boston: G. K. Hall, 1983), #185. Figure 3 reproduces the orthography of the actual note as it appears in French. The numbered notes are reproduced as facsimile scraps, with the French and English print versions at the bottom of the page. Slash marks indicate the end of the line in the handwritten version. The book is unpaginated.

20. Thierry de Duve, *Pictorial Nominalism on Marcel Duchamp's Passage from Painting to the Readymade,* trans. Dana Polan with the author (Minneapolis: University of Minnesota Press, 1991), 126–27.

21. See Andrew Clearfield, "Pound, Paris, and Dada," *Paideuma* 7, no. 1 & 2 (spring and fall 1978): 113–40.

22. Richard Sieburth, "Dada Pound," *South Atlantic Quarterly* 83, no. 1 (winter 1984): 44–68; see 60.

23. See my "Dada without Duchamp; Duchamp without Dada: Avant-Garde Tradition and the Individual Talent," *Stanford Humanities Review* 7, no. 1 (1999): 48–78.

24. Canto 78/500–501, lines 62–88. For convenience, I have numbered the lines here starting with 1.

25. "It is sometimes said in the village / that a helmet has no use / none at all / It is only good to give courage / to those who don't have any at all." See Carroll F. Terrell, ed., *A Companion to the Cantos of Ezra Pound,* 2 vols. (Berkeley: University of California Press, 1980–1984), 2: 418. The *Companion* does not tell us whether this stanza is meant to be spoken or sung.

26. The line *"E fa di clarità l'aer tremare"* has its particular resonances for Pound. In his 1910 introduction to his early Cavalcanti translations, Pound takes on the poet's early editors, complaining that they transcribed Cavalcanti's manuscript incorrectly: *e fa di clarità tremar l'are,* perhaps this version is more "musical." But in Sonneto VII—as Pound prints it, the line Sonneto 7 itself—the line in question is *"Che fa di clarità l'aer tremare,"* which Pound, ignoring the relative pronoun, translates in his best "archaic" style as "And making the air to tremble with a bright clearness" (see Pound, *Translations I* [New York: New Directions, 1967], 24, 38–39). As Wallace Martin has pointed out to me (e-mail, 25 March 2002), "Pound's fanaticism about the shades of difference between manuscripts and between reciting and singing a poem" aligns his nominalism with Duchamp's *infrathin.*

27. See Humphrey Carpenter, *A Serious Character: The Life of Ezra Pound* (London: Faber & Faber, 1988), 30.

28. Pierre Cabanne, *Dialogues with Marcel Duchamp*, trans. Ron Padgett (New York: Viking, 1971), 41–43.

29. In French, the title of the *Large Glass* (*Verre Grand*)—*La Mariée mise à nu par ses célibataires, même*—contains a host of puns: e.g., *Mariée/m'art y est/Mar(cel) y est; célibataires/sel y va taire; même/m'aime.*

30. Yunte Huang, e-mail to author, 17 April 2002.

Chapter 4

1. William H. Gass, *Reading Rilke: Reflections on the Problems of Translation* (New York: Alfred A. Knopf, 1999), 57–58.

2. See Marjorie Perloff, "Reading Gass Reading Rilke," *Parnassus* 25, no. 1 & 2 (2001): 486–508.

3. Eva Hesse and Heinz Ickstadt, eds., *Amerikanische Dichtung von den Anfängen bis zur Gegenwart* (Munich: Beck, 2000), 374–75.

4. Ludwig Wittgenstein, *Tractatus-Logico-Philosophicus* [German-English parallel text], trans. C. K. Ogden (1922; London: Routledge, 1990). References are to numbered sections. *Wittgenstein's Lectures, Cambridge, 1930–1931; From the Notes of John King and Desmond Lee*, ed. Desmond Lee (Chicago: University of Chicago Press, 1989), 112. Subsequently cited in the text as *Lectures* 1.

5. Wittgenstein, *Philosophical Investigations* [German-English parallel text], eds. G. E. M. Anscombe and Rush Rhees, 2nd edition (1953; Oxford, UK: Blackwell, 1999). References are to sections of part 1 and to pages of part 2.

6. Jacques Bouveresse, *Le Mythe de l'interiorité; expérience, signification et langage privé chez Wittgenstein* (Paris: Éditions de Minuit, 1987), 464.

7. Ludwig Wittgenstein, *Culture and Value* [German-English parallel text], ed. G. H. von Wright, in collaboration with Heikki Nyman, trans. Peter Winch (Oxford, UK: Blackwell, 1980), 24. There is no exact English equivalent of the German verb *Dichten*. The closest would be something like *poetize*, but this is not an actual English word. Peter Winch translates the sentence in question as "Philosophy ought really to be written only as a poetic composition." This seems to me to rationalize the German excessively, so I have used, for this passage, David Antin's idiomatic translation ("Wittgenstein among the Poets," *Modernism, Modernity* 5, no. 1 [Jan. 1998]: 161). The verb *Dichten* also means "to make thick or dense" and "to fictionalize." Given these variations, it may be objected that, like Rilke's language, Wittgenstein's defies translation. But there is a significant difference: however awkward translations of the word *Dichten* may be, the basic meaning of the construction—that philosophy to be more like its seeming opposite, poetry or fiction, the thickening of language—remains the same.

8. Ludwig Wittgenstein, *Lectures and Conversations on Aesthetics, Psychology, and Religious Belief*, ed. Cyril Barrett (Berkeley: University of California Press, 1966), 11.

9. See *Briefwechsel*, ed. B. F. McGuinness and G. H. von Wright. Correspondence with B. Russell, G. E. Moore, J. M. Keynes, F. Ramsey, et al. In German, with original

version of Wittgenstein's own letters in English, in an appendix; German translations by J. Schulte (Frankfurt am Main: Suhrkamp, 1980), 47, 22, 47, 78, respectively.

10. See *Briefwechsel*, 78; *Culture and Value*, 67, 41.

11. Franz Parak, "Wittgenstein in Monte Cassino," in Ludwig Wittgenstein, *Geheime Tagebücher, 1914–1916*, ed. W. Baum (Wien: Turia & Kant, 1991), 146, 152.

12. See Marjorie Perloff, *Wittgenstein's Ladder: Poetic Language and the Strangeness of the Ordinary* (Chicago: University of Chicago Press, 1996), 42–43.

13. Ludwig Wittgenstein, *Zettel* [German-English parallel text], ed. G. E. M. Anscombe and G. H. von Wright, trans. G. E. M. Anscombe (1945–1948; Berkeley: University of California Press, 1970). References are to numbered propositions.

14. Sol LeWitt, "Paragraphs on Conceptual Art," in *Artforum* 5, no. 10 (summer 1967): 80. There are, of course, other important aspects of Conceptualism: see the excellent entries on "Conceptual Art," including the LeWitt reference, in Michael Kelly, ed., *Encyclopedia of Aesthetics*, 4 vols. (New York: Oxford University Press, 1988), I: 414–27. "The grand strategy," writes Yair Guttmann, "was to resist the attempts to sever the art object from its context" (I: 422). The relation of Joseph Kosuth to Wittgenstein is discussed in I: 426–27.

15. Ludwig Wittgenstein, *Wittgenstein's Lectures, Cambridge 1932–1935; From the Notes of Alice Ambrose and Margaret MacDonald*, ed. Alice Ambrose (Chicago: University of Chicago Press, 1979), 13.

16. Ludwig Wittgenstein, *Les Cours de Cambridge, 1932–1935*, ed. Alice Ambrose; trans. Elisabeth Rigal (Mauvezin, France: Trans-Europ-Repress), 26.

17. Ludwig Wittgenstein, *Philosophical Occasions, 1912–1951* [German-English parallel texts where appropriate], ed. James Klagge and Alfred Nordmann (Indianapolis: Hackett, 1993), 167.

18. Antin, "Wittgenstein among the Poets," 263. Cf. Marjorie Perloff, "Introduction," David Antin, *Talking* (1972; Elmwood Park, IL: Dalkey Archive, 2001), iv–v.

19. The *Larousse* defines a lipogram as "a literary work in which one compels oneself strictly to exclude one or several letters of the alphabet." See Harry Mathews, in Harry Mathews and Alistair Brotchie, eds., *Oulipo Compendium* (London: Atlas, 1998), 174–75.

20. Warren F. Motte Jr., ed. and trans., *Oulipo: A Primer of Potential Literature* (Lincoln: University of Nebraska Press, 1986), 16–17.

21. Jacques Roubaud, *Quelque chose noir* (Paris: Gallimard, 1986); Rosmarie Waldrop, trans., *some thing black* (Elmwood Park, IL: Dalkey Archive, 1990). Note that in Waldrop's translation, the space between "some" and "thing" (like "quelque" and "chose") suggests that the reference is not only to something black but to some black thing. All further references to the poetic sequence are to these two texts.

22. Jacques Roubaud, "The *Oulipo* and the Combinatorial Art," in *Oulipo Compendium*, 38.

23. Dante, *La Vita Nuova*, trans. Barbara Reynolds (Baltimore: Penguin, 1969), 29.

24. See Ann Beer, "Beckett's Bilingualism," in *The Cambridge Companion to Beckett*, ed. John Pilling (Cambridge, Eng.: Cambridge University Press, 1994), 209–21.

25. Samuel Beckett, *Molloy* (1955; New York: Grove Weidenfeld, 1989), 7; Erich Franzen, trans., Beckett, *Molloy* (Frankfurt am Main: Suhrkamp, 1975), 5.

Chapter 5

1. Eugene Jolas, *Man from Babel*, ed. Andreas Kramer and Rainer Rumold (New Haven, CT: Yale University Press, 1998), 5.

2. Henry James, *The Question of Our Speech; The Lesson of Balzac: Two Lectures* (Boston: Houghton Mifflin, 1905), 3, 16, 43. For further discussion of this astonishing essay, see Peter Quartermain, *Disjunctive Poetics: From Gertrude Stein and Louis Zukofsky to Susan Howe* (Cambridge, Eng.: Cambridge University Press, 1992), 9–12.

3. The following Stein pieces were published in *transition*, subsequently cited as T: "An Elucidation," T 1 (April 1927): 64–78; "As a Wife Has a Cow," T 3 (June 1927): 10–14; "Studies in Conversation," T 6 (September 1927): 74–78; "Made a Mile Away," T 8 (November 1927): 155–65; "A Novel of Desertion," T 10 (January 1928): 9–13; "Dan Raffel, A Nephew," T 12 (March 1928): 51–52; "Descriptions of Literature," T 13 (summer 1928): 50–53; "An Instant Answer or a Hundred Prominent Men," T 13 (summer 1928): 118–30; "Four Saints in Three Acts, An Opera to be Sung," T 16–17 (June 1929): 39–72; "She Bowed to Her Brother," T 21 (March 1932): 100–03. And further, *transition* 14 (February 1929) contains a complete Stein bibliography of writings to date, see 47–55.

4. In *transition* 3 (June 1927), which contained Stein's "As a Wife Has a Cow" as lead-off piece, as well as Laura Riding's "The New Barbarism and Gertrude Stein," the editorial praises Stein as an "abstract artist," who "compos[es] her word patterns without an accompanying text of obvious explanations" (177). In the December 1927 issue, Jolas defends Stein against the notorious attack by Wyndham Lewis (see 172). And in "The Revolution of Language and James Joyce," *transition* 11 (February 1928), Jolas writes: "Miss Gertrude Stein attempts to find a mysticism of the word by the process of thought thinking itself. In structurally spontaneous compositions in which words are grouped rhythmically, she succeeds in giving us her mathematics of the word, clear, primitive and beautiful" (111). The note for the *Anthologie*, longer than any of the others, declares "*Tender Buttons*, paru il y a quelques années, l'a montrée comme possédant un vrai génie d'innovation dans le style, et ses derniers livres n'ont aucun rapport avec les genres littéraires que nous connaissons" (217).

5. Jolas's "proclamation" of "The Revolution of the Word" has been reproduced in Jerome Rothenberg, *The Revolution of the Word: A New Gathering of American Avant-Garde Poetry, 1914–1945* (New York: Seabury Press, 1974), 150; rpt. Exact Change, Boston, 1998. The signatories were Kay Boyle, Whit Burnett, Hart Crane, Caresse Crosby, Harry Crosby, Martha Foley, Stuart Gilbert, A. L. Gillespie, Leigh Hoffman, Eugene Jolas, Elliot Paul, Douglas Rigby, Theo Rutra (a Jolas pseudonym), Robert Sage, Harold J. Salemson, and Laurence Vail.

6. Samuel Beckett, "Dante . . . Bruno. Vico..Joyce," in *Our Exagmination Round His Factification for Incamination of Work in Progress* (Paris: Shakespeare and Co.,

1929); rpt. in *Disjecta: Miscellaneous Writings and a Dramatic Fragment,* ed. Ruby Cohn (New York: Grove Press, 1984), 27–28.

7. Samuel Beckett, letter to Charles Prentice, 23 March 1931, cited in James Knowlson, *Damned to Fame: The Life of Samuel Beckett* (New York: Simon & Schuster, 1996), 156. Chatto & Windus turned down Beckett's manuscript almost immediately.

8. James Joyce, *Finnegans Wake* (1939; New York: Penguin, 1976), 214. The passage first appeared in *transition* 8 (November 1927) as follows: "Do you tell me that now? I do in troth. And didn't you hear it a deluge of times? You deed, you deed! I need, I need!" For a discussion of the revisions and an explication of etymologies and derivations, see A. Walton Litz, *The Art of James Joyce: Method and Design in Ulysses and Finnegans Wake* (New York: Oxford University Press, 1964), 105–08.

9. Jean-Michel Rabaté, *James Joyce, Authorized Reader* (Baltimore: Johns Hopkins University Press, 1991), 120–23, 145.

10. Eugene Jolas, "Slanguage: 1929," T 16–17 (June 1928): 32–33.

11. T 21 (March 1932): 323–25.

12. *Man from Babel,* 18. The lines read: "I stand on the battlements, reaching up to the sky; / Alone in the sunset glow; / The wild city roars violently around me; / My dreambound heart beats in steel and stone."

13. The version cited in *Man from Babel* (109) is slightly different. "Ivilley" is "ivlleyo"; "morrowlei" is "lorroley"; "meaves" is "neaves"; "sardinewungs" becomes "sardine-swungs"; "flight" becomes "light"; "mickmecks" becomes "mickmacks." It is not clear whether these are transcription errors, misprints, or intentional changes.

14. The subtitle first appears in *transition* 21 (March 1932), when Jolas began to turn increasingly inward in response to the two great totalitarianisms of the day. This issue contains the roundtable "Crisis of Man," in which Stein, Jung, Benn, and Frobenius, among others, comment on the "evolution of individualism and metaphysics under a collectivist regime" (107).

15. T 23 (July 1935): 65. The title, "Mots-Frontiere," is odd: the correct grammar and spelling would make it "Mots-frontières." Again, "neumond," "wunder," and "tal" should be capitalized. Throughout this and related poems, Jolas tends to reproduce German nouns without the required initial capital.

16. Dougald McMillan, *Transition: The History of a Literary Era, 1927–1938* (New York: George Braziller, 1976), 117.

17. "Contrastes," the third of Cendrars's *Dix-neuf poèmes élastiques,* begins with the line "Les fenêtres de ma poésie sont grand'ouvertes sur les boulevards et dans ses vitrines"; see Blaise Cendrars, *Du Monde entier au coeur du monde* (Paris: Denoël, 1947), 56.

18. "Intrialogue" and "Verbairrupta of the Mountainmen" appeared in T 22 (February 1933): 21–23, "Frontier-Poem" in the final (tenth anniversary) issue, T 27 (1938).

19. See, on this point, Jerome Rothenberg and Pierre Joris, *Poems for the Millen-*

nium: The University of California Book of Modern and Postmodern Poetry, vol. 2, From Postwar to Millennium (Berkeley: University of California Press, 1998), "Introduction," especially 11–12, as well as the many examples of polyglot works in the text.

20. Kamau Brathwaite, *Trench Town Rock* (Providence, RI: Lost Roads, 1994), 9.

21. Alfred Arteaga, *Cantos* (Berkeley, CA: Chusma House, 1991), 20.

22. Theresa Hak Kyung Cha, *Dictee* (Berkeley: University of California Press, 2001), cited from *Poems for the Millennium,* vol. 2, 838.

23. Edward Kamau Brathwaite, *History of the Voice: The Development of Nation Language in Anglophone Caribbean Poetry* (London: New Beacon Books, 1984), 13.

24. Joan Dayan, "Who's Got History: Kamau Brathwaite's 'Gods of the Middle Passage,'" *World Literature Today: Kamau Brathwaite,* 1994 Neustadt International Prize for Literature Issue, 68, no. 4 (autumn 1994): 727.

25. Kamau Brathwaite, *Barabajan Poems, 1492–1992* (Kingston: Savacou North, 1994), 378. In "Wordsongs & Wordwounds/Homecoming: Kamau Brathwaite's *Barabajan Poems*" (*World Literature Today: Kamau Brathwaite,* 750–57), Elaine Savory discusses the poet's "video style." "Bob'ob" was Brathwaite's grandfather's brother, a carpenter; "Kapo" is a Jamaican folk wood sculptor called Mallacai Reynolds whom Brathwaite knew in the mid-1970s (see "Wordsongs," 756, note 5).

26. See "Wordsongs," 751.

27. See Michael Holquist and Caryl Emerson, "Glossary," in M. M. Bahktin, *The Dialogic Imagination: Four Essays,* ed. Michael Holquist, trans. Caryl Emerson and Michael Holquist (Austin: University of Texas Press, 1981), 425.

28. See Walter K. Lew, *Excerpts from Dikte for Dictée* (Seoul, Korea: Yeul Eum, 1992), cited in *Poems for the Millennium,* vol. 2, 844.

29. While I was completing this essay, I received issue 5 of *Chain,* "Different Languages" (1998), ed. Jena Osman and Juliana Spahr. Most of the work in this issue is bilingual (often English and Spanish) or multilingual, in keeping with the aesthetic of Brathwaite and Cha rather than the internationalism of Jolas, although many of the experiments, like Will Lavender's "Glossolalia" (125–29) and Jessie Jane Lewis and Peter Rose's "Pressures of the Text" (130–37), interpret multilingualism as the insertion, into the English structure, of technological languages, dialects, pictograms, visual devices, and so on. In any case, as we see in *Chain,* multilingualism is very much in the air.

Chapter 6

1. See Raymond Kuhn, *The Media in France* (London: Routledge, 1995), 87–89; James Knowlson, *Damned to Fame: The Life of Samuel Beckett* (New York: Simon & Schuster, 1996), 305–08.

2. Michel Serres, "Platonic Dialogue" (1968), in Serres, *Hermes: Literature, Sci-*

ence, Philosophy, ed. Josué V. Harari and David F. Bell (Baltimore: Johns Hopkins University Press, 1982), 65.

3. Martin Esslin, "Samuel Beckett and the Art of Radio," *Mediations: Essays on Brecht, Beckett, and the Media* (New York: Grove Press, 1982), 125–54; rpt. in *On Beckett: Essays and Criticism,* ed. S. E. Gontarski (New York: Grove Press, 1986), 366. In a related essay, "The Mind as Stage—Radio Drama" (*Mediations,* 171–87), Esslin relates "blind" radio to the silent cinema but observes that the analogy breaks down because radio "can evoke the visual element by suggestion alone" (172).

4. Klaus Schöning, "The Contours of Acoustic Art," in *Theatre Journal* 43, no. 3 (October 1991): Special issue, "Radio Drama," ed. Everett Frost, 312. Schöning's is one of the best treatments I have seen on the larger issues involved in radio art.

5. Don Druker, "Listening to the Radio," *Theatre Journal* 43: 334.

6. For discussions of the productions themselves, see Clas Zilliacus, *Beckett and Broadcasting: A Study of the Works of Samuel Beckett for and in Radio and Television,* Acta Academiae Aboensis, Ser. A. Humaniora, vol. 51, no. 2 (Abo, Finland: Abo Akademi, 1976), 76–98; Jonathan Kalb, "The Mediated Quixote: The Radio and Television Plays, and *Film,*" in *The Cambridge Companion to Beckett,* ed. John Pilling (Cambridge, Eng.: Cambridge University Press, 1994), 124–44; Katharine Worth, "Beckett and the Radio Medium," in *British Radio Drama,* ed. John Drakakis (Cambridge, Eng.: Cambridge University Press, 1981), 202–08; and Donald Wicher, "'Out of the Dark': Beckett's Texts for Radio," in *Beckett's Later Fiction and Drama: Texts for Company,* ed. James Acheson and Kateryna Arthur (New York: St. Martin's Press, 1987), 8–10.

7. The designation "skullscape" is Linda Ben Zvi's, "soulscape" is Ruby Cohn's, both in the recorded discussion that follows the production of *Embers* for the Beckett Festival of Radio Plays, recorded at the BBC Studios, London, in January 1988. The director/producer for *Embers,* as for *Words and Music* (see the next section), was Everett Frost; the associate producer, Faith Wilding; and the project originator, Martha Fehsenfeld. In the BBC production, Barry McGovern played Henry, Billie Whitelaw played Ada, Michael Deacon was the Riding Master/Music Master, Tika Viker-Bloss was Addie, and Henry Strozier, the host for the production. In *Words and Music,* David Warrilow played Words (Joe) and Alvin Epstein, Croak; the music was performed by the Bowery Ensemble, conducted by Nils Vigeland. National Public Radio broadcast the five-part series of radio plays on Beckett's birthday, April 13, 1989. The Beckett Festival cassettes are available from the Pacifica Radio Archive (818–506–1077, or through their Web site at http://www.pacificaradioarchives.org).

For Cohn's analysis of *Embers,* see also her *Just Play: Beckett's Theater* (Princeton, NJ: Princeton University Press, 1980), 84–86. *Embers,* writes Cohn, "is a paradigm of most of Beckett's subsequent author-character combinations. Set in a human mind, spare of referential content, dramatic stories condense toward incantation" (86).

8. Even at this level, however, there are problems. Kalb says, for example, that Henry "may or may not be walking by the sea with his daughter Addie nearby," thus

ignoring the complex time shifts: in the present of the play's opening, Addie has long been dead. Kalb also refers oddly to Ada as Henry's "companion" rather than what she so evidently is—his wife—and the two, as I will suggest later, by no means merely "reminisce about old times."

9. Samuel Beckett, letter to Barney Rosset, his U.S. publisher (Grove Press), 27 August 1957, cited in Zilliacus, *Beckett and Broadcasting*, as frontispiece; and in Everett C. Frost, "A 'Fresh Go' for the Skull: Directing *All That Fall*, Samuel Beckett's Play for Radio," in *Directing Beckett*, ed. Lois Oppenheim (Ann Arbor: University of Michigan Press, 1997), 191.

10. John Pilling, *Samuel Beckett* (London: Routledge and Kegan Paul, 1973), 98.

11. *Embers*, in Samuel Beckett, *Collected Shorter Plays* (New York: Grove Press, 1984), 91–104, see 96. All references to *Embers* are to this edition. For an interesting discussion of mediumistic evocation in *Embers* in relation to Yeats's *Words upon the Window-Pane*, see Worth, "Beckett and the Radio Medium," 196–208.

12. *Embers*, 93. Although my reading here and throughout is based on the Beckett Festival recording in conjunction with the text, I use the text as score, since Beckett indicates what the quality of voice is meant to be. Such scoring has its problems; it is not quite true to the actual experience of hearing a work a single time (or even several times) on the air. Following Beckett's written text allows me to reread, reconsider, and compare passages in nonlinear ways. But since presumably Beckett would have wanted us to study a given recording, not just listen to it once, the use of text as score, in conjunction with the recording, is not, I hope, a violation of his purpose.

13. See my "Between Verse and Prose: Beckett and the New Poetry," *Critical Inquiry* 9, no. 2 (December 1982): 415–34; rpt. in Gontarski, *On Beckett*, 191–206.

14. Zilliacus, *Beckett and Broadcasting*, 85. Zilliacus argues that the Henry-Bolton parallel is more convincing than the father-Bolton one, "because it leaves the play more coherent. . . . Henry's father, whether he committed suicide or not, found a way out: his story has been finished. Henry, like Bolton, has to go on: the Bolton story is doomed to remain unfinished because Henry himself is not finished." Cf. Ludovic Janvier, *Pour Samuel Beckett* (Paris: Les Éditions de Minuit, 1966), 126, 129; John Fletcher and John Spurling, *Beckett: A Study of His Plays* (London: Eyre Methuen, 1972), 97.

15. Wicher, "'Out of the Dark,'" 10. Again, Ruby Cohn follows Hersh Zeifman's lead in taking the characters to be "embers of the Christian faith, with an implied equation between Henry-Bolton-victim Christ and father-Holloway-savior Christ"; see Cohn, *Just Play*, 85, and cf. Hersh Zeifman, "Religious Imagery in the Plays of Samuel Beckett," in Ruby Cohn, ed., *Samuel Beckett: A Collection of Criticism* (New York: McGraw-Hill, 1975), 90.

16. Samuel Beckett, *Company* (New York: Grove Press, 1980), 18.

17. H. Porter Abbott, *Beckett Writing Beckett: The Author in the Autograph* (Ithaca, NY: Cornell University Press, 1996), 17.

18. Charles Grivel, "The Phonograph's Horned Mouth," in *Wireless Imagina-*

tion: Sound, Radio, and the Avant-Garde, ed. Douglas Kahn and Gregory Whitehead (Cambridge, MA: MIT Press, 1992), 35.

19. *Archives of Silence, 1997: Q3, 4'33"* The Box Set, http://www.newalbion.com/artists/cagej/silence/html/1997q3/0117.h tml, 20 July 1997.

20. See Katharine Worth, "Words and Music Perhaps," in *Samuel Beckett and Music,* ed. Mary Bryden (New York: Clarendon Press, 1998), 9–20. I have not heard the Searle score, but Worth's discussion suggests that it was much more mimetic than Feldman's in its treatment of the Beckett text.

21. For the background of the relationship, see Everett Frost, "The Note Man on the Word Man: Morton Feldman on Composing the Music for Samuel Beckett's *Words and Music* in *The Beckett Festival of Radio Plays,*" in Bryden, *Samuel Beckett and Music,* 47–55. The bulk of this article is an interview with Feldman, most of which is reproduced on the cassette tape itself. See also Knowlson, *Damned to Fame,* 557–58. Cf. the *Apmonia* Web site compiled and written by Tim Conley and A. Ruch, http://www.themodernword.com/beckett/beckett_feldman.html. This site contains key biographical information about Feldman as well as analyses of each of the "Beckett" pieces.

22. Katharine Worth implies the same thing throughout "Words and Music Perhaps." Humphrey Searle is praised for underscoring Beckett's meanings; his position is assumed to be secondary.

23. Gregory Whitehead, "Out of the Dark; Notes on the Nobodies of Radio Art," in Kahn and Whitehead, ed., *Wireless Imagination,* 253–63, see 254.

24. See, for example, Fletcher and Spurling, *Beckett: A Study of His Plays,* 99–100; Eugene Webb, *The Plays of Samuel Beckett* (Seattle: University of Washington Press, 1972), 102; Vivian Mercier, *Beckett/Beckett: The Classic Study of a Modern Genius* (London: Souvenir Press, 1993), 155.

25. See "Words and Music," Beckett, *Collected Short Plays,* 127–134, 132.

26. Herbert Lindenberger, *Opera, The Extravagant Art* (Ithaca, NY: Cornell University Press, 1984), 108–09, and see chapter 3 passim.

Chapter 7

1. See, for example, Maggie O'Sullivan's anthology, *Out of Everywhere: Linguistically Innovative Poetry by Women in North America and the UK* (London: Reality Street Editions, 1996).

2. Ron Silliman, "Language, Realism, Poetry," Preface to *In the American Tree,* ed. Ron Silliman (1986; Orono, ME: National Poetry Foundation, 2001), xv, xix.

3. Charles Bernstein, "An Interview with Tom Beckett," *The Difficulties* 2, no. 1 (1982); rpt. in *Content's Dream: Essays, 1975–1984* (Los Angeles: Sun & Moon), 408.

4. Charles Bernstein, "Stray Straws and Straw Men," *Content's Dream,* 41.

5. Compare the Beckett interview (Bernstein, "An Interview with Tom Beckett," 407, 408), where Bernstein remarks, "*Voice* . . . is inextricably tied up with the organizing of the poem along psychological parameters," "a self-constituting project."

"To try to unify the style of work around this notion of self is to take the writing to be not only reductively autobiographical in trying to define the *sound* of me but also to accept that the creation of a persona is somehow central to writing poetry" (407). And again, "It's a mistake, I think, to posit the self as the primary organizing feature of writing."

6. See, for example, Steve McCaffery, "Nothing Is Forgotten but the Talk of How to Talk: An Interview by Andrew Payne" (1984), in *North of Intention: Critical Writings, 1973–1986* (New York: Roof Books, 1986), 111–12, where McCaffery dismisses early experiments in sound poetry as bedeviled by the "dominant mythology of Origin: a privileging of the pre-linguistic, child-sound, the Rousseauist dream of immediate-intuitive communication, all of which tended to a reinscription of a supposed pre-symbolic order in a present, self-authenticating instant."

And cf. Michael Davidson, "'Hey Man, My Wave!': The Authority of Private Language," in *Poetics Journal* 6: "Marginality: Public and Private Language," ed. Barrett Watten and Lyn Hejinian (1986): 33–45. "The ideal of subjectivity itself," writes Davidson, "is not so much the source as the product of specific sociohistorical structures. The subject upon which the lyric impulse is based, rather than being able to generate its own language of the heart, is also constituted within a world of public discourse. The lyric 'I' emerges as a positional relation. Its subjectivity is made possible by a linguistic and ultimately social structure in which 'I' speaks" (41).

For comparable statements by women poets, see the section "Poetics and Exposition" in Mary Margaret Sloan, ed., *Moving Borders: Three Decades of Innovative Writing by Women* (Jersey City, NJ: Talisman House, 1998). Rosmarie Waldrop, for example, dismisses the Romantic notion that "the poem is an epiphany inside the poet's mind and then 'expressed' by choosing the right words." Rather, "The poem is not 'expression,' but a cognitive process that, to some extent, changes me" (609–10).

7. Roland Barthes, "The Death of the Author" (1968), in *Image, Music, Text* (New York: Farrar, Straus, 1968), 142, 145–47, my emphasis. And cf. "From Speech to Writing" (1974), in *The Grain of the Voice: Interviews 1962–1980/Roland Barthes*, trans. Linda Coverdale (New York: Farrar, Straus, 1985), 3–7.

8. Michel Foucault, "What Is an Author?" in Foucault, *Language, Counter-Memory, Practice: Selected Essays and Interviews*, ed. Donald F. Bouchard, trans. Donald F. Bouchard and Sherry Simon (Ithaca, NY: Cornell University Press, 1977), 116, 124, 138.

9. Fredric Jameson, "The Cultural Logic of Late Capitalism," *Postmodernism; or, the Cultural Logic of Late Capitalism* (Durham, NC: Duke University Press, 1991), 11.

10. See "The Cultural Logic of Late Capitalism," *New Left Review* 146 (July–August 1984): 53–92.

11. Ron Silliman, et al., "Aesthetic Tendency and the Politics of Poetry: A Manifesto," *Social Text* 19/20 (fall 1988): 264.

12. See *New Poems for the Millennium: The University of California Book of Modern and Postmodern Poetry*, ed. Jerome Rothenberg and Pierre Joris, 2 vols. (Berkeley: University of California Press, 1995, 1998).

13. Ron Silliman, "Who Speaks: Ventriloquism and the Self in the Poetry Reading," in *Close Listening: Poetry and the Performed Word*, ed. Charles Bernstein (New York: Oxford University Press, 1998), 362.

14. Bernstein, "The Revenge of the Poet-Critic; or, The Parts Are Greater Than the Sum of the Whole," *My Way: Speeches and Poems* (Chicago: University of Chicago Press, 1998), 8–9.

15. Charles Bernstein, "What's Art Got to Do with It? The Status of the Subject of the Humanities in an Age of Cultural Studies," *My Way*, 45, 48.

16. *Oxford English Dictionary*, 1928 edition (Oxford: 2003), s.v. "signature."

17. Michel Foucault, *Les Mots et les choses: une archéologie des sciences humaines* (Paris: Gallimard, 1966), 41, 44, my translation. Ironically, the English translation bears the title *The Order of Things*, which eliminates Foucault's own stress on the relation of word to thing as the important one.

18. Jacques Derrida, "Signature Event Context," trans. Samuel Weber and Jeffrey Mehlman, *Glyph* 1 (1977); rpt. in *Limited Inc* (Evanston, IL: Northwestern University Press, 1988), 9.

19. Ron Silliman, "Albany," *ABC* (Berkeley, CA: Tuumba Press, 1983), unpaginated; Susan Howe, "Frame Structures," *Frame Structures: Early Poems, 1974–1979* (New York: New Directions, 1996).

20. See Silliman, "The New Sentence," *The New Sentence* (New York: Roof Books, 1987), 63–93, and compare Bob Perelman, "Parataxis and Narrative: The New Sentence in Theory and Practice," *The Marginalization of Poetry: Language Writing and Literary History* (Princeton, NJ: Princeton University Press, 1996), 59–78.

21. Jed Rasula, "Ron Silliman," *Contemporary Authors* (Detroit: St. James Press, 1996), 1009.

22. Charles Olson, "Projective Verse," *Collected Prose of Charles Olson*, ed. Donald Allen and Benjamin Friedlander (Berkeley: University of California Press, 1997), 247.

23. Michael Palmer, "Autobiography," *At Passages* (New York: New Direction, 1995), 84; Barrett Watten, "City Fields" (1978) in *Frame (1971–1990)* (Los Angeles: Sun & Moon, 1997), 137.

24. Jasper Johns, "Sketchbook Notes, 1963–64," in Jasper Johns, *Writings, Sketchbook Notes, Interviews*, ed. Kirk Varnedoe (New York: Museum of Modern Art, 1996), 54. Johns's famous entry reads:

Take an object
Do something to it
Do something else to it
  "   "   "   "   "

25. Ludwig Wittgenstein, *Tractatus Logico-Philosophicus*, trans. D. F. Pears and B. F. McGuinness (1921; New York, 1961), §1.1.

26. Gertrude Stein, "What Are Master-Pieces?" *Writings, 1932–1946* (New York:

Library of America, 1998), 355. Stein repeated this sentence frequently: see, for example, "Geographical History of America," *Writings*, 424.

27. David Levi Strauss, "Aporia and Amnesia" (review of Michael Palmer's *At Passages*), *The Nation*, 23 December 1996, 27.

28. Silliman, letter to the author, 10 January 1998; my emphasis.

29. Ron Silliman, "Under *Albany*" (Detroit: Gale Research Center, 1997, in *Contemporary Authors Autobiography Series*, vol. 29, ed. Joyce Nakamura, Gale Research, Detroit, MI, 1998, 309–52). It would be interesting to compare Silliman's to a number of other Language poets' autobiographical memoirs written for the Gale series, especially Charles Bernstein's "An Autobiographical Interview conducted by Loss Pequeño Glazier," *Contemporary Authors Autobiography Series* 24 (Detroit: Gale Research, 1997), 31–50. For Bernstein, "autobiography" and "poetry" remain separate entities, his métier being the hybridization of the poetic/theoretical rather than of the poetic/autobiographical. Cf. Rae Armantrout's autobiography, *True* (Berkeley, CA: Atelos, 1998), which, like Bernstein's, does not introduce "poetry" into autobiography.

30. See Marjorie Perloff, "The Portrait of the Language Poet as Autobiographer: The Case of Ron Silliman," *Quarry West* 34, Special issue, "Ron Silliman and the Alphabet," ed. Tom Vogler (1998): 167–81. The present discussion of "Albany" is a recasting of this earlier discussion.

31. William Blake, "London," *Songs of Experience [1794]*, *The Poetry and Prose of William Blake*, ed. David V. Erdman (Garden City, NY: Doubleday, 1970), ll. 3–4, 26.

32. Mark DeWolfe Howe, *Touched with Fire: The Civil War Letters and Diary of Oliver Wendell Holmes Jr., 1861–1864* (Cambridge, MA: Harvard University Press, 1947). Howe's transformations of particular historical sources have been explored by many critics, before and after my essay appeared in 1999, ranging from Hank Lazer's early "Singing into the Draft: Susan Howe's Textual Frontiers," *American Book Review* 13, no. 4 (October–November 1991), rpt. in Lazer, *Opposing Poetries*, vol. 2, Readings (Evanston, IL: Northwestern University Press, 1996), 60–69, to Peter Nicholls, "Unsettling the Wilderness: Susan Howe and American History," *Contemporary Literature* 37.4 (1996): 586–601, to Rachel Bach's full-length study *The Poetry and Poetics of Susan Howe* (Tuscaloosa: University of Alabama Press, 2002). Such extensive commentary suggests in itself that Howe's mode is by no means merely classifiable as "Language" writing.

33. Robert Lowell, "91 Revere Street," *Life Studies*, in *Life Studies and For the Union Dead* (1964; New York: Farrar, Straus & Giroux, 1967), 46.

34. Susan Howe, *Cabbage Gardens*, in *Frame Structures*, 74.

35. Ludwig Wittgenstein, *Philosophical Investigations*, 3rd edition, trans. G. E. M. Anscombe (New York: Macmillan, 1958), §115.

36. *Frame Structures*, 13. Cf. Joan Retallack's *Afterrimages* (Middletown, CT: Wesleyan University Press, 1995), where poetry itself is treated as complex afterimage.

37. In his excellent "SHUFFLE OFF TO BUFFALO: Susan Howe's *Frame Structures*," *The Germ* 1 (fall 1997): 211, Thomas A. Vogler points out that "Flinders" is "an archaic

word, from the root *splei* = to splice, split, by way of the Scandinavian and Middle English [*flenderis*], meaning bits, fragments, splinters."

38. I owe this insight to a superb essay on *Cabbage Gardens* by Molly Schwartzburg, a PhD candidate at Stanford University.

39. Ron Silliman, Interview with Vogler and Thomas Marshall, *Quarry West* 34 (1998): 24–25.

40. Charles Wright, "Disjecta Membra," in James Tate, ed., *The Best American Poetry 1997*, Series ed., David Lehman (New York: Scribner, 1997), 194.

41. The first issue of the little mimeo-journal *L=A=N=G=U=A=G=E*, ed. Bruce Andrews and Charles Bernstein, appeared in 1978. Many of the texts in this and subsequent issues have been collected in *The L=A=N=G=U=A=G=E Book*, ed. Bruce Andrews and Charles Bernstein (Carbondale: Southern Illinois University Press, 1984).

42. Marjorie Perloff, "Dada without Duchamp/Duchamp without Dada: Avant-Garde Tradition and the Individual Talent," *Stanford Humanities Review* 7, no. 1 (1999): 48–78.

43. The irony is that Eliot was the avowed enemy of the New York Poets; Frank O'Hara, for example, was given to statements like "Lord! Spare us from any more Fisher kings!" (see my *Frank O'Hara: Poet among Painters*, 2nd edition, [Chicago: University of Chicago Press, 1998], 25, 9–12). In his recent *The Last Avant-Garde: The Making of the New York School of Poets* (New York: Doubleday, 1998), David Lehman tries to revive the case for a distinct New York School, emphasizing the group affiliations of Ashbery, Frank O'Hara, and Kenneth Koch at Harvard, the relations with painters in New York, and the legacy to the so-called Second Generation of New York Poets. But the bulk of his book, ironically enough, contains individual chapters on his chosen four (Ashbery, O'Hara, Koch, James Schuyler), the unanticipated effect being to stress difference, both in quality and in mode, rather than group allegiance.

44. For these terms, see Edward Kamau Brathwaite, *History of the Voice: The Development of Nation Language in Anglophone Caribbean Poetry* (London: New Beacon Books, 1984), 13 and passim; Elaine Savory, "Wordsongs & Wordwounds/Homecoming: Kamau Brathwaite's *Barabajan Poems*," *World Literature Today: Kamau Brathwaite Special Issue*, vol. 68, no. 4 (autumn 1994): 750–57.

Chapter 8

1. Robert Sheppard, *Poetics and Linguistically Innovative Poetry, 1978–1997* (Exeter, UK: Stride, 1999).

2. Walter Benjamin, "The Work of Art in the Age of Mechanical Reproduction," *Illuminations*, ed. Hannah Arendt (New York: Schocken Books, 1969), 238.

3. *L=A=N=G=U=A=G=E*, edited by Bruce Andrews and Charles Bernstein, was a mimeograph magazine, whose first issue appeared in spring 1978. *This*, first edited by Robert Grenier and then by Barrett Watten, began publication in 1971; *Hills*, edited by Bob Perelman, began in 1973. Frank Davey's *Open Letter*, published in Toronto, was founded in 1972. These foundational journals as well as such projects as Lyn

Hejinian's Tuumba Chapbook series were thus in place by the mid-seventies. The whole run of *L=A=N=G=U=A=G=E* and related journals is now available online in Craig Dworkin's *Eclipse* project: http://www.princeton.edu/eclipse.

4. See Steve McCaffery, "Diminished Reference and the Model Reader," *North of Intention: Critical Writings, 1973–1986* (New York: Roof Books, 1986), 13–29; Bruce Andrews, "Text and Context," *Paradise & Method; Poetics & Praxis* (Evanston, IL: Northwestern University Press, 1996), 6–16; Charles Bernstein, "Stray Straws and Straw Men," *Content's Dream: Essays 1975–1984* (Los Angeles: Sun & Moon Press, 1986), 40–49.

5. *L=A=N=G=U=A=G=E*, Supplement Number One (June 1980), front page, unpaginated. For the sake of convenience, I shall supply page numbers.

6. See especially Jakobson, "Linguistics and Poetics," *Language in Literature*, ed. Krystyna Pomorska and Stephen Rudy (Cambridge, MA: Belknap Press, 1987), 62–94. Many of the essays in this collection are relevant to the topic—for example, "The Dominant," "Problems in the Study of Language and Literature," and "Two Aspects of Language and Two Types of Aphasic Disturbances."

7. See William R. Paulson, *The Noise of Culture: Literary Texts in a World of Information* (Ithaca, NY: Cornell University Press, 1988), chapter 2, "Science at Work," passim.

8. Charles Bernstein, "Stray Straws and Straw Men," *Content's Dream*, 40–41.

9. In his essay "1973," in *The Mechanics of the Mirage: Postwar American Poetry*, ed. Michel Delville and Christine Pagnoulle (Liège: Université de Liège, 2000), 49–66, Peter Middleton begins to engage the thorny issue of seventies poetry. He relates the demise of Clayton Eshleman's *Caterpillar*, whose last issue was in 1973, and the founding of *American Poetry Review* (1972) to post-Vietnam, Watergate politics and the new distrust of public speech, and the increasing separation of the white avant-garde from black writing. Middleton takes into account such important poetic developments as Jerome Rothenberg's projects to place cultural difference and the recognition of non-Western poetries on the agenda, David Antin's turn toward improvisation, and Michael Palmer's incorporation of French avant-garde poetics into his work. But he notes that at the moment when Barrett Watten's *This* was devoting a whole issue to Clark Coolidge (1973), the dominant poetic discourse valorized poets like Robert Lowell, Maxine Kumin, and William Stafford.

10. Sharon Bryan, "Hollandaise," in *The Morrow Anthology of Younger American Poets*, ed. Dave Smith and David Bottoms (New York: William Morrow, 1985), 107–08. Bryan, born in 1943, holds an MFA from the University of Iowa and has published a book called *Salt Air* from Wesleyan University Press (1983). In their introduction, Smith and Bottoms describe the typical Morrow Younger Poet as one whose "knowledge, while eclectic, seems focused on the psychological and mythical resonances in the local surface, event, or subject. . . . He seems to jog more than to write literary criticism" (19).

11. *Naked Poetry: Recent American Poetry in Open Forms*, ed. Stephen Berg and Robert Mezey (Indianapolis: Bobbs-Merrill, 1969).

12. Allen Ginsberg, "First Thought, Best Thought," *Loka: A Journal from Naropa Institute,* ed. Rick Fields (Garden City, NY: Anchor/Doubleday, 1975); rpt. in Ginsberg, *Composed on the Tongue,* ed. Donald Allen (Bolinas, CA: Grey Fox, 1980), 106–17. Again and again Ginsberg speaks of "natural" speech, spontaneity, the breath as guide to measure, and so on.

13. See Ron Silliman, "Who Speaks: Ventriloquism and the Self in the Poetry Reading," in *Close Listening: Poetry and the Performed Word,* ed. Charles Bernstein (New York: Oxford University Press, 1998), 365. Silliman's is a seminal essay for understanding the limitations of reader-response theory. See essay 7 of the present text for discussion of Silliman's point.

14. See, on this point, George Hartley, *Textual Politics and the Language Poets* (Bloomington: Indiana University Press, 1989). This, the first book-length study of Language poetry, was largely devoted to the movement's politics, drawing heavily on Ron Silliman, Bob Perelman, and Barrett Watten.

15. The most notable exception is Lyn Hejinian, who contributed essays and manifestos to the early issues of *L=A=N=G=U=A=G=E,* for example "If Written Is Writing," and was coeditor, with Barrett Watten, of *Poetics Journal.* Another very different exception is Susan Howe, who combined not poetry and theory so much as poetry and historical scholarship, negotiating in fascinating ways between the two in *My Emily Dickinson* (Berkeley, CA: North Atlantic Books, 1985).

A key volume that includes a number of women poets writing as theorists is Bob Perelman's *Writing/Talks* (Carbondale: Southern Illinois University Press, 1985). The book contains Rae Armantrout's "Poetic Silence," Beverly Dahlen's "A Reading: a Reading," Carla Harryman's "The Middle," Fanny Howe's "Artobiography," and Lyn Hejinian's now well-known "The Rejection of Closure," rpt. in Hejinian, *The Language of Inquiry* (Berkeley: University of California Press, 2000), 40–58.

16. See, for example, Rod Mengham, *Textual Practice* 3, no. 1 (spring 1989): 115–24; D. S. Marriott, "Signs Taken for Signifiers: Language Writing, Fetishism and Disavowal," and Anthony Mellors, "Out of the American Tree: Language Writing and the Politics of Form," both in *fragmente* 6 (1995): 73–91. Marriott's essay, for example, begins with the sentence, "It will be the argument of this paper that language writing, in its systematic attempt to empty the linguistic sign of its referential function, replaces representation with a fetishistic substitute, that of the signifier" (73), the reference being to essays by McCaffery, Bernstein, Silliman, and Andrews.

17. Since 1999, when I wrote this essay, there have been a number of studies of women Language poets. See, for example, Ann Vickery, *Leaving Lines of Gender: A Feminist Genealogy of Language Writing* (Hanover, NH: Wesleyan University Press, 2000). Vickery provides an excellent corrective to earlier studies; at the same time, by treating women poets in isolation, one loses the larger picture in which male and female Language poets—for example, Charles Bernstein and Susan Howe—were best friends and close associates. Again, since 1999 many women Language poets— Kathleen Fraser, Lyn Hejinian, Joan Retallack—have published collections of their essays, and so we now have a very different sense of the Language scene.

18. Parenthetical numbers with # sign refer to issue numbers of *Temblor*.

19. "Two Stein Talks" is reprinted, in revised form with a headnote and the addition of footnotes for the many references, in Lyn Hejinian, *Language of Inquiry*, 83–130.

20. Farrah Griffin, Michael Magee, and Kirsten Gallagher, "A Conversation with Harryette Mullen," *Combo* #1 (summer 1998), ed. Michael Magee, as reprinted on Harryette Mullen Web site, http://epc.buffalo.edu/authors/mullen, 1–2.

21. Barbara Henning, "An Interview with Harryette Mullen," *Poetry Project Newsletter* (1999): 2. See the Poetry Project Web site, http://www.poetryproject.com/newsletter/mullen.html.

22. Harryette Mullen, *Trimmings* (New York: Tender Buttons, 1994), 9.

23. Unpublished lecture delivered at Intersection for the Arts, San Francisco, 24 May 1993. I owe my knowledge of this lecture to Aldon Lynn Nielsen's important study *Black Chant: Languages of African-American Postmodernism* (New York: Cambridge University Press, 1997), 35–37.

24. Kate Pearcy, "A Poetics of Opposition: Race and the Avant-Garde," unpublished essay read at the " 'Poetry and the Public Sphere' Conference on Contemporary Poetry," 24–27 April 1997.

25. Harryette Mullen, *Muse & Drudge* (Philadelphia: Singing Horse Press, 1995), 1.

26. In *Everybody's Autonomy: Connective Reading and Collective Identity* (Tuscaloosa: University of Alabama Press, 2001), Juliana Spahr points out that *Sappho's Lyre* (Berkeley: University of California Press, 1991) is the title of Diane J. Rayor's translations of archaic lyric and women poets of Ancient Greece, and adds, "Only here Sappho is marked as the African-American Sapphire. Resonating here is the 'locus of confounded identities' that Hortense Spillers notes at the beginning of 'Mama's Baby, Papa's Maybe: An American Grammar Book': 'Let's face it. I am a marked woman, but everybody knows my name. 'Peaches' and 'Brown Sugar,' 'Sapphire' and 'Earth Mother,' " 114.

27. Spahr (112–13) cites the Steve Miller Band's "The Joker" as a source of this image: "No don't worry mama. / Cause I'm right here at home. / You're the cutest thing / That I ever did see / Really love your peaches / Wanna shake your tree." And there are related songs by Blind Lemon Jefferson and Ma Rainey that stand behind the peach image as well as the "juicy fruit" that follows.

28. Ann Lauterbach, "Pragmatic Examples: the Nonce," *Moving Borders: Three Decades of Innovative Writing by Women*, ed. Mary Margaret Sloan (Jersey City, NJ: Talisman House, 1998).

29. Beverly Dahlen, "In Re 'Person,' " *Moving Borders*, 664.

30. As cited by Mullen, Poetry Project Web site.

31. *UbuWeb* is located at http://www.ubu.com.

32. The Electronic Poetry Center Web site is located at http://epc.buffalo.edu.

33. Marjorie Perloff, "Screening the Page/Paging the Screen: Digital Poetics and the Differential Text," forthcoming in Thomas Swiss and Adelaide Morris, eds., *The Language of New Media* (Cambridge, MA: MIT Press, 2004).

34. Gertrude Stein, "An Acquaintance with Description" (1929), in *A Stein Reader,* ed. Ulla E. Dydo (Evanston, IL: Northwestern University Press, 1993), 507.

Chapter 9

1. Mary Ellen Solt, *Concrete Poetry: A World View* (Bloomington: Indiana University Press, 1971), 71.

2. Dick Higgins, "Concrete Poetry," *Encyclopedia of Poetry and Poetics,* ed. Alex Preminger and T. V. F. Brogan (Princeton, NJ: Princeton University Press, 1993), 233.

3. Solt explains: "In 1952 . . . three poets in Sao Paulo, Brazil—Haroldo de Campos, Augusto de Campos and Decio Pignatari—formed a group for which they took the name *Noigandres* from Ezra Pound's Cantos. In Canto XX, coming upon the word in the works of Arnaut Daniel, the Provençal troubadour, old Lévy exclaimed: 'Noigandres, eh, noigandres / Now what the DEFFIL can that mean!' This puzzling word suited the purposes of the three Brazilian poets very well; for they were working to define a new formal concept" (*Concrete Poetry,* 12).

4. Rosmarie Waldrop, "A Basis of Concrete Poetry," *Bucknell Review* (fall 1976): 141–51, 143–44.

5. Ibid., 141. The "Pilot Plan" of *Noigandres* similarly talks of "space-time structure instead of mere linear-temporistical development" (Solt, *Concrete Poetry,* 71).

6. Solt, *Concrete Poetry,* 101. For her own translation, see page 102. In her notes, as recorded by Haroldo himself in a note to the author, Solt gives the following verbal equivalents. *Fala* means both "speech" and "speak" (imperative verb); *cala* is also an imperative verb, which means "be quiet," and, by analogy to *fala,* can be read as "silence." *Cara* = "heads" (literally "face"), *coroa* = "tails" (literally "crown"), *para* = "to stop," and *clara* = "clear." The poem dates from 1962.

7. Solt (102) reads the poem somewhat differently: "When the play stops, silence may turn to silver, speech may turn to gold (but only if speech is clear)." The reference to the clarity of language makes this, according to Solt, a reference to the Concrete poem itself.

8. Ron Silliman, "The New Sentence," *The New Sentence* (New York: Roof Books, 1992), 63–93. In "Parataxis and Narrative: The New Sentence in Theory and Practice," *The Marginalization of Poetry: Language Writing and Literary History* (Princeton, NJ: Princeton University Press, 1996), 61, Bob Perelman summarizes the "new sentence" as follows: "A new sentence is more or less ordinary itself, but gains its effect by being placed next to another sentence to which it has tangential relevance. . . . Parataxis is crucial: the autonomous meaning of a sentence is heightened, questioned, and changed by the degree of separation or connection that the reader perceives with regard to the surrounding sentences. This is on the immediate formal level. From a larger perspective, the new sentence arises out of an attempt to redefine genres; the tension between parataxis and narrative is basic" (61).

9. R. P. Draper, "Concrete Poetry," *New Literary History* 2, no. 2 (winter 1971): 329–40, 337.

10. Steve McCaffery and bpNichol, *Rational Geomancy: The Kids of the Book-Machine. The Collected Research Reports of the Toronto Research Group, 1973–1982* (Vancouver: Talonbooks, 1992).

11. James Tate, "Casting a Long Shadow," *The Prose Poem: An International Journal* 8 (1998): 78.

12. Steve McCaffery, "Symphosymposium on Contemporary Poetics and Concretism," in K. David Jackson, Eric Vos, and Johanna Drucker, eds., *Experimental—Visual—Concrete: Avant-Garde Poetry Since the 1960s* (Atlanta: Rodopi, 1996), 372.

13. Charles Baudelaire, *Paris Spleen*, trans. Louise Varèse (New York: New Directions, 1970), ix–x. For the original, see Charles Baudelaire, *Le Spleen de Paris* (Texte de 1869), ed. Y. G. Le Dantec; révisée par Claude Pichois (Paris: Gallimard: Bibliothèque de la Pléiade, 1961), 229.

14. Haroldo de Campos, "Sanscreed Latinized: The *Wake* in Brazil and Hispanic America," *Tri Quarterly* 38 (winter 1977): 56. For the translations themselves, see Augusto and Haroldo de Campos, *Panorama do Finnegans Wake* (São Paulo: Editôra Perspectiva, 1971). Augusto de Campos reprints "Dos Fragmentos do *Finnegans Wake*" along with an essay about them in his *A margem da margem* (São Paulo: Companhia das Letras, 1989), 35–48. For Augusto de Campos's Stein translations, see "Gertrude é uma gertrude," *O Anticrítico* (São Paulo: Companhia das Letras, 1986), 177–89. The Stein influence on the prose poem, which would be the subject of another essay, has to do with the way repetition and permutation of monosyllabic and disyllabic words creates visual as well as verbal patterning.

15. Augusto de Campos, "Theory of Concrete Poetry: Introduction," trans. Jon M. Tolman, *Studies in the Twentieth Century*, no. 7 (spring 1971), 48, and cf. Augusto de Campos, "Yale Symphosymposium," in Jackson, Vos, and Drucker, eds., *Experimental—Visual—Concrete*, 376. Augusto cites "the vocabulistic kaleidoscope of *Finnegans Wake* and its textual polyreadings" and the "experimental, minimalist, and molecular prose of Gertrude Stein" as important sources for *Noigandres*.

16. James Joyce, *Finnegans Wake* (1939; New York: Penguin, 1976), 260–308. All further references are to this edition.

17. Haroldo de Campos, "The Open Work of Art" (1955), trans. Maria Lucia Santaella Braga, in *Dispositio: Revista Hispánica de Semiótica Literaria* 6, no. 17/18 (summer–fall 1981): 5–8. In his preface to the Brazilian edition of his *Opera Aperta*, Umberto Eco wrote, "It is certainly curious that some years before I wrote *Opera Aperta*, Haroldo de Campos, in a short article, anticipated my themes to an astounding degree, as if he reviewed the book which I had not yet written and would yet write without having read his article" (*Dispositio,* 5).

18. James Joyce, *Letters,* vol. 1, ed. Stuart Gilbert (New York: Viking Press, 1957), 213.

19. See Haroldo de Campos, "Poetic Function and Ideogram/The Sinological Argument," *Dispositio,* 9–39. *Ideograma,* 2nd edition, was published by Editora da Universidade de São Paulo in 1986.

20. Haroldo de Campos, *Galáxias* (São Paulo: Editora ex Libris, 1984), Afterword, unpaginated, reprinted as headnote to Oseki-Dépré's French translation (see note 24

below). In the afterword, Haroldo writes that the *Galáxias* were first published in the journal *Invenção* (São Paulo, 1964) and were subsequently published irregularly in various places until 1976.

21. Roland Greene, "From Dante to the Post-Concrete: An Interview with Augusto de Campos," in *Harvard Library Bulletin*, "Material Poetry of the Renaissance/ The Renaissance of Material Poetry," 3, no. 2 (summer 1992): 20.

22. Gertrude Stein, *How to Write* (1931; Los Angeles: Sun & Moon, 1995), 248.

23. For an excellent discussion of Stein's abstract visual word designs in various texts, see Ulla Dydo, "Stop Look and Listen: A Digression on the Picture of a Page of Gertrude Stein," *Big Allis* 6 (1993): 15–27.

24. See Haroldo de Campos, *Galaxies,* traduit, Inés Oseki-Dépré & l'auteur (Paris: La Main courante, 1998), unpaginated; Haroldo de Campos, "de Galáxias," trans. Suzanne Jill Levine (from a basic version by Jon Tolman), in *Desencontrários/ Unencontraries: 6 poetas brasileiros/6 Brazilian Poets,* ed. Josely Vianna Baptista (São Paulo: Bamerindus, 1995), 70–73. There is to date no complete translation of the *Galáxias* into English.

25. See Marjorie Perloff, *Radical Artifice: Writing Poetry in the Age of Media* (Chicago: University of Chicago Press, 1991), 115–20.

26. Rosmarie Waldrop, *Lawn of Excluded Middle* (Providence, RI: Tender Buttons, 1993), 13.

27. Ludwig Wittgenstein, *Philosophical Investigations,* 3rd edition, trans. G. E. M. Anscombe (New York: Macmillan, 1958), #115.

28. Rosmarie Waldrop, *Reluctant Gravities* (New York: New Directions, 1999), 4.

29. Steve McCaffery, "Aenigma," in "Hegel's Eyes," *Theory of Sediment* (Vancouver: Talonbooks, 1991), 38.

30. Joan Retallack, *How to Do Things with Words* (Los Angeles: Sun & Moon, 1998), 105–06.

31. Kenneth Goldsmith, *No. 111 2.7.93—10.20.96* (Great Barrington, MA: The Figures, 1997), 3, and online at http://www.ubuweb.com/111/0001-0100/02.html.

Chapter 10

1. Peter O'Leary, "Quod Vides Scribe in Libro," Introduction to *To Do as Adam Did: Selected Poems of Ronald Johnson* (Jersey City, NJ: Talisman House, 2000), xii. Citations from this volume are reproduced using, as far as possible, the same size font as in the original.

2. Ronald Johnson, Preface, *Songs of the Earth* (San Francisco: Grabhorn-Hoyem, 1970), unpaginated; rpt. in O'Leary, *Selected Poems of Ronald Johnson,* 63–78.

3. Henry-Louis de La Grange, *Gustav Mahler,* vol. 3, Vienna, Triumph and Disillusion (1904–1907) (New York: Oxford University Press, 2000), 102–05.

4. Eugen Gomringer, "The Poem as a Functional Object" from the Foreword to *33 Konstellazionen,* in Mary Ellen Solt, ed., *Concrete Poetry: A World View* (Bloomington: Indiana University Press, 1971), 69–70.

5. Augusto de Campos, Decio Pignatari, and Haroldo de Campos, "Pilot Plan for Concrete Poetry" (1958), in Solt, *Concrete Poetry,* 71–72.

6. Ibid.

7. Oyvind Fahlström, "Hatila Ragulpr Pä Fätskliaben: Manifesto for Concrete Poetry" (1953), in Solt, *Concrete Poetry,* 74–78.

8. See my *Twenty-first-Century Modernism: The "New" Poetics* (Malden, MA: Blackwell, 2002), chapter 4 passim.

9. Steve McCaffery, "Synchronicity, Ronald Johnson and the Migratory Phrase," *Vort* 3, no. 3, Guy Davenport-Ronald Johnson Issue (1976): 116. See also McCaffery, "Corrosive Poetics: The Relief Composition of Ronald Johnson's *Radi os,*" *Pretexts: literary and cultural studies* 11, no. 2 (2002): 121–32. The following comment on *Radi os* is apropos here: "It is precisely in this manner, as a reader-poacher, that Johnson enters the textual space of *Paradise Lost* to realize a negative production of detours, erasures and new articulations. There is a coupling of meaningfulness to a shifting materiality of language" (126).

10. Eugen Gomringer, *konstellazionen* (Berne: Spiral Press, 1953); rpt. as Figure 4 in Solt, *Concrete Poetry,* 93.

11. Peter O'Leary, Interview with Ronald Johnson, November 19, 1995, http://www.trifectapress.com/johnson/interview.html.

Chapter 11

1. Jacques Roubaud, *La vieillesse d'Alexandre. Essai sur quelques états récents du vers français* (Paris: Editions Ramsay, 1988), 7.

2. Stephane Mallarmé, "Crise de vers," in *Variations sur un sujet, in Oeuvres complètes,* ed. Henri Mondor et G. Jean-Aubry (Paris: Gallimard, Bibliothèque de la Pléiade, 1946), 362. Translation mine.

3. Jacques Roubaud, "Introduction," *The Oulipo and Combinatorial Art* (1991); rpt. in Harry Mathews and Alastair Brotchie, eds., *Oulipo Compendium* (London: Atlas Press, 1998), 42.

4. Michel Bénabou, "Alexandre au greffoir," *La Bibliothèque Oulipienne,* vol. 2 (Paris: Editions Ramsay, 1987), 202–33.

5. Ibid., 227. A literal translation would be "Lovers devoted to impassive rivers / Are equally devoted, in the shadow of the forests, / To cats and sweet like the flesh of children / Who like them are sensitive to the chill in the cold darkness."

6. Again a literal translation: "Fervent lovers and austere scholars / In their ripe season, are equally fond / of cats, strong and soft, the pride of the household, / Who, like them, are sensitive to the cold and, like them, sedentary."

7. Harry Mathews, "35 Variations on a Theme from Shakespeare," *Shiny* 9/10 (1999): 97–101.

8. The N + 7 method involves replacing each noun (N) with the seventh following it in the dictionary. Much depends upon the dictionary chosen: the shorter the dictionary, the more discordant the next word is likely to be. See *Oulipo Compen-*

dium, 198–99. For a discussion of Cage's use of constraints in *Roaratorio,* see my "The Music of Verbal Space: John Cage's 'What You Say,'" in *Sound States: Innovative Poetics and Acoustical Technologies,* with accompanying CD, ed., Adalaide Morris (Chapel Hill: University of North Carolina Press, 1997), 129–48.

9. The poems, in the order cited, may be found in *The Norton Anthology of Modern and Contemporary Poetry,* vol. 2, ed. Jahan Ramazani, Richard Ellmann, and Robert O'Clair (New York: W. W. Norton, 2003): Yusef Komunyakaa, "My Father's Love Letters," 863; James Fenton, "Dead Soldiers," 901; Jorie Graham, "The Dream of the Unified Field," 927; Rita Dove, "Claudette Colvin Goes to Work," 986; Thylias Moss, "Interpretation of a Poem by Frost," 1001; Cathy Song, "Sunworshippers," 1022; Henri Cole, "Folly," 1038. In all fairness, the anthology does contain a sampling of "alternate" poetries—for example, Charles Bernstein, Susan Howe, Lyn Hejinian, and Michael Palmer—and there are of course poets like Paul Muldoon who use sound in interesting ways. But the dominant mode is the one I describe here.

10. I discuss what I call "the linear fallacy" in an essay by that name for *The Georgia Review* 35 (winter 1981): 855–69.

11. Language poetry and related experimental modes of the nineties differ from this model in that syntax is often fractured, continuity fragmented, and puns multiple. But, interestingly, the aural dimension of poetry generally plays no greater part here than in the more mainstream poems above. Here are two typical poems published in Douglas Messerli's *From the Other Side of the Century: A New American Poetry, 1960–1990* (Los Angeles: Sun & Moon, 1994)—Ray Di Palma's "The Wrong Side of the Door":

> Supplementary to the account
> Are a series of tangled memories
> And observations at random
> Written in a logbook bound in burlap. (661)

And James Sherry's "Pay Cash Only":

> She shakes feathers toward him
> to ward off buttering his own
> small bills, filled with soldiers
> of diverse excess, caught up
> in an investment in lunch.
> As they say, "Hog tied to penny rolls,
> his car won't go down the road straight." (707)

Again, however complex their irony and wordplay, the form of the poems is lineated prose.

12. See *The New Princeton Encyclopedia of Poetry and Poetics,* ed. Alex Preminger

and T. V. F. Brogan (Princeton, NJ: Princeton University Press, 1993), 14. The article on African poetry is by George Lang.

13. Christian Bök, *Eunoia* (Toronto: Coach House Books, 2001), 103. All further page references are to this edition.

14. As of the preparation of the present text, the headnote and complete text of "Via" have not yet been published.

15. *How 2* 1, no. 6 (2001). The Web site is http://www.scc.rutgers.edu/however/ v1_6_2001/current/in-conference/bergvall.html.

16. An excerpt from "About Face" is published as an appendix to my interview with Caroline Bergvall, "ex/Crème/ental/eaT/ing," *Sources: Revue d'études Anglophones:* Special issue, "20th-Century American Women's Poetics of Engagement," 12 (spring 2002): 123–35. Like "Via," "About Face" will appear in Bergvall's new book, *Mesh.*

17. E-mail from Caroline Bergvall to me, 14 March 2003.

18. See Retallack's "Narrative as Memento Mori" in essay 9 of the present text.

19. Hugh Kenner, "Something to Say," *A Homemade World: The American Modernist Writers* (New York: Alfred A. Knopf, 1975), 60.

Chapter 12

1. Tom Raworth, *Visible Shivers* (Oakland, CA: O Books, 1987).

2. Raworth is evidently the oldest living open-heart surgery survivor, treated in the UK in the first round of heart operations conducted there in the fifties. The surgery for atrial septal defect (the most benign and common form of congenital heart disease), which then took eight hours to perform, is now no longer necessary; generally, the defective opening can be closed without subcutaneous incision.

3. I owe this and much other incidental information about specifics of English culture in these years to Nate Dorward.

4. John Barrell, "Subject and Sentence: The Poetry of Tom Raworth," *Critical Inquiry* 17 (winter 1991): 386–409, see 393.

5. Tom Raworth, *Contemporary Authors Autobiography Series,* vol. 11, ed. Mark Zadrozny (Detroit: Gale Research Group, 1990), 297–311.

6. See e-mail from Tom Raworth to me, 22 October 2002. Ellipses are Raworth's.

Chapter 13

1. Rae Armantrout, *The Pretext* (Los Angeles: Green Integer, 2001).

2. Since this essay was completed, Armantrout has published *Veil: New and Selected Poems* with the Wesleyan University Press (2001), and a second collection is forthcoming from Wesleyan in 2004. If this move from small presses to Wesleyan is not exactly the imprimatur of the Establishment, it nevertheless marks a new level of success for Armantrout's poetry.

3. *Pretext*, 7. "Birthmark" is reprinted in *Veil*, 91. I cite the poem from this version because the Wesleyan page is of normal size as opposed to the "pocket" format of Green Integer, and so the contrast between prose and verse is heightened, as it should be. The question of layout is, of course, relevant to the interpretation of this or any poem and should be taken up in class discussion.

4. Lyn Hejinian, "An Interview with Rae Armantrout," *A Wild Salience: The Writing of Rae Armantrout*, ed. Tom Beckett (Cleveland: Burning Press, 1999), 16.

5. Brian Reed, "Hart Crane's Victrola," *Modernism/Modernity* 7, no. 1 (2000): 99–125.

6. Jorie Graham, "Evolution," *Never* (New York: Ecco/Harper Collins, 2002), 21–25. "Evolution" was first published in *The London Review of Books*, 5 July 2001. Graham chose "Evolution" to be distributed in a special edition by The Poetry Center, Chicago, when she gave a reading there on 12 December 2001. For this occasion, "Evolution" was specially printed on Somerset paper, prefaced by a line drawing by Jennie Bastian. The broadside was designed by Amy Rowan and The Poetry Center.

7. I am counting the run-on particles as part of the preceding lines; if these are counted as separate entities, the poem has thirty lines.

Chapter 14

1. Frank O'Hara, "Naptha," *The Collected Poems of Frank O'Hara*, ed. Donald Allen (Berkeley: University of California Press, 1995), 338.

2. Michael Scharf, "The Vendler/Perloff Standoff/Handoff," *Writers and Critics* 28, no. 1 (January/February 2000): 19–23.

3. In revised form, this essay appears here as essay 7, "Language Poetry and the Lyric Subject." The controversial pages on Scalapino—which had actually served as no more than an example of different voice possibilities among San Francisco Language poets—have been excised.

Index

Sustained discussions of a particular author or work are indicated in boldface. Figures are denoted by italics.